Film
Review
1988-9

Film
Review
1988-9

INCLUDING VIDEO RELEASES

F. Maurice Speed

WITH
JAMES CAMERON-WILSON

COLUMBUS BOOKS
LONDON

FILM REVIEW's Film Personality of the Year Poll

Who made the most impact on the big screen in 1987/8? Here's your chance to vote for the most outstanding film performance of the year.

Make your choice from the films listed in this book under 'Releases of the Year' and write, on a postcard:

    (1) name of actor/actress
    (2) name of film
    (3) in a few words, the reason why you think this was the best film performance of the year.

Add your own name and address and send your card, by 31 May 1989, to the Editorial Department at Columbus Books (address below).

The five readers who supply the best reasons for their choice will each receive a Columbus film book.

Results of the Film Personality Poll and names of the winning readers will be published in the 1989/90 edition of *Film Review*. Winners will also be notified by post, no later than 30 June 1989.

First published in Great Britain in 1988 by
COLUMBUS BOOKS LIMITED
19-23 Ludgate Hill
London EC4M 7PD

Copyright © 1988 F. Maurice Speed

British Library Cataloguing in Publication Data
Film Review
1. Cinema films – Serials
791.43′05

ISBN 0–86287–940–X
ISBN 0–86287–939–6 Pbk

Designed by Fred Price

Phototypeset by Falcon Graphic Art Ltd
Wallington, Surrey

Printed and bound by Scotprint Ltd., Musselburgh, Scotland

Contents

Introduction

F. MAURICE SPEED surveys the cinematic year

They are making too many movies! At least, they are in the United States, and statistics prove it. Of the films produced by the so-called independents – those companies which are not the major Hollywood studios (Paramount, Warner, Columbia and Universal etc.) – 37 per cent received no cinema showing at all during 1987, the majority of them going directly into the video lists in order to recover some of their production costs.

The same set of statistics shows that the 200-plus independent features made during the year, at a total cost of about $630 million, brought back (from American cinema showings only and ignoring all subsidiary income) only $165 million. To make up the shortfall the producers had to look to foreign sales (including in some cases slim pickings from UK showings), video-cassette cash, cable TV and other outlets which at best could only hope to lessen the deficit. During 1986 161 films were made by independents at a cost of about $500 million, bringing back only $150 million from cinema releases. The sad fact emerges that whereas some truly bad films, in terms of taste, artistry, imagination and craftsmanship, earned a pot of gold for their makers, by exploiting the baser side of human nature and by sensational and clever advertising, many a good, literate, original and beautifully crafted movie ended up as a flop at the box office and a financial disaster for its backers. This situation, often a cause for critical complaint, is likely to continue for the foreseeable future.

Still on the subject of too many films: a total of more than 500 features (511, according to *Variety*) made in the United States and on location by American companies during 1987, a 7 per cent rise above the 1986 total, meant that about 10 new films were available to the cinemas every week of the year. Yet here in Britain, it is a rare week when more than four or five new productions have their first showing, a situation which results in even a good film having to wait up to a year after its American premiere to get a booking in Britain. Ironically, whereas a few years ago there were too many cinemas and too few moviegoers to fill them, resulting in a vast number of closures, there are now not enough cinemas to show even a small proportion of the films waiting to cross the Atlantic. It is not only American films that suffer: at the 1988 Cannes Festival a common complaint by British producers concerned the long gap between complet-

Director/producer Richard Attenborough on the set of his major 1987–8 UIP release Cry Freedom.

ing a film and getting it shown, and the consequent delay before it starts to earn money.

American cinema statistics make absorbing reading for anyone interested in the movies, and it is a great pity that there has been nothing like them in Britain for several years. However, new Board of Trade questionnaires are to be sent out in the near future to all exhibitors in Great Britain and will, it is hoped, make accessible on a yearly basis a more comprehensive set of data than ever before available.

One interesting fact to be gathered from the American data is that the number of foreign-language films dubbed into English (American, to be more precise) during 1987 fell to just 9, whereas the number of imports released in subtitled form rose to 75, which shows which way that particular controversial wind of change is blowing. During the same period, the number of British and Commonwealth films released in the United States doubled to 62.

During 1987–8 hard-core pornographic production in the USA virtually ceased, at least in terms of cinema production; though the number of such movies made directly for video is anybody's guess.

More facts and figures of interest: while, of the Hollywood majors, Warner and Universal showed a slight rise in the total of films completed, Tri-Star and Fox showed a decrease, while at MGM and Paramount the 1987 figures were virtually identical to those of 1986. The biggest variation was at Cannon, where 1987's very high total of 41 films dipped to just 17 planned for 1988; but, in the light of the turmoil that has afflicted the company, this sort of belt-tightening was to be expected.

My favourite piece of film journalism of the year appeared in the *Daily Telegraph* on 28 November 1987. Entitled 'The Invasion of Bad Taste' and written by Jeffrey Richard, it said much of what I've long been thinking: 'Good taste used to be universally admired; bad taste deplored and discouraged. The late twentieth century, with its characteristic perversity, has reversed this view, coming to regard bad taste as liberated and gutsy. Bad taste has, in short, become a virtue and has crept into every area of life and leisure.' Modern American films, Mr Richard continued, 'have produced two nauseating and apparently unending genres: the so-called "Gross-Out" comedies . . . and present-day horror films, which consist entirely of repulsive scenes of slaughter and blood-letting.' My own feelings entirely – though I must in fairness add that I think Mr Richard's controversial comments are sometimes a little too sweeping and, although he doesn't include them in his attack, not all

Danish director/scenarist Gabriel Axel (right) with his opera singer star Jean-Philippe Lafont in the former's culinary masterpiece Babette's Feast – Babettes Gaestebud *(an Artificial Eye release), which won the Oscar for Best Foreign Language Film.*

British films are innocent of the charges. Certainly there has never been such bad taste as that which is exhibited, too often, in the cinema nowadays. Hardened as I am after some 60 years of moviegoing, I now find it frequently necessary, for personal comfort, to avert my eyes from the screen or close my ears to the appalling, needlessly foul dialogue.

Let's return to some hard facts. Every year the film industry is plagued with strikes or threats of strikes; in fact, since the beginning of the 'eighties, the directors have gone on strike once and threatened a walk-out on one other occasion, the screen actors have officially stopped acting once, the musicians have withdrawn their services once and the screen extras called out their members once, in 1987. Top of the 'everybody out' ladder, however, are the members of the Writers' Guild of America, who have laid down their pens in anger in 1981, 1985 and now, for the third time, in 1988, when the strike lasted a record six months. It finally fizzled out in early August, having cost the industry nearly £15 million.

Technically there is not much to record this year. Almost inevitably there has been an announcement about yet another 'revolutionary' 3-D system in the pipeline; but so many of these 3-D promises have been made and not kept that one must be sceptical. I hope the new Aspex system proves to be the exception, and that there is some substance in the claim that, while it will still be necessary to wear those awful cardboard glasses to view the film in perfection, it will be watchable even without them and the viewer will still get some of the three-dimensional effect.

The British film industry appears to be flourishing mightily in terms both of production and attendance, after its long spell in the doldrums. The year 1988 started off with five new films going into production and apparently many more are lined up, which suggests that, even taking into account those projects which will inevitably fall by the wayside, enough will be produced to make 1988–9 something of a boom period. Although official figures are not currently issued (a situation soon likely to be corrected, as I have mentioned) there is no question about the continued rise in moviegoing in Britain, and a fairly reliable estimate suggests that the 1987 attendance total was in the region of 76 million, an increase over 1986 of about 4 million. In 1988 this cheerful trend continues, with a box-office intake for the year likely to be about £100 million. All this has led to a flurry of new cinema building, mostly multiscreen complexes.

However, while the two pioneers, at Milton Keynes and High Wycombe, have apparently been a huge success, some later arrivals have not been spinning gold. It is being realized that the siting of these new cinema complexes is all-important, the danger being a phenomenon termed 'dilution'. When built in places where there is already a flourishing cinema, the complex does not increase the total number of moviegoers or the number of films they go to see. Instead, business is split between the rival cinemas, and is indifferent for both as a result. So we are back to square one, indifferent business being the main cause of all those closures just a few years ago.

So far it has been the Americans who have been opening these multiscreen cinemas. American MultiCinemas, the pioneers in this country, has promised it will open seven more during 1988–9 and has plans to bring its total up to 25 by the early 1990s. Cineplex Odeon, the largest chain of cinemas in North America, announced its intention of moving into Britain in a big way by opening about 100 screens before the end of the 1990s. 'We see great opportunities in Europe, especially England,' the company said. In summer 1988, ownership of the Maybox 10-screen complex, opened in Slough in late 1987, was transferred to Cineplex Odeon, thus giving the company the first of its projected British chain. In London, too, the 'multis' are on the march. America's CIC Group plans to spend £4 million on a new complex at the old Whiteley's store site in Queensway, and Cannon's plans for a 17-screen cinema in Piccadilly still seem to be on course, even if the starting date has been considerably delayed.

Warner Brothers has thrown its hat in the ring with the building of a new multi-screen cinema in Manchester, and has said it won't be stopping there. All this has spurred the Odeon circuit on to a reversal of its recent policy of cinema closures and it now has a building programme which will result in its present total of 208 screens in 75 cinemas rising to 300 screens in 80 cinemas by late 1988 or early 1989. There are plenty more plans and promises around, enough to produce a generally optimistic picture for the future.

The long-running Cannon crisis has continued into 1988, though this year the dark clouds seem to be lifting somewhat. What has emerged as a near certainty is that Cannon will continue in its primary business of making and showing movies, with its twin executive big guns (Menahem Golan and Yoram Globus) firing the shots, though it may well emerge a leaner and lesser outfit than in its expansive prime. It appears that the organization's crisis was virtually ended in spring 1988 with a vast sale-and-leaseback deal of Cannon's British cinemas with a Madrid property company, followed by a $100-million injection from Italian financier Giancarlo Parreti, which, apart from giving the Cannon Group a new and healthy lease of life, will surely also give Mr Parreti a say in the company's future affairs . . .

Meanwhile, Cannon cinemas were enjoying a very successful 1987, their 460 British screens producing some £52 million (a 6 per cent rise over 1986) and promising even better things for 1988, with the January receipts alone touching £6 million, approximately £1½ million up on the January 1987 figure. It is no wonder that Cannon plans to extend what is already Britain's largest cinema chain. Incidentally, the news that Kenneth Rive has taken over the Cannon distribution arm in Britain was very welcome, in view of his past record: when he had his own small chain of specialist cinemas, he introduced a string of first-class

Bestselling author Norman Mailer who wore, not very memorably, the director's hat for his adaptation of his own novel Tough Guys Don't Dance *– a Cannon release.*

foreign films otherwise unlikely to have been seen in the UK.

The optimistic mood now prevailing in the British film industry was confirmed by the announcement that the giant Granada group had set up a film division, the first results of which we will soon be seeing when *The Tree of Hands* (with Lauren Bacall and Peter Firth) and the Irish-set drama *Joyriders* are premièred in late 1988 or early 1989. The distributing company, Entertainment, has also launched into movie production in a big way with a major, £13-million, Pinewood-based movie entitled *Slipstream*.

In contrast to the expansion of the cinema business in Britain, French cinemas are doing so badly that an estimated 10 per cent of them closed down during 1987, the blame for waning attendances being placed on TV. India's film industry, the largest in the world, has also been suffering, with the number of movies produced falling from 1986's total of 840 to a still-massive 806 in 1987. India's film exports have also fallen, from 505 in the 1985–6 period to 406 during 1986–7.

Another long-running saga which continued from 1987 well into the summer of 1988 was the David Puttnam story. In a very long and painstaking two-part investigative feature entitled 'The Rise and Fall of the Coca-Cola Kid', *Variety* (18 and 25 May 1988) covered in detail the whole complicated and controversial business of Puttnam's appointment

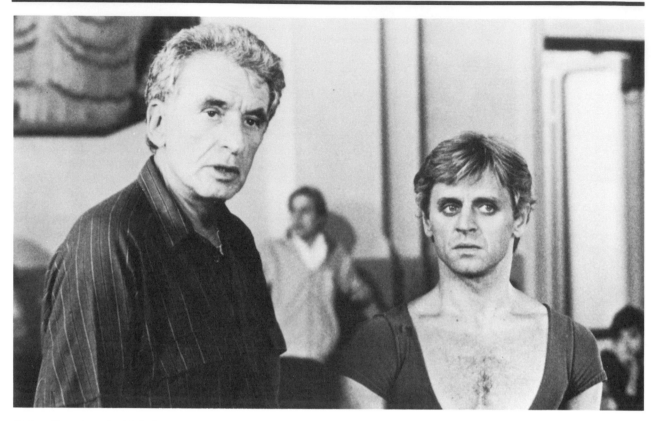

Herbert Ross pictured with ballet star Mikhail Baryshnikov while making Dancers *(a Cannon release), which was about the making of a film of* Giselle. *Actor-dancer-director-choreographer Ross made his first movie (a musical version of* Goodbye, Mr Chips) *in 1969 after a successful career on Broadway.*

to, and abrupt resignation from, the Hollywood hot seat as Columbia Pictures production boss, and tried to answer such pertinent questions as: was Puttnam pushed or did he jump? who was in the right, who in the wrong? This review probably comes the closest we will ever get to the whole truth, suggesting that the friction created by Puttnam's outspoken comments about Hollywood ways and means, and Hollywood's annoyance at seeing a Briton at the top of their American celluloid ladder were at least ingredients in Puttnam's sudden departure. According to *Variety*, Puttnam walked out of Columbia with a $7-million severance settlement cheque in his pocket; and in another article he was reported as saying: 'It's been the best year of my life, the most productive one, the one in which I have learnt most.'

Somehow, although the stories are in many ways so dissimilar, the Puttnam affair reminds me of Bryan Forbes's reign at Associated British in 1969–70, when his policy of making superior movies sadly failed to bring in enough cash (though he is most unlikely to have walked out with a golden handshake on the Puttnam/Columbia scale). Both stories point to the miserable conclusion that it isn't easy for a good producer who aims to raise standards to become a successful moviemaking boss.

I suppose that, in view of the inevitable commercialism of the cinema, the kind of people who generally control production, the overwhelming need to make a profit and the cut-throat game of musical chairs played by executives at the top of the industry, we should be thankful for small mercies, such as the occasional, often unexpected gem which thoroughly deserves its commercial success. One such gem this year was John Boorman's critically acclaimed and very popular *Hope and Glory*, a convincing and beautifully made movie which will almost certainly emerge as one of the most successful British-made movies of 1988.

The year 1988 has seen the opening of cinema/film museums on both sides of the Atlantic, in London the BFI's Museum of the Moving Image, next to the National Film Theatre on the South Bank (one of the exhibits of which is the very first, 1944–5 edition of *Film Review*) and, in New York, after seven years' preparatory work, the American Museum of the Moving Image.

So many British film actors and technicians of all sorts are now working and living in Hollywood and other American centres of film-making that they have formed their own version of the British Academy of Film and Television Arts, with 300 members. Though affiliated to the original BAF-TA, it claims not to be just a branch but an entirely self-supporting organization, which plans to offer monthly events and provide a meeting place for expatriate Britons.

Many international celebrities – such as Monica Vitti, Robert Altman, Gina Lollobrigida, Pierre Richard, etc. – attended the second Funny Film Festival (a non-competitive affair) now held annually at the Italian spa town of Darfo Boario Germe. The programme presented the world première of *According to Pontius Pilate* and included Britain's *Wish You Were Here*. *Variety* commented: 'If the films live up to comedy promise, the Funny Film Festival sincerely believes it can write participants a clean bill of health for years to come.' The Festival's twin mottoes were 'Smile and the world smiles with you' and 'Laugh for a better life'.

Versatile director/writer/producer Robert Altman during the filming of his latest work, Cannon's Fool for Love, *looking remarkably like the leading character in his 1976 production* Buffalo Bill and the Indians.

One of the most expensive films of 1988–9 is likely to be Terry Gilliam's epic *The Adventures of Baron Munchausen*. If reported costs of $33 million and still rising are true, its backers may have a long, if not endless, wait for it to make a profit.

Jack Lemmon, who in March 1988 received the American Film Institute's Life Achievement award, had some pertinent comments to make on the occasion about today's ludicrously inflated film production costs. 'Money doesn't make good movies,' was Lemmon's message. He recalled that his Oscar-winning movie *Save the Tiger* cost $1 million when it was made in 1973, but even if the budget had been twice that figure, he didn't think the movie could have been any better. He pointed out that to make the same film today would cost anything between $12 and $14 million – and it *still* wouldn't be any better. He agreed that stars' enormous salaries were one of the main causes of this inflation and suggested that they follow the example set by Julie Andrews and himself in Blake Edwards's *That's Life!* and take the same risks as the directors and producers, by working for a minimum salary and then sharing in the profits – or losses.

At about the time that Lemmon was saying this, Jack Valenti, President of MPAA, was going on record as saying that, while box-office returns were reaching new heights, so were production costs, with the average cost of today's movies reaching $20 million and with half as much again needed for print costs, advertising and publicity, the total

showing a 15 per cent rise over last year and a staggering 113 per cent leap from the 1980 figure.

Remember last year's uproar about the many plans to colour old black-and-white films? It seems to have completely died down and one now hears practically nothing about such projects. One exception concerns Jacques Tati's *Jour de fête*. Few moviegoers will be aware that Tati intended the film to be made in colour and had a colour camera on the set. He finally decided to make the movie in black-and-white, only after the trouble-beset Thomas-Houston company, whose system he was using, closed down their laboratory. Now plans are afoot to make a colour print based on Tati's original colour material, so here will be one reasonably uncontroversial example of colorization.

Though it is still a pretty slow business, women are getting more of the executive jobs in the international film business. In 1987 many of them met in Georgia, USSR, to form the Cinema Women International Federation, the aim of which is to establish an international organization to improve the opportunities and rights of women film professionals throughout the world.

A pretty impressive show of women's work in international moviemaking occurred at the 3rd Annual Women in Films Festival in Hollywood in October 1987, kicking off with the West Coast premiere of *The Whales of August*, a marvellous movie starring Lillian Gish, Bette Davis and Ann Sothern.

That seems a positive note on which to end this review of the film year, both in and out of the cinema. As usual, there has been a great deal of rubbish on offer, but the occasional flashes of brilliance make everything worthwhile. After some 60 years of professional moviegoing, I remain firmly hooked. Good viewing!

Releases of the Year

In this section you will as usual find details of all the films released in Great Britain from 1 July 1987 to the end of June 1988 – the period covered by all the reference features in the book. The precise dating of some of these releases is a little tricky in view of the current lack of any rigidity in the release pattern, but dates given refer to the general release and not pre-release.

In the case of films sent out on a 'floating' release the date of the film's first London showing has been added because usually this is also the first British showing.

The normal abbreviations operate as follows: Dir – for Director; Pro – for Producer; Assoc Pro – for Associate Producer; Ex Pro – for Executive Producer; Pro Ex – for Production Executive; Pro Sup – for Production Supervisor; Co-Pro – for Co-Producer; Pro Co-Ord – for Production Co-Ordinator; Ph – for Photographer; Ed – for Editor; Art – for Art Director; Pro Des – for Production Designer; M – for Music; and a few others which will be obvious.

Abbreviations for the name of film companies are also pretty obvious when used, such as Fox for 20th Century-Fox, Rank for Rank Film Distributors, UKFD for United Kingdom Film Distributors and UIP for Universal International Pictures. Where known, the actual production company is given first, the releasing company last.

The nationality of the film is noted wherever possible – titles for which no country of origin is mentioned can usually be taken as being American – but in these days of increasing international co-productions between two, three or even four countries it is sometimes difficult to designate a national identity.

Finally, unless otherwise specified (i.e. in black-and-white), it can safely be taken that the film is made in Technicolor or some similar colour process.

Censorship certificates: *U* represents films suitable for persons of any age; *PG* (Parental Guidance) represents films which some parents might consider unsuitable for their children; *15* means no persons under that age will be admitted; and films certified with an *18* (approximately the old 'X' certificate) means that nobody under that age will be admitted to the cinema while that film is showing.

Note: 'No cert' means that no certificate had been issued by the *initial showing of the film* but this does not mean that one was not or will not be issued at a later date.

The Adventures of Buckaroo Banzai Across the 8th Dimension. Young, good-looking, athletic and intellectual Buckaroo, brilliant neuro-surgeon, physicist and successful rock star, drives his jet-powered car through the base of an impenetrable mountain and is launched into the eighth dimension. There he encounters the preposterously evil Dr Lizardo (John Lithgow, way over the top), and a loathsome posse of bad guys. It's like nothing you've ever seen, but at the same time it's a bizarre pot-pourri of every film genre you've heard of – sci-fi, comedy, thriller, fantasy, love story, western, adventure . . . that manages to be funny by keeping its face straight.

Rest of cast: Peter Weller (Buck), Ellen Barkin, Jeff Goldblum, Christopher Lloyd, Lewis Smith, Pepe Serna, Clancy Brown, Vincent Schiavelli, Ronald Lacey, Rosalind Cash, Robert Ito, Matt Clark, William Traynor, Carl Lumbly, Dan Hedaya, Mariclare Costello, Bill Henderson, Damon Hines, Billy Vera, Laura Harrington, Michael Santoro, Kent Perkins, Jonathan Banks, Robert Gray, Gary Bisig, Kenneth Magee, James Keane, John David Ashton, Takov Smirnoff, Leonard Gines, Francine Lembi, John Walter Davis, Read Morgan, James Rosin, Raye Birk, Jane Marla Robbins, Kevin Sullivan, Jessie Lawrence Ferguson, Radford Polinsky, Sam Minsky, Robert Hummer, Gerald Peterson. Dir and Co-Pro (with Neil Canton): W.D. Richter. Ex Pro: Sidney Beckerman. Assoc Pro: Dennis Jones. Screenplay: Earl Mac Rauch. Ph: Fred J. Koenekamp. Ed: Richard Marks and George Bowers. Pro Des: J.M. Riva. Art: Richard Carter and Stephen Dane. M: Michael Boddicker. (Sherwood Pro-Orbit). Rel: floating; first shown London (Brixton Ritzy) 10 July 1987. 102 mins. Cert PG.

The Adventures of Mark Twain. Technically fascinating animated cartoon feature in Claymation, a sort of plasticine which gives the characters a three-dimensional reality and fluidity of movement. This first example of the method took three and a half years to make, with 24 adjustments to the sculptured figures per second of running time – adding up to some 130,000 painstaking changes for the film. Equally painstaking is the script, of which nearly every word is Mark Twain's own. The story, almost inevitably less arresting, is about the author's pursuit of Halley's Comet through space, in his Heath Robinson-style airship.

Voices: James Whitmore (Twain), Chris Ritchie (Tom Sawyer), Gary Krug (Finn), Michele Mariana, John Morrison, Carol

Edelman, Dallas McKennon, Herb Smith, Marley Stone, Wilbur Vincent, Wally Newman, Tim Conner, Todd Tolces, Billy Scream, Wilf Innton, Tom Gasek, Compton Downs, Billy Victor. Dir and Pro: Will Vinton. Ex Pro: Hugh Tirrell. Screenplay: Susan Shadburne. M: Billy Scream. Animation: W.F. Fiesterman, Tom Gasek, Mark Gustafson etc. (Entertainment). Rel: floating; first shown London (ICA) 18 December 1987. 83 mins. Cert U.

Allan Quartermain and the Lost City of Gold. A remake of Harry Alan Towers's film, never released on the large screen to my knowledge, based on Rider Haggard's *Allan Quartermain* novel, to which it bears scant relation. This version of the story of Allan (played by Richard Chamberlain) and his search for gold and a lost white African tribe is not much more successful than the earlier film.

Rest of cast: James Earl Jones, Henry Silva, Robert Donner, Doghmi Larbi, Aileen Marson, Cassandra Peterson, Martin Rabbett etc. Dir: Gary Nelson (Add Dir: Newt Arnold). Pro: Menahem Golan and Yoram Globus. Screenplay: Gene Quintano, Alex Phillips and Frederick Elmes. Ed: Alain Jakubowicz. Pro Des: Trevor Williams and Leslie Dilley. M: Michael Linn. (Cannon Group). Rel: 14 August 1987. 111 mins. Cert PG.

Amazing Stories. A stitching job of three assorted and contrasting SF stories from the old American TV series of the same title. The first is about a trapped gunner in a Second World War bomber who, when the under-carriage fails, gets out pen and paper and draws a new one, which lands the crippled aircraft; the second features an actor playing a mummy who suddenly has to face the real thing; the third is about a teacher who dies under a spell but is brought back to life with a detachable head. With Kevin Costner, Kiefer Sutherland, Mary Stuart Masterson, Casey Siemaszko, etc.

Dir: Steven Spielberg, William Dear and Robert Zemeckis. Ex Pro: Spielberg. (Amblin Entertainment for Universal-UIP). Rel: floating. 110 mins. Cert 15.

Mark Twain and, above, his revolutionary spaceship in the Clubhouse Pictures/ Entertainment release The Adventures of Mark Twain – *the first feature to be made in Claymation, a new animation system.*

The Russian mouse family which emigrates to the New World in UIP's An American Tail. *The odd cat out, Tiger (left), helps lost little Fievel to rejoin his family.*

An American Tail. In terms of draughtsmanship, character creation, simple humour and those scary sequences beloved of the late Walt, this Steven Spielberg animated cartoon feature is the nearest anyone has ever approached to the earlier, vintage work of Disney: only the final inimitable touch of magic is missing. But this is still very good fun for the young and the young at heart. The story follows the fortunes of a perky little mouse hero and his family, who emigrate from Russia to escape their fearsome feline enemies, only to find that America is not, as promised, cat-free.

Voices: Cathianne Blore, Dom DeLuise, John Finnegan, Phillip Glasser, Amy Green, Madeline Kahn, Pat Musick, Nehemiah Persoff, Christopher Plummer, Neil Ross, Will Ryan, Erica Yohn. Dir: Don Bluth. Pro: Bluth, John Pomeroy and Gary Goldman. Ex Pro: Steven Spielberg, David Kirschner, Kathleen Kennedy and Frank Marshall. Screenplay: Judy Freudberg and Tony Geiss; from a story by Kirschner, Freudberg and Geiss. Ed: Dan Molina. M: James Horner (songs by Horner, Cynthia Weil and Barry Mann). (Universal-UIP). Rel: 24 July 1987. 81 mins. Cert U.

Angel Dust – Poussière d'ange. The second film by Edouard Niermans following his debut some five years ago with *Anthracite* confirms this writer-director's talent for the medium. He has not been wholly idle in the interim, but has been making material for French TV. Here he has taken a more or less routine *film noir* crime story and told it in an individual, stylish and, some may find, rather confusing way. Paris detective Blount is on a long-term big bender after his wife has left him for another man, but slowly sobers up as he becomes involved with an attractive teenager who, he gradually discovers, is both devious and deadly beneath all her young charm. As he slowly unravels the case – which is what it becomes – he turns up a few surprises both for himself and for the audience, which lead to a violent, exciting and bloody climax and an unethical – in cop-movie terms – ending. What lifts all this several notches above the norm are the touches of wry humour (one especially amusing right at the start), pace and polished performances, particularly by Bernard Giraudeau as the cop and fascinating Fanny Bastien as the girl.

Rest of cast: Fanny Cottençon, Jean-Pierre Sentier, Michel Aumont, Gérard Blain, Luc Lavandier, Véronique Silver, Daniel Laloux, Yveline Ailhaud, Patrick Bonnel, Bertie Cortez, Henri Marteau, Daniel Russo, Louis Audubert, James Bakech, Pierre Belot, Valerie Deronzier, Max Fournel, François Giombini, Jean-Pierre Hutinet,

Shabby private eye Angel (Mickey Rourke) earns his fee from mysterious Mr Cyphre (Robert De Niro, top right) in Alan Parker's Tri-Star/Columbia thriller Angel Heart. *Bottom right: Epiphany the Voodooist (Lisa Bonet).*

Jean-Marie Lemaire, Marie Matheron, Georges Montillier, Marie-Therese Orain, Alexandra Pandev, Patrick Paroux, Pascal Pistacio, Juliette Rennes, Serge Ridoux, Luc Rosello, Alain Stern. Dir and Screenplay (latter with Jacques Audiard and Alain Le Henry): Edouard Niermans. Pro: Jacques-Eric Strauss. Ph: Bernard Lutic. Ed: Yves Deschamps and Jacques Witta. Art: Dominique Maleret. M: Léon Senza and Vincent-Marie Bouvot. (President Films/Top 1/Films de la Saga/FR3 Films Pro/La Sofia Co-Pro-Palace Pictures). Rel: floating; first shown London (Renoir) 12 February 1988. 95 mins. Cert 15.

Angel Heart. Masterly *film noir*, with Mickey Rourke as Harry Angel, an unprepossessing private detective in 1955 New York. A mysterious, pony-tailed stranger (Robert De Niro) hires Angel to unravel the whereabouts of a swing band singer, gone missing ten years earlier. Murder and mayhem lead him to New Orleans, where the dishevelled detective becomes a murder

suspect and is lured into a violent world of voodoo and worse. A superb piece of film artistry, with the atmosphere laid on with a trowel; excellent photography, production design and music, and an ingenious plot.

Rest of cast: Lisa Bonet, Charlotte Rampling, Stocker Fontelieu, Brownie McGhee, Michael Higgins, Elizabeth Whitcraft, Eliott Keener, Charles Gordone, Dann Florek, Kathleen Wilhoite, George Buck, Judith Drake, Gerald L. Orange, Peggy Severe, Pruitt Taylor Vince, David Petit-jean, Rick Washburn, Neil Newlon, Oakley Dalton, Yvonne Bywaters, Loys T. Bergeron, Joshua Frank, Ernest Watson, Rickie Monie. Dir: Alan Parker. Pro: Alan Marshall and Elliott Kastner. Ex Pro: Mario Kassar and Andrew Vajna. Screenplay: Alan Parker; based on the novel *Falling Angel* by William Hjortsberg. Ph: Michael Seresin. Ed: Gerry Hambling. Pro Des: Brian Morris. M: Trevor Jones. (Tri-Star – Columbia). Rel: 30 October 1987. Cert 18.

Les Anges du péché. It has taken 44 years for Robert Bresson's first feature film to be shown in a public cinema in Britain and one wonders why; for, typical of this great French director's sparse and uncompromising style, this

tragic story of relationships within a Dominican convent in France is compelling to watch.

Cast: Renée Faure, Jany Holt, Sylvie, Marie-Hélène Daste, Yolande Laffon, Mila Parely, Paula Debrelly, Sylvia Monfort, Gilberte Terbois, Louis Seigner, Georges Colin. Dir: Robert Bresson. Pro: Synops-Robert Tual. Screenplay: Father Bruckberger, Jean Giraudoux and Bresson. Ph: Philippe Agostini. Ed: Yvonne Martin. Set Design (Art): René Renoux. M: Jean-Jacques Grunewald. (Electric). Rel: shown to celebrate Bresson's 80th birthday at Everyman, Hampstead, for a season from 11 September 1987. 91 mins. Cert PG.

Appointment with Death. Hercule Poirot, Agatha Christie's lovable Belgian sleuth, is on holiday in Israel with a gaggle of suspects when the tyrannical Mrs Emily Boynton is murdered. Everybody wanted her dead, but whodunit? Michael Winner directs with a sledgehammer; even the normally reliable John Gielgud looks uncomfortable; Piper Laurie belts out a caricature as Mrs Boynton; while some of the younger members of the cast are just plain embarrassing. Only Jenny Sea-

Comfortably plump detective Hercule Poirot (Peter Ustinov) peers over the shoulder of the Colonel (John Gielgud) in Cannon's Appointment with Death. *On the right is Jenny Seagrove, as Dr Sarah King.*

grove shines, as a beautiful doctor, while Peter Ustinov, as always, is beguiling as Poirot.

Rest of cast: Lauren Bacall, Carrie Fisher, Hayley Mills, David Soul, John Terlesky, Valerie Richards, Nicholas Guest, Mike Sarne, Doug Sheldon, Amber Bezer. Dir and Pro: Michael Winner. Ex Pro: Menahem Golan and Yoram Globus. Screenplay: Anthony Shaffer, Peter Buckman and Michael Winner. Ph: David Gurfinkel. Ed: Arnold Crust (Michael Winner). Pro Des: John Blezard. M: Pino Donaggio. (Cannon). Rel: floating; first shown London (Cannons Haymarket and Shaftesbury Ave) 27 May 1988. 108 mins. Cert PG.

Asterix in Britain – Astérix chez les Bretons. Somewhat surprisingly, the famous French cartoon character of the brave little Gaul has not previously had the enormous success in Britain that it has enjoyed elsewhere in Europe and, indeed, around the world. But this second Asterix film, made in the

Gaumont studios specially created for these cartoon features, may well put that right. It tells how Asterix and his fat, amusingly dim-witted sidekick, Obelix, come to Britain to defend the rotund Gaul's cousin against the Roman legions. It may not rock you off your seat with laughter but the characters have an endearing quality and it will certainly amuse the youngsters.

With the voices of Roger Carel (Asterix), Pierre Tornade (Obelix), Pierre Mondy (Cetinlapsus), Serge Sauvion (César). Dir: Pino Van Lamsweerde. Pro: Yannick Piel. Screenplay: Pierre Tchernia; based on the cartoon creations of René Goscinny and Alberto Uderzo. Ph: Philippe Laine. Ed: Robert and Monique Isnardon. Art: Michel Guerin. M: Vladimir Cosma. Animation Dir: Keith Ingham. (Gaumont/Dargaud/Gutenberghus-Palace Pictures). Rel: floating; first shown London (Cannon Tottenham Court Road) 25 March 1988. 75 mins. Cert U.

Aria. A splendid idea by the British producer Don Boyd resulted in this collection of ten loosely linked short films, each based on a different operatic extract, interpreted by a different director. They range from the more conven-

tional (such as Nicolas Roeg's reconstruction of the attempted assassination of King Zog in Vienna, to the music of Verdi's *Un ballo in maschera*) to the less so (as in the case of Jean-Luc Godard's ludicrous concentration on female nudes and male muscles, with scant respect to the music of Lully's *Armide*), with interesting if uneven contributions by Robert Altman, Bruce Beresford, Bill Bryden, Ken Russell etc. Incidentally, there's quite a lot of nudity . . . opera seems to give film directors erotic ideas. The linking of the segments is awkward and the film does not quite work as a whole; but there is enough superb singing, wonderful music and visual splendours and enough striking ideas to make this one of the year's most original and fascinating movies, if, sadly, one of rather limited achievement and appeal.

Segment 1, Un ballo in maschera Dir: Nicolas Roeg. Cast includes Theresa Russell, Stephanie Lane, Arthur Vox, Dennis Holmes, Paul Brightwell, Frank Baker, Chris Hunter etc. Assoc Pro: Richard Bell and Luc Roeg. Ph: Harvey Harrison. Art: Diana Johnstone. *Segment 2*, Verdi's *La vergine degli angeli*. Dir: Charles Sturridge. Cast: Nicola Swain, Jack Kyle, Marianne McLoughlin. Assoc Pro: Paul Spencer. Ph: Gale Tattersall. Art: Andrew McAlpine. Ed: Matthew Longfellow. *Segment 3*, Lully's *Armide*. Dir: Jean-Luc Godard. Cast: Marion Peters and Valerie Allain, with lots of well-muscled bodybuilders. Ph: Carolyn Champetier (and Pierre Mignot). Pro Des: Stephen Altman. *Segment 4*, Verdi's *Rigoletto*. Dir: Julian Temple. Cast: Buck Henry, Anita Morris, Beverly D'Angelo, Gary Kasper, John Hostetter (as Elvis Presley impersonator) etc. Assoc Pro: Amanda Temple. Ph: Oliver Stapleton. Art: Piers Plowden. Writer: Charlie Coffer. *Segment 5*, Korngold's *Das Glück das Mir*. Dir: Bruce Beresford. Cast: Elizabeth Hurley, Peter Birch. Assoc Pro: Iain Brown. Ph: Dante Spinotti. Ed: Marie-Thérèse Boiche. Art: Andrew McAlpine. *Segment 6*, Rameau's *Les Boréades*. Dir: Robert Altman. Assoc Pro: Scott Bushnell. Ed: Steve Dunn. Cast: Bertrand Bonvoison, Cris Campion, Anne Canovas, Sandrine Dumas, Jody Guelb, Julie Hagerty, Philipine Leroy-Beaulieu, Genevieve Page, Delphine Rich, Louis-Marie Taillefer. *Segment 7*, Wagner's 'Liebestod' from *Tristan und Isolde*. Dir: Franc Roddam. Assoc Pro: Joni Sighvasson. Ph: Fred Elmes. Art: Matthew Jacobs. Ed: Rick Elgood. Cast: Bridget Fonda, James Mathers. *Segment 8*, Puccini's *Turandot* ('Nessun dorma'). Dir: Ken Russell. Assoc Pro: Paul Spencer. Ph: Gabriel Beristain. Art: Paul Dufficey. Ed: Mike Bradsell.

Scenes from half of the ten short films which made up the musically delightful and otherwise interesting but not wholly successful Virgin release Aria. Clockwise, from above: Theresa Russell, as King Zog, in Nicolas Roeg's opening film based on Verdi's Un ballo in maschera; Valerie Allain and a muscleman in *Jean-Luc Godard's piece – Lully's Armide; Anita Morris in Julian Temple's Rigoletto extract; Linzi Drew in Ken Russell's extravagant visual interpretation of Puccini's Turandot; John Hurt, link man to the various sections; the audience in Robert Altman's contribution, Rameau's Les Boréades.*

Cast: Linzi Drew, Andreas Wisniewski, Kwabena Manso, Bella Enahoro, Bunty Mathias, Angela Walker. *Segment 9*, Charpentier's *Depuis le jour*. Dir: Derek Jarman. Assoc Pro: James Mackay. Ph: Mike Sothon. Ed: Peter Cartwright and Angus Cook. Pro Des: Christopher Hobbs. Cast: Tilda Swinton, Spencer Leigh, Amy Johnson. *Segment 10*, Leoncavallo's *I pagliacci* ('Vesti la giubba'). Dir: Bill Bryden. Assoc Pro (GB): Paul Spencer. Ph: Gabriel Beristan. Ed: Mike Cragg and Paul Naisbitt. Cast: John Hurt, Sophie Ward. Singers: 1: Leontyne Price, Carlo Bergonzi, Robert Merrill, Shirley Verrett and Reri Grist. 2: Leontyne Price, Giorgio Tozzi, Ezio-Flagello. 3: Rachel Yakar. 4: Alfredo Kraus, Anna Moffo, Annadi Stasio. 5: Carol Neblett, Rene Collo. 6: Jennifer Smith, Anne-Marie Rodd, Philip Langridge. 7: Leontyne Price. 8: Jussi Bjoerling. 9: Leontyne Price. 10: Enrico Caruso. Pro (the whole film) Don Boyd. Ex Pro: Jim Mervis: Tom Kuhn and Charles Itchell, Co-Pro: Al Clark and Mike Watts. Co-ordinating Ed: Marie Thérèse Boiche and Mike Cragg. (RVP Pro/Virgin Vision). Rel: floating; first shown London (Lumiere) 30 October 1987. 89 mins. Cert 18.

The Armour of God – Long Xiong Hu Di. A minor Hong Kong production which starts and finishes in fine, sun-lit style but sinks into something of an abyss in between. Jackie Chan stars and directs himself in a tale of heroes and villains in search of a priceless suit of Crusader's armour, and performs all those remarkable stunts himself.

Rest of cast: Alan Tam, Rosamund Kwan, Lola Forner, Bosidale Sumiljanik, Ken Boyle, Mars, Brackie Fong, Alicia Shawnte, Marcia Chizam, Vivian Wickliff, Linda Denly, John Ladalski, Robert O'Brien, Boris Gregoric, Stephanie Evans, William Williams. Dir: Jackie Chan. Pro: L.K.C. Ho and, Chua Lam. Ex Pro: Raymond Chow. Screenplay: Edward Tang and others; based on a story by Barry Wong. Ph: Bob Thompson and Peter Ngor etc. Ed: Cheung Yiu Chung. Art: William Cheung. M: Michael Rai. (Golden Harvest-Video/Target). Rel: floating; first shown London (Cannon Group) 9 October 1987. 90 mins. Cert 15.

Babette's Feast – Babettes Gaestebud. From Denmark and Karen Blixen (author of *Out of Africa*) comes this gourmet classic about a famous Parisian woman chef (from the Café Anglais) who is forced into exile and becomes servant-cook to the daughters of a deceased pastor-prophet in a village on the wild and inhospitable Danish coast. When she unexpectedly wins 10,000 francs in the French lottery, Babette spends the lot on supplies from Paris in order to prepare a marvellous banquet for the villagers, whose normal meals consist of soup, rough bread and dried fish. How this wonderful wine and food transforms and humanizes them! Quietly amusing yet moving, with a slightly ironic philosophical undercurrent, this is a lovely and mouth-watering movie, brilliantly acted by Stéphane Audran (as the chef) and the rest of the small cast.

Rest of cast: Jean-Philippe Lafont, Gudmar Wivesson, Jarl Kulle, Bibi Andersson, Hanne Steensgord, Bodil Kher, Vibeke Hastrup, Birgitte Federspiel, Bent Rothe, Ebbe Rode, Lizbeth Movin, Preben Lerdorff Rye, Poul Kern, Kai Kristiansen, Axel Strøbye, Michel Bouquet (the voice of the narrator). Dir: Gabriel Axel. Pro: Bo Christensen. Ex Pro: Just Betzer. Screenplay: Axel; based on the novella by Karen Blixen/Isak Dinesen. Ph: Henning Kristiansen. Ed: Finn Henriksen. Art: Sven Wichman. M: Per Norgaard. (Just Betzer–Panorama Film International, in co-operation with Nordisk Film A/S and Danish Film Institute-Artificial Eye). Rel: floating; first shown London (Lumiere) 4 March 1988. 105 mins. Cert U.

Baby Boom. A frantic workaholic sales executive (Diane Keaton) – 'Worry is my middle name' – inherits a 13-month-old child and finds her life transformed – for better and for worse. Yet another addition to the recent crop of baby movies, this time with a feminist angle – and not so funny. A handful of witty lines battle in vain against a contrived plot, melodramatic situations and a bland score.

Rest of cast: Harold Ramis, Sam Wanamaker, Sam Shepard, James Spader, Pat Hingle, Britt Leach, Kristina and Michelle Kennedy (as the baby), Linda Ellerbee, Elizabeth Bennett, Beverly Todd, Patti Johns, Annie Golden, Jennifer Balgobin, Victoria Jackson, Carol Gillies, Paxton Whitehead, Hansford Rowe, Mary O'Sullivan, Lisa Fuller, Elizabeth Philbin. Dir: Charles Shyer. Pro: Nancy Meyers. Assoc Pro: Bruce A. Block. Screenplay: Nancy Meyers and Charles Shyer. Ph: William A. Fraker. Ed: Lynzee Klingman. Pro Des: Jeffrey Howard. M: Bill Conti. Costumes: Susan Becker. (MGM/UA-UIP). Rel: 18 March 1988. 110 mins. Cert PG.

Barfly. Charles Bukowski, the poet laureate of American low-life, typically showed no interest in this project until he found out how much money he might make. Movie-hater that he is, Bukowski has turned in an amazing, semi-autobiographical story of a bum poet with pride. Mickey Rourke, at his sleaziest yet, pumps his character with self-respect and Scotch, a no-good king of the gutter who quotes Tolstoy like invective. A very funny, well acted eye-opener on the world of the alcoholic.

Rest of cast: Faye Dunaway (sensational), Alice Krige, Jack Nance, J.C. Quinn, Frank Stallone (Sly's brother), Sandy Martin, Roberta Bassin, Gloria Leroy, Joe Unger, Harry Cohn, Pruitt Taylor Vince, Joe Rice, Julie 'Sunny' Pearson, Donald L. Norden, Wil Albert, Hal Shafer, Zeek Manners, Pearl Shear, Rik Colitti, Michael Collins, Ron Joseph, Damon Hines, Lahmard J. Tate, Carlos Cervantes, Peter Conti, Vance Colvig, Stacey Pickren, Leonard Termo, Gary Cox, Fritz Feld, Albert Henderson, Sandy Rose, Madalyn Carol, George Marshall Ruge, Debbie Lynn Ross. Dir: Barbet Schroeder. Pro: Barbet Schroeder, Fred Roos and Tom Luddy. Ex Pro: Menahem Golan and Yoram Globus. Assoc Pro: Jack Baran. Screenplay: Charles Bukowski. Ph: Robby Müller. Ed: Eva Gardos. Pro Des: Bob Ziembicki. M: Classical extracts. (Cannon). Rel: 4 March 1988. 99 mins. Cert 18.

*batteries not included. A tenement brownstone in New York is up for demolition, but its tenants refuse to uproot. In come the heavies – complete with baseball bats – but they are kept at bay by a family of miniature flying saucers. Steven Spielberg, as executive producer of this ill-named fantasy, reaches new depths of mawkishness and predictability, plundering his own well-trodden *Close Encounters*, *E.T.* and even an episode from *Twilight Zone – The Movie*. He has handed the directorial reins to Matthew Robbins (*Dragonslayer*), who in turn creates some self-indulgent hokum of the worst kind. The sentimentality is so thick that it drips off the screen.

Cast: Hume Cronyn, Jessica Tandy, Frank McRae, Elizabeth Peña, Michael Carmine, Dennis Boutsikaris, Tom Aldredge, Jane Hoffman, John DiSante, John Pankow, MacIntyre Dixon, Michael Greene, Doris Belack, Wendy Schaal etc. Dir: Matthew Robbins. Pro: Ronald L. Schwary. Ex Pro: Steven Spielberg, Kathleen Kennedy and Frank Marshall. Screenplay: Matthew Robbins, Brad Bird, Brent Maddock and S.S.

Wilson; based on a story by Mick Garris. Ph: John McPherson. Ed: Cynthia Scheider. Pro Des: Ted Haworth. Art: Angelo Graham. M: James Horner. (Universal-UIP). Rel: 25 March 1988. 106 mins. Cert PG.

The Beekeeper – O Melissokomos. Fascinating Greek-French co-production with a meandering story about an elderly retired schoolteacher making his annual visit to his various far-flung beehives. He picks up a young girl on the way – and nothing yet everything happens. The ambiguous ending is apt for a film full of nuances and quiet pleasures, which offers Marcello Mastroianni yet another opportunity for an outstanding performance.

Rest of cast: Nadia Mourouzi, Serge Reggiani, Jenny Roussea, Dinos Iliopoulos, Vassia Panagopolou, Dimitris Poulikakos, Nikos Kouos, Yannis Savradinos, Chris Nezer. Dir: Theodorus Angelopoulos. Ex Pro: Nikos Angelopoulos. Screenplay: Theodorus Angelopoulos, in collaboration with Dimitris Nollas. Ph: Giorgos Arvanitis. Ed: Takis Yannopoulos. Art: Mikes Karapiperis. M: Helen Karaindrou. (Greek Film Centre/Angelopoulos/ERTI, Athens/MK2 Pro., Paris-Artificial Eye). Rel: floating; first shown London (Renoir) 8 January 1988. 122 mins. Cert 18.

The Believers. Weird *Marathon Man*-style horror thriller, splashed with blood and guts, from John Schlesinger. His expertise and feel for pace paper over the holes for the most part in a complicated and not always easy-to-follow plot about a phoney faith called Santeria which calls for human sacrifice. The film's opening sets the mood with two horrible, apparently unrelated New York murders which are subsequently investigated by police psychotherapist Cal (Martin Sheen), whose wife was one of the victims. At some length he comes up with the answer: cult rituals. Even the superior production qualities and assured direction cannot lessen the visual nastiness and violence which are the movie's mainsprings.

Rest of cast: Helen Shaver, Harley Cross, Elizabeth Wilson, Harris Yulin, Robert Loggia, Richard Masur, Lee Richardson, Carla Pinza, Jimmy Smits, Raul Davils, Malick Bowens, Janet Laine Green, Larry Ramon, Philip Corey, Jennifer Lee, Nonnie Griffin, Bob Clout, Joan Kaye, Eddie Jones, John Bendel, Joseph Pantangelo, Joseph Wilkins etc. Dir: John Schlesinger. Pro: Schlesinger, Michael Childers and Beverly

Wanda (Faye Dunaway) and shabby, unshaven Henry (Mickey Rourke) share a moment of exuberance in Cannon's Barfly.

Camhe. Ex Pro: Edward Teets. Screenplay: Mark Frost; based on the book *The Religion* by Nicholas Conde. Ph: Robby Müller. Ed: Peter Honess. Pro Des: Simon Holland. Art: John Kasarda and Carol Spier. M: J.

Jessica Tandy looks in awe at the mini spaceship which has arrived in her home in Universal/UIP's *batteries not included.

Peter Robinson. (Orion-Rank). Rel: 8 April 1988. 113 mins. Cert 18.

Bell Diamond. Another idiosyncratic film by John Jost, this account of the break-up of a marriage has even less general appeal than usual.

Cast: Marshall Gaddis, Sarah Wyss etc. Dir, Pro, Screenplay, Ed and Ph: John Jost. Screenplay: improvised. M: John English, (Jost-ICA). Rel: floating; first shown London (ICA) 31 March 1988. 96 mins. No cert.

Bellman and True. A tough, gritty story about a man called Hiller (Bernard Hill), a failed computer systems engineer forced to work for a ruthless team of bank robbers. Deserted by his wife and dumped with her son, Hiller decides to help his captors in order to secure a decent future for his ward. A rather bleak affair, without a likeable character in sight.

Rest of cast: Kieran O'Brien (as the boy), Richard Hope, Frances Tomelty, Derek Newark, John Kavanagh, Ken Bones, Arthur Whybrow, Peter Howell, Jim Dowdall, Richard Strange, William Sleigh, Badi Uzzaman, Ann Carroll, Chris Sanders, Kate McEnery, Stephen Churchett, Roger McKern, Peter Jonfield, Richard Walsh, Andrew Paul, Camilla Nash, Alisa Bosschaert, Alan Downer, Michael Bertenshaw. Dir: Richard Loncraine. Pro: Michael Wearing and Christopher Neame. Ex Pro: George Harrison, Denis O'Brien, John Hambley and Johnny Goodman. Screenplay: Desmond Lowden, Richard Loncraine and Michael Wearing. Ph: Ken Westbury. Ed: Paul Green. Pro Des: John Bunker. M: Colin Towns. (HandMade-Recorded Releasing). Rel: 15 April 1988. 121 mins. Cert 15.

Ken Bones, Bernard Hill and Richard Hope in an unhappy moment for the blackmailed middle man in the Recorded Releasing thriller Bellman and True.

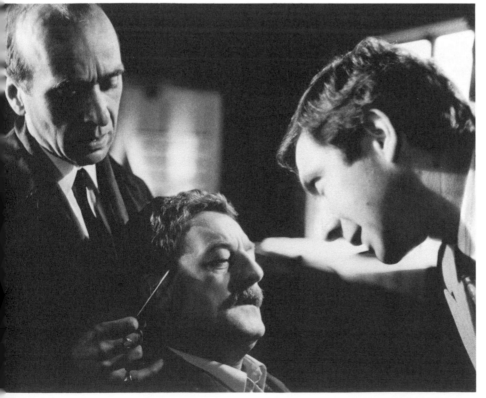

The Belly of an Architect. Peter Greenaway's third film is far and away his best, and of the widest appeal. None the less, however artistic, and sometimes arty, it may be, it is still more likely to win festival awards and provoke some long, psychologically slanted reviews than to attract the paying patrons. Superbly photographed in Italy, always wonderful visually, it is also far too long and always vaguely distasteful. It very coldly tells the story of an American architect attempting to stage an exhibition in Rome of the work of his eighteenth-century French hero Boullée. The main complications are provided by his jealousy of an Italian architect who is taking his wife away from him and his increasing awareness that the agony in his belly is a fatal cancer. Brian Dennehy plays the ample American, Chloe Webb is irritating – especially her voice – as the wife, and the supporting cast gives the impression that nobody concerned with the production had much regard for putting blood in the veins or flesh on the bones of their characters. Did someone whisper 'magnificent intellectual failure'?

Rest of cast: Lambert Wilson, Sergio Fantoni, Stephania Casini, Vanni Corbellini, Alfredo Varelli, Geoffrey Copleston, Francesco Carnelutti, Claudio Spadaro, Riccardo Ussani, Enrica Scrivano, Julian Jenkins, Marino Mase, Andrea Prodan, Marne Maitland, Fabio Sartor, Stephano Gragnani, Rate Furlan. Dir and Screenplay: Peter Greenaway. Pro: Colin Callender and Walter Donohue. Assoc Pro: Conchita Airoldi and Dino di Dionisio. Ph: Sacha Vierny. Ed: John Wilson. Art: Luciana Vedovelli. M: Wim Mertens (Add M: Glenn Branca). (Film Four International and British Screen in assoc with Hemdale and Sacis-Monial Ltd London/Tangram Film Rome-Recorded Releasing). Rel: floating; first shown London (Gate Notting Hill and Screen-on-the-Hill) 16 October 1987. 118 mins. Cert 15.

Bernadette. Veteran Jean Delannoy's sincere, straightforward and uninvolved story of the young Bernadette Soubirous, the sickly girl, daughter of a French miller, who had visions of the Virgin in a grotto and so established it as the holy shrine of Lourdes, the world-famous place of miracles. Bernadette is played without charisma but with simple charm by (dubbed) American actress Sydney Penny.

Rest of cast: Jean-Marc Bory, Michele Simonnet, Roland Lesaffre, Bernard Dheran, François Dalout, Stephan Garcin, Arlette Didier, Beata Tyszhiewicz, Frank David. Dir: Jean Delannoy. Pro: Jacques Quintard. Screenplay: Delannoy and Robert Arnaut. Ph: Jean-Bernard Penzer. Ed: Annick Charvein. Art: Alain Paroutaud. M: Francis Lai. (Films de l'Etoile d'Or/Bernadette Assoc. International-Cannon). Rel: floating; first shown London (Cannon Shaftesbury Ave) 15 April 1988. 105 mins. Cert U.

Best Seller. A former hit-man from a large multi-national corporation (James Woods) teams up with a detective-novelist (Brian Dennehy) to help expose the murderous doings of Woods's ex-employer (Paul Shenar). As the unlikely duo hop between Los Angeles and New York to unveil the evidence, Dennehy embarks on an expository novel, but becomes increasingly suspicious of the identity of his colleague. An unusual, nasty and always compelling thriller – with plenty of black laughs – well played by the steely, ferret-like Woods, working off the equally impressive, stolid, ursine Dennehy.

Rest of cast: Victoria Tennant, Allison Balson, George Coe, Ann Pitoniak, Mary Carver, Sully Boyar, Kathleen Lloyd, Harold Tyner, E. Brian Dean, Jeffrey Josephson, Edward Blackoff, Branscombe Richmond,

At an exclusive Rome restaurant, inebriated Brian Dennehy reveals The Belly of an Architect *to the disgusted diners in the Film Four/Recorded Releasing British film of that title.*

J.P. Blumstead, William Bronder, Jenny Gago, Michael Crabtree, Clare Fields, Claudio Stenke, David Byrd, Loyda Ramos, Obaka Adedunyo, Ted Markland, Phil Hoover, David Blackwood, David Ursin, Jay Ingram, Daniel Trent, Gary Kirk, Dean Abston, David Cass, Bill Mitchell, John Howard Swain, Dennis Acree, Mark Venturini, Larry Holt, Jeff Ramsey, James Winburn, Peter Stader, Samuel V. Baldoni, Hank Woessner, Brian Gaffikin, Michael White, Martin West, Wally Burr, Arlin Miller, Sands Hall. Dir: John Flynn. Pro: Carter De Haven. Ex Pro: John Daly and Derek Gibson. Screenplay: Larry Cohen. Ph: Fred Murphy. Ed: David Rosenbloom. Pro Des: Gene Rudolf. M: Jay Ferguson. (Orion/Hemdale – Rank). Rel: floating; first shown London (Leicester Square Theatre) 27 November 1987. 95 mins. Cert 18.

The ill-assorted team of detective (Brian Dennehy) and hit-man (James Woods, right) work together to expose the villainy of the latter's boss in the Orion/Rank thriller Best Seller.

Investigating Eddie Murphy illustrates the old-fashioned way of obtaining information from a suspect in Paramount/UIP's comedy Beverly Hills Cop II.

Beverly Hills Cop II. Noisy, frenetic sequel to the world's second most successful comedy (the first is *Ghostbusters*), with Eddie Murphy called back to Beverly Hills to solve a series of brutal 'Alphabet Crimes'. The laughs are pretty thin on the ground, the jokes geared either to sex or to Sylvester Stallone and/or Rambo. The blank spots are filled in by car chases, accompanied by loud music. It's obviously time for Murphy to reassess his career strategy.

Rest of cast: Judge Reinhold, Jürgen Prochnow, Ronny Cox, John Ashton, Brigitte Nielsen, Allen Garfield, Paul Reiser, Gil Hill, Dean Stockwell, Paul Guilfoyle, Robert Ridgley, Brian O'Connor, Alice Adair, Eugene Butler, Glenn Withrow, Stephen Liska, Gilbert Gottfried, Tom Bower, Valerie Wildman, Hugh M. Hefner (as himself), Carrie Leigh, Frank J. Pesce, Vic Manni, Sheri Levinsky, Ray Murphy Sr, Todd Susman, Chris Rock, Susan Lentini, Anthony D'Andrea, Robert Pastorelli, Kopi Sotiropulos, Richard Tienken, Teal Roberts, Peggy Sands, Larry Carroll, Carlos Cervantes, Dayna O'Brien, Ola Ray. Dir: Tony Scott. Pro: Don Simpson and Jerry Bruckheimer. Ex Pro: Robert D. Wachs and Richard Tienken. Screenplay: Larry Ferguson, Warren Skaaren, David Giler and Dennis Klein, from a story by Eddie Murphy and Robert D. Wachs, based on characters created by Danilo Bach and Daniel Petrie Jr. Ph: Jeffrey L. Kimball. Ed: Billy Weber, Chris Lebenzon and Michael Tronick. Pro Des: Ken Davis. M: Harold Faltermeyer, with songs by Bob Seger, The Pointer Sisters, Jermaine Jackson, James Ingram, George Michael, Charlie Sexton etc. (Paramount – UIP). Rel: 9 October 1987. 103 mins. Cert 15.

Beyond Therapy. Three characters in search of a psychiatrist. Typical Robert Altman comedy, based on Christopher Durang's play, in which an ensemble of wacky characters collides in a French restaurant in New York (filmed in Paris). An undisciplined affair that tries too hard to shock and degenerates into puerile farce – a serious waste of thespian talent.

Cast: Julie Hagerty, Jeff Goldblum, Glenda Jackson, Tom Conti, Christopher Guest, Genevieve Page, Cris Campion, Sandrine Dumas, Bertrand Bonvoisin, Nicole Evans, Louis-Marie Taillefer, Matthew Lesniak, Laure Killing, Gilbert Blin, Vincent Longuemare. Dir: Robert Altman. Pro: Steven M. Haft. Assoc Pro: Scott Bushnell. Ex Pro: Roger Berlind. Screenplay: Christopher Durang and Robert Altman; from Durang's play. Ph: Pierre Mignot. Sup Ed: Steve Dunn. Ed: Jennifer Agué. Pro Des: Stephen Altman. M: Gabriel Yared. (Sandcastle 5/New World – Entertainment). Rel: floating; first shown London (Cannons Haymarket and Chelsea) 16 October 1987. 94 mins. Cert 15.

The Big Bang – Le Big Bang. A feast of animated bad taste from France and Belgium, with the focus on big 'boobs' and bottoms and the like, in a story set in the post-atomized world of 1995, where mutated males and females live in opposing colonies.

Voices include those of David Lander, Carole Androsky, Marshall Efron, Alice Playten, Marvin Silbersher, Joanna Lehman, Jerry Bledsoe, Josh Daniel, Bob Kaliban, George Osterman, Ray Owens, Deborah Taylor, Ron Vernon, Roberta Wallach. Dir: Picha. Pro: Boris Szulzinger. Screenplay: Tony Hendra. Ed: Nicole Garnier-Klipfel. M: Roy Budd. (Zwanz, Paris/Comedia, Brussels-Entertainment). Rel: floating; first shown London (Cannons Panton St and Edgware Rd) 17 July 1987. 74 mins. Cert 18.

The Big Easy. Lieutenant McSwain (Dennis Quaid), astute, charming and handsome, relishes the perks of being a cop, which allow him to bend the law to his gain and comfort. Committed to his job, he has only one other thing on his mind: Anne Osborne (Ellen Barkin), astute, charming and beautiful, and committed to her job as a DA prosecutor. She has only one thing on her mind: police corruption. It's no easy task, but they fall in love and McSwain falls foul of the law (and Miss Osborne). *The Big Easy* kicks the clichés out of the window and concentrates on entertaining its audience with style. Dennis Quaid makes an unusual, engaging lead, while Ellen Barkin projects the sort of potential that could make her the next Meryl Streep. Good score, interesting New Orleans locations, a great movie.

Rest of cast: Ned Beatty, Ebbe Roe Smith, John Goodman, Lisa Jane Persky, Charles Ludlam, Thomas O'Brien, Judge James Garrison, Carole Sutton, David Petitjean, Nick Hagler, Marc Lawrence, Jim

Chimento, Grace Zabriski, Steve Broussard, Solomon Burke, Eliott Keener, Gailard Sartain, Edward St Pe, Robert Lesser, Cheryl Starbuck, Terrance Simien, Margie O'Dair, Arden Lo, Rickey Pierre, Nick Krieger, Gary Sturgis, Byron Nora, Archie Sampier, Jeff Hollis, Joy Houck Jr, August Krinke, John Schluter, Zephirin Hymel 4, Jack Harris, George Dureau, Patrick Frederic, Lane Trippe, Don Lutenbacher, Peter Gabb, Buddy Quaid, The Dewey Balfa Band, The Mallet Playboys Band, Dennis Curren, Rico Wheat, St Augustine's Marching Hundred (Band), Robert Kearney, Joseph Vatalanotto. Dir: Jim McBride. Pro: Stephen Friedman. Ex Pro: Mort Engelberg. Screenplay: Daniel Petrie Jr., with Jack Baran. Ph: Affonso Beato. Ed: Mia Goldman. Pro Des: Jeannine Oppewall. M: various, inc. Dennis Quaid. (Kings Road – Recorded Releasing). Rel: 2 October 1987. 100 mins. Cert 18.

Big Foot and the Hendersons (US: *Harry and the Hendersons*). Generally slight and mildly amusing comedy (with a few moral lessons, such as the evils of the gun in human hands, packed into the footage) about a gentle giant brought home from the forest by the Henderson family and the various reactions by friend and foe to the creature's arrival in town.

Cast: John Lithgow, Melinda Dillon, Margaret Langrick, Joshua Rudoy, Kevin Peter Hall, David Suchet, Lainie Kazan, Don Ameche, M. Emmet Walsh, Bill Ontiverous, David Richardt, Jacqueline Moscou, Laura Kenny, Richard E. Arnold, Scan Morgan, Nick Flynn, David MacIntyre, Peggy Platt, Orene Anderson, William Dear, Laurie O'Brien, Michael Loggins, James King, Nathaniel Ellis, Juleen Murray, Connie Craig, Mark Mitchell, Dana Middleton, Richard Foley, Larry Wansley, Steve Sheppard-Brodie, Mickey Gilbert, Tom Hammond, Stuart Schwarz, Justin Mastro, Michael Goodell, Church McCullum, Vern Taylor, Stan Sturing, Robert Isaac Lee, Debbie Carrington, John F. Bloom, Britches, William Frankfather. Dir and (with W.E. Martin and Ezra D. Rappaport) Screenplay. William Dear. Pro: Dear and Richard Vane. Ph: George Koblasa. Ed: Donn Cambern. Pro Des: James Bissell. Art: Don Woodruff. M: Bruce Broughton. (Amblin Entertainment for Universal-UIP). Rel: floating; first shown London (Plaza) 11 December 1987. 111 mins. Cert PG.

The Big (Military) Parade – Da Yuebing. From the director of *Yellow Earth* comes another Chinese film which reveals the new, more liberal attitude to the artist in China, as in the USSR, even if in this case the Red Army did insist on changes to some of the dialogue and a new ending to the film. It tells the story of six soldiers preparing for their part in the celebrations of the 35th anniversary of the birth of the Chinese Republic. Assured direction, superb photography and a fascinating moral undertone as the selected six try to retain some sort of individuality as they are trained to be cogs in a massive military machine.

Cast: Wang Xueqi, Sun Chun, Lu Lei, Wu Ruofu, Guan Qiang, Kang Hua and members of the People's Liberation Army. Dir: Chen Kaige. Pro: Chen Liguo. Screenplay: Gao Lili. Ph: Zhang Yimou. Ed: Zhou Xinxia. Art: He Qun. M: Qu Xiaosongand Zhao Jiping (Guangxi Film Studio – ICA Projects). Rel: floating; first shown London (ICA) 11 March 1988. 103 mins. Cert 15.

The Big Town. A gambling drama, starring Matt Dillon as a crap shooter with a lucky streak who journeys to Chicago to make his fortune. There he finds nothing but trouble, and a little sex. This is *film noir* for kids, with the accent more on production design (we are in 1957) than on characterization, although Suzy Amis – as a single parent – comes off well.

Rest of cast: Diane Lane, Tommy Lee Jones, Bruce Dern, Tom Skerritt, Lee Grant, David Marshall Grant, Don Francks, Del Close, Meg Hogarth, Cherry Jones, Mark Danton, David Elliott, Steve Yorke, Chris Owens, Sean McCann, Kevin Fox, Marc Strange, Don Lake, Angelo Rizacos, Chris Benson, Gary Farmer, Diego Matamoros, Sarah Polley, Kirsten Bishop, Ken McGregor. Dir: Ben Bolt (son of Sir Robert). Pro: Martin Ransohoff. Co-Pro: Don Carmody. Ex Pro: Gene Croft. Screenplay: Robert Roy Pool; based on the novel *The Arm* by Clark Howard. Ph: Ralf D. Bode. Ed: Stuart Pappe. Assoc Ed: Kim Secvist. Pro Des: Bill Kenney. M: Michael Melvoin. (Columbia-Rank). Rel: 2 October 1987. 110 mins. Cert 15.

Black and White – Noir et blanc. The winner of the Camera d'Or award for Best First Film at the Cannes Film Festival is an uncomfortable French movie filmed in black-and-white with a minimum of dialogue and is certainly no crowd-puller. Written and directed by Claire Devers, it explores a sadomasochistic relationship between a humble little white accountant and a hefty black masseuse which soon becomes obsessional, leading to a horrifying, explosive and unexpected-if-logical climax.

Dennis Quaid as the detective with dubious ethics and Ellen Barkin as the corruption-fighting DA find they have something in common – love – in The Big Easy *from Recorded Releasing.*

It will be interesting to see how this disturbing new talent develops.

Cast: Francis Frappat, Jacques Martial, Josephine Fresson, Marc Berman, Benôit Régent, Christophe Galland, Claire Rigollier, Catherine Belkodia, Arnaud Carbonnier and Rhapsodes Choir. Dir and Screenplay: Claire Devers. No Pro credit. Ph: Daniel Desbois, Christopher Doyle, Alain Lesfargues and Jean Paul da Costa. Ed: Fabienne Alvarez and Yves Sarda. Art: Anne Isabelle Estrada. (Films du Volcan with assist. of French Ministry of Culture – Electric/Everyman). Rel: floating; first shown London (Everyman) 18 March 1988. 80 mins. Cert 18.

The Black Cannon Incident – Hei Pao Shi Jian. Only now (and maybe not for much longer) could such a film emerge from China and be shown there, for it is highly critical of some of the workings of the regime. The 'black cannon' of the title is a chess piece, lost by a young translator whose innocent efforts to get

Investigator Debra Winger and suspected murderess Theresa Russell (left) begin an ambiguous relationship in a fascinating psychological thriller from Fox, Black Widow.

it replaced bring official suspicion of his being a spy. As a result he is sacked and in spite of his explanation he is refused reinstatement. Five times his case is discussed by local bureaucratic bosses at meetings during which the split between the new- and old-guard thinking is revealed; and the criticisms would probably be even more explosive if one didn't have to rely on the subtitles. A film likely to mark the apex of new critical attitudes in China and as such of some historical significance.

Cast includes Liu Zifeng, Gao Ming and Gerhard Olschewski. Dir: Huang Jianxin. Screenplay: Li Wei. Ph: Wang Xinsheng and Feng Wei. (Xi'an Film Studios–ICA). Rel: floating; first shown London (ICA) 30 October 1987. 98 mins. Cert PG.

Black Widow. Handsome, polished and generally very good psychological thriller which could easily have been even better: this just about sums up

Bob Rafelson's first feature direction since his remake of *The Postman Always Rings Twice* some six years ago. He concentrates on the admittedly fascinating psychological angles rather than the thrills in this story about a bored, desk-bound US Department of Justice assistant who becomes obsessed with her suspicion that natural causes weren't to blame for the convenient deaths of the several rich husbands of a certain lovely lady. When she begs time off to follow up her theory that murder plays a part in the story and meets up with her suspect, a strange, ambiguous relationship springs up between them. The two roles are beautifully played by Debra Winger and Theresa Russell.

Rest of cast: Sami Frey, Dennis Hopper, Nicol Williamson, Terry O'Quinn, James Hong, Diane Ladd, D.W. Moffett, Lois Smith, Leo Rossi, Danny Kamekona, Rutanya Alda, Mary Woronov, Wayne Heffley, Raleigh Bond, Donegan Smith, Christian Clemenson, Arnsenio 'Sonny' Trinidad, Darrah Meeley, Kate Hall, George Ricord, Richard E. Arnold, Bea Kiyohara, Chris S. Ducey, Tee Dennard, David Mamet, Johnny 'Sugarbear' Willis, Gene Callahan, Thomas Hill, Juleen Murray, Ed Pang, Allen

Nause, Denise Dennison, Robert J. Peters, Rick Shuster, Al Cerullo, David Kasparian, Mick Muldoon. Dir: Bob Rafelson. Pro: Harold Schneider. Ex Pro: Laurence Mark. Screenplay: Ronald Bass. Ph: Conrad L. Hall. Ed: John Bloom. Pro Des: Gene Callahan. M: Michael Small. (Fox in assoc. with Americent Films and American Entertainment Partners-Fox). Rel: 17 July 1987. 102 mins. Cert 15.

Blind Date. Typical, top-flight – which means often very funny – Blake Edwards comedy with odd touches of vulgarity and plenty of slapstick sequences all beautifully timed. It's a wild farce about a lovely young lady who is charming when she's sober but a danger to society when drunk.

Cast: Kim Basinger, Bruce Willis, John Larroquette, William Daniels, George Coe, Mark Blum, Phil Hartman, Stephenie Faracy, Alice Hirson, Graham Stark, Joyce Van Patten, Jeannie Elias, Sacerdo Tanney, Georgeann Johnson, Sab Shimono, Momo Yashima, Armin Shimerman, Brian George, Ernest Harada, Emma Walton, Elaine Wilkes, Susan Lentini, Barry Sobel, Arlene Lorre, Timothy Stack, Jack Gwillim, Diana Bellamy, Seth Isler, Paul Carafotes, Bob Ari, Don Sparks, Bill Marcus, Michael

Bruce Willis, Kim Basinger and a bottle of 'bubbly' start the string of disasters that make the Blake Edwards Tri-Star/Columbia comedy Blind Date *uproariously funny.*

Genovese, Randall Bowers, John Demy, Jon Smet, Noele de Saint Gall, Julia Jennings, Dick Durock, Stanley Jordan; Billy Vera and the Beaters. Dir: Blake Edwards. Pro: Tony Adams. Ex Pro: Gary Hendler and Jonathan D. Krane. Co-Ex Pro: David Permut. Assoc Pro: Trish Caroselli. Screenplay: Dale Launer. Ph: Harry Stradling. Ed: Robert Pergament. Pro Des: Rodger Maus. M: Henry Mancini. (Tri-Star–Columbia) Rel: 4 September 1987. 95 mins. Cert 15.

Bliss. Harry Joy is a happily married, successful advertising executive with an ideal life. One day he dies of a heart attack – for four minutes. When he returns, he finds his life much changed: his wife is having an affair with his partner, his son is having sex with his daughter and an elephant has sat on his car. Suddenly, Harry realizes life is hell! *Bliss*, the directorial debut of Ray

It's all so puzzling for Barry Otto, who finds everything changed after his four-minute death in Entertainment's *comedy release* Bliss.

Lawrence, swept up Australian Oscars for Best Film, Best Direction and Best Screenplay, but is, for the most part, a plodding, indulgent mess, with sporadic glimpses of magic.

Cast: Barry Otto (as Harry Joy), Lynette Curran, Helen Jones, Miles Buchanan, Gia Carides, Tim Robertson, Jeff Truman, Bryan Marshall (excellent), Paul Chubb, Robert Menzies, Nique Needles, Jon Ewing, Kerry Walker, Sara de Teliga, Saskia Post, George Whaley, Marco Colombani, Tommy Dysart, Les Foxcroft, Alexander Hay, Allan Penney, Rob Steele, Paul Kean, Nicole Black, Manning Clark, Gerry Duggan, Katy Edwards, Peter Carmody, David Nettheim, John Doyle, Alan Beecher, Peter Carlow, Richard Singer, Jack Cheslyn, Stephen Wall, Chrissy James, Mike Chandler, Sam Gilchrist, Hayden Topperwein, Marc Cristan, Ernest Wade, Philip Dodd, Robert Rosenberg, Aimee Gleason, Gerry Corpey, Diana Adams, Anna Phillips, Vic Hunter, Lester Morris, Patrick Mitchell, Mark Butler, Ben Lawrence, Jamie Morrison. Dir: Ray Lawrence. Pro: Anthony Buckley. Screenplay: Ray Lawrence and Peter Carey; from the latter's novel. Ph: Paul Murphy. Ed: Wayne Leclos. Art: Owen Paterson. M: Peter Best. (Entertainment). Rel: 4 December 1987. 111 mins. Cert 18.

Boy Meets Girl. The odd film out. This moody 1983 French film, made in black-and-white, by writer-director Leos Carax (a promising debut), is an *avant-garde* effort which, while certainly not every moviegoer's *tasse de thé*, is of interest to a minority who will find

plenty of scope for interpreting its story about a young man's encounters with various, often odd characters in the shadier parts of Paris. Not easy to dismiss, or to forget.

Cast: Denis Lavant, Mireille Perrier, Elie Poicard, Caroll Brooks, Christian Cloarec, Anna Baldaccini, Maite Nahyr. Dir and Screenplay: Leos Carax. Pro: Patricia Moraz. Ex Pro: Alain Dahan. Ph: Jean-Yves Escoffier and Pascal Rabaud. Ed: Nelly Meunier and Francine Sandberg. Art: Serge Marzoloff and Jean Bauer. M: Jacques Pinault. (Abilene–Other Cinema). Rel: floating; first shown London (Metro) 10 July 1987. 100 mins. Cert 18.

Brain Damage. Nasty little thriller about a brain-sucking Thing which lives in the bath and does no good at all to friend or foe alike. Ugh.

Cast: Rick Herbst, Jennifer Lowry, Gordon Macdonald, Theo Barnes, Lucille Saint-Peter, 'Elmer', Vicki Darnell, Joe Gonzales, Bradlee Rhodes, Michael Bishop, Beverly Bonner, Ari Roussimoff, Micael Rubenstein, Angel Figueroa, John Reichert, Dan Henenlotter, Kenneth Packard, Artemis Pizarro, Slam Wedgehouse, Kevnin Vanhentenryck. Dir and Screenplay: Frank Henenlotter. Pro: Edgar Levins. Ex Pro: André Blay and Al Eicher. Assoc Pro: Charles Bennett and Ray Sundlin. Ph: Bruce Torbet. Ed: James Y. Kwei and Henenlotter. Art: Ivy Rosovsky. M: Gus Russo and Clutch Reiser. (Henenlotter-Palace Pictures). Rel: floating; first shown London (Scala) 4 March 1988. 90 mins. Cert 18.

Bright Lights, Big City. In 1986 United Artists acquired the rights to Jay McInerney's acclaimed, bestselling novel. Tom Cruise expressed interest in

playing the young hero; Joyce Chopra (*Smooth Talk*) was signed to direct. Everybody, it seemed, wanted to be involved. But as with all leviathan productions, stars come and go, directors are fired and budgets escalate. Enter Michael J. Fox, desperate to change his image as light male juvenile lead, and director James Bridges, still smarting from the failure of his last film, *Perfect*. The result is an overblown, unintelligible, unbelievable tale of a yuppie research editor (Fox, trying hard, but miscast) in New York going through hell (broken marriage, cocaine addiction, job loss) and taking us with him. A good cast (particularly Kiefer Sutherland and Frances Sternhagen) and some interesting ideas cannot salvage this flash turkey.

Rest of cast: Phoebe Cates, Dianne Wiest, Swoosie Kurtz, Tracy Pollan, John Houseman, Charlie Schlatter, Jason Robards, David Warrilow, Alec Mapa, William Hickey, Gina Belafonte, Sam Robards, Zette, Marika Blossfeldt, Jessica Lundy, Kelly Lynch, Peter Boyden, Annabelle Gurwitch, Russell Horton, Peter Maloney, Maria Pitillo, Susan Traylor, Nicholas Guest, Reni Santoni, Wendy Schaal, Jonathan Stark, Arnold Turner, Claudette Wells. Dir: James Bridges. Pro: Mark Rosenberg and Sydney Pollack. Ex Pro: Gerald R. Molen. Screenplay: Jay McInerney; from his novel of the same name. Ph: Gordon Willis. Ed: John Bloom. Pro Des: Santo Loquasto. M: Donald Fagen. Costumes: Bernie Pollack. (UA-UIP). Rel: 27 June 1988. 107 mins. Cert 18.

Broadcast News. Highly convincing and consistently entertaining picture of the cut-and-thrust happening on the other side of your television screen. It stars William Hurt as the charismatic anchor man whose deviousness is exposed as his ambition flowers, Albert Brooks as the wholly professional reporter who never gets his just reward (the anchor chair), and Holly Hunter – brilliant – as the dedicated, gifted, whirligig producer whose only escape from the tensions of the job lies in the occasional quiet flood of tears. The professional relationships of the trio are paralleled by an intriguing romantic triangle. The only slight flaw in this beautifully scripted, directed and played movie (to which Jack Nicholson contributes a small but telling, officially uncredited role) is the awkward and unnecessary epilogue.

Rest of cast: Robert Prosky, Lois Chiles, Joan Cusack, Peter Hackes, Christian

Michael J. Fox as the New York yuppie going through hell in the UA/UIP release Bright Lights, Big City.

Clemenson, Robert Katims, Ed Wheeler, Stephen Mendillo, Kimber Shoop, Dwayne Markee, Gennie James, Leo Burmester, Amy Brooks, Jonathan Benya, Frank Doubleday, Sally Knight, Manny Alvarez, Luis Valderrama, Francisco Garcia, Richard Thomsen, Nathan Benchley, Marita Geraghty, Nicholas D. Blanchet, Maura Moynihan, Chuck Lippman, Nannette Rickert, Tim White, Peggy Pridemore, Emily Crowley, Gerald Ender, Josh Billings, David Long etc. Dir, Screenplay and Pro: James L. Brooks. Co-Pro: Penney Finkelman Cox. Assoc Pro: Kristi Zea, Suan Zirinsky. Ex Pro: Polly Platt. Ph: Michael Ballhaus. Ed: Richard Marks. Pro Des: Charles Rosen. M: Bill Conti. (Gracie Films-UKFD/Fox). Rel: floating; first shown London (Odeon Haymarket) 8 April 1988. 132 mins. Cert 15.

Bullet Proof. An 'expendable' mission in an expendable movie. This casually constructed action melodrama centres on a terror group established in Mexico and the mission to destroy it led by ex-CIA agent, now Los Angeles cop, 'Bulletproof' Frank McBain (Gary Busey).

Rest of cast: Darlanne Fluegel, Henry Silva, Thalmus Rasulala, L.Q. Jones, Rene Enriquez, Mills Watson, James Andronica, R.G. Armstrong, William Smith, Luke Askew, Lincoln Kilpatrick, Lydie Denier, Ramon Franco, Juan Fernandez, Jorge Severa Jr, Lucy Lee Flippin, Redmond M. Gleeson, Ken Medlock, Don Pike, Danny Trejo, Gray Frederickson, Arnold Diaz, Drew Fischer, Ron Shipp, Laura Crosson, Christopher Doyle, Bobbie Cummings, James Haley, Perry Blackburn, Frank Holtry, Gary Pike, Brad Orrison. Dir: Steve Carver. Pro: Paul Hertzberg. Co-Pro: N.C. Lundell. Assoc Pro: Fred Olen Ray. Ex Pro: Lisa M. Hansen. Screenplay: T.L. Lankford and Steve Carver; from a story by Lankford and Ray. Ph: Francis Grumman. Ed: Jeff Freeman. Pro Des: Adrian H. Gorton. Art: Monette Goldman and Gary Tolby. M: Tom Chase and Steve Rucker. (Bullet-proof Pro-Virgin). Rel: floating; first shown London (Cannons Panton St and Edgware Rd) 11 December 1987. 94 mins. Cert 15.

Burglar – Vzlomshchik. A film from the USSR providing proof that Heavy Metal and all that jazz has, surreptitiously or not, been invading the Soviet heart-

Three stars who give brilliant performances in Fox's outstanding Broadcast News: *Holly Hunter (left) as the dedicated producer, William Hurt (top right) as the ambitious anchorman and Albert Brooks (bottom right) as the ace reporter.*

land from its Western bases – whether you feel glad or sorry about the event will depend on your musical tastes. Beyond that, this pleasant little film shows plenty of promising talent and gives a rather surprising view of some facets of life in Soviet Russia. It is seen through the eyes of a 12-year-old lad who adores his 'outsider' elder brother and turns to crime in the hope of stopping his hero's criminal activities. As for the soundtrack . . . well, you can always take your ear plugs along.

Cast includes: Oleg Yelikomov, Konstantin Kinchev, Y. Teapnik, S. Gaitan, P. Petrenko etc. Dir: Viktor Valery Ogorodnikov. Ex Pro: Irina Oprakundina. Screenplay: Viktor Priyomikhov. Ph: V. Mironov. Ed: T. Demsovoi. Art: Viktor Ivanov. M: V. Kisin. (Lenfilm Studio – The Other Cinema). Rel: floating; first shown London (Metro) 2 October 1987. 89 mins. No cert.

Glenda Jackson winning back her job and husband John Thaw (inset) at the same time in the British film Business as Usual, *made and released by Cannon.*

Business As Usual. A topical, well constructed, acted and credibly written British film, owing more than a little to the kitchen-sink era. Glenda Jackson, at her cloth-cap working-class best, plays the manageress of a gown shop who is sacked by the boss when she defends her girls from his lecherous attentions. She fights back with increasing vigour until, with the help of the union, she wins back her job – and her husband (John Thaw).

Rest of cast: Cathy Tyson, Mark McGann, Buki Armstrong, Stephen McGann, Philip Foster, Natalie Duffy, Eamon Boland, James Hazeldine, Jack Carr, Mel Martin, Michelle Byatt, Robert Keegan, Angela Elliot, Christine Moore, Stephen Dillon, Eithne Browne, Lucy Sheene, John Flanagan, Peter Christian, Christopher Quinn, Kathy Jamieson, Rachel Laurence, Will Tracy, Craig Charles, Sharon Power, Ann Aris, Tom Pepper, Dev Sagoo, Roland Oliver, Graham Callan, Simon Barrett. Dir and Screenplay: Lezli-An Barrett. Pro: Sara Geater. Ex Pro: Menahem Golan and Yoram Globus. Ph: Ernie Vincze. Ed: Henry Richardson. Art: Hildegarde Betchler. (London Cannon Films-Cannon Film Dist). Rel: floating; first shown London (Cannon Haymarket and other Cannon cinemas) 11 September 1987. 90 mins. Cert 15.

Can't Buy Me Love. Run-of-the-mill teenage comedy about the high-school boy with such an inferiority complex that he hires his pretty and personable neighbour to be his girlfriend for a month – just to show 'em. The result is predictable.

Cast: Patrick Dempsey, Amanda Peterson, Courtney Gains, Seth Green, Tina Caspary, Devin Devasquez, Darcy de Moss, Eric Bruskotter. Dir: James Foley. Pro: Thom. Mount. Ex Pro: Jere Henshaw and Ron Beckman. Co-Pro: Mark Burg. Screenplay: Michael Swerdlick. Ph: Peter Lyons Collister. Ed: Jeff Gourson. Pro Des: D.J. Harris. M: Robert Folk. (Touchstone-Warner). Rel: 27 May 1988. 94 mins. Cert PG.

The Care Bears' Adventure in Wonderland! This third Canadian-made Care Bear feature may well please the youngsters. The best of the trio, it has non-stop entertainment for them as Grumpy and his Care Bear pals pull a not very enthusiastic Alice through her looking glass into the strange world on the other side. Moral lessons, allusions to other fairy tales, pleasant music and reasonable animation should ensure a long life for the film, both on the large screen and thereafter on video.

With the voices of Colin Fox and many others not named. Dir: Raymond Jafelice. Pro: Michael Hirsch, Patrick Loubert and Clive A. Smith. Screenplay: Susi Snooks and John DeKlein; from the story by Peter Sauder. M: Trish Cullen; songs written and sung by John Sebastian. (Nelvana Pro-Fox). Rel: 25 March 1988. 75 mins. Cert U.

China Girl. On New York's Lower East Side, where Chinatown borders Little Italy, an Italian Romeo falls in love with a Chinese Juliet, sparking off a ruthless gang war between the so-called 'gooks' and 'greaseballs'. Abel Ferrara, fast becoming a Scorsese for the 'eighties with such films as *Driller Killer*, *Ms 45* and *Fear City*, creates a grim, compelling portrait of the underbelly of New York with some stark, atmospheric film-making. The weakness of the acting is more than made up for by the fine camerawork, sharp editing and a pounding rock score. Fascinating stuff.

Cast: James Russo, David Caruso, Sari Chang (as Juliet), Richard Panebianco (as Romeo), Russell Wong, Joey Chin, Judith Malina, James Hong, Robert Miano, Paul Hipp, Doreen Chan, Randy Sabusawa, Keenan Leung, Lum Chang Pan, Sammy Lee, Johnny Shia, Stephen Chen, Raymond Moy, Josephina Gallego-Diaz, Caprice Benedetti, Anthony Dante, Robert Lasardo, Chi Moy, David Kelsey Reilly, Joseph Pentangelo, Anthony Esposito, Diane Cheng, Frank Young, John Ciarcia, Jon Orofino, Ida Bernadini, Nancy Moo. Dir: Abel Ferrara. Pro: Michael Nozik. Ex Pros: Mitchell Cannold and Steve Reuther. Screenplay: Nicholas St John. Ph: Bojan Bazelli. Ed: Anthony Redman. Pro Des: Dan Leigh. M: Joe Delia. (Vestron). Rel: floating; first shown London (Metro and Cannons Oxford St and Edgware Rd) 29 January 1988. 90 mins. Cert 18.

A Chinese Ghost Story – Qian Nu Youhun. A young tax collector is forced to spend a night in the haunted temple of Lan Ro where he gradually falls in love with a beautiful ghost. Extraordinary Cantonese horror-comedy, looking like *The Evil Dead* directed by a young Kurosawa. A haunting experience, with some memorable scenes and stunning visuals, including an unbelievable Samurai rap. The subtitles (in both Mandarin and English) are hilarious: 'Don't let he sees you', 'You're wasting the times', etc.

Featuring singing superstar Leslie Cheung as the tax collector, Wong Tsu Hsien as the ghost and Wo Ma as the Samurai (no other cast details available). Dir: Ching Sio Tung. Pro: Tsui Hark. Ex Pro: Claudie Chung. Screenplay: Yeun Kai Chi. Ph: Poon Hang Seng, Sander Lee, Tom Lau and Wong Hang. Ed: Cinema City Co. Ltd. Art: Yee Chung Man. M: Romeo Diaz and James Wong. (Cinema City-Metro). Rel: floating; first shown London (Metro) 22 January 1988. 98 mins. No cert.

Cobra Verde. Extraordinary, epic piece of film-making about a Brazilian bandit, Cobra Verde (Klaus Kinski), who is taken on as foreman of a prosperous sugar cane plantation. After he impregnates all three (under-age) daughters of the plantation owner, he is dispatched to West Africa on a futile mission to catch slaves. The bandit is expected to die, but nobody has reckoned on the resilience of Cobra Verde.

The Comrades *(l. to r. Keith Allen, William Gaminara, Robin Soans, Stephen Bateman, Philip Davis, Jeremy Flynn) – in Curzon's Bill Douglas film about the Tolpuddle Martyrs. Right: a despairing martyr (Robin Soans) is watched by Heather Page.*

Mesmeric imagery, deranged performances and some startling *cinéma vérité* add fuel to a most unusual, haunting drama, as original and compelling a masterpiece in its way as *El Topo* and *The Tin Drum*. For the record, this is the fifth screen partnership of filmmaker Werner Herzog and star Klaus Kinski.

Rest of cast: King Ampaw, Jose Lewgoy, Salvatore Basile, His Royal Highness Nana Agyefi Kwame II de Nsein. Dir: Werner Herzog. Pro: Lucki Stipetic. Ex Pro: Walter Saxer and Salvatore Basile. Screenplay: Werner Herzog. Ph: Viktor Ruzicka and Thomas Mauch. Ed: Maixmiliane Mainka. Pro Des: Fabrizio Carola. M: Popol Vuh. (ZDF and Ghana Film Industry Corp./ACCRA-Palace). Rel: floating; first shown London (Renoir and Gate Notting Hill) 22 April 1988. 101 mins. Cert 15.

Comrades. Discerning moviegoers with good memories may recall with pleasure Bill Douglas as the creator of three fascinating, shortish films, released in the 'seventies, about his growing up in poor circumstances in Scotland. This is virtually his first long – alas, far, far too long – feature film: the

story of the forerunners of Trade Unionism, the Tolpuddle Martyrs, a group of peasant tradesmen whose demand for higher wages in the 1830s led to their being shipped to Australia as criminals. Initially the film marvellously creates the feel and detail of the rural life of the period, but when it follows the 'martyrs' to Australia it gets a bit bogged down. It helps if you know the historical facts before seeing the film, otherwise it may all seem confusing. But Douglas's skill with and feeling for the medium makes many of its 180 minutes very watchable.

Cast: Robin Soans, Imelda Staunton, Amber Wilkinson, William Gaminara, Katy Behean, Stephen Bateman, Sandra Voe, Philip Davis, Valerie Whittington, Harriet Doyle,

James Woods (above) as the Cop. *Also involved in this Entertainment release, Lesley Ann Warren and Charles Durning (right).*

Patrick Field, Heather Page, Keith Allen, Patricia Healey, Jeremy Flynn, Shane Down, Robert Stephens, Joanna David, Michael Hordern, Freddie Jones, Barbara Windsor, Murray Melvin, Trevor Ainsley, Malcolm Terris, Dave Atkins, Collette Barker, Michael Clark, Alex McCrindle, Jack Chissick, Sarah Reed, Nicola Hayward; and, in Australia, Vanessa Redgrave, James Fox, Arthur Dignam, John Hargreaves, Simon Parsonage, Charles Yunipingu, Simon Landis, Anna Volska, Brian Mac-Dermott, Shane Briant, Tim Eliot, David Netheim, Patrick Field, Jeremy Flynn, Mark Brown, Sophie Randall, Emma Tuck, John and Jan Holman, Bevan James, John Lee, Ralph Cotterill, David McWilliams, Lynette Curran, Alex Norton. Dir and Screenplay: Bill Douglas. Pro: Simon Relph. Assoc Pro: Redmond Morris and David Hannah. Ph: Gale Tattersall. Ed: Mick Audsley. Pro Des: Michael Pickwoad. Art: Derrick Chetwyn. M: Hans Werner Henze and David Graham. (Curzon Films/ National Film Finance Corp/Film Four International-Curzon). Rel: floating; first shown London (Curzon West End) 28 August 1987. 180 mins. Cert PG.

Cop. James Woods stars as a cop with a conscience in this superbly atmospheric thriller about a serial killer in Hollywood. As Lloyd Hopkins, Woods has seldom been better as he alienates his family, friends and his own police department in his quest to nail the murderer. Attention to detail, suspense and fine acting lifts this potential B-melodrama into a class of its own.

Rest of cast: Lesley Ann Warren, Charles Durning, Charles Haid, Raymond J. Barry, Randi Brooks, Steven Lambert, Christopher Wynne, Jan McGill, Vicki Wauchope, Melinda Lynch, John Petievich, Dennis Stewart, Randi Pelish, Annie McEnroe, Rick Marotta, Michael V. Allen, Helen Page Camp, Scott Sandler, Christopher Blane, Matt Almond, Banks Harper, Jim Wilkey, Jimmy Woodward, Lisa McCullough. Dir, Pro and Screenplay: James B. Harris; based on the novel *Blood On the Moon* by James Ellroy. Co-Pro: James Woods. Ex Pro: Thomas Coleman and Michael Rosenblatt. Ph: Steve Dubin. Ed: Anthony Spano. Pro Des: Gene Rudolf. M: Michael Colombier. (Atlantic-Entertainment). Rel: floating; first shown London (Cannons Panton St and Edgware Road) 10 June 1988. 110 mins. Cert 18.

The Courier. A terrible film, with interesting credentials. Cait O'Riordan, erstwhile bass player for the Pogues, is the female lead, supplying the weight of feminine reason; her husband, billed here as Declan MacManus but better known as Elvis Costello, wrote the score; Neil Jordan, director of *Mona Lisa*, guests as executive producer; and Irish stalwarts Gabriel Byrne and Ian Bannen provide some acting backbone. A brave, fresh look at Dublin today and its attendant life of armed robbery and heroin addiction, *The Courier* is marred by some undisciplined direction, slack editing, poor sound and impenetrable diction.

Rest of cast: Padraig O'Loingsigh (as the Courier), Patrick Bergin, Andrew Connolly, Michelle Houlden, Mary Ryan, Dave Duffy, Joe Savino, Caroline Rothwell, Mary Elizabeth Burke Kennedy, Stuart Dunne, Martin Dunne, Mick Egan, Mark Flanagan, Anne Enright, Liz Bono, Lucy Vigne-Welsh, Owen Hyland, Kevin Doyle, Albert Fahy, Alec Doran, Aidan Murphy, Aisling Cronin, Tony Coleman, Seay Ledwidge. Dir: Frank Deasy and Joe Lee. Pro: Hilary McLoughlin. Co-Pro: Stephen Woolley. Ex Pro: Neil Jordan, Nik Powell and John

Will he? A moment of terror for Padraig O'Loingsigh (Mark) with Gabriel Byrne (Val) holding his life in his hand in Palace's The Courier.

Hambley. Screenplay: Frank Deasy. Ph: Gabriel Beristain. Ed: Derek Trigg and Annette D'Alton. Pro Des: Dave Wilson. M: Declan MacManus (Elvis Costello). (City Vision/Euston-Palace). Rel: floating; first shown London (Cannon Haymarket) 19 February 1988. 86 mins. Cert 15.

Creepshow 2. A wooden carving of an Indian warrior comes menacingly to life; an oil slick on a lonely lake devours a gang of teenagers; and a moribund, blood-splattered hitchhiker refuses to die in this arbitrary collection of horror-comic tales. The special effects are fine, the stories somewhat thin but the tone is suitably tongue-in-cheek. You can find a lot worse on prime-time TV.

Cast: Lois Chiles, George Kennedy, Dorothy Lamour and Tom Savini as 'the Creep'; rest of cast (in order of appearance): Domenick John, Philip Doré, Maltby Napoleon, Tyrone Tonto, Frank S. Salsedo, Holt McCallany, David Holbrook (son of Hal), Don Harvey, Dan Kamin, Deane Smith, Shirley Sonderegger, Paul Satterfield, Jeremy Green, Daniel Beer, Page Hannah, David Beecroft, Tom Wright, Richard

Lois Chiles, as Annie, is attacked by a hitchhiker (Tom Wright) in Creepshow 2, *from Entertainment.*

Parks, Stephen King, Cheré Bryson, Joe Silver. Dir: Michael Gornick. Pro: David Ball. Ex Pro: Richard P. Rubinstein. Assoc Pro: Mitchell Galin. Screenplay: George A. Romero, based on stories by Stephen King. Ph: Dick Hart and Tom Hurwitz. Ed: Peter Weatherly. Pro Des: Bruce Miller. M: Les Reed. Additional M: Rick Wakeman. (New World-Entertainment). Rel: 20 November 1987. 90 mins. Cert 18.

A head for heights, too! Australian hero Paul Hogan and baddie Vincent Gerosa have differing reactions to high-rise New York in UA's 'Crocodile' Dundee II. Inset: Hogan with Linda Kozlowski.

'Crocodile' Dundee II. Mick Dundee (Paul Hogan) is back in the Big Apple, romancing journalist Sue Charlton (Linda Kozlowski) and on the run from a gang of drug dealers. This time Dundee seems too smooth, too indestructible to gain audience sympathy, but his adventures are engaging enough. In its first nineteen days of release in the USA the film grossed over (US) $61 million.

Rest of cast: John Meillon, Ernie Dingo, Hechter Ubarry, Juan Fernandez, Charles Dutton, Kenneth Welsh, Stephen Root, Dennis Boutsikaris, Carlos Carrasco, Luis Guzman, Marilyn Sokol, Gregory Jbara,

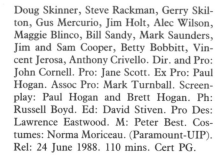

Doug Skinner, Steve Rackman, Gerry Skilton, Gus Mercurio, Jim Holt, Alec Wilson, Maggie Blinco, Bill Sandy, Mark Saunders, Jim and Sam Cooper, Betty Bobbitt, Vincent Jerosa, Anthony Crivello. Dir. and Pro: John Cornell. Pro: Jane Scott. Ex Pro: Paul Hogan. Assoc Pro: Mark Turnball. Screenplay: Paul Hogan and Brett Hogan. Ph: Russell Boyd. Ed: David Stiven. Pro Des: Lawrence Eastwood. M: Peter Best. Costumes: Norma Moriceau. (Paramount-UIP). Rel: 24 June 1988. 110 mins. Cert PG.

Cry Freedom. Richard Attenborough attempting the impossible and achieving something very near, by making a well documented anti-apartheid tract into an always interesting, constantly gripping and very human motion picture. He does it by opening with a sickeningly impressive and convincing portrayal of the evils inherent in the South African racial system, with all its inevitable brutality, then switching to a lengthy but exciting central escape and chase sequence, and finally reverting to the propaganda angle by a spectacular recreation of the 1986 slaying of some 500 schoolchildren during a riot in the black township of Soweto. All this is based on the detailed experiences, set down in his two books (*Biko* and *Asking for Trouble*), of an outspoken, liberal white newspaper editor, Donald Woods, whose house arrest ended in his escape with his family to England in 1987.

Cast: Kevin Kline (splendid as Woods), Penelope Wilton, Denzel Washington (also impressive as black activist Biko), John Hargreaves, Alec McCowen, Kevin McNally, Zakes Moke, Ian Richardson, Josette Simon, John Thaw, Timothy West, Miles Anderson, Tommy Buson, Jim Findlay, Julian Glover, Kate Hardie, Alton Kumalo, Louis Mahoney, Maw Makondo, Joseph Marcell, John Matshikiza, Sophie Mgcina, John Paul, Wabei Siyolwe, Gwen Watford, Juanita Waterman, Graeme Taylor, Adam Spring and Hamish Stuart Walker, Evelyn and Xoliswa Sithole, James Coine, Albert Ndinda, Andrew Whaley, Shelley Borkum, Patricia Gumede, Angela Gavaza, Nocebo Mlambo, Walter Matemavi, Clement Muchachi, Ruth Chinamando, Basil Chidyamathamba, Marcy Mushore, Lawrence Simbarashe, Carl Chase, Morgan Sheppard, Tichatonga Mazhindu, Neil McPherson, Hepburn Graham, Claude Maredza, Carlton Chance, Glen Murphy, Russell Keith Grant, Munyaradzi Kanaventi, George Lovell, Andrew McCulloch, Graham Fletcher Cook, Karen Drury, Niven Boyd, Tony Vogel, Christopher Hurst, Gerald Sim, Pet-

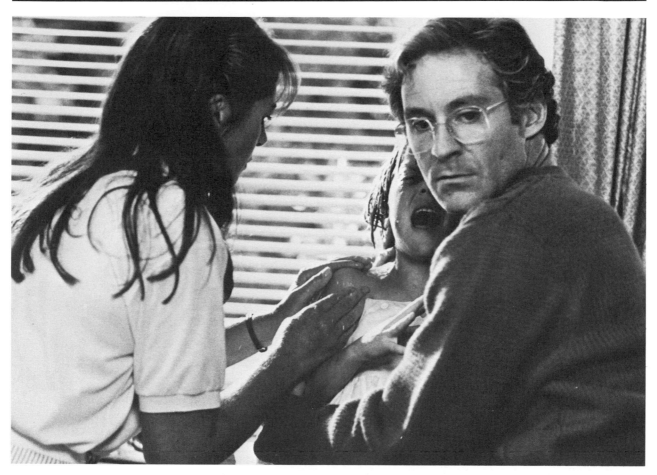

Liberal editor Kevin Kline and wife Penelope Wilton try to comfort their daughter – Spring Stuart-Walker – after she has suffered acid burns in Richard Attenborough's magnificent anti-apartheid film Cry Freedom *(a UIP release).*

er Cartwright, Gary Whelan, Dudley Dickin, David Trevena, Badi Uzzaman, Robert Phillips, Fishoo Tembo, Peggy Marsh, Gwyneth Strong, Philip Bretherton, Paul Herzberg, Robert MacNamara, Hans Sittig, Kimpton Mativenga, David Henry, Michael Turner, Kalie Hanekom, Paul Jerricho, Star Ncube, David Guwaza, Hilary Minster, James Aubrey, Peter Cary, Dominic Kanaventi, Sam Mathambo, Walter Muparutsa, Judy Cornwall, Michael Graham Cox, John Hartley, Simon Shumba, Garrick Hagon, Nick Tate, Marilyn Poole, William Marlowe. Dir and Pro: Richard Attenborough. Co-Pro: Norman Spencer and John Briley. Ex Pro: Terence Clegg. Screenplay: John Briley. Ph: Ronnie Taylor. Ed: Lesley Walker. Pro Des: Stuart Craig. M: George Fenton and Jonas Gwangwa. 2nd Unit Ph/Dir: Peter MacDonald. (Marble Arch Pro-Universal-UIP). Rel: 18 February 1988. 159 mins. Cert PG. (Filmed in Zimbabwe, Kenya and UK).

Cry from the Mountain. Billy Graham Foundation production with quite a bit going for it, including beautifully photographed backgrounds of the wild Alaskan mountains, where most of the film was made on location. It tells the story of an eventful holiday there by a father and son which results in a decision to cancel the parents' divorce plans and, thanks to the wife's attendance at a Graham revival meeting, a happy-ever-after ending.

Cast: Wes Parker, Rita Walker, Chris Kidd, James Cavan, Coleen Gray, Jerry Ballew, Allison Argo, Glen Alsworth, Myrna Kidd, Billy Graham. Dir: J.F. Collier. Pro: W.F. Brown. Assoc Pro: Jerry Balew. Screenplay: D.L. Quick. Ph: Gary D. Baker. Ed and Pro Des: J. Michael Hooser. M: J.A.C. Redford. (Billy Graham Film Ministry-International). Rel: floating; first shown London (several Cannon cinemas) 16 October 1987. 75 mins. Cert PG.

Dancers. Backstage ballet film about a dancer who has come to maturity without growing up and is revitalized by a new young dancer. The best parts of it are the later sections which deal with the performance of the ballet *Giselle* – which, apparently, was the film's original title. Something of a bio-pic, perhaps, about the production's talented star, Mikhail Baryshnikov.

Rest of cast: Alessandra Ferri, Leslie Browne, Thomas Rall, Lynn Seymour, Victor Barbee, Julie Kent, Mariangela Melato, Leandro Amato, Gianmarco Tognazzi, Desmond Kelly, Chrisa Keramidas, Amy Werba, Jack Brodsky, Robert Argand, Amanda McKerrow, Bonnie Moore, and the dancers of the American Ballet Theatre Co. Dir: Herbert Ross. Pro: Menahem Golan and Yoram Globus. Assoc Pro: Charles France and John Thompson. Ex Pro: Nora Kaye and Jack Brodsky. Screenplay: Sara Kernochan. Ph: Ennio Guarnieri. Ed: William Reynolds. Pro Des: Gianni Quaranta. Art: Luigi Marchione. M: *Giselle* by Adolph Adam; incidental music by Pino Donnagio. (Golan/Globus in assoc. with Hera/Baryshnikov-Cannon Rel). Rel: floating; first shown London (Cannon Shaftesbury Ave) 8 December 1987. 99 mins. Cert PG.

The Dark Side of the Moon – Manden I Manen. In view of its expressionistic style, imaginative treatment and somewhat gloomy Germanic artistry (in

Above: at the annual Christmas get-together Gabriel (Donal McCann) gives thanks to his hosts. Left: later that night, back at their hotel, he learns for the first time from his wife (Anjelica Huston) about an old romance with painful memories. This last, marvellous movie made by John Huston, The Dead, *was released by Vestron.*

Rest of cast: Catherine Poul Jupont, Christina Bengtsson, Kim Jansson, Yavuzer Cetinkaya, Roy Richards, Berthe Quistgaard, Erik Truxa, Anne Nojgard, Marianne Mortensen, Stig Hoffmeyer. Dir and Screenplay: Erik Clausen. Ex Pro: Tivi Magnusson. Assoc Pro: Per Arman. Ph: Morten Bruus. Ed: Ghita Beckendorf. Pro Des: Leif Sylvester Petersen. M: John Hoybe, songs by Robert Broberg (perf. by Broberg, Lotte Romer, Oyvind Ougard, Maria Bramsen, Thomas Grue and Henning Pold). (Film Cooperative, Danmark/Metronome Pro. A/S for Danish Film Institute-Cannon). Rel: floating; first shown London (Cannon Premiere) 18 March 1988. 94 mins. Cert 15.

addition to the outstanding debut performance of Peter Thiel), the fact that this powerful Danish movie has won eight international awards and an Oscar nomination should surprise nobody. Writer-director Erik Clausen illustrates his theme of the darker side of love in his story of a man who murders his beloved wife when she suddenly announces she is leaving him for another man. After a six-year jail sentence he emerges into a world in which he feels he has no part, a world in which he is the true outsider, as he searches for his estranged daughter and seeks her forgiveness.

The Dead. John Huston's final film is a magnificent chamber-piece epitaph to a master moviemaker: a beautifully crafted adaptation – by John's son Tony – of a short story from James

Joyce's early collection, *Dubliners*. The carefully detailed story of an annual Christmas family party in snow-draped Dublin, 1904, and the moving aftermath when, back in their hotel, one of the wives confesses to her husband a long-ago love for a boy for whose death she feels responsible, is exquisitely reconstructed. Magnificent performances are given by all the predominantly Irish cast, especially, by Donal McCann and Huston's actress daughter Anjelica as the couple.

Rest of cast: Rachael Dowling, Cathleen Delany, Helena Carroll, Ingrid Craigie, Dan O'Herlihy, Frank Patterson, Donal Donnelly, Marie Kean, Maria McDermottroe, Seán McClory, Kate O'Toole, Maria Hayden, Bairbre Dowling, Lyda Anderson, Dara Clarke, Colm Meany, Cormac O'Herlihy, Paul Grant, Patrick Gallagher, Amanda Baird, Paul Carroll, Redmond M. Gleason, Brendon Dillon. Dir: John Huston. Pro: Wieland Schulz-Keil and Chris Sievernich. Ex Pro: William J. Quigley. Screenplay: Tony Huston; from one of James Joyce's *Dubliners* stories. Ph: Fred Murphy. Pro Des: Stephen Grimes. M: Alex North. (Vestron Pictures/Zenish-Vestron/Miracle). Rel: floating; first shown London (Lumiere) 11 December 1987. 82 mins. Cert U.

Dead of Winter. Aspiring New York actress Kate McGovern (Mary Steenburgen) is given the chance of a lifetime – to take over the lead role in a celluloid thriller. Driven to the isolated, snow-bound residence of its producer, 'Dr' Joseph Lewis (Jan Rubes), the actress soon discovers that all is not as it seems and that her life is in danger. In the tradition of *Wait Until Dark* and *My Name Is Julia Ross* (the latter directed by Joseph H. Lewis, by the way), this theatrical, melodramatic suspenser makes the most of its ingenious plot turns and thankfully doesn't take itself too seriously. Totally unbelievable, the film is nevertheless an engaging roller-coaster ride of Gothic camp capped by a splendid performance from Ms Steenburgen. Predictable, but fun.

Rest of cast: Roddy McDowall, William Russ, Ken Pogue, Wayne Robson, Mark Malone, Michael Copeman, Sam Malkin, Pamela Moller, Dwayne McLean, Paul Welsh. Dir: Arthur Penn. Pro: John Bloomgarden and Marc Shmuger. Assoc Pro: Michael MacDonald. Screenplay: Marc Shmuger and Mark Malone. Ph: Jan Weincke. Ed: Rick Shaine. Pro Des: Bill Brodie. M: Richard Einhorn. (MGM/UA-UIP). Rel: floating; first shown London

Mary Steenburgen, who finds only terror when applying for a job in MGM/UIP's thriller Dead of Winter.

(Cannons Panton St and Fulham Rd) 5 February 1988. 100 mins. Cert 15.

Death Wish 4: The Crackdown. Charles Bronson is back as Paul Kersey, the wooden vigilante, who this time single-handedly sets about destroying the Los Angeles drug trade. Plenty of action, tacky production values and buckets of gratuitous violence, but at least this is better directed than the last three films as J. Lee Thompson takes over the reins from Michael Winner.

Rest of cast: Kay Lenz, John P. Ryan, Perry Lopez, Soon-Teck Oh, George Dickerson, Dana Barron, Jesse Dabson, Peter Sherayko, James Purcell, Michael Russo, Mike Moroff, Dan Ferro, Tom Everett, Tim Russ, Hector Mercado, Derek Rydall, Mark Pellegrino. Dir: J. Lee Thompson. Pro: Pancho Kohner. Ex Pro: Menahem Golan and Yoram Globus. Screenplay: Gail Morgan Hickman, based on characters created by Brian Garfield. Ph: Gideon Porath. Ed:

Peter Lee Thompson. Art: Whitney Brooke Wheeler. M: Paul McCallum, Valentine McCallum and John Bisharat. (Cannon). Rel: 15 April 1988. 99 mins. Cert 18.

Didn't You Kill My Brother? Obviously bound-for-TV satirical comedy from *Fawlty Towers* director Bob Spiers and the Comic Strip group. The conflict between East End twin brothers (both played by Alexei Sayle) provides the excuse to take swipes at various facets of life in the 'eighties.

Rest of cast: Beryl Reid, Graham Crowden, Pauline Melville, Peter Richardson, David Stafford, Benjamin Rufus Zephaniah, Kevin Allen, Janet Palmer, Laura Hill, Nigel Louis-Marie, Zoe Nathenson, Dexter Fletcher, Eddie Yeoh, James Hickling, Jack Galloway, Mark Wing-Davey, Ben Aris, Danny Webb, Jack Ellis, John Quarmby, Robert Pereno, Moloki Chrystie, David Beames, Graham Fletcher-Cook, Danny Cunningham, Brian Croucher, Richard Cordery, Bonny Brigg, Leslie Guinn, Tom Lock, Richard Sampson, James Adah, Daniel Adegwe, Christian Solari, Giovanni Rennalls, Suza Horvat, Les Bull, Matthew Marsh, Helen Shah, Andros Adamou,

Rachel Briggs, Debbie Cleal, Nina Shah. Dir: Bob Spiers. Pro: Simon Wright. Assoc Pro: Mandy Ruben. Pro Co-Ord: Cate Arbeid. Ex Pro: Michael White. Screenplay: Alexei Sayle, Pauline Melville and David Stafford. Ph: Peter Jessop. Ed: Geoff Hogg. Pro Des: Deborah Gillingham. Art: Denise Ruban. M: Kenny Craddock and Colin Gibson. (Comic Strip Ltd for Channel 4- Recorded Releasing). Rel: floating; first shown London (Scala and Cannon Baker St) 6 November 1987. 52 mins. Cert 15.

Dirty Dancing. *Romeo and Juliet* updated to 1963 and processed into a nostalgic dance movie, complete with parental bigotry, the good guy from the wrong side of the tracks, and an action-packed soundtrack (Eric Carmen, The Drifters, The Shirelles, The Ronettes, etc.) A major hit with audiences, the film benefits from some good performances (particularly Jennifer Grey –

Joel's daughter – as a love-struck Jewish princess) and an occasionally witty script. But tread carefully over the clichés.

Rest of cast: Patrick Swayze, Jerry Orbach, Cynthia Rhodes, Jack Weston, Jane Bruckner, Kelly Bishop, Lonny Price, Max Cantor, Charles Honi Coles, Neal Jones, 'Cousin Brucie' Morrow, Wayne Knight, Paula Trueman, Alvin Myerovich, Miranda Garrison, Garry Goodrow, Antoine Pagan, Tom Cannold. Dir: Emile Ardolino. Pro: Linda Gottlieb. Co-Pro: Eleanor Bergstein. Ex Pro: Mitchell Cannold and Steven Reuther. Screenplay: Eleanor Bergstein. Ph: Jeff Jur. Ed: Peter C. Frank. Pro Des: David Chapman. M: John Morris. Choreography: Kenny Ortega. (Vestron). Rel: 16 October 1987. 88 mins. Cert 15.

Dogs in Space. Like hard drugs and whisky, *Dogs in Space* is an acquired taste. If you can sit through the first

agonizing 30 minutes then the rest is not so bad. An antipodean *Sid and Nancy*, the film is an exposé of 'bohemian' life in 1978 Melbourne, set in a ramshackle house in which a horde of brain-damaged druggies sing, lust and vomit their way through an aimless existence. Of interest is that Michael Hutchence, lead singer of rock group INXS, makes his film debut in a role of a drugged-out, no-good singer. You have been warned.

Rest of cast: Saskia Post, Nique Needles, Deanna Bond, Tony Helou, Chris Haywood, Peter Walsh, Laura Swanson, Adam Briscomb, Sharon Jessop, Edward Clayton-Jones, Martii Coles, Chuck Meo, Caroline Lee, Fiona Latham, Stephanie Johnson, Gary Foley, Glenys Osborne, Allanah Hill, Robyn McLellan, Troy Davies, John Murphy, Owen Robertson, Helen Phillips, Kelly Hoare, Robyn Lowenstein, Robert Ratti, Barbara Jungwirth, Beamish Elliot, Noel Pennington, Ted Fahrner. Dir and Screenplay: Richard Lowenstein. Pro: Glenys Rowe. Ex Pro: Robert Le Tet and Dennis Wright. Ph: Andrew De Groot. Ed: Jill Bilcock. Art: Jody Borland. M: Dogs In Space, Whirlywirld, Thrush and the C...s, Primitive Calculations, etc. (Skouras-Atlantic-Recorded Releasing). Rel: floating; first shown London (Gate Notting Hill, Renoir and Cannon Oxford St) 10 June 1988. 108 mins. Cert 18.

Dragnet. Fast and furious, crisply-written spoof of the cult 'sixties TV series, with plenty of gags, girls and action. Ill-matched detectives Joe Friday (Dan Aykroyd) and Pep Streebek (Tom Hanks) take it upon themselves to save the future of Los Angeles from the evil clutches of an evangelical Jim Bakker figure (Christopher Plummer) and a Hefneresque soft-porn tycoon (Dabney Coleman). Very funny, Concorde-paced interweaving of comedy styles, with Aykroyd and Hanks striking sparks off each other.

Rest of cast: Harry Morgan (as Bill Gannon, repeating his role from TV), Alexandra Paul, Jack O'Halloran, Elizabeth Ashley, Kathleen Freeman, Bruce Gray, Lenka Peterson, Julia Jennings, Lisa Aliff, Joe Altmark, Nina Arvesen, Fred Asparagus, Peter Aykroyd, Larry Bilzarian, Jim Boeke, Sandra Canning, William Chalmers, Donald Craig, Karen Criswell, Josh Cruze, Jennifer Curry, Gray Daniels, Gary Lee Davis, Susan Deemer, Juli Donald, Sandra Eng, Ava Fabian, Lisa London, Christopher Man-

Detective Dan Aykroyd finds a new angle to his job in UIP's Dragnet.

kiewicz, Dona Speir. Dir: Tom Mankiewicz. Pro: David Permut, Robert K. Weiss. Ex Pro: Bernie Brillstein. Assoc Pro: Don Zepfel. Screenplay: Dan Aykroyd, Alan Zweibel and Tom Mankiewicz. Ph: Matthew F. Leonetti. Ed: Richard Halsey and William D. Gordean. Pro Des: Robert F. Boyle. M: Ira Newborn. (Universal-UIP). Rel: 26 February 1988. 106 mins. Cert PG.

Dudes. This is a kind of *Death Wish* with a punk haircut, directed by Penelope Spheeris, America's most outrageous female director. Three punks (Jon Cryer, Daniel Roebuck and Flea), disillusioned with the Big Apple, aim for California but are waylaid by a gang of rednecks in Arizona. An extraordinary mish-mash of genres, *Dudes* is sometimes sentimental, occasionally funny, often violent and even predictable, while the standard of production veers from the amateur to the stylish. A curate's egg.

Rest of cast: Catherine Mary Stewart, Lee Ving, Michael Balzary, Peter Willcox, Read Morgan, Witcliffe Young, Calvin Bartlett, Glen Withrow. Dir: Penelope Spheeris. Pro: Herb Jaffe and Miguel Tejada Flores. Ex Pro: Mort Engelberg. Screenplay: John Randall Johnson (his first). Ph: Robert Richardson. Ed: Andy Horvitch. Pro Des: Robert Ziembicki. M: Charles Bernstein, with songs by The Vandals, Faster Pussycat, The Little Kings, The Leather Nun, The Tail Gators, W.A.S.P., Legal Weapon, etc. (New Century/Vista-Recorded Releasing). Rel: floating; first shown London (Cannon Tottenham Court Road) 22 May 1988. 90 mins. Cert 15.

Eat the Rich. A coarse and black-edged British satirical farce from the Comic Strip production group, with such specialized (and limited) appeal that it has every promise of becoming a cult film. Like the characters involved, it never makes much sense or gives a clear indication of its intent, but superficially it is about a small group of highly unlikely revolutionaries led by an ambiguously-sexed ex-waiter (at top-flight restaurant 'Bastards'), a smooth governmental 'mole' (ex-*Crossroads* star Ronald Allen) and a Home Secretary of low mental but high physical prowess (an impressive performance in its way by ex-stuntman Nosher Powell).

Rest of cast: Kevin Allen, David Beard, Rowena Bently, Angie Bowie, Simon Brint, Rene Bruchet, Lez Bubb, Kathy Burke, Robert Cartwithen, Katrin Cartlidge, 'Cayenne' (S. American band), Sean Chap-

Top: the bow-and-arrow brigade of revolutionaries (Ron Tarr, Lanah Pellay, Fiona Richmond and Jimmy Fagg) goes into action in Recorded Releasing's Eat the Rich. *Above left: MI5 Mole (Crossroads' Ronald Allen) and Soviet paymaster (Lemmy); and, above right, Nosher Powell (excellent) as a Home Secretary with more brawn than brain.*

man, Robbie Coltrane, Miles Copeland, Hugh Cornwell, Neil Cunningham, Robert Davis, Neil Dickson, Sandra Dorne, Simon Drake, Adrian Edmondson, Jimmy Fagg, Norman Fisher, Bob Flagg, Peter Fontaine, Dawn French, Fran Fullenwider, Adrian Funnell, Joanne Good, Cathryn Harrison, Jools Holland, Lemmy, Debbie Lindon, Sue Lloyd, Paul McCartney, Shane McGowan, Christopher Malcolm, Rik Mayall, Frank Murray, Derren Nesbitt, Daniel Peacock, Lamar Pellay, Nigel Planer, Avril Rankin, Miranda Richardson, Peter Richardson, Pete Richens, Fiona Rich-

mond, Marika Rivera, Roland Rivron, Tricia Ronane, Peter Rosengard, Jennifer Saunders, Barney Sharp, Sandie Shaw, Spider Stacey, Koo Stark, Jonathan Stratt, Ron Tarr, Tim Van Rellim, Rupert Vansittart, Steve Walsh, John Wilson, Bill Wyman, Terence Wood, Eddie Yeon. Dir: Peter Richardson. Pro: Tim Van Rellim. Ex Pro: Michael White. Assoc Dir: Pete Richens. Screenplay: Richardson and Richens. Pro Co-Ord: Maggie Tyler. Ph: Witold Stok. Ed: Chris Ridsdale. Art: Jock Scott. M: (written and performed by) Motorhead. (Iron Fist Pictures in assoc with British Screen, Film Four International, New Line, Recorded Releasing, Smart Egg Pictures and The Cast etc.-Recorded Releasing). Rel: 13 November 1987. 90 mins. Cert 18.

Eddie Murphy Raw – (alternative title **Pieces of My Mind**). 'Raw' is the operative word in this film record of

Jim (Christian Bale) is about to be separated from his parents (Emily Richard and Rupert Frazer) in the panic caused by the Japanese invasion of Shanghai. Left: he later finds unexpected friendship from a young Japanese pilot, in Spielberg's Empire of the Sun *(a Warner release).*

Murphy's personal appearance at the Felt Forum in New York. Almost wilfully offensive, with its stream of four-letter words and virulent attacks on anyone or anything from women to homosexuals. It's a pity because, hidden somewhere underneath the vocal garbage, a good, intelligent and gifted performer sometimes seems to be peeping out. Dir: Robert Townsend. Pro: R.D. Wachs and K.I. Wayans. Ex Pro: Murphy and R. Tieken. Ph: Ernest Dickerson. Ed: Lisa Day. (Murphy/Paramount-UIP). Rel: 13 May 1988. 90 mins. Cert 18.

Empire of the Sun. Overlong (153 minutes), with too many touches of sentimentality and old-hat cinematic gimmicks (such as a celestial choir bursting into song at the drop of a hat), this earthbound Spielberg spectacular still offers plenty of expertly tailored entertainment. Stoppard's screenplay (showing little of his touch), based on the J.G. Ballard book, is about an 11-year-old English boy who is separated from his parents in Shanghai during their flight from the advancing Japanese army and spends the major part of the war in an internment camp where he becomes a shrewd little survivor. Christian Bale carries the major acting role on his small shoulders with considerable energy, though it is left to John Malkovich to provide the film's only fleshed-out role. Some splendidly spectacular scenes, unfamiliar backgrounds, good photography and a scrupulously balanced attitude towards the Japanese compensate for the film's length.

Rest of cast: Miranda Richardson, Nigel Havers, Joe Pantoliano, Leslie Phillips, Masato Ibu, Emily Richard, Rupert Frazer, Peter Gale, Takatoro Kataoka, Ben Stiller, David Neidorf, Ralph Seymour, Robert Stephens, Zhai Nai She, Guts Ishimatsu, Emma Piper, James Walker, Jack Dearlove, Anna Turner, Ann Castle, Yvonne Gilan, Ralph Michael, Sybil Maas, Eric Flynn, James Greene, Simon Harrison, Barrie Houghton, Paula Hamilton, Thea Ranft, Tony Boncza, Nigel Leach, Sheridan Forbes, Peter Copley, Barbara Bolton, Francesca Longrigg, Samantha Warden, Kieron Jecchinis, Michael Crossman, Gary Parker, Ray Charleson, Burt Kwouk, Tom Danaher, Kong-Guo-Jun, Takao Yamada, Hiro Arai, Paul McGann, Marc de Jonge, Susan Leong, Nicholas Dastor, Edith Platten, Shirley Chantrell, John Moore, Ann Queensberry, Sylvia Marriott, Frank Duncan, Ronald Eng. Dir: Steven Spielberg. Pro: Spielberg, Kathleen Kennedy and Frank Marshall. Ex Pro: Robert Shapiro. Assoc Pro: Chris Kenny. Screenplay: Tom Stoppard; based on the J.G. Ballard novel. Ph: Allen Daviau. Ed: Michael Kahn. Pro Des: Norman Reynolds. M: John Williams. (Amblin Entertainment-Warner). Rel: 25 March 1988. 153 mins. Cert PG.

Every Time We Say Goodbye. Sincere, old-fashioned love story in which a Canadian pilot (Tom Hanks) falls in love with a local Sephardic Jewess (Cristina Marsillach). Set in Jerusalem during the Second World War, the film makes the most of its exotic backgrounds, contrasting effectively with the rigid mores of the Jewish people. Essentially a kosher *Romeo and Juliet*, it is a well-crafted, well acted and often quite engaging comedy-drama, spoilt only by the predictability of this genre. Tom Hanks, in his most dramatic

The sheriff and the Texas Ranger team (Rip Torn and Nick Nolte) prepare to attack drug-trafficking farmers in Guild Films' Extreme Prejudice.

screen role to date, has never been better, and is well served under the helmsmanship of Moshe Mizrahi (*I Love You, Rosa; Madame Rosa*).

Rest of cast: Benedict Taylor, Anat Atzmon, Gila Almagor, Monny Moshanov, Avner Hizkiyahu, Caroline Goodall, Esther Parnass, Daphne Armony, Orit Weisman, Ronit Lors, Moshe Ivgi, David Menachem, Nissim Azikry, Avi Keidar, Alan Abovtboul, Jacky Banian, Rivka Gour, Jack Cohen, Danni Muja, Orna Porat, Gordy Mass, Ofera Ariav, Ilan Machora, Hora Jerusalem, Anat Ben-Yehoshua. Dir: Moshe Mizrahi. Pro: Jacob Kotzky and Sharon Harel. Screenplay: Moshe Mizrahi, Rachel Harel and Leah Appet; from a story by Moshe Mizrahi. Ph: Giuseppe Lanci. Ed: Mark Burns. Art: Micky Zahar. M: Philippe Sarde. (Tri-Star-Columbia-Cannon-Warner). Rel: floating; first shown London (Cannon Tottenham Court Road) 18 September 1987. 97 mins. Cert 15.

Extreme Prejudice. *The Wild Bunch* meets *Coogan's Bluff* and there's little blood left over. Tough ol' Walter Hill, director of *The Long Riders* and *Southern Comfort*, pitches an unsympathetic, slimmed-down Nick Nolte, as a Texas ranger, against a drug king and a small army of ex-soldiers turned bad. Tough question: are there more corpses or plot twists? The dialogue, too, is classically bad. One redneck (William Forsythe) yells lasciviously at an attractive passer-by, 'Hey, lady, as long as I've got a

face, you've got a place to sit.' *Extreme Prejudice* classifies itself as a glorified B-movie resurrected from the 'sixties.

Rest of cast: Powers Boothe, Michael Ironside, Maria Conchita Alonso, Rip Torn, Clancy Brown, Matt Mulhern, Larry B. Scott, Dan Tullis Jr, John Dennis Johnston, Luis Contreras, Carlos Cervantes, Tom 'Tiny' Lister Jr, Marco Rodriguez, James Lashly, Tony Frank, Mickey Jones, Kent Lipham, Sam Gauny, Gil Reyes, Rick Garcia, Richard and Larry Duran, Christiana Garcia, Charles Lewis, Humberto de la Torre, Fred Eisenlohr, Anthony Galvan 3, Eric Bowden, Frank Lugo, Jimmy Ortega, Lin Shaye, Anthony Lattanzio, Ken Medlock, Michelle Lynn Rosen. Dir: Walter Hill. Pro: Buzz Feitshans. Assoc Pro: Mae Woods. Ex Pro: Mario Kassar and Andrew Vajna. Screenplay: Deric Washburn and Harry Kleiner, from a story by John Milius and Fred Rexer. Ph: Matthew F. Leonetti. Ed: Freeman Davies. Pro Des: Albert Heschong. M: Jerry Goldsmith. (Carolco-Guild). Rel: 25 September 1987. 105 mins. Cert 18.

Fatal Attraction. As a thriller, *Fatal Attraction* should go down in the annals alongside *Psycho*; as sexual drama, it should stand shoulder-to-shoulder with *Last Tango*. The adult hit of '87, the film embodies every married man's nightmare. Michael Douglas, a successful lawyer and contented husband, spends one night with an attractive book editor, Glenn Close. As consenting adults, they agree to a no-strings fling. But Miss Close, bordering on Lady Macbeth, decides she wants Douglas to herself – even if she has to kill to get him. A taut, efficient drama

Alex (Glenn Close) refuses to accept that the affair is over and accuses her married lover (Michael Douglas) in Paramount/UIP's brilliant sex thriller Fatal Attraction.

with the emotional force of a stiletto. Notice Maurice Jarre's perfect score and look out for Anne Archer's excellent performance as the unknowing wife.

Rest of cast: Ellen Hamilton Latzen, Stuart Pankin, Ellen Foley, Fred Gwynne, Meg Mundy, Tom Brennan, Lois Smith, Mike Nussbaum, Sam J. Coppola, Eunice Prewitt, Jane Krakowski, Justine Johnston, Mary Joy, Christine Farrell, Marc McQue, James Eckhouse, Faith Geer, Carol Schneider, David Bates, Anna Levine, Alicia Perusse, Christopher Rubin, Thomas Saccio, Greg Scott, Chris Manor, Barbara Harris. Dir: Adrian Lynne. Pro: Stanley R. Jaffe and Sherry Lansing. Screenplay: James Dearden, based on his screenplay *Diversion*. Ph: Howard Atherton. Ed: Michael Kahn and Peter E. Berger. Pro Des: Mel Bourne. M: Maurice Jarre. (Paramount-UIP). Rel: 15 January 1988. 119 mins. Cert 18.

A Flame in My Heart – Une Flamme dans mon coeur. An actress goes off the rails after leaving her Arab boyfriend and falling for a timid journalist. This extraordinary film was conceived over a cup of coffee between Swiss film-maker Alain Tanner and leading lady Myriam Mézières, notable for one of the most sexually abandoned performances ever given by a professional actress on screen. Filmed in black-and-white, it could be a pornographic home movie for intellectuals.

Rest of cast: Aziz Kabouche, Benoît Régent, Biana, Jean Yves Berthelot, André Marcon, Anne Rucki, Jean-Gabriel Nordmann. Dir: Alain Tanner. Pro: Paolo Branco. Ex Pro: Dominique Vignet. Screenplay: Myriam Mézières and Alain Tanner. Ph: Acacio De Almeida. Ed: Laurent Uhler. M: J.S. Bach played by Neill Gotkovsky. (Garance/La Sept/Filmograph-Mainline). Rel: floating; first shown London (Cannon Piccadilly) 15 April 1988. 110 mins. Cert 18.

Flowers in the Attic. 'Fathers die, Christopher,' whines a pouting Kristy Swanson (the cyborg in Wes Craven's *Deadly Friend*), 'even if they're young, handsome and we need them.' Craven, better known for starting the chain of nightmares on Elm Street, wanted to film Virginia Andrews's bestseller. It's a shame he didn't. This appalling screen version follows the attic antics of four drippy children incarcerated in Grandmother's house after the death of their father. Louise Fletcher, as Granny, sets the low tone of acting. The script creaks, the photography fluctuates (from out-of-focus to grainy) and the pace drags. The man to blame is director Jeffrey Bloom, previously unknown for *Blood Beach*, *Dogpound Shuffle* and *The Stick-Up*.

Rest of cast: Victoria Tennant (as Mother), Jeb Stuart Adams (son of Nick Adams), Ben Ganger, Lindsay Parker, Marshall Colt (as Father), Nathan Davis, Brooke Fries, Alex Coba, Leonard Mann, Bruce Neckels, Gus Peters, Clare C. Peck (as Narrator). Dir: Jeffrey Bloom. Pro: Sy Levin and Thomas Fries. Ex Pro: Charles Fries and Mike Rosenfeld. Screenplay: Jeffrey Bloom; based on the novel by Virginia C. Andrews. Ph: Frank Byers and Gil Hubbs. Ed: Gregory F. Plotts. Pro Des: John Muto. M: Christopher Young. (New World-Entertainment). Rel: 22 April 1988. 92 mins. Cert 15.

Four Adventures of Reinette and Mirabelle – Quatre Aventures de Reinette et Mirabelle. A minor but

Lee Ermey as the fearsome US Marine drill sergeant in Stanley Kubrick's superb, award-winning martial epic Full Metal Jacket, *a Warner release.*

quietly amusing addition to Eric Rohmer's steady flow of highly individual movies, this is the story, in four episodes, of two girls – a city girl and a country lass – who, despite having little in common, become friends and share adventures in Paris. The girl from the country – a delightful performance by newcomer Joëlle Miguel – steals most of the thunder as we see her changing under the Parisian influence. Part 1 is about the girls' meeting and is easily the least interesting of the quartet. Part 2 shows the country innocent becoming acquainted with city ways. Part 3 explores the girls' differing moral values. The final part concerns Reinette's efforts to sell a painting to an art dealer. All very inconsequential, just like life.

Cast: Episode 1. *The Blue Hour – L'Heure bleue*: Joëlle Miguel, Jessica Forde, the Housseau family. 2. *The Waiter – Le Garçon de café*: Miguel, Forde and Philippe Laudenbach. 3. *The Beggar, Kleptomaniac, Hustler – Le Medicant, La Cleptomane, L'Ar-

maqueuse*: Miguel, Forde, Yasmine Haury, Marie Riviere, Beatrice Romand, Gérard Courant, David Rocksavage, Jacques Auffray, Haydee Caillot. 4. *Selling the Picture – La Vente du tableau*: Miguel, Forde, Fabrice Luchini, Marie Bouteloup, Françoise Valier. Dir and Screenplay: Eric Rohmer. Ph: Sophie Maintigneux. Ed: Maria-Luisa Garcia. M: Ronan Girre and Jean-Louis Valero. (Compagnie Eric Rohmer-Les Films du Losange-Artificial Eye). Rel: floating; first shown London (Chelsea Cinema and Renoir) 8 January 1988. 99 mins. Cert U.

Friendship's Death. A very talkative movie with a political background about a woman from the planet Procryon, bound for the Institute of Technology in Massachusetts. However, she slips up on her earth-entry plan and lands in Amman (in 1970) where she becomes involved with, among other things, the Palestinian/Jordanian fighting. 'Other things' include a journalist on the job there. Somebody, somewhere pigeonholed this strange movie as a 'film essay' and that seems a pretty apt label for an interesting but limited-appeal production.

Cast: Tilda Swinton, Bill Paterson, Patrick Bauchau, Ruby Baker, Joumana Gill. Dir

and Screenplay: Peter Wollen. Pro: Rebecca O'Brien. Ex Pro: Colin MacCabe. Pro Ex: Jill Pack. Ph: Witold Stok. Ed: Robert Hargreaves. Pro Des: Gemma Jackson. M: Barrington Pheloung. (Modelmark for the BFI in assoc with Channel 4). Rel: floating; first shown London (Camden Plaza) 20 November 1987. 78 mins. Cert 15.

Full Metal Jacket. This, Stanley Kubrick's first film for seven years, is no more just another Vietnam movie than *2001: A Space Odyssey* was just another science-fiction film, or *The Shining* another horror flick. *Full Metal Jacket* is a film about war, about the dehumanization of the American marine, about the duality of man. True, no Kubrick film is like another, but every scene of every Kubrick film bears the Master's stamp – that mark of authority, of importance, even. A great movie: demanding, numbing and often very funny. Oddly enough, *Full Metal Jacket* was shot entirely in England.

Cast: Matthew Modine, Adam Baldwin, Vincent D'Onofrio, Lee Ermey, Dorian Harewood, Arliss Howard, Kevyn Major Howard, Ed O'Ross, John Terry, Ian Tyler, Herbert Norville, Bruce Boa, Kieron Jecchinis, Kirk Taylor, Sal Lopez, Gary Landon

The young recruit (D.B. Sweeney) celebrates his wedding with Vietnam veterans James Caan and James Earl Jones (right) in Francis Coppola's Gardens of Stone *(Tri-Star/ Columbia).*

Mills, Papillon Soo, Peter Edmund, Ngoc Le, Leanna Hong, Tan Hung Kopel, Keith Hodiak, Peter Merrill, Peter Norville, Nguyen Hue Phong, Duc Hu Ta etc., Parris Island Recruits and Vietnam Platoon. Dir and Pro: Stanley Kubrick. Co-Pro: Philip Hobbs. Assoc Pro: Michael Herr. Ex Pro: Jan Harlan. Screenplay: Stanley Kubrick, Michael Herr and Gustav Hasford; based on the novel *The Short Timers* by Gustav Hasford. Ph: Douglas Milsome. Ed: Martin Hunter. Pro Des: Anton Furst. M: Abigail Mead. (Warner). Rel: floating; first shown London (Warner) 11 September 1987. 116 mins. Cert 18.

Gaby – A True Story. Heart-warming, intellectually challenging story of a Mexican girl with cerebral palsy who overcomes the limitations forced on her by society. Norma Aleandro, as Gaby's keeper, won an Oscar nomination, but it is Rachel Levin in the title role who holds the film together. An intelligent, well acted feature that reaffirms our

belief in the value of life, although how strictly 'true' the story is may be a matter of some doubt.

Rest of cast: Liv Ullmann, Robert Loggia (as Gaby's parents), Lawrence Monoson (remarkable as another victim of CP), Robert Beltran, Beatriz Sheridan, Tony Goldwyn, Danny De La Paz, Paulina Gomez, Enrique Lucero, Hugh Harleston, Carolyn Valero. Dir: Luis Mandoki. Pro: Pinchas Perry. Story developed by Luis Mandoki (as told to him by Gaby Brimmer). Screenplay: Martin Salinas and Michael James Love. Ph: Lajos Koltai. Ed: Garth Craven. Art: Alejandro Luna. M: Maurice Jarre. (Tri-Star-Columbia). Rel: floating; first shown London (Cannon Tottenham Court Road) 10 June 1988. 114 mins. Cert 15.

Gardens of Stone. 1968, Virginia, USA. Intelligent adult drama about America's old guard during the Vietnam war. James Caan, following a five-year hiatus to raise his son, returns to the screen as a grizzled Vietnam veteran whose job it is to train new recruits for the front line. The film follows his friendships, both romantic and platonic, his spiralling anger, and his frustration at being stuck on the wrong side of the war. An unusual, considered

stance on Vietnam and a surprising antidote to Coppola's *Apocalypse Now*. Slow, maybe, but well acted, written and photographed.

Rest of cast: Anjelica Huston, James Earl Jones, D.B. Sweeney, Dean Stockwell, Mary Stuart Masterson, Dick Anthony Williams, Lonette McKee, Sam Bottoms, Elias Koteas, Larry Fishburne, Casey Siemaszko, Peter Masterson, Carlin Glynn, Erik Holland, Bill Graham, Terrence Currier, Terry Hinz, A.V. Gorman Jr, Louis Rangel, Lisa-Marie Felter, William Williamson, Joseph A. Ross Jr, Matthew Litchfield, Nick Mathwick, Robert Frerichs, Grant Lee Douglass, Mark Frazer, Terry Foster, M. Sizemore, Steve Barcanic, H.O. Moss. Dir: Francis Coppola. Pro: Michael I. Levy and Francis Coppola. Ex Pro: Stan Weston, Jay Emmett and Fred Roos. Co-Ex Pro: David Valdes. Screenplay: Ronald Bass, based on the novel by Nicholas Proffitt. Ph: Jordan Cronenweth. Ed: Barry Malkin. Pro Des: Dean Tavoularis. M: Carmine Coppola. (Tri-Star-Columbia). Rel: floating; first shown London (Cannon Shaftesbury Ave) 22 January 1988. 111 mins. Cert 15.

The Glass Menagerie. Faithful, expertly filmed version of the Tennessee Williams play, eschewing the more melodramatic tendencies of the author.

Karen Allen (as Laura, left), Joanne Woodward (Amanda, centre) and John Malkovich (Tom) in Paul Newman's faithful adaptation of the Tennessee Williams play The Glass Menagerie *(Columbia).*

Set in St Louis, Missouri, it explores the friction that erupts between a brother and sister and their dominating mother before the visit of a gentleman caller 'from the outside world of reality'. Not since *Sleuth* has an entire cast acted so brilliantly – encouraged by Michael Ballhaus's camerawork and Paul Newman's direction.

Cast: Joanne Woodward, John Malkovich, Karen Allen, James Naughton. Dir: Paul Newman. Pro: Burtt Harris. Assoc Pro: Joe Caracciolo. Playwright: Tennessee Williams. Ph: Michael Ballhaus. Ed: David Ray. Pro Des and Costumes: Tony Walton. M: Henry Mancini. (Columbia). Rel: floating; first shown London (Cannon Haymarket) 15 January 1988. 143 mins. Cert PG.

Good Morning Babylon. In 1913 two Italian brothers leave Tuscany for America, where they hope to utilize their skills as stonemasons. Moving west, they encounter other Italian architects who have been commissioned to build the majestic Tower of Jewels at the San Francisco Exposition of 1915. After seeing their work, film director D.W. Griffith invites the brothers to help construct his Babylonian set for *Intolerance*. The Taviani brothers' first English-language film, often visually arresting – and with a memorable performance from Charles Dance as D.W. Griffith – is only partly successful. The Tavianis, together one of the best

A double wedding for the emigré Italian brothers (Joaquim de Almeida and Vincent Spano), with their brides (Désirée Becker and Greta Scacchi) in the Taviani brothers' first American film, Artificial Eye's Good Morning Babylon.

The good wife (Rachel Ward) who turns bad through sexual obsession in the Entertainment-released Australian film, The Good Wife. *Real-life husband Bryan Brown (top right) plays the spouse and Sam Neill (bottom right) plays the object of her mad desire.*

directing forces in Italy, would be wise to concentrate in future on more indigenous subjects, with which they have shown themselves to be masterful.

Rest of cast: Vincent Spano (as Nicola), Joaquim de Almeida (as Andrea), Greta Scacchi, Désirée Becker, Omero Antonutti, Bérangère Bonvoisin, David Brandon, Brian Freilino, Margarita Lozano, Massimo Venturiello, Andrea Prodan. Dir: Paolo and Vittorio Taviani. Pro: Giuliani G. De Negri. Exec Pro: Edward Pressman. Screenplay: the Tavianis, in collaboration with Tonino Guerra, from an idea by Lloyd Fonvielle. Ph: Giuseppe Lanci. Ed: Roberto Perpignani. Art: Gianni Sbarra. M: Nicola Piovani. (Filmtre/Rome/MK2 Productions, Paris/Edward R. Pressman Film Corporation/RAI 1 and Films A2 – Artificial Eye). Rel: floating; first shown London (Lumiere) 28 August 1987. 116 mins. Cert 15.

The Good Wife (Australia: *The Umbrella Woman*). A young wife's boredom with her monotonous, lonely life and the crude lovemaking of her logger husband – and his almost moronic younger brother – leads to her increasingly wild sexual obsession with the newly arrived hotel barman from the big city, whose sophisticated manners soon have most of the local women in a tizzy and several of them in his bed. Weak, silly and generally unsympathetic leading characters – however uncomfortably close to life they may be – do not help this more-than-competently directed, finely acted but unevenly written Australian romantic drama, set in a lovingly recreated small backwoods community in 1939.

Cast: Rachel Ward, Bryan Brown (husband and wife in the film and in real life), Steven Vidler, Sam Neill, Jennifer Claire, Bruce Barry, Peter Cummins, Carole Skinner, Clarissa Kaye-Mason, Barry Hill, Susan Lyons, Helen Jones, Lisa Hensley, May Howlett, Maureen Green, Garry Cook, Harold Kissin, Oliver Hall, Sue Ingleton, Robert Barrett, Maurice Hughes, Margarita Haynes, Bill Bader, Dick May, Trevor Thomas, Philip Wilton, Craig Fuller, Peter Ford. Dir: Ken Cameron. Pro: Jan Sharp. Assoc Pro: Helen Watts. Pro Ex: Michael Nolin. Screenplay: Peter Kenna. Ed: John Scott. Ph: James Bartle. Pro Des: Sally Campbell. M: Cameron Allan. (Laughtin Kookaburra Pro-Entertainment). Rel: floating; first shown London (Cannon Tottenham Court Road) 25 September 1987. 97 mins. Cert 15.

A Great Wall (US: *The Great Wall is a Great Wall*, which was President Nixon's comment about China's world wonder). The first American film to be made in China (Peking) since the Revolution is a simple, charming and understandably somewhat superficial comedy about the differences between the two cultures, explored through the story of a Chinese-American computer executive who decides to take his family on a visit to his sister and her family whom he hasn't seen for twenty years. Unusual locations, warm performances and a mixture of English and Mandarin Chinese dialogue make this a real collector's piece.

Cast: Peter Wang, Sharon Iwai, Kelvin Han Yee, Li Qinqin, Hu Xiaoguang, Shen Guanglan, Wan Xiu Jian, Ran Zhijuan, Han Tan, Jeannette Pavini, Howard Frieberg, Bill Neilson, Teresa Roberts. Dir: Peter Wang. Pro: Shirley Sun. Ex Pro: Wu Yangchian, Zhu Youjun and E.N. Wen. Screenplay: Wang and Sun. Ph: Peter Stein and Robert Primes. Ed: Graham Weinbren. Pro Des: Wing Lee. Art: Cheung Ming Ming and Feng Yuan. M: David Liang and Ge Ganru. (W and S/Nanhai Film Co-Pro-Mainline Pictures). Rel: floating; first shown London (Screen-on-the-Hill and Cannon Tottenham Court Road) 10 July 1987. 102 mins. Cert PG.

Hail! Hail! Rock 'n' Roll. Feature documentary on Chuck Berry, self-proclaimed 'prime minister of rock 'n' roll', complete with live concert footage and rave assessments from Bruce Springsteen, Bo Diddley, Little Richard, Jerry Lee Lewis, Roy Orbison and the Everly Brothers. John Lennon once said, 'If you tried to give rock 'n' roll another name you might call it Chuck Berry'. If you tried to give Chuck Berry another name it might be 'perfectionist', 'dynamic', 'loyal' or 'difficult'. Director Taylor Hackford (*The Idolmaker, La Bamba*) sets out to verify Lennon's claim. An authentic and witty document on a legend still going strong at 62.

Venues include the Fox Theatre in St Louis, Missouri; the Cosmopolitan Club, East St Louis, Illinois; and the star's home, Berry Park, in Wentzville, Missouri. Guest singers and musicians include Eric Clapton, Robert

Americanized Chinese son (Kelvin Han Yee) and mother (Sharon Iwai) in Peking in Mainline's made-in-China comedy A Great Wall.

Cray, Johnnie Johnson, Etta James, Steve Jordan, Julian Lennon, Bobby Keys, Keith Richards, Chuck Leavell, Linda Ronstadt, Joey Stampinato, Ingrid Berry. Dir: Taylor Hackford. Pro: Stephanie Bennett and Chuck Berry. Assoc Pro: Albert Spevak and Jane Rose. Ph: Oliver Stapleton. Ed: Lisa Day. Concert Pro Des: Kim Colefax. (Universal-UIP). Rel: floating; first shown London (Plaza) 12 February 1988. 121 mins. Cert PG.

Hamburger Hill. Yet another in the 1987 spate of Vietnam war films. This one, set *circa* 1969, is less convincing than the prizewinning *Platoon*, although its authenticity should be assured: the screenplay comes from the hand of a soldier who served in the conflict, and the director was also in the thick of it as a cameraman taking official war film. But, however technically excellent, it is somehow uninvolving. The characters are inhuman and it is too often difficult to understand what they are saying. The story concerns the bloody, high-fatality assault on the hill of the title which, once won, is almost immediately abandoned.

Cast: Anthony Barrile, Michael Patrick Boatman, Don Cheadle, Michael Dolan, Don James, Dylan McDermott, M.A. Nickles, Harry O'Reilly, Daniel O'Shea, J.C. Palmore, Tim Quill, Tommy Swerdlow, Courtney B. Vance, Steven Weber, Tegan West, Kieu Chinh, Doug Goodman, J.D. Van Sickle. Dir: John Irvin. Pro: Marcia Nasatir and James Carabatsos. Co-Pro: Larry de Waay. Ex Pro: Jerry Offsay and David Korda. Screenplay: Carabatsos. Ph: Peter MacDonald. Ed: Peter Tanner. Pro Des: Austen Spriggs. M: Philip Glass. (RKO Pictures – Palace Pictures). Rel: 2 October 1987. 118 mins. Cert 15.

A Handful of Dust. Impeccable dramatization of Evelyn Waugh's novel of tragedy within the English upper crust of 1932. Charles Sturridge, who directed ITV's magnificent *Brideshead Revisited*, captures perfectly the dark mood of the original, in which Tony Last, landed gentleman, finds his wife has been cheating on him. A tremendous story, well told, with first-rate performances, photography,

The high cost of a futile victory, surveyed by the survivors of the attack during the Vietnam War. From Palace Pictures' Hamburger Hill.

music, production design *et al*, it could turn out to be the best British film of 1988.

Cast: James Wilby (as Tony), Kristin Scott Thomas (excellent as Brenda Last), Rupert Graves, Anjelica Huston, Judi Dench, Alec Guinness, Beatie Edney, Pip Torrens, Christopher Godwin, Stephen Fry, Graham Crowden, Cathryn Harrison, Richard Beale, Jackson Kyle, Norman Lumsden, Jeanne Watts, Kate Percival, Richard Leech, Roger Milner, Tristram Jellinek, John Quentin, Timothy Bateson, Moyra Fraser, Marsha Fitzalan, Annabel Brooks, Tamsin Olivier, Maureen Bennett, Hugh Simon, Alan Hay, Matthew Ryan, Alice Dawnay, John Junkin, Peggy Aitchison, Jeannette Baillie, Julian Infante, William Gonzalez. Dir: Charles Sturridge. Pro: Derek Granger. Ex Pro: Jeffrey Taylor and Kent Walwin. Assoc Pro: David Wimbury. Screenplay: Charles Sturridge, Tim Sullivan and Derek Granger. Ph: Peter Hannan. Ed: Peter Coulson. Pro Des: Eileen Diss. M: George Fenton. Costumes: Jane Robinson. (Premier Releasing). Rel: floating; first shown London (Cannon Shaftesbury Ave) 14 June 1988. 118 mins. Cert PG.

Hearts of Fire. Pleasant but unremarkable rock musical with the numbers strung on the familiar story line of a youngster making the big time from small beginnings. Fiona Flanagan is pretty enough until her face contorts in her efforts to raise the roof with her voice – which drives the on-screen audiences wild with excitement. Supporting her, as fictional wooers, are real-life rock singers Bob Dylan and Rupert Everett.

Rest of cast: Lesley Donaldson, Barbara Barnes-Hopkins, Myra Fried, Arlene Duncan, Maury Chaykin, Bill Block, David Blacker, Kevin Fox, Jeremy Ratchford, Tony Rasato, Richard Comar, Robert Lannon, Raymond Mason, Ian Dury, Richie Havens, Suzanne Bertish, Julian Glover, Larry Lamb, Tim Cappello, Steve Bolton, Mark Rylance, Stella Duncan-Petley, Zoe Nathenson, Honey Hazel, Norman Gregory, Allan Corduner, Peter Sugden, Tony Aitken, Robin Brunskill, Julian Firth, Sidney Livingstone, Susannah Hoffmann, Colt's Band (Red Beach, Fred Fairbrass, Laura McDonald, David Rosenberg, Chris Botti, Philip Poppa, Tony Carlucci, Michael Skinner, Taborah Johnson, Cree Summer Franks). Dir: Richard Marquand. Pro: Marquand, Jennifer Miller and Jennifer Alward. Co-Pro: Iain Smith. Ex Pro: G.W. Abrams and Doug Morris. Screenplay: Scott Richardson and Joe Eszterhas. Ph: Alan Hume. Ed: Sean Barton. Pro Des: Roger Murray-Leach. M: John Barry. M Dir: Beau Hill. (Lorimar/Phoenix Entertainment

Group-Fox/UKFD). Rel: floating; first shown London (Odeon Marble Arch) 9 October 1987. 95 mins. Cert 15.

Hello Again. Light and frothy *Diary of a Dead Housewife*, or *Peggy Sue Got Killed*. Shelley Long, an accident-prone Long Island housewife, chokes on a South Korean chicken ball, dies and is raised to the living a year later by her sister (Judith Ivey), a crazy medium. She (Miss Long) has a lot of explaining to do, and doesn't believe it herself; in her absence a lot has been going on, including the marriage of her son (Thor Fields) and the re-marriage of her husband (Corbin Bernsen from *L.A. Law*). Daft, deftly slapstick comedy of absurdity, crowned by a delightful, bewildered performance from Miss Long.

Rest of cast: Gabriel Byrne, Sela Ward, Austin Pendleton, Carrie Nye, Robert Lewis, Madeleine Potter, John Cunningham, I.M. Hobson, Mary Fogarty, Tony Sirico, Elkan Abramowitz, Shirley Rich, Kaiulani Lee, John Rothman, Kate McGregor-Stewart, Lynne Thigpen, Royce Rich, Chip Zien, Anna Marie Wieder, Robert Lempert, Susan Isaacs, Marcell Rosenblatt, Catherine Tambini, Everett Quinton, John Tillinger, Debra D. Stewart, Patricia Gage, Mary Armstrong, Colin R. Fox, Rose Indri, Elyzebeth Chrystea, Suzanne Barnes, Karen Shallo, Paul Royce, Illeana Douglas. Dir and Pro: Frank Perry. Ex Pro: Salah M. Hassanein. Screenplay: Susan Isaacs. Ph: Jan Weincke. Ed: Peter C. Frank and Trudy Ship. Pro Des: Edward Pisoni. M: William Goldstein. Costumes: Ruth Morley. (Touchstone-Warner). Rel: 10 June 1988. 96 mins. Cert PG.

Hellraiser. Thoroughly repellent British blood-and-guts sci-fi horror movie without any notable mitigating qualities in the way of scripting, direction or performances. A ludicrous story about a mysterious box which, when opened, lets out the forces of evil. Strictly for strong-stomached horror fans.

Cast: Andrew Robinson, Clare Higgins, Ashley Laurence, Sean Chapman, Oliver Smith, Robert Hines, Anthony Allen, Leon Davis, Michael Cassidy, Frank Baker, Kenneth Nelson, Gay Barnes, Niall Buggy. Dir and Screenplay: Clive Barker; based on his book *The Hellbound Heart*. Pro: Christopher Figg. Ex Pro: David Saunders, Christopher Webster and Mark Armstrong. Ph: Robin Vidgeon, R. Marden. Art: Jocelyn James. M: Christopher Young. (Film Futures/New World-Entertainment). Rel: floating; first shown London (Cannon Prince Charles) 11 September 1987. 93 mins. Cert 18.

Hidden City. Writer Stephen Poliakoff's directorial debut is a mixed bag of credits and debits. It is a meandering, overlong story about a statistician who is drawn into an officially disapproved search by a film technician for some missing pieces of film which, she suspects, when welded into a whole, will reveal a government scandal. The search leads through bizarre, hidden parts of London, such as an old tram depot below Holborn, a vast air-raid shelter beneath Tottenham Court Road, a huge rubbish tip, a canal tunnel and various other eerily atmospheric locations. Visually it is fascinating but, sadly, it lacks the pace and incisive direction which could have made it a minor masterpiece.

Cast: Charles Dance, Cassie Stuart, Bill Paterson, Richard E. Grant, Alex Norton, Tusse Silberg, Richard Ireson, Saul Jephcott, Michael Mueller, Stevan Rimkus, Gerard Horan, Campbell Morrison, Robin Soans, Noreen Kershaw, Chris Jury, Michelle Fairley. Dir and Screenplay: Stephen Poliakoff. Pro: Irving Teitelbaum. Assoc Pro: Ron Purdie. Ph: Witold Stok. Ed: Peter Coulson. Pro Des: Martin Johnson. Art: Alastair Paton. M: Michael Storey. (Hidden City Films for Films Four International-The Other Cinema). Rel: floating; first shown London (Metro) 24 June 1988. 107 mins. Cert 15.

Hibiscus Town. Another of the new Chinese films, this is a political drama about two contrasting women caught up in the trauma of the infamous Cultural Revolution and translated into terms of melodrama on the grand scale as it follows the terrible, turbulent period between 1964 and 1979.

Cast: Liu Xiaoqin and Jiang Wen as the two women, with supporting cast. Dir: Xie Jin. (ICA). Rel: floating; first shown London (ICA) 3 June 1988. 135 mins. No cert.

Hollywood Shuffle. Robert Townsend financed this movie with credit cards (and no bank account), and that's as interesting as it gets. It's an amateurish attempt to show up the bias of Hollywood casting directors towards blacks, while spitting out anti-Eddie Murphy jokes and filling the screen with 'jive-ass niggers'. At its best, *Hollywood Shuffle* is a promising springboard for actor-producer-writer-director Townsend, at its worst a ramshackle collection of unfunny and farcical sketches. The message is fine, it's the megaphone that's the problem.

Bombed and burnt out: mother (Sarah Miles) and son (Sebastian Rice-Edwards) in John Boorman's prize-winning Columbia British release Hope and Glory. *Right: a punting lesson from grandfather (Ian Bannen) when the family moves to his more peaceful Thames-side home.*

Rest of cast: Anne-Marie Johnson, Starletta Dupois, Helen Martin, Craigus R. Johnson, Domenick Ierrera, Paul Mooney, Lisa Mende, Robert Shafer, John Witherspoon, Franklin Ajaye. Dir, Pro, Screenplay: Robert Townsend. Ex Pro: Carl Craig. Co-Screenplay: Keenen Ivory Wayans. Ph: Peter Deming. Ed: W.O. Garrett. Art: Melba Katzman Farquhar. M: Patrice Rushen and Udi Harpaz. (Goldwyn-Virgin). Rel: floating; first shown London (Metro and Brixton Ritzy) 25 March 1988. 82 mins. Cert 15.

Hope and Glory. Written, directed and produced by John Boorman, with three of his family in the cast, *Hope and Glory* is closely based on his experiences as a schoolboy during the Second World War. It is divided into two parts: family life in a badly bombed London suburb and, later, an almost idyllic existence in his grandparents' lovely house on the banks of the upstream Thames. A sensitive, realistic and pretty convincing mixture of comedy, dra-ma and tragedy, beautifully observed and vividly recalled, with a sharp insight into the minds and behaviour of children. The best performance comes from Ian Bannen as the richly realized grandfather.

Rest of cast: Sarah Miles, David Hayman, Derrick O'Connor, Susan Wooldridge, Sammi Davis, Sebastian Rice-Edwards, Jean-Marc Barr, Annie Leon, Amelda Brown, Jill Baker, Katrine Boorman, Geraldine Muir, Nicky Taylor, Gerald James, Sara Langton, Barbara Pierson, Charley Boorman, Susan Brown, Colin Higgins, Peter Hughes, Arthur Cox, Ann Thornton, Andrew Bicknell, Hannah Nicol, Imogen Cawrse, Shelagh Fraser, David Parkin, Christine Crowshaw, William Armstrong, Colin Dale, Jodie Andrews, Nicholas Askew, Jamie Bowman, Carlton Taylor,

Scotland's master director Bill Forsyth retains his originality in his first Hollywood production, Housekeeping. *Here Sylvie (Christine Lahti) exults in her freedom. Inset: two promising newcomers in this Columbia film, Andrea Burchill (left) and Sara Walker.*

Emma Buckley. Dir, Pro and Screenplay: John Boorman. Co-Pro: Michael Dryhurst. Ex Pro: Jake Eberts and E.F. Gross. Ph: Philippe Rousselot. Ed: Ian Crafford. Pro Des: Anthony Pratt. Art: Don Dossett. M: Peter Martin. (Columbia Pictures in assoc with Nelson Entertainment and Goldcrest Films). Rel: 9 October 1987. 113 mins. Cert 15.

Horse Thief – Daomi Zei. Not so much a movie, more an exposé of Tibetan religious rituals. Still, it is a powerful and vivid picture of Tibetan life, withdrawn from Chinese circulation because of its realistic content. Some scenes linger long in the memory, such as the live burial of diseased goats and the (religious) distribution of millions of pieces of paper over the Himalayas. Raw, forceful cinema and an eye-opener for Western audiences.

Cast (mostly amateur): Cexiang Rigzin, Dan Zhiji, Daiba, Gaoba, Jayang Jamco, Drashi.

Dir: Tian Zhuangzhuang. Pro: Xi'an Film Studio. Ex Pro: Wu Tianming. Screenplay: Zhang Rui. Ph: Hou Yong and Zhao Fei. Art Dir: Huo Jianqi. M: Qu Xiaosong. (Xi'an Film Studio – ICA). Rel: floating; first shown London (ICA) 14 August 1987 (and at the Edinburgh Film Festival). 98 mins. Cert PG.

Housekeeping. Two orphan girls are brought up in a remote town in British Columbia by a series of aged great-aunts – until the arrival of eccentric Aunt Sylvia (Christine Lahti) who changes their lives. An extraordinary, leisurely study of a woman at odds with conformity (a role originally intended for Diane Keaton), *Housekeeping* is director Bill Forsyth's first cinematic foray outside Scotland, and his most serious to date. Although there are many memorable scenes, the film as a whole proves to be an unsatisfactory, unsettling experience.

Rest of cast: Sara Walker, Andrea Burchill, Anne Pitoniak, Barbara Reese, Bill Smillie, Wayne Robson, Margot Pinvidie. Dir: Bill Forsyth. Pro: Robert L. Colesberry. Screenplay: Bill Forsyth; based on the novel by Marilynne Robinson. Ph: Michael Coulter. Ed: Michael Ellis. Pro Des: Adrienne Atkin-

son. M: Michael Gibbs. (Columbia). Rel: floating; first shown London (Chelsea Cinema and Renoir) 4 December 1987. 116 mins. Cert PG.

House of Games. An extraordinary piece of cinema, a veritable mystery tour of the world of con men – like a carefully contrived parlour game for intellectuals. David Mamet, playwright of *Glengarry Glen Ross*, *American Buffalo* and *Edmund*, and scenarist of *The Postman Always Rings Twice*, *The Verdict* and *The Untouchables*, makes his directorial debut with stylistic confidence. A successful psychologist (Lindsay Crouse, Mamet's wife) working in Seattle, Washington, finds she has too little time to 'enjoy' herself any more and sets about remedying the problem – to dramatic effect.

Rest of cast: Joe Mantegna, Mike Nussbaum, Lilia Skala, J.T. Walsh, Willo Hausman, Karen Kohlhaas, Steve Goldstein, Jack Wallace, Ricky Jay, G. Roy Levin, Bob Lumbra, Andy Potok, Allen Soule, Ben Blakeman, Scott Zigler, W.H. Macy, John Pritchett, Meshach Taylor, Sugarbear Willis, Josh Conescu, Julie Mendenhall, Rachel Cline, Patricia Wolff, Paul Walsh, Robert Maguire, Jacqueline De La Chaume. Dir:

The Orion/Rank House of Games *marks the polished and stylish directorial debut of scenarist and playwright David Mamet. Something of an intellectual exercise, the film stars Joe Mantegna and Lindsay Crouse.*

David Mamet. Pro: Michael Hausman. Screenplay: David Mamet, from a story by Jonathan Katz and David Mamet. Ph: Juan Ruiz Anchia. Ed: Trudy Ship. Pro Des: Michael Merritt. M: Alaric Jans. (Orion-Rank). Rel: floating; first shown London (Cannon Haymarket etc.) 20 November 1987. 101 mins. Cert 15.

Innerspace. *Fantastic Voyage* meets *All of Me* in this preposterous, entertaining original. Briefly, Dennis Quaid is miniaturized until invisible to the naked eye and is accidentally injected into the rear end of Martin Short. Utilizing all the sci-fi available to him, Quaid plugs his high-tech gadgetry into Martin Short's sensory organs, and the latter becomes two men – a kind of Short circuit. This opens up no end of narrative possibilities and the film exploits most of them to superb comic and dramatic effect. In fact, why this wasn't the hit film of 1987 is a mystery.

Steven Spielberg was the executive producer.

Rest of cast: Meg Ryan, Kevin McCarthy, Fiona Lewis, Vernon Wells, Robert Picardo, Wendy Schaal, Harold Sylvester, Henry Gibson, William Schallert, John Hora, Mark L. Taylor, Orson Bean, Kevin Hooks, Kathleen Freeman, Archie Hahn, Dick Miller, Kenneth Tobey, Joe Flaherty, Andrea

Exciting times for Meg Ryan as she desperately holds on to Martin Short's leg in Spielberg's Warner-released sci-fi fantasy Innerspace.

Martin, Jason Laskay, Frank Miller, Shawn Nelson, Grainger Hines, Chuck Jones, Jeffrey Boam, Charles Aidman. Dir: Joe Dante. Pro: Michael Finnell. Co-Pro: Chip Proser. Ex Pro: Steven Spielberg, Peter Guber and John Peters. Co-Ex Pro: Frank

Down and out in New York in the 'thirties; an almost unrecognizable Meryl Streep with Jack Nicholson in the Palace Pictures release Ironweed.

Marshall and Kathleen Kennedy. Screenplay: Jeffrey Boam and Chip Proser; from a story by Proser. Ph: Andrew Laszlo. Ed: Kent Beyda. Pro Des: James H. Spencer. M: Jerry Goldsmith. (Warner). Rel: 27 November 1987. 119 mins. Cert PG.

Ironweed. Slow-moving, thoughtful film version of William Kennedy's acclaimed novel, with Jack Nicholson as the Albany (New York) down-and-out haunted by the ghosts of his past. An engrossing, heartfelt look at the underbelly of America in 1938, the film is blessed with some outstanding performances, particularly from Nicholson, Tom Waits as his companion-in-the-gutter and Meryl Streep, unrecognizable as a former pianist reduced to a world of humiliation and penury, a mere shell of her former self. Grim going, but a film with insight and humanity.

Rest of cast: Carroll Baker (as Nicholson's wife), Michael O'Keefe, Fred Gwynne,

Margaret Whitton, Jake Dengel, Nathan Lane, James Gammon, Will Zahrn, Laura Esterman, Joe Grifasi, Hy Anzell, Bethel Leslie, Richard Hamilton, Black-Eyed Susan, Louise Phillips, Marjorie Slocum, Lena Spencer, Lola Pashalinski, Paul A. DiCocco Jr, Priscilla Smith, James Dukas, Jared Swartout, Ted Levine, Martin Patterson, Terry O'Reilly, Michael O'Gorman, Frank Whaley, Jordan Valdina, Louis St Louis, Lois Barden Stilley, Ean Egas, Nebraska Brace, William Duell. Dir: Hector Babenco. Pro: Keith Barish and Marcia Nasatir. Ex Pro: Joseph H. Kanter, Denis Blouin and Rob Cohen. Co-Pro: Gene Kirkwood and C.O. Erickson. Screenplay: William Kennedy, based on his novel. Ph: Lauro Escorel. Ed: Anne Goursaud. Pro Des: Jeannine C. Oppewall. M: John Morris. (Tri-Star/Home Box Office-Palace). Rel: floating; first shown London (Odeon Haymarket) 20 May 1988. 135 mins. Cert 15.

Ishtar. If this had been a vehicle for Chevy Chase and Dan Aykroyd they would have ditched it (so would Cannon and Ball have done, for that matter). As it is, this is a turbulent comedy fashioned for Warren Beatty and Dustin Hoffman – or re-fashioned, as Hoffman plays a womanizer and Beatty a

romantic loser. OK, maybe Beatty, after his po-faced *Reds*, and Hoffman, after *Death of a Salesman*, wanted to let their hair down, but why – after so long away from the screen (Beatty, six years; Hoffman, five) – choose something so spectacularly infantile and expensive (reputed cost: $50 million)? The shameless duo play songwriters dispatched to Morocco on a dubious assignation where they become involved with the CIA, KGB and a blind camel. By comparison, *Three Amigos* looks like a masterpiece.

Rest of cast: Isabelle Adjani, Charles Grodin, Jack Weston, Tess Harper, Carol Kane, David Margulies, Aharon Ipale, Rose Arrick, Fuad Hageb, Julie Garfield, Christine Rose, Bob Girolami, Abe Kroll, Hannah Kroll, Herb Gardner, Bill Moor, Edgar Smith, J.C. Cutler, Ron Berglass, Matt Frewer, Alex Hyde White, Stefan Gryff, Mark Ryan, Warren Clarke, Arthur Brauss. Dir: Elaine May. Pro: Warren Beatty. Assoc Pro: David L. MacLeod and Nigel Wooll. Screenplay: Elaine May. Ph: Vittorio Storaro. Ed: Stephan A. Rotter, William Reynolds and Richard Cirincione. Pro Des: Paul Sylbert. Costumes: Anthony Powell. M: John Strauss; original songs by Paul Williams and Elaine May. (Columbia). Rel: 27 November 1987. 108 mins. Cert PG.

Ivan's Childhood. First shown at the old Jacey cinema in London in January 1964 and now re-released by Artificial Eye, this first Andrei Tarkovsky feature film is about the war as seen through the eyes of a prematurely aged boy of twelve, who becomes a soldier, penetrates the German lines and is eventually hanged when caught. The film was the debut of a film artist of outstanding quality and with its many brilliant scenes foreshadows Tarkovsky's later, more complex work.

Cast: Kolya Burlyaev, Valentin Zubkov, Ye Zharikov, S. Krylov, N. Grinko, D. Milyutenko, V. Malyavina, I. Tarkovsky. Dir: Andrei Tarkovsky. (Artificial Eye). Rel: floating; first shown London (Renoir) 20 May 1988. 95 mins. Cert PG.

I've Heard the Mermaids Singing. A strange, poetic, engaging tale of an accident-prone temp (Sheila McCarthy, in her film debut) hired to work in a Toronto art gallery. There, she comes to terms with her own lack of talent as a photographer and with her love for the curator (Paule Baillargeon). Essentially a character study, this is a brave, whimsical first work from director-producer-writer-editor Patricia Rozema, a well-scripted comedy that is proud to be Canadian.

Rest of cast: Ann-Marie MacDonald, John Evans, Brenda Kamino, Richard Monette. Dir, Pro, Screenplay and Ed: Patricia Rozema. Co-Pro: Alexandra Raffe. Ex Pro: Don Haig. Ph: Douglas Koch. Art: Valanne Ridgeway. M: Mark Korven; Ludwig van Beethoven (5th Symphony), Leo Delibes ('Viens, Mallika, les lianes en fleurs' from his opera *Lakmé*). (Ontario Arts Council/Canada Council/National Film Board/Ontario Film Development Corporation/Telefilm Canada-Contemporary/Electric). Rel: floating; first shown London (Screen-on-the-Green, Gate Notting Hill and Cannon Tottenham Court Road) 4 March 1988. 84 mins. Cert 15.

Jane and the Lost City. Based on the *Daily Mirror* comic strip 'Jane', about a flighty British agent in the Second World War, this is an adventure featuring savage warriors, dotty colonels, active volcanoes, treacherous Nazis, pilot-less aircraft and breathtaking

Sheila McCarthy making a very successful screen debut in the poetic Canadian production I've Heard the Mermaids Singing, *the Contemporary/Electric release which marked the equally successful debut of writer-director Patricia Rozema.*

Warren Beatty and Dustin Hoffman play singer-songwriters in Columbia's expensive but undistinguished Ishtar.

painted backdrops. American hunk Sam Jones (*Flash Gordon*) supplies the brawn, Kirsten Hughes is a mediocre Jane and newcomer Elsa O'Toole steals the film as a Roedean-educated jungle queen.

Rest of cast: Maud Adams, Jasper Carrott (dreadful), Robin Bailey, Graham Stark, John Rapley, Ian Roberts. Dir: Terry Marcel. Pro: Harry Robertson. Ex Pro: Terry Ramsden. Screenplay: Mervyn Haisman; from a story by Mervyn Haisman, Terry

Michael Caine steers the boat into the jaws of watery death in the fourth giant shark saga, Jaws – The Revenge. A Universal-UIP release.

Marcel and Harry Robertson. Ph: Paul Beeson. Ed: Alan Jones. Pro Des: Michael Pickwoad. M: Harry Robertson. (Marcel-Robertson-Blue Dolphin). Rel: floating; first shown London (Odeon Marble Arch and Cannon Panton Street) 12 May 1988. 91 mins. Cert PG.

Jaws (4) – The Revenge. Fourth in this increasingly daft series throws the last vestige of credibility to the winds with the creature, which apparently hates the entire Brody family, actually following his quarry down from New England to the Bahamas to get another bite. The finale is uproarious farce, nearly swamping some surprisingly good performances from a cast that includes Michael Caine and Lorraine Gary.

Rest of cast: Lance Guest, Mario Van Peebles, Karen Young, Judith Barsi, Lynn Whitfield, Mitchell Anderson, Jay Mello, Cedric Scott, Charles Bowleg, Melvin Van Peebles, Mary Smith, Edna Billotto, Fritzi Jane Courtney, Cyprian R. Jube, Lee Fierro, John Griffin, Diane Hetfield, Daniel J. Manning, W.E. Marks, James Martin, David Wilson, Romeo Farringdon, Anthony Delaney, Heather Thompson, Levant Carey, Darlene Davis. Dir and Pro: Joseph Sargent. Screenplay: Michael de Guzman. Ph: John McPherson. Ed: Michael Brown. Pro Des: John Lloyd. M: Michael Small. (Universal-UIP). Rel: 14 August 1987. 100 mins. Cert 18.

Jean de Florette. The first of two two-hour films (made simultaneously) adapted from a two-part Marcel Pagnol story (the second, though written first, is *Manon des sources*) about Provence and the Provençals. Against the harsh, arid, rocky background of Haute Provence, it follows the cruel and callous machinations of a local patriarch and his dim-witted nephew to gain possession of a parcel of land on which there is a spring. The old man surreptitiously blocks up the spring to conceal it from the new inheritor owner from town, who consequently kills himself trying to keep his crops alive. Successful at last, the connivers' secret (safe with the clanny locals) is discovered by the young daughter only after her father's death, leading to her later grim revenge, related in the second film. The most expensive French film ever made, its characters are marvellously well delineated and the actors perform superbly under the inspired direction of Claude Berri, resulting in a classic, memorable film equal in power, visual splendour and character perception to the late Pagnol's own great films.

Cast: Yves Montand, Gérard Depardieu, Daniel Auteuil, Elisabeth Depardieu, Ernestine Mazurowna, Marcel Champel, Armand Meffre, André Dupon, Pierre Nougaro, Marc Betton, Jean Maurel, Roger Souza, Bertino Benedetto, Margarita Lozano, Pierre Jean Rippert, Didier Pain, Fransined, Christian Tamisier, Marcel Berbert, Jo Doumerg, Chantal Liennel. Dir and Screenplay (latter with Gérard Brach): Claude Berri; from the novel by Marcel Pagnol. Ex Pro: Pierre Grunstein. Assoc Pro: Alan Poire. Ph: Bruno Nuytten. Ed: Arlette Langmann, Hervé de Luze and Noëlle Boisson. Pro Des: Bernard Vezat. M: Jean-Claude Petit. (Renn Pro/Films A2/Rai 2/DD Pro-Cannon Film Dist.) Rel: floating; first shown London (Curzon Mayfair) 24 July 1987. 120 mins. Cert PG.

King Lear. Yet another of Jean-Luc Godard's typically shapeless celluloid creations, full of bits and pieces adding up to plenty of spice but very little substance.

Cast: Burgess Meredith (Lear), Peter Sellars (Shakespeare), Molly Ringwald, Jean-Luc Godard, Norman Mailer, Kate Miller, Woody Allen. Dir, Screenplay and Ed: Jean-Luc Godard. Pro: Menahem Golan and Yoram Globus. Assoc Pro: Tom Luddy. Ph: Sophie Maintigneux. No other details available. (Cannon). Rel: floating; first shown London (ICA and Cannon Premiere) 29 January 1988. 90 mins. Cert 15.

The Kitchen Toto. The second film in Cannon's gift to first-time directors, *The Kitchen Toto* is not the story of a domesticated dog but a serious, frugal slice of film-making about the Mau Mau uprising in Kenya, *circa* 1950, as seen through the eyes of a 12-year-old native hired as a kitchen toto, or cook's help. The boy, stolidly played by the non-professional Edwin Mahinda, finds his loyalties divided between his white employers and his own tribesmen, albeit the killers of his father, as he witnesses the escalation of bloody events leading to the British declaration of a State of Emergency in 1952. The director, 27-year-old Harry Hook, a Kenyan native from the age of four, handles his first screenplay with competence, if few surprises, and makes the most of the cultural contrast between the British and Kikuyu ways of life. He is also well served by Roger Deakins's crisp photography and a peremptory, engaging performance from Bob Peck as the Chief of Police.

Rest of cast: Phyllis Logan, Robert Urquhart, Kirsten Hughes, Edward Judd, Nathan Dambuza Mdledle, Ann Wanjugu, Job Seda, Leo Wringer, Nicholas Charles, Ronald Pirie. Dir and Screenplay: Harry Hook. Pro: Ann Skinner. Ex Pro: Menaham Golan and Yoram Globus. Ph: Roger

Edwin Mahinda as The Kitchen Toto *in the Cannon release concerning life in Kenya during the Mau-Mau troubles.*

Deakins. Ed: Tom Priestley. Pro Des: Jamie Leonard. M: John Keane. (British Screen/Film Four International/Skreba Film-Cannon). Rel: 27 November 1987. 95 mins. Cert 15.

La Bamba. The stirring story of Ritchie Valens, the 17-year-old rock star who rocketed to brief fame until his death in a plane accident in 1959 (which also killed Buddy Holly and the Big Bopper). A passionate film, realized with admirable simplicity, and serviced with excellent production values and a top-notch cast, particularly Rosana De Soto as Ritchie's long-suffering mother. A sensational soundtrack from Los Lobos includes the Valens hits 'Donna, Come On Let's Go' and 'La Bamba', and other songs of the period.

Rest of cast: Esai Morales, Elizabeth Peña, Joe Pantoliano, Lou Diamond Phillips (as Ritchie), Danielle von Zerneck, Rick Dees, Marshall Crenshaw (as Buddy Holly), Howard Huntsberry (as Jackie Wilson), Brian Setzer (as Eddie Cochran), Daniel Valdez, Felipe Cantu, Eddie Frias, Mike Moroff, Geoffrey Rivas, Sam Anderson, Maggie Gwinn, Jeffrey Alan Chandler (as Alan Freed), Stephen Lee (as Big Bopper), John Quade, Lettie Ibarra, Tony Genaro, Allison Robinson, Hunter Payne, Diane Rodriguez, Kati Valdez, Gloria Balcorta, Ernesto Hernandez, Noble Willingham, Thom Pintello, Stephen Schmidt, Rosanna Locke, Kim Sebastian, Dyana Ortelli, Andy Griggs, Art Koustik. Dir and Screenplay: Luis Valdez. Pro: Taylor Hackford and Bill Borden. Assoc Pro: Daniel Valdez. Ex Pro: Stuart Benjamin. Ph: Adam Greenberg. Ed: Sheldon Kahn and Don Brochu. Pro Des: Vince Cresciman. M: Carlos Santana and Miles

The girl-watcher is French director Leos Carax, one of the many unexpected players to appear in Jean-Luc Godard's odd version of King Lear *(a Cannon release).*

Goodman. (New Visions Productions – Columbia). Rel: 7 November 1987. 108 mins. Cert 15.

The Last Emperor. The last Chinese god-ruler was a Manchurian boy who at the age of three became the country's last 'Son of Heaven'; although deposed at the age of six, he was allowed to stay on in the Forbidden City until thrown out by a warlord who captured Peking. Thereafter he became a playboy in Tientsin and a Japanese-controlled puppet-emperor of Manchukuo, suffered ten years' imprisonment by the Communists and, free at last, became a humble, happy gardener in the Peking park. Nearly 60 years of China's cataclysmic history is captured in marvellously spectacular manner in three hours of superb cinema by Bernardo (*Last Tango*) Bertolucci, who won the distinction of helming the first Western film to be made (almost) wholly in China with active official Chinese parti-

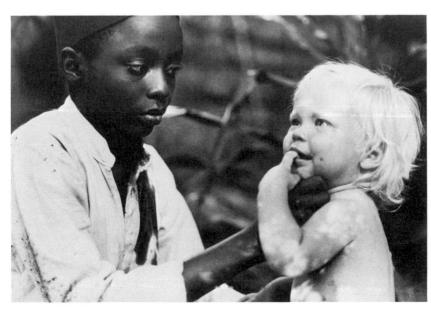

Richard Vuu in the title role in Bernardo Bertolucci's Oscar-laden Columbia release The Last Emperor. *Left: John Lone as the former emperor with his first wife (Joan Chen).*

cipation. *The Last Emperor* is memorable for its scope, its outstanding photography, the handling of its vast crowd scenes, its intelligent condensation of history, its music and its generally very high level of production quality. There are notable performances, too, more especially by John Lone (the emperor in adulthood), Joan Chen (his first wife), Richard Vuu (the Imperial 3-year-old) and Peter O'Toole (the English tutor). Not surprisingly, the film won nine 1987 Oscars.

Rest of cast: Ying Ruocheng, Victor Wong, Dennis Dun, Ryuichi Sakamoto, Maggie Han, Ric Young, Wu Jun Mei, Cary Hiroyuki Tagawa, Jade Go, Fumihiko Ikeda, Tijger Tsou, Wu Tao, Fan Guang, Henry Kyi, Alvin Riley III, Lisa Lu, Hideo Takamatsu, Hajime Tachibana, Basil Pao, Jian Xireng, Chen Kai Ge, Zhang Liangbin, Huang Wenjie, Liang Dong, Dong Zhendong, Dong Jiechen, Constantine Gregory, Soong Huaikeui, Shao Ruzhen, Li Yu, Li Guangli, Xu Chunqing, Zhang Tianmin, Luo Honghian, Yang Baozong, Cai Hong-xiang, Yu Shihong, Wu Jun, Lucia Hwong, Cui Jingping, Wu Hai, Gu Junguo, Xu Tongrui, Li Fusheng, Chen Shu, Cheng Shuyan, Luo Shigang, Zhang Daxing, Zu Ruigang, Jin Yuan, Akira Ikuta, Ma Guang, Cui Xinmin, Li Zhenduo, Yang Hong-chang, Wang Biao, Michael Vermaaten, Matthew Spender, Martin Reynolds. Dir: Bernardo Bertolucci. Pro: Jeremy Thomas. Assoc Pro: Franco Giovale and Joyce Her-lihy. Screenplay: Mark Peploe with Berto-lucci (initial screenplay collaboration Enzo Ungari). Ph: Vittorio Storaro. Ed: Gabriella Cristiani. Pro Des: Ferdinando Scarfiotti. M: Ryuichi Sakamoto, David Byrne and Cong Su. Pro Sup: Mario Cotone. (Columbia). Rel: floating; first shown London (Odeon Leicester Square) 26 February 1988. 162 mins. Cert 15.

The Last of England. This self-indulgent collection of Derek Jarman's home movies (shot on 8 mm film blown up), documentary-style snippets of de-relict streets, and other sad bits and pieces is a bit of a mess, adding up to a grim and depressing picture of England. Impressionistic, poetic, puzzling, puckish, superficial – you name it, you'll find it here. For the occasional few minutes the vision is arresting, during others it is just boring, and the only fun to be had is picking out the good bits from the bad.

Cast: Spring, John Phillips, Gay Gaynor, Gerrard McCarthur, Matthew Hawkins, Tilda Swinton, Spencer Leigh and with the voice of Nigel Terry. Dir: Derek Jarman. Pro: James Mackay and Don Boyd. No screenplay credit listed. Ph: (in colour and black-and-white) Jarman, Christopher Hughes, Cerith Wyn Evans, Richard Hes-lop. Pro Des: Christopher Hobbs. Lighting Des: Christopher Hughes. Ed: Peter Cart-wright, Angus Cook, Sally Yeadon and John Maybury. M: Simon Turner, Andy Gill, Mayo Thompson, Albert Oehlen, Barry Adamson and El Tito. (Anglo International/ British Screen/Channel 4/ZDF-Tartan Films/Blue Dolphin). Rel: floating; first shown London (Cannon Prince Charles) 23 October 1987. 87 mins. Cert 18.

Lethal Weapon. Mel Gibson takes the title role, a human killing machine: expert in jujitsu, one of the world's best marksmen and a potential suicide case.

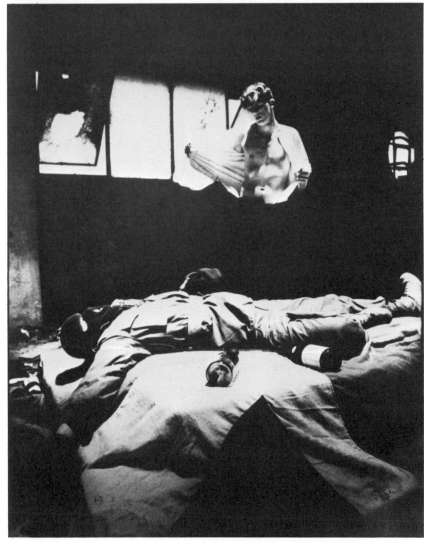

Two scenes from Derek Jarman's gloomy cinematic forecast of things to come, from the Blue Dolphin release The Last of England.

Luckily, he's on the side of the law, a top homicide cop in the Los Angeles Police Department. But *Lethal Weapon* is more than a *Rambo*-in-blue, it's a film about a policeman's lot. It is also one of the most exciting crime thrillers of the year, with excellent photography (from Britain's Stephen Goldblatt), an atmospheric score (Eric Clapton) and engaging performances from Gibson and Danny Glover as contrasting spirits out to bust an international heroin ring. Efficient entertainment.

Rest of cast: Gary Busey, Mitchell Ryan, Tom Atkins, Darlene Love, Traci Wolfe, Jackie Swanson, Damon Hines, Ebonie Smith, Bill Kalmenson, Lycia Naff, Patrick Cameron, Don Gordon, Jimmie F. Skaggs, Jason Ronard, Blackie Dammett, Gail Bowman, Robert Fol, Selma Archerd, Richard B. Whitaker, Mary Ellen Trainor, Steve Kahan, Jack Thibeau, Grand Bush, Ed O'Ross, Gustav Vintas, Frank Reinhard, Paul Tuerpe, Chad Hayes, Chris D. Jardins, Sven Thorsen, Peter DuPont, Gilles Kohler, Credric Adams, James Poslof, Al Leong, Michael Shaner, Natalie Zimmerman, Lenny Juliano, Deborah Dismukes, Cheryl Baker, Terri Lynn Doss, Sharon K. Brecke, Donald Gooden, Alphonse Philippe Mouzon, Shaun Hunter, Everitt Wayne Collins Jr, Henry Brown, Teresa Kadotani, John O'Neill, Tom Noga plus Burbank the cat and Sam the dog. Dir: Richard Donner. Pro: Donner and Joel Silver. Assoc Pro: Jennie Lew. Screenplay: Shane Black. Ph: Stephen Goldblatt. Ed: Stuart Baird. Pro Des: J. Michael Riva. M: Eric Clapton and Michael Kamen. (Warner). Rel: 28 August 1987. 109 mins. Cert 18.

Let's Hope It's a Girl – Speriamo che sia femmina. Leisurely, sunny, consistently captivating Mario Monicelli film with an outstanding cast in a story that wanders happily along, touched by tragedy, black comedy and lightly etched farce. It is about the return to the family's Tuscan farm of the estranged husband of a countess, who is running it with her daughters and her indispensable maid. He seeks cash for one of his crazy schemes but is killed in a farcical accident which throws everything into chaos and the family into mutual recriminations. But, after upheaval and threatened dispersal, fate takes a hand and the household of women settles down, deciding that the only solution to their various problems is to stay together and work things out without male help or interference. The film has a beautiful performance by Liv Ullmann as the countess, superbly

backed up by Catherine Deneuve (as her sister), Philippe Noiret (the count), Bernard Blier (the vague uncle), Athina Cenci (the domineering home help) and Lucrezia Lante Della Rovere (the unmarried, pregnant daughter). The film won the 1986 Italian Critics' Prize.

Rest of cast: Giuliana De Sio, Stefania Sandrelli, Giuliano Gemma, Paolo Hendel. Dir: Mario Monicelli. Pro: Giovanni Di Clemente. Pro Dir: Raimondo Castelli and Bruno Ridolfi. Screenplay: Tullio Pinelli, Suso Cecchi D'Amico, Piero De Bernardi and Monicelli. Ph: Camillo Bazzoni. Ed: Ruggero Mastroianni. Art: Enrico Fiorentini. M: Nicola Piovani. (Clemi Cinematografica, Italy/Producteurs Associés/Soprofilms/ Films A2, France-Artificial Eye). Rel: floating; first shown London (Renoir) 6 November 1987. 119 mins. Cert 15.

Letters from a Dead Man – Pisma Myortvovo Cheloveka. Powerful, compelling and salutary Soviet film about the aftermath of a nuclear disaster which, though made before the Chernobyl explosion, has clear associations with it. Obviously sincere, it packs a powerful plea for sanity in a world now permanently overshadowed by the threat of the Bomb, by presenting a few dying survivors living in cellars beneath a blue-sepia world of dim, endless, muddy desolation. It's a sobering, frightening movie and an astonishingly mature one from this new director.

Cast: Rolan Bykov, I. Ryklin, V. Mikailov, A. Sabinin, V. Lobanov, N. Gryakalova, V. Mayorova, V. Dvorzhetski, S. Smirnova, N. Alkanov. Dir: Konstantin Lopushansky. Screenplay: Lopushansky, Vyacheslav Rybakov and Boris Strugatsky. Ph: (in colour and black-and-white): Nikolai Pokoptsev. Art: Yelena Amshinskaya and Viktor Ivanov. M: Alexander Zhurbin, Faure and Messaien. (Lenfilm Studio/Sovexportfilm-Artificial Eye). Rel: floating; first shown London (Renoir) 25 September 1987. (Winner of the Grand Prix at Mannheim Festival in 1986.)

Little Dorrit. Long, theatrical and intimate version of Charles Dickens's novel about life in the Marshalsea, London's infamous debtors' prison. Often heavy-going and claustrophobic in its setting, the film is not an ideal example of the greatness of Dickens, although the social message is clear. Hardly cinematic, it might have been tremendous on television.

Cast: Derek Jacobi, Alec Guinness, Cyril Cusack, Eleanor Bron, Michael Elphick,

Bill Fraser, Joan Greenwood, Patricia Hayes, Miriam Margolyes, Roshan Seth, Max Wall, Sarah Pickering (as Little Dorrit), Amelda Brown, Edward Burnham, Daniel Chatto, Roger Hammond, Pauline Quirke, Richard Stirling, Luke Duckett, Sophie Ward, Kathy Staff, Patricia Napier, John Savident, Brian Pettifer, John Harding, Alec Wallis, Michael Mears, Ken Morley, Stuart Burge, Donald Bisset, Harold Innocent, David Pugh, David Doyle, Kate Wiliams, Betty Turner, Howard Goorney, Liz Smith, Celia Bannerman, Murray Melvin, Darlene Johnson, Dermot Crowley, Heathcote Williams, John McEnery, Richard Clifford, Olivier Pierre, Tusse Silberg, Ian Hogg, Robert Morley, Alan Bennett, Brenda Bruce, Jonathan Cecil, Malcolm Tierney, Trevor Ray, Rosalie Crutchley, Betty Marsden, Paul Rhys, Arthur Hewlett, John Tordoff, Christopher Hancock, Jo Warne, Danny Schiller, Eric Richard. Dir and Screenplay: Christine Edzard. Pro: John Brabourne and Richard Goodwin. Ph: Bruno de Keyzer. Ed: Olivier Stockman. M: Giuseppe Verdi, arranged and conducted by Michael Sanvoisin. (A Sands Film-Curzon Films). Rel: floating; first shown London (Curzon West End) 11 December 1987. Shown in two parts: part 1: 177 mins; part 2: 183 mins. Cert U.

The Living Daylights. A strictly Bond-formula movie, with all the required ingredients of spectacular thrills, weird and wonderful lethal gadgets, a dash of romance (pretty, innocent agent Maryam D'Abo), some nice touches of humour, lovely international backgrounds and a contrived, confusing story to fit all the bits and pieces into a polished and technically acceptable film. The new 007 (No. 4) Timothy Dalton gives a sound, formula performance, a little lacking in the old Connery/ Moore charisma and sly sense of fun. But it's good to see the old Aston Martin back, complete with a cargo of even more fanciful survival accessories.

Rest of cast: Jeroen Krabbe, Joe Don Baker, John Rhys-Davies, Art Malik, Andreas Wisniewski, Thomas Wheatley, Desmond Llewelyn, Robert Brown, Geoffrey Keen, Walter Gotell, Caroline Bliss, John Terry, Virginia Hey, John Bowe, Julie T. Wallace, Kell Tyler, Catherine Rabett, Dulice Licier, Nadim Sawalha, Alan Talbot, Carl Rigg,

Sarah Pickering in the title role in the Sands/ Cannon celluloid marathon (six hours long) based on the Charles Dickens classic Little Dorrit. *Inset: Patricia Hayes as Affrey and the late Joan Greenwood as Mrs Clennam.*

Not a very promising welcome from jail-keeper Ken Sharrock to new prisoners Maryam D'Abo and the new 007 Timothy Dalton in the UA/UIP release The Living Daylights. *Left: the same couple in a more relaxed situation.*

Tony Cyrus, Atik Mohamed, Michael Moor, Sumar Khan, Ken Sharrock, Peter Porteous, Antony Carrick, Frederick Warder, Glyn Baker, Derek Hoxby, Bill Weston, Richard Cubison, Heinz Winter, Leslie French. Dir: John Glen. Pro: Albert R. Broccoli and Michael G. Wilson. Assoc Pro: Tom Pevsner and Barbara Broccoli. Screenplay: Richard Maibaum and M.G. Wilson. Ph: Alec Mills (2nd Unit Dir and Ph: Arthur Wooster). Ed: John Grover and Peter Davies. Pro Des: Peter Lamont. Art Sup: Terry Ackland-Snow. M: John Barry. (Theme song intro by Barry and Pal Waaktaar). (Broccoli/IUA-UIP). Rel: 14 August 1987. 130 mins. Cert PG.

The Lost Boys. A flashy, exhilarating thriller-comedy for the teenage market, *The Lost Boys* succeeds on practically all counts. Newcomer Jason Patric stars as the new kid in town, which happens to be Santa Cruz, murder capital of the world. Patric, idiot that he is, falls in love with 'half-vampire' Jami Gertz and is lured, reluctantly, into the dark world of the Undead. Although scary, there are lots of laughs, some memorable imagery, great songs and excellent performances from Corey Feldman (at fifteen, America's youngest successful comedian), Kiefer Sutherland as leader of the vampires, and Edward Herrmann and Dianne Wiest as the adults. Joel (*St Elmo's Fire*) Schumacher directed.

Rest of cast: Corey Haim, Barnard Hughes, Jamison Newlander, Brooke Carter, Billy Wirth, Alexander Winter, Chance Michael Corbitt, Alexander Bacon Chapman, Nori Morgan, Todd Feder, Christopher Peters, Keith Butterfield, Gerald Younggren, Eric Graves, J. Dinan Myrtetus, Kelly Jo Minter, Timmy Cappello, Jim Turner, Tony Cain, Melanie Bishop, Sandra E. Garcia, Ian Guindon, Jane Bare, B. Lowenberg, Captain Colourz, Inez Pandalfi, with Cody as Nanook and Folsom as Thorn. Dir: Joel Schumacher. Pro: Harvey Bernhard. Ex Pro: Richard Donner. Screenplay: Janice Fischer, James Jeremias and Jeffrey Boam, from a story by Janice Fischer and James Jeremias. Ph: Michael Chapman. Ed: Robert Brown. Pro Des: Bo Welch. M: Thomas Newman; with songs sung by Lou Gramm, INXS, Jimmy Barnes, Roger Daltrey, Echo and the Bunnymen, Run

Those teeth (belonging to Kiefer Sutherland) give the game away in the Warner release The Lost Boys – *a thrill-and-giggle job.*

D.M.C., The Rascals, etc. (Warner). Rel: 29 January 1988. 92 mins. Cert 18.

The Love Child. Modestly made, kitchen-sink-style British movie about life on a South London council estate. The 'child', an orphan lad, whose hippy parents were killed in a car smash, falls in love with a squatter artist who, along with a couple of flower children throwbacks with whom he becomes friends, does his work prospects no good at all; in fact they get him the sack. But it all ends cheerfully and there are moments of good, well observed comedy along the way. As the lad's grandmother Sheila Hancock goes her own sweet and excellent way; standing firm by her ideas of the script while all around are conforming to lesser effect.

Rest of cast: Peter Capaldi, Percy Herbert, Lesley Sharp, Alexei Sayle, Arthur Hewlett, Cleo Sylvestre, Stephen Lind, Ajaykumar, Andrew Seear, Kevin Allen, Robert Blythe, Cathy Murphy, Stephen Frost, Steven

O'Donnell, Eric Kent, Jon Raymond, Leon Berton, Christopher McHallem, Lee Cornes, Evie Garratt, Valerie Buchanan, Kerryann White, Ray Kingsley, Marsha

Sheila Hancock pours tea for her nephew Peter Capaldi in Frontroom's kitchen-sink-style Love Child, *a British film about life on a London council estate.*

Millar, Nicola Lawrence, Geoff Ward, Andy Sutton, Gaylie Runciman, Christopher Whittingham, Irene Marot, Jack Fortune, Isaac Grand. Dir: Robert Smith. Pro: Angela Topping. Screenplay: Gordon Hann. Ph: Thaddeus O'Sullivan. Ed: John Davies. Pro Des: Caroline Hanania. M: Colin Gibson and Kenny Craddock. (Frontroom Pro in assoc with BFI, Channel 4 TV and VPRO

59

TV Holland-BFI). Rel: floating; first shown London (Metro and Cannon Chelsea) 16 October 1987. 101 mins. Cert 15.

Gareth Bushill, Caroline Milmoe and Georgina Hulme look into the deceptively harmless window of their new home at The Magic Toyshop, *an emporium run by their unpleasant uncle (Tom Bell, right) in the Palace Pictures release.*

Made in Heaven. Boy loses girl, boy dies, boy falls in love with angel, boy loses angel – boy, is this guy unlucky! God, alias Debra Winger, gives him one last chance and sends him back to earth where his angel is now a human baby. He has 30 years to catch her. Suddenly, Alan Rudolph's extraordinary film turns from whimsical fantasy to *Love Story* with wings and halo. A wonderful, wonderful movie trying to escape from a terrible one. Great soundtrack, though.

Rest of cast: Timothy Hutton (as the boy), Kelly McGillis (as the angel), Maureen Stapleton, Don Murray, Marj Dusay, Ray Gideon, Zack Finch, Ann Wedgeworth (excellent), James Gammon, Mare Winningham, Neil Young, Tom Robbins, James Tolkan, Ric Ocasek, Vyto Ruginis, Gailard Sartain, Leon Martell, Matraca Berg, Tom Petty, John Considine, Rob Kneeper, Robert Gould, Debra Dusay and Ellen Barkin, etc. Dir: Alan Rudolph. Pro: David Blocker, Raynold Gideon and Bruce Evans. Assoc Pro: Stuart Besser. Pro Ex: Dana Mayer.

Screenplay: Raynold Gideon and Bruce Evans. Ph: Jan Kiesser. Ed: Tom Walls. Pro Des: Paul Peters. Art: Steve Legler. M: Mark Isham; songs sung by Martha Davis, Luther Vandross, R.E.M., etc. (Lorimar-Fox). Rel: floating; first shown London (Renoir) 23 October 1987. 103 mins. Cert PG.

The Magic Toyshop. This toyshop is definitely not one for the kiddies, with thinly veiled sexual sadism, incest and magic going on in the back parlour. A strangely disturbing, haunting mixture of the factual and the faery, it is about three suddenly orphaned children – the eldest is a girl of sixteen who is very aware of her physical sexuality – taken in by their Cockney uncle, a toyshop owner who makes bizarre life-sized puppets, and rules with an iron hand. British-made, near-surrealistic, poetically imaginative and altogether one of the most original films of the year, even

if its appeal isn't likely to be wide. Caroline Milmoe gives a lovely performance as the girl and the support she gets is first-class. Though made for TV, the film deservedly had its premiere release on the large screen. Bill Connor's music merits a special commendation.

Rest of cast: Tom Bell, Kilian McKenna, Patricia Kerrigan, Lorcan Cranitch, Marlene Sidaway, Gareth Bushill, Georgina Hulme, Marguerite Porter, Lloyd Newson. Dir: David Wheatley. Pro: Steve Morrison.

Screenplay: Angela Carter; based on her book of the same title. Ph: Ken Morgan. Ed: Anthony Ham. Pro Des: Stephen Fineren. M: Bill Connor. (Granada Television-Palace Pictures). Rel: floating; first shown London (Gate Notting Hill and Camden Plaza) 31 July 1987. 103 mins. Cert 15.

Making Mr Right. *Love Story* meets *Short Circuit* in this wacky, thoroughly delightful romantic-comedy with relative newcomer Ann Magnuson as a publicity consultant who falls head-over-heels for a blond, beautiful and barmy client – Ulysses (John Malkovich), an android. Ulysses thinks he's alive – and in love, too – and exhibits more human emotion than his inventor, Dr Jeff Peters (also Malkovich). So Dr Jekyll meets Mr Hyde in an extraordinary twist. Malkovich, increasingly different from film to film, is wonderful in his two opposing roles, and is well supported by heaps of incidental humour and some pacey direction.

The Professor (John Malkovich) makes last-minute adjustments to his android Ulysses during Making Mr Right, *the Orion/Rank release which presented star Ann Magnuson (pictured below with the missing part).*

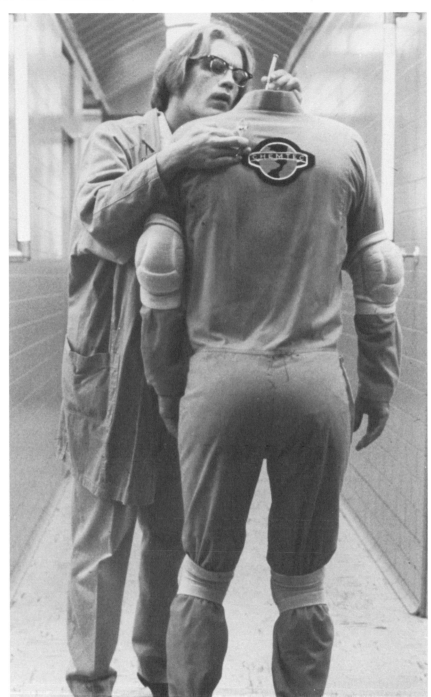

Rest of cast: Glenne Headly (Mrs Malkovich), Ben Masters, Laurie Metcalf, Polly Bergen, Harsh Nayyar, Hart Bochner, Susan Berman, Polly Draper, Christian Clemenson, Merwin Goldsmith, Sid Raymond, Sidney Armus, Robert Trebor, John Hambrick, Susan Lichtman, Steve Rondinaro, Sherry Diamont, Ruthe Geier, Mike Hanly, Donna Rosae, P.B. Floyd, Trip Hamilton, Jill Mallorie, Eve Mash, Ronnie Rosado, Roy Datz, Frank Sangineto, Stephen McFarland, Tom Schwartz, Ruth Mullen, Michael Seidelman, James F. Murtaugh, Ralph Gunderman, Bob Cruz, Harry Chase, Ken Ceresne, Janice Frank, Stanley Kirk, Garitt Kono, Kevin Williams, Clayton Ludovitch, Alan D. Minor, Jose Ramirez, Luisa Rodriguez, Guy Trusty, Gerald Owens. Dir: Susan Seidelman. Pro: Mike Wise and Joel Tuber. Ex Pro: Seidelman and Dan Enright. Screenplay: Floyd Byars and Laurie Frank. Ph: Edward Lachman. Ed: Andrew Mondshein. Pro Des: Barbara Ling. M: Chaz Jankel. (Orion-Rank). Rel: floating; first shown London (Chelsea Cinema) 6 May 1988. 98 mins. Cert 15.

Mala Noche (Bad Night). A one-man-band, inexpensive, black-and-white feature from a new writer-director-producer who will almost certainly do better things in the future. It is an adaptation of a short novel, apparently at least in part autobiographical, about a homosexual shop worker in Portland, Oregon who develops a great lust for an itinerant Mexican who actually prefers the luster's sister and passes along a friend as substitute. The latter is killed

61

He-Man Dolph Lundgren does battle with one of the baddies in Cannon's spectacular Masters of the Universe. *Left: Skeletor (Frank Langella) and Evil-Lyn (Meg Foster) plot to destroy He-Man.*

by the cops, the Mexican vanishes . . . to turn up again in a hurried finale.

Cast: Tim Strecter, Doug Cooeyate, Ray Monge, Nyla McCarthy, Sam Downey, Bob Pitchlynn, Eric Pedersen, Marty Christiansen, Bad George Connor, Don Chambers, Walt Curtis, Kenny Presler, Conde Benavides, Cristo Stoyos, Matt Cooeyate, Maruya Munoz, Arturo Torres, Marsellus Allen, Anne Buffen, Dieter Reshhe, Frank Euward, John Benneth, Pat Switzler, Steve Young, Fred Portra, G.H. Mackie, Judy Ann Leach, Katherine Serlo, Pablo Telles, Chris Monlux, Steve Foster, Havier Valle, Steven Hulse, Denny Chericone. Dir, Pro, Ed and Screenplay: Gus Van Sant; based on the short novel by Walt Curtis. Ph: John Campbell. M: Creighton Lindsay. (Northern Film Co-Respectable Films-Other Cinema). Rel: floating; first shown London (Metro) 24 July 1987. 78 mins. Cert 18.

The Man from Majorca – Nannen fran Mallorca.

That most meticulous of Swedish writer-director-editors Bo Widerberg certainly doesn't make things too easy for his audience in this brilliantly crafted 1984 crime thriller about corruption in high places, which, if a shade on the long side, is pretty consistently absorbing. The complicated story starts with a post office robbery in which a nearby police car crew becomes involved. When the murder of two witnesses follows, they are suddenly taken off the case, but continue their sleuthing in their spare time and eventually track down the high-placed Special Branch killer and his accomplices – only to see them helped off the pair's painstakingly lowered hook by orders from above – well above. Splendidly acted against a background of cold and Christmassy Stockholm.

Cast: Sven Wollter, Tomas von Bromssen, Hakan Serner, Ernst Gunther, Thomas Hellberg, Sten Lonnert, Nina Gunke, Niels Jensen, Gun Karlsson, Karin Bergstrand, Hans Villius, Tommy Johnson. Dir, Screenplay and Ed: Bo Widerberg; based on the book *Griss-festen* by Leif G.W. Persson. Ex Pro: Goran Lindstrom. Ph: Thomas Wahlberg. Art: Jan Oquist. M: Bjorn Gunnarsson. (Drakfilm/Svensk Filmindustrie/Svenska Filminstitutet/Swedish Television SVT2/Filmhuset/Crone Film Sales-Cannon). Rel: floating; first shown London (Cannon Premiere) 14 August 1987. 105 mins. Cert 15.

Manon of the Springs – Manon des sources.

A continuation, ten years on, of the Marcel Pagnol story begun in *Jean de Florette*. The sequel recounts the tragedy of the Provençal patriarch César Soubeyran ('Le Papet'), whose obsession with the successful continuation of the family name leads him to greed and dishonesty and brings about his eventual shame. Though maybe just a shade below Pagnol's original film, this is still a magnificent example of pure cinema, increasingly powerful and moving as it reaches the final sequences, which have all the inevitability of Greek tragedy. A marvellous performance by Yves Montand as 'Le Papet' and an almost equally impressive one by Daniel Auteuil as the nephew whom love changes from a cunning buffoon to a figure of almost noble proportions. A remarkable achievement for all concerned, especially director and writer (with Gérard Brach) Claude Berri.

Rest of cast: Emmanuelle Béart, Hippolyte Girardot, Elisabeth Depardieu, Gabriel Bacquier, Margarita Lozano, Lucien Damiani, Tiki Olgado, Armand Meffre, André Dupon, Pierre Nougaro, Marc Betton, Roger Souza, Jean Maurel, Pierre Jean Rippert, Didier Pain, Fransined, Jean Bouchaud, Yvonne Gamy, Chantal Liennel, Françoise Trompette. Dir and (with Gérard Brach) Screenplay: Claude Berri; based on the Marcel Pagnol novel *L'Eau des collines*, which in turn was based on Pagnol's 1953 film. Ex Pro: Pierre Grunstein. Assoc Pro: Alain Poiré. Ph: Bruno Nuytten. Ed: Arlette Langmann, Geneviève Louveau, Hervé de Luze and Noëlle Boisson (various sources give various of these names). Pro Des: Sylvie Gautrelet. Art: Bernard Vezat. M: Jean-Claude Pettit (theme music adapted from Verdi's opera *The Force of Destiny*). A French-Italian-Swiss co-pro. (Renn Pro/Antenne 2 TV France/Films A2/DD Pro, Paris/RAI TV, Rome/Television Suisse Romande, Geneva, with participation of the French Ministry of Culture and the Centre National de la Cinematographie-Cannon Releasing). Rel: floating; first shown London (Curzon) 20 November 1987. 114 mins. Cert PG.

Mascara.

In this case too many cooks – French, Belgian and Dutch – certainly appear to have spoilt this English-speaking, pretty unpalatable celluloid offering. The often ambiguous, always confusing story concerns a police inspector (Michael Sarrazin) with homosexual tastes and incestuous inclinations, his cold-eyed sister (Charlotte Rampling) who passes final judgement and carries out the well-deserved sentence on him, her lover (Derek De Lint) and an assorted crew of transvestites who, in bizarre make-up and costumes, mime operatic arias in the underground seafront nightclub where most of the unsavoury action takes place. But in all the mish-mash there is one tremendously effective and unforgettable scene, where a lovely, excitingly contoured and beautifully breasted girl (Eva Robins) slowly disrobes and turns to face the camera . . . revealing a full set of male genitals.

Rest of cast: Romy Haag, Herbert Flack, Serge-Henri Valcke, Jappe Claes, John van Dreelen, Harry Cleven, Norman Christine Deumner, Pascale Jean-Louis, Alexandra Van Der Noot, Mark Verstraete, Hugo Van Den Burghe, Charlotte Berden, Marie-Luce Bonfanti, Carmela Locantore, Lois Chacon, Michel Laborde, Alain Zerar, Lida Lobo,

Rupert Graves as Alec and James Wilby as Maurice in the triumphant Merchant Ivory adaptation of E.M. Forster's Maurice, *released by Enterprise Pictures.*

Natalie Fritz, Serge 'Lydie' Lambert, Katja Delvos, Lou De Projck, Terry Fischer. Dir: Patrick Conrad. Pro: Pierre Drouot, Rene Solleveld and Henry Lange. Line Pro: Dany Geys. Assoc Pro: Peter Weijdeveld. Pro Co-Ord: Ilse Somers. Ex Pro: Menahem Golan and Yoram Globus. Screenplay: Conrad, Hugo Claus and Pierre Drouot. Ph: Gilbert Azevedo. Ed: Susana Rossberg. Art: Dirk Debou and Misjel Vermeiren. M: Egisto Macchi, with a series of numbers by Kris Kristofferson, Woody Herman etc. (Iblish Films, Brussels-Prakino Pictures, Amsterdam-Dedalus, Paris-Atlantic Consolidated Enterprises (Ace), New York-Gala Releasing). Rel: floating; first shown London (Cannon Premiere) 6 November 1987. 96 mins. Cert 18.

Masters of the Universe. A junior *Star Wars* spectacular based on the bestselling He-Man toys, with plenty of the familiar planetary ironware, lots of in-space battles, a forgettable script and some arresting make-up, as bold, brave and all-good He-Man fights the powers of darkness in the person of Skeletor and his minions. Strictly a young people's film . . . just the thing to keep the kids amused during the holidays.

Cast: Dolph Lundgren, Frank Langella, Meg Foster, Billy Barty, Courteney Cox,

James Tolkan, Christina Pickles, Robert Duncan McNeil, Jon Cypher, Chelsea Field, Tony Carroll, Pons Maar, Anthony De Longis, Robert Towers, Barry Livingstone, Jessica Nelson, Gwynne Gilford, Walter Scott, Walt P. Robles, Cindy Eyman. Dir: Gary Goddard. Pro: Menahem Golan and Yoram Globus. Assoc Pro: Evzen Kolar. Ex Pro: Edward R. Pressman. Co-Pro: Elliot Schick. Screenplay: David O'Dell. Ph: Havania Baer. Ed: Anne V. Coates. Pro Des: William Stout. Art: Robert Howland. M: Bill Conti. (Golan/Globus Pro in assoc with Edward R. Pressman Film Corp-Cannon Releasing). Rel: 26 December 1987. 106 mins. Cert U.

Maurice. A powerful and articulate love story about a young man painfully coming to terms with his homosexuality, executed with taste, expert craftsmanship and an accurate eye for detail. Based on E.M. Forster's 1914 novel – publication of which was suppressed until after his death – *Maurice* is a maturer work than the same director's *A Room with a View*, eschewing the earlier film's overt sentimentality and tendency towards caricature. A triumph of British film-making.

Cast: James Wilby, Hugh Grant, Rupert Graves, Denholm Elliott, Simon Callow,

Billie Whitelaw, Barry Foster, Judy Parfitt, Phoebe Nichols, Patrick Godfrey, Mark Tandy, Ben Kingsley, Helena Michell, Kitty Aldridge, Michael Jenn, Peter Eyre, Catherine Rabett, Mark Payton, Maria Btrineva, John Elmes, Alan Foss, Philip Fox, Olwen Griffiths, Chris Hunter, Gerard McArthur, Breffini McKenna, Miles Richardson, Phillada Sewell, Mathew Sim, Andrew St Clair, Harriet Thorpe, Julian Wadham, Richard Warner, Alan Whybrow, Orlando Wells, Helena Bonham-Carter. Dir: James Ivory. Pro: Ismail Merchant. Assoc Pro: Paul Bradley. Screenplay: Kit Hesketh-Harvey and James Ivory. Ph: Pierre Lhomme. Ed: Katherine Wenning. Pro Des: Brian Ackland-Snow. Art Dir: Peter James. M: Richard Robbins. (Merchant Ivory Productions/Cinecom/Film Four-Enterprise). Rel: floating; first shown London (Cannons Shaftesbury Ave and Fulham Road) 11 September 1987. 140 mins. Cert 15.

Maybe Baby (US: *For Keeps*). Let's face it, Molly Ringwald is growing up. Gone is the freckled virgin of the high-school prom, gone the daddy's girl with the padlocked knees. After puberty: motherhood. Here Hollywood's favourite teenage innocent tackles sex, motherhood and marriage and makes an intriguing mess of it. This story of two cute teenagers forced into the competitive world of adult responsibility

Randall Batinkoff and Molly Ringwald face up to the problems of young marriage and parenthood in Tri-Star/Columbia's Maybe Baby.

Colin Firth and Kenneth Branagh as the two First World War survivors who find rural life a healer in Warner's A Month in the Country.

(and how they fall flat on their faces) comes in a coyly sentimental package, but with enough home truths to make us care. Ringwald has never been better and is well matched by newcomer Randall Batinkoff as her ingenuous suitor.

Rest of cast: Kenneth Mars, Miriam Flynn, Conchata Ferrell, Sharon Brown, Jack Ong, Robert Ruth, Marty Zagon, Hailey Ellen Agnew, Roger Hampton, Tino Insana, Renee Estevez, Helen Siff, Robert Nadder, Shane McCabe, Allison Roth, Patricia Patts, Brandon Douglas, Kimberly Bailey. Dir: John G. Avildsen. Pro: Jerry Belson and Walter Coblenz. Screenplay: Tim Kazurinsky and Denise DeClue. Ph: James Crabe. Ed: John G. Avildsen. Pro Des: William J. Cassiddy. M: Bill Conti. (Tri-Star-Columbia). Rel: floating; first shown London (Cannons Haymarket and Oxford St) 17 June 1988. 98 mins. Cert 15.

Miss Mary. The story of an English governess (Julie Christie) entrusted to care for the children of a rich Argentinian landowner. Although set against the turbulent years (1930–45) of Argentinian history – paving the way for the Perón regime – *Miss Mary* is essentially a chamber piece, from the director of the Oscar-nominated (Best Foreign Film) *Camila*. Julie Christie struggles bravely with the difficult role of the arrogant (i.e. English) Miss M. who

must, by profession, be subservient, but the actress cannot save the film from its awkward and confusing flashback structure, a most annoying and dreary device.

Rest of cast: Nacha Guevara, Luisina Brando, Eduardo Pavlovsky, Gerardo Romano, Iris Marga, Guillermo Battaglia, Sofia Viruboff, Donald McIntyre, Barbara Bunge etc. Dir: Maria Luisa Bemberg. Pro: Lita Stantic. Assoc Pro: Joan Baribeault and Carlos Gaustein. Screenplay: Jorge Goldenberg and Maria Luisa Bemberg, from an idea by Bemberg, Beda Docampo Feijoo and Juan Bautista Stagnaro. Ph: Miguel Rodriguez. Ed: Cesar D'Angiolillo. M: Luis Maria Serra. (New World-Entertainment). Rel: floating; first shown London (Curzon Phoenix) 18 September 1987. 100 mins. Cert 15.

A Month in the Country. A sparse story of two so-called 'intact' survivors of the Great War who converge on the sleepy Yorkshire parish of Oxgodby. There, Birkin is to resurrect a church mural, Moon to excavate a medieval grave. And that's about it. Economically and intelligently written, Simon Gray's screenplay creaks with subtext, and is well interpreted by Colin Firth and Kenneth Branagh, two of Britain's finest young actors. Though a slim film, overloaded with its own importance, for the most part it is an aesthetic and literate pleasure.

Rest of cast: Natasha Richardson, Patrick Malahide, Tony Haygarth, Jim Carter, Richard Vernon, Vicky Arundale, Martin

O'Neil, Lisa Taylor, Tim Barker, David Gillies, Eileen O'Brien, Barbara Marten, Elizabeth Anson, Judy Gridley, Maurice D. Iley, David Garth, Ken Kitson, Andrew Wilde, John Atkinson, Mary Wray. Dir: Pat O'Connor. Pro: Kenith Trodd. Ex Pro: John Hambley and Johnny Goodman. Screenplay: Simon Gray; based on the novel by J.L. Carr. Ph: Ken MacMillan. Ed: John Victor Smith. Pro Des: Leo Austin. M: Howard Blake. (Film Four International-Warner). Rel: floating; first shown London (Warner and Gate Notting Hill) 20 November 1987. 96 mins. Cert PG.

Moonstruck. The trials and tribulations of an Italian-American family in and out of love in Brooklyn, New York. An agreeable, heartfelt farce, blessed by the perceptive pen of John Patrick Shanley (*Five Corners, The January Man*) and some wonderful performances.

Cast: Cher, Nicolas Cage, Danny Aiello, Julie Bovasso, Feodor Chaliapin, Olympia Dukakis, Vincent Gardenia, Anita Gillette, Louis Guss, John Mahoney, Nada Despotovich, Joe Grifasi, Gina DeAngeles, Robin Bartlett, Helen Hanft, David S. Howard, Robert Weil, Amy Aquino, Lisa Howard, Cynthia Dale, Martha Collins, Catherine Scorsese. Dir: Norman Jewison. Pro: Patrick Palmer and Norman Jewison. Screenplay: John Patrick Shanley. Ph: David Watkin. Ed: Lou Lombardo. Pro Des: Philip Rosenberg. M: Dick Hyman. Costumes: Theoni V. Aldredge. (MGM-UIP). Rel: 29 April 1988. 102 mins. Cert PG.

Mr Jolly Lives Next Door. Brutal and bloody 'comedy' from the Comic Strip crew which takes fun to the point of repulsion. Roughly, very roughly, it's all about a couple of drunken goons attempting to fulfil their £3,000 contract to kill Nicholas Parsons.

Cast: Adrian Edmondson, Rik Mayall, Peter Cook, Peter Richardson, Gerard Kelly, Granville Saxon, Gordon Kane, Basil Otoin, Tommy Windward, Basil Ho-Yen, Ian Bartholomew, Steve Whyment, Derek Van Weenan, Derek Hunt, Christian Fletcher, Shirley McKenzie, Danielle Carter, Thomas Wheatley, Dawn French, Michael Cule, Jennifer Saunders, Philip Locke, Harriet Thorpe. Dir: Stephen Frears. Pro Sup: Elaine Taylor. Pro Co-Ord: Katy Radford. Ex Pro: Michael White. Screenplay: Adrian Edmondson, Rik Mayall and Roland Rivron. Ph: Oliver Stapleton. Ed: Rob Wright. Pro Des: Grant Hicks. Art: Jonathan McKinstry. M: Roland Rivron. (Comic Strip Ltd for Channel 4-Recorded Releasing). Rel: floating; first shown London

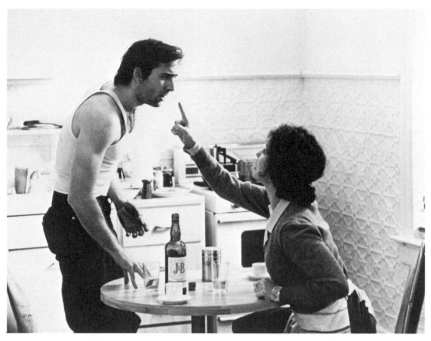

Cher becomes involved with her prospective brother-in-law (Nicolas Cage) in MGM-UIP's Moonstruck.

(Cannon Baker St and Scala) 6 November 1987. 52 mins. Cert 15.

My Friend Ivan Lapshin – Moi Drug Ivan Lapshin. The third and most outstanding film to be made by Russian director Alexei Guerman, made back in 1982 but not seen until the summer of 1986, when it was shown on Soviet TV. Technically and artistically dazzling, original and inventive; mixing colour with sharp black-and-white and

Rik Mayall and Adrian Edmondson in the not-so-jolly Comic Strip comedy Mr Jolly Lives Next Door, *from Recorded Releasing.*

variously tinted photography as it relates 'dear memories' of the unsettled 'thirties (recalled, incidentally, by a narrator we never see), some sad, some happy, some haunting and some funny, a perfect mirror of life. Friend Lapshin is a police investigator (of low financial and social status) in love with an actress, who admits to him she loves his more dashing friend. Woven into this story is one about the pursuit and capture of a dangerous criminal, which leads to the investigator's friend being seriously injured and his own revengeful killing of the unarmed prey. Not a minute of the film's 92 minutes is superfluous and that in this day of painfully padded movies is really something.

Cast: Andrei Boltnev, Nina Rousisnova, Andrei Mironov, Alexei Jarkov, Z. Adamovich, A. Filippenko, Yu Kuznetsov, V. Fililnov, A. Slivnikov, A. Dudarenko etc. Dir: Alexei Gherman. Ex Pro: V. Goroshnikova and V. Izvekov. Screenplay: Ediuard Volodarskl. Ph: Valeri Fedosov. Ed: L. Semionovi. Art: Yuri Pougatch. M: Arkadi Gagulachvili. (Lenfilm/Sovexport-Other Cinema). Rel: floating; first shown London (Metro) 9 October 1987. 100 mins. Cert 15.

My Girlfriend's Boyfriend – L'Ami de mon amie. After slipping a bit from his normally high standard with his more recent movies (allowing, it is said, his young players to write a lot of their own dialogue), Eric Rohmer is right back on his old, sure course. This is the sixth of

Hunted by ruthless baddies, Nadine (Kim Basinger) and separated husband (Jeff Bridges) are forced into a high, tight corner in the Tri-Star/Columbia comedy thriller.

his 'Comedies and Proverbs' series, for which he wrote every word of the screenplay himself – and it shows. Heavily dialogue-weighted, as one would expect, and on the long side for such slim material, it is nevertheless a wholly delightful, very Gallic movie about four young people who dance a sedate little round dance, exchanging partners, suffering pangs of conscience and uncertainty about *l'amour*. Beautiful performances from all concerned help to make this fictional 'slice of life' seem four-dimensionally real.

Cast: Emmanuelle Chaulet, Sophie Renoir, Anne-Laure Meury, Eric Vieillard, François-Eric Gendron. Dir and Screenplay: Eric Rohmer. Pro: Margaret Menegoz. Ph: Bernard Lutic and Sabine Lanceline. Ed: Luisa Garcia. No art credits. M: Jean-Louis Valero. (AAA/Films du Losange-Artificial Eye). Rel: floating; first shown London (Chelsea Cinema and Camden Plaza) 24 June 1988. 102 mins. Cert PG.

My Sweet Little Village – Vesnicko má Středisková. Jiri Menzel, the Bill Forsyth of Czechoslovakia, shows us that the spirit of his people has not been broken under the weight of the Communist regime. The small village of Krekovice – picturesque on the outside, a hornet's nest within – is the setting for this simple story of a retarded truck driver's mate who is forced to move to Prague. Practically every character is portrayed as a scheming busybody, but there is plenty of warmth and a minimum of artifice.

Cast: János Bán, Marian Labuda, Rudolf Hrusinsky, Milena Dvorska, Ladislav Zupanic, Petr Cepek, Libuse Safrankova, Jan Hartl, Evzen Jegorov, Oldrich Vlach. Dir: Jiri Menzel. Pro: Jan Suster. Screenplay: Zdenek Sverak. Ph: Jaromir Sofr. Ed: Jiri Brozeck. Pro Des: Zbyner Hoch. M: Jiri Sust. (Barrandon Film Studio '85-Cannon). Rel: floating; first shown London (Cannon Premiere) 4 December 1987. 100 mins. Cert PG.

Nadine. Slim of story but commendably strong on laughs, this comedy-cum-romance-cum-murder thriller set in small-town Texas is concerned with the plans for a big road development which could earn a major fortune for anyone with advance knowledge. With a stolen copy of the plans in his files, the local 'art' photographer is planning to sell them to the local bigwig crook (Rip Torn, in a grand, meaty performance), but he is murdered when he asks too much. The sole witness of the murder is the local manicurist, Nadine, who discovers the plans in her folder of nude photographs and becomes the crook's next main target. Also involved is her divorcing but ever-loving husband. All very familiar but in this case quite funny stuff, lifted by an often witty script, well-paced direction and splendid performances by Kim Basinger as Nadine, Jeff Bridges as the husband and, in a small supporting role, Gwen Verdon.

Rest of cast: Glenne Headly, Jerry Stiller, Jay Patterson, William Youmans, Gary Grubbs, Mickey Jones, Blue Deckert, Harlan Jordan, Norman Bennett, James Harrell, John Galt, Joe Berryman, Linwood P. Walker III, Ray Walker, Shelby Brammer, Lloyd Catlett, Sidney Brammer. Dir and Screenplay: Robert Benton. Pro: Arlene Donovan. Ex Pro: Wolfgang Glattes. Ph: Nestor Almendros. Ed: Sam O'Steen. Pro Des: Paul Sylbert. M: Howard Shore. (Tri-

Star/ML Delphi Pro-Columbia). Rel: floating; first shown London (Cannons Oxford St and Panton St) 29 January 1988. 83 mins. Cert PG.

Near Dark. Superior vampire movie with some pretty horrific scenes, in which the bloodsuckers kill for sport as well as for their dinner. The story concerns a cowboy type picking up an attractive member of a coven of killers and, smitten and bitten, starts to get wise only when he finds they are drooling over the prospect of adding his family to their tally. So he decides to try to do the supposedly impossible and kill them off.

Cast: Adrian Pasdar, Jenny Wright, Lance Henriksen, Bill Paxton, Jenette Goldstein, Tim Thomerson, Joshua Miller, Marcie Leeds, Kenny Call, Ed Corbett, Troy Evans, Bill Cross, Roger Aaron-Brown, Thomas Wagner, Robert Winley, James LeGros, Jan King, Danny Kopel, Billy Beck, S.A. Griffin, Bob Terhune, W.T. Lane, Garry Littlejon, Paul Michael Lane, Eddie Mulder, Don Pugsley, Neith Hunter, Theresa Randle, Tony Pierce, Gordon Haight, Leo Geter, Gary Wayne Cunningham. Dir: Kathryn Bigelow. Pro: Steven-Charles Jaffe. Co-Pro: Eric Red. Assoc Pro: Diane Nabatoff and Mark Allan. Ex Pro: E.S. Feldman and C.R. Meeker. Screenplay: Eric Red and Kathryn Bigelow. Ph: Adam Greenberg. Ed: Howard Smith. Pro Des: Stephen Altman. Art: Dian Perryman. M: Tangerine Dream. (Scotti Bros/Intl. Video Entertainment-Entertainment). Rel: 8 January 1988. 94 mins. Cert 18.

The Night Is Young – Mauvais Sang. The second film from new, young French director-writer Léos Carax – and a very curious, seemingly wilfully complex and confusing crime thriller. It features a gang plotting to steal a newly developed medical culture to combat the spread of a rampant sex disease, a secret formula of which a rival gang, led by an American woman, would also like to get hold. The film has odd interpolations in the style of Chaplin (with his *Limelight* playing on the soundtrack), Godard and others; an unattractive young leading player; a lot of unusual photographic effects and sombre lighting; all adding up to a sorry mess.

Cast: Denis Lavant, Juliette Binoche, Michel Piccoli, Hans Meyer, Julie Delpy, Carroll Brooks, Hugo Pratt, Serge Reggiani, Mireille Perrier. Dir and Screenplay: Léos Carax. Ex Pro: Alain Dahan. Pro: Philippe Diaz. Ph: Jean-Yves Escoffier. Ed: Nelly

Fearsome Freddy (Robert Englund) bites off more than he can chew but victim Patricia Arquette looks pretty casual about the whole thing, in the Palace Pictures release A Nightmare on Elm Street 3 – Dream Warriors.

Quettier. Art: Michael Vandestien, Thomas Peckre and Jack Dubus. M: Prokofiev, Britten and Chaplin, with songs by Bowie, Aznavour and Serge Reggiani. (Les Films Plain Chant/Soprofilms/FR3 Films-Artificial Eye). Rel: floating; first shown London (Chelsea Cinema and Renoir) 18 September 1987. 119 mins. Cert 15 (Winner of the Louis Deluc Prize for 1986).

A Nightmare on Elm Street Part 3: Dream Warriors. Freddy, everyone's favourite nightmare, is back and bloodier, his sense of humour unimpaired. Wes Craven, director of the original, helped pen this most successful sequel (in America it has grossed more than double the first film) but can't salvage the wear and tear on the old story. However, he has added some unique visuals and at times *Dream Warriors* proves as ingenious and as imaginative (if not more so) than its predecessors. Heather Langenkamp returns as a psychiatrist specializing in 'dream disorders', assigned to a clinic of suicide cases (or are they?). Ten out of ten for originality.

Rest of cast: Patricia Arquette (sister of Rosanna), Priscilla Pointer, Larry Fishburne, Craig Wasson, Robert Englund (as Freddy), John Saxon, Dick Cavett, Zsa Zsa Gabor, Brooke Bundy, Rodney Eastman, Bradley Gregg, Ira Heiden, Ken Sagoes,

Penelope Sudrow, Jennifer Rubin, Clayton Landey, Nan Martin, Stacey Alden, Kristin Clayton, Sally Piper, Rozlyn Sorrell, James Carroll, Jack Shea, Michael Rougas, Paul Kent, Mary Brown, Melanie Doctors, Donna Durham. Dir: Chuck Russell. Pro: Robert Shaye. Co-Pro: Sara Risher. Ex Pro: Wes Craven and Stephen Diener. Screenplay: Wes Craven and Bruce Wagner. Ph: Roy Wagner. Ed: Terry Stokes. Art: Mick Strawn and C.J. Strawn. M: Angelo Badalamenti and Don Dokken. (New Line/Heron Communications/Smart Egg Pictures-Palace Pictures). Rel: 30 October 1987. 97 mins. Cert 18.

Night of the Creeps. Another routine horror movie with echoes from many of its predecessors, little originality and a sparse ration of giggles, about the 'things' let loose in a college fraternity which turn their victims into zombies.

Cast: James Lively, Steve Marshall, Jill Whitlow, Tom Atkins, Wally Taylor, Bruce Solomon, Vic Polizos, Allan J. Kayser, Ken Heron, Alice Cadogan, June Harris, David Paymer, David Oliver, Evelyn Smith, Ivan E. Roth, Daniel Frishman, Kevin Thompson, J.S. Griffo, Katherine Britton, Leslie Ryan, Dave Alan Johnson, Suzanne Snyder, Jay Wakeman, Elizabeth Cox, Emily Fiola, Russel Moss, Richard De Haven, John J. York, Tim Townsend, Tex Donaldson, J. Arlen Jones, Craig Schaefer, Richard Sassin, Robert Herman, Jack Lightsy, Elizabeth Alda, David B. Miller, Arick Stillwagon, Ted Rae, Howard Berger, Earl Ellis, Robert Kurtzman, Keith Werle, Beal Carrotes, Robert Kino, Todd Bryant, Dawn Schroder, Chris Dekker, Brian McGregor, Dick Miller. Dir and Screenplay: Fred Dekker.

What starts out as a night's babysitting for Elisabeth Shue (centre) ends in a wild adventure on the streets of Chicago in the Disney/Warner release A Night on the Town. *Also in the picture: Maia Brewton, Anthony Rapp and Keith Coogan.*

Pro: Charles Gordon. Ex Pro: William Finnegan. Ph: (in black-and-white and colour) Robert C. New. Ed: Michael K. Knue. Pro Des: George Costello. Art: Mario Caso. M: Barry De Vorzon. (Tri-Star/Columbia). Rel: 3 July 1987. 88 mins. Cert 18.

A Night on the Town. Originally entitled *Adventures in Babysitting*, this splendid adventure marks the directorial debut of Chris Columbus, scriptwriter of Spielberg's *Gremlins*, *The Goonies* and *Young Sherlock Holmes*. A beautiful 17-year-old student (Elisabeth Shue) is left to babysit for the evening and is catapulted into a wild and dangerous rollercoaster ride through the streets of Chicago. Inventive, briskly paced and great fun, the film is aided by excellent performances from the four young leads and no less by the supporting cast, particularly Calvin

Levels as a smiling, worldly-wise car thief.

Rest of cast: Keith Coogan, Anthony Rapp, Maia Brewton, Vincent Phillip D'Onofrio, Penelope Ann Miller, George Newbern, John Ford Noonan, Bradley Whitford, Ron Canada, John Chandler, Dan Ziskie, Allan Aarons, Marcia Bennett, Rummy Bishop, David Blacker, Lolita David, John Dee, Monica Devereux, Clarke Devereux, Rick Goldman, Deryck Hazel, John Hemphill, Frank Hill, Philip Honey, Clark Johnson, Maryann Kelman, Kirsten Kieferle, Peter Lavender, Kevin Lund, Southside Johnny, Allan Merovitz, Sam Moses, Les Nirenberg, Juan Ramirez, Richard Rebiere, Diane Robin, Sandi Ross, Charlene Shipp, Sandra Shuman, Linda Sorensen, Walt Woodson. Dir: Chris Columbus. Pro: Debra Hill and Lynda Obst. Screenplay: David Simkins. Ph: Ric Waite. Ed: Fredric Steinkamp and William Steinkamp. Pro Des: Todd Hallowell. M: Michael Kamen. (Touchstone-Warner). Rel: floating; first shown London (Warner) 19 February 1988. 102 mins. Cert PG.

90 Days. That's the period in which 'Blue' (Stefan Wodoslawsky) has to decide whether he will marry the oriental mail-order girl he has selected from a Korean catalogue. Blue is in direct

contrast to his pal Alex (Sam Grana), an irrepressible Don Juan thrown out, along with his golf clubs, by his exasperated wife. Made in that mixture of semi-documentary and fictional style that has come to be essentially Canadian, with the cast (a mixture of professional and amateur) surely ad-libbing some of their lines. The pace is reasonable, the humour quiet and sometimes very effective, and the end warm and charming, making the whole film, if variable in tone, extremely likeable.

Rest of cast: Christine Pak, Farnanda Tavares, Daisy de Bellefeuille, Katy de Volpi, Claudine Beaudine, Claudia Pak, Tedros Mikael, Jeanine Basile, J.R. Lee, Richard Todd, Goupi and Michael Brunet, Andy Thomson, Paul Cowan, Anthony Kent. Dir: Giles Walker. Pro and Screenplay: Walker and David Wilson. Ex Pro: Andy Thomson. Ph: Andrew Kizanuk. Ed: David Wilson. No art credit. M: Richard Gresko. (National Film Board of Canada-The Other Cinema). Rel: floating; first shown London (Minema) 19 February 1988. 99 mins. Cert 15.

No End – Bez Konca. Deadly solemn Polish film about a youngish woman (Grazyna Szapolowska) coming to terms with her husband's death. Political subterfuge, masturbation and a chance encounter with an Englishman (Daniel Webb) lighten the load, but it's an uphill haul. What can one say about a film that opens in a graveyard and ends with a suicide?

Rest of cast: Maria Pakulnis, Aleksander Bardini, Jerzy Radziwilowicz, Artur Barcis, Michal Bajor. Dir: Krzysztof Kieslowski. Pro: The Polish Corporation for Film Production Zespoly Filmowe. Screenplay: Krzysztof Kieslowski and Krzysztof Piesiewicz. Ph: Jacek Petrycki. Ed: Krystyna Rutkowski. Art: Allan Starski. M: Zbigniew Preisner. (Zespoly Filmowe-Artificial Eye). Rel: floating; first shown London (Renoir) 11 March 1988. 108 mins. Cert 18.

November Moon – Novembermond. West German-French co-production and a fairly minor one at that: the story of a Jewish refugee fleeing from Germany, with its growing Nazi menace, in 1933 and becoming involved in a lesbian love affair in Paris. Neither cast nor script has much to offer.

Cast: Gabriele Osburg, Christine Millet, Daniele Delorme, Bruno Pradal, Stephane Garcin, Louise Martini, Gerhard Olschews-

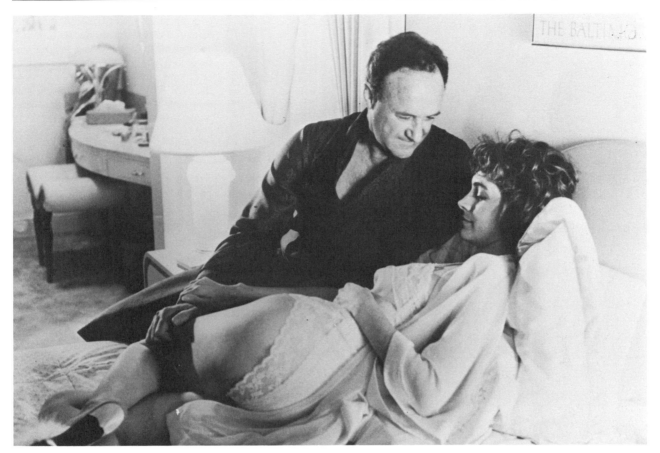

Above: Gene Hackman, as US Defense Secretary, with the mistress (Sean Young) he subsequently murders in the Rank release No Way Out. *Left: the sailor investigator of the crime (Kevin Costner).*

ki, etc. Dir and Screenplay: Alexandra von Grote. Ph: Bernard Zitzermann. Ed: Susann Lahaye. Art: Helger Gross and Jean-Pierre Balzerolla. M: Egisto Macchi. (Ottokar Runze Film, Berlin/Sun 7 Pro, Paris-ICA). Rel: floating; first shown London (ICA) 26 October 1987. 106 mins. No cert.

No Way Out. Although heavily disguised, *No Way Out* is a remake of the 1948 Charles Laughton *film noir* classic *The Big Clock*. A racy, sometimes rather confusing story of murder in high places; the culprit is the US Secretary of State, who is subsequently shielded from the consequences by his nasty homosexual assistant who, finding that the young naval officer assigned to the murder investigation was also the dead girl's lover, proceeds to pin the crime on him. It takes a while to set sail, but once under way the story grips right to the silly, confected ending which could and should be removed. Otherwise it is a well-crafted movie with some good performances including those of Kevin Costner as the chaser chased, Gene Hackman as the callous killer, Will Patton as his shield and Sean Young as the good-time girl.

Rest of cast: Howard Duff, George Dzundza, Jason Bernard, Iman, Fred Dalton Thompson, Leon Russom, Dennis Burkley, Marshall Bell, Chris D, Michael Shillo, Nicholas Worth, Leo Geter, Matthew Barry, John DiAquino, Peter Bell, Tony Webster, Matthew Evans, Gregory Le Noel, Gregory Avellone, Jeremy Glenn, David Paymer, Charles Walker, Bob Courts, Bruce Dobus, Eugene Robert Glazer, Darryl Henriques, John Hostetter, Michael Hungerford, Robert Kerman, Joan McMurtrey, Jay Arlen Jones, Rob Sullivan, Edith Fields, Frederick Allen, Scott Freeman, Noel Manchan, June Chandler, Lee Shael, Jeffrey Sudzin, Gordon Needham, Austin Kelly, Charles Middleton, Stephen R. Asinas, Terrance Cooper, Dorothy Parke, and Maori dancers Jill Clark, Cindy and Steve Keung, Lorna Martyn, Arona McDonald. Dir: Roger Donaldson. Pro: Laura Ziskin and Robert Garland. Assoc Pro: Glenn Neufeld. Ex Pro: Mace Neufeld. Screenplay: Robert Garland; from Kenneth Fearing's novel *The Big Clock*. Ph: John Alcott and Alun Bollinger. Ed: Neil Travis. Pro Des: Dennis Washington. M: Maurice Jarre. (Orion-Rank Film Dist.). Rel: 26 February 1988. 114 mins. Cert 15.

The Nutcracker – The Motion Picture. Beautifully staged and presented classical ballet which, unlike many productions, recalls the slightly sombre atmosphere of E.T.A. Hoffman's ori-

A new kind of role for Barbra Streisand in Warner's Nuts – *as a prostitute accused of manslaughter.*

ginal fairy story, *The Nutcracker and the Mouse King*. The film is based on the Pacific Northwest Ballet company's production of 1983 and it seems set to become a classic.

Cast: Hugh Bigney, Vanessa Sharp, Patricia Barker, Wade Walthall and the Pacific Northwest Ballet. Co-Dir: Carroll Ballard. Pro: Willard Carroll, Donald Kushner, Peter Locke and Thomas Wilhite. Ex Pro: Thomas Coleman and Michael Rosenblatt. Ph: Stephen M. Burum. Ed: John Nutt and Michael Silvers. Art: Peter Horne. M: Tchaikovsky. (Hyperion/Kushner-Locke-ICA/Entertainment Film Dist). Rel: floating; first shown London (ICA) 1 April 1988. 85 mins. Cert U.

Nuts. A prostitute (Barbra Streisand) is indicted for manslaughter, but is considered too mentally unstable to testify in court. A hearing is called and Richard Dreyfuss steps in to defend the prostitute's sanity. Based on the stage play by Tom Topor, *Nuts* is a dream vehicle for an actress, but unfortunately Streisand turns in a performance of such mega-

wattage that she obscures the reality of the character underneath. Dreyfuss, as always, is excellent in an entertaining production that looks as if it might well have escaped from the small screen.

Rest of cast: Maureen Stapleton, Eli Wallach, Robert Webber, James Whitmore, Karl Malden, Leslie Nielsen, William Prince, Dakin Matthews, Paul Benjamin, Warren Manzi, Elizabeth Hoffman, Castulo Guerra, Stacy Bergman, Hayley Taylor-Block, Matt Riivald, John Wesley, Sarina Grant, Tyra Ferrell, Nicole Burdette, Valentina Quinn, Carlos Cervantes, Ron Cummins, Gerry Okuneff, Conni Marie Brazelton, Roydon Clark, Dana Dru Evenson, Bruce Barbour, Suzanne Kent. Dir: Martin Ritt. Pro: Barbra Streisand. Ex Pro: Teri Schwartz and Cis Corman. Screenplay: Tom Topor, Darryl Ponicsan and Alvin Sargent, based on Topor's play of the same name. Ph: Andrzej Bartowiak. Ed: Sidney Levin. Pro Des: Joel Schiller. M: Barbra Streisand. (Warner). Rel: floating; first shown London (Warner) 12 February 1988. 116 mins. Cert 18.

On the Black Hill. Long, necessarily episodic, lovingly made life story of a pair of identical twins, the sons of a rough Welsh farmer from the Brecon Beacons and an English vicar's refined daughter, a marriage with class undercurrents. Marvellously and authentical-

ly atmospheric, with fine photography of the Welsh-English border country and powerful acting by a largely unfamiliar cast. There's a gritty feeling of real, hard rural life on the Beacons at the turn of the century and after. This is a largely sombre record, only very occasionally touched by humour.

Cast: Mike Gwilym, Robert Gwilym (the twins), Bob Peck, Gemma Jones, Jack Walters, Nesta Harris, Huw Toghill, Gareth Toghill, Lynn Gardner, Claire Evans, Eyrl Phillips, Rhys and Aled Baker, Lillian Evans, Ceri Morgan, Eric Wynn, Iona Banks, Terry Jackson, Nicola Beddoe, Ronan Vibert, Mark Jones, Lyndon Lewis, Sion Probert, Jill Richards, Geoffrey Hutchings, Robert Page, James Warrior, Rob Edmunds, William Vaughan, Ken Caswell, Kim Dunn, Huw Evans, Benjamin Whitrow, James Bree, Antonia Pemberton, Patrick Godfrey, Tricia George, Mark Dignam, Anthony Benson, Rodney Wood, David Garfield, Catherine Schell, Ben Marloe. Dir and Screenplay: Andrew Grieve; from the novel by Bruce Chatwin. Pro: Jennifer Howarth. Ph: Thaddeus O'Sullivan. Ed: Scott Thomas. Art: Jocelyn James. M: Robert Lockhart. (BFI Pro. for Channel 4 in assoc with British Screen Finance Ltd). Rel: countrywide from 13 May to 1 August 1988. 117 mins. Cert 15.

Opera do Malandro. An odd but surprisingly successful hybrid: a Ruy Guerra screen version of a Chico Buarque (both are Brazilian) stage musical which was based on the Brecht-Weill (German) musical play *The Threepenny Opera*, with the background switched to one of Rio's less salubrious quarters, *circa* 1941, with its assortment of lowlife characters – and nearly all Brecht's political angles removed. Made wholly in the studio, it is reminiscent of the American musical films of the 1940s, with some lively dance numbers and peppy music.

Cast: Edson Celulari, Claudia Ohana, Elba Ramalho, Ney Latorraca, Fabio Sabag, J.C. Violla, Wilson Grey, Maria Silvia, Claudia Gimenez, Andreia Dantas, Ilva Nino, Zenaide, Djenane Machado, Katia Bronstein, Luthero Luiz etc. Dir and Co-Pro (with Marin Karmitz): Ruy Guerra. Ex Pro: Alberto Graca. Screenplay: Chico Buarque, Orlando Senna and Guerra; based on the Buarque musical of the same title. Ph: Antonio Luis Mendes. Ed: Mair Tavares, Ide Lacreta and Kenout Peltier. M: Buarque. (MK2/France/Brazil and TF-1, Paris, with participation of the French Ministry of Culture-Artificial Eye). Rel: floating; first shown London (Lumiere) 31 July 1987. 105 mins. Cert 15.

The twin brothers (played by real-life twins Mike and Robert Gwilym) work their land on the Welsh-English border in the impressive BFI film On the Black Hill.

Orphans. High-powered adaptation of Lyle Kessler's play about two social misfits in New Jersey who kidnap a crime lord. Albert Finney is magnificent as the Chicago gangster, doling out measured bouts of kindness and wisdom, and is well supported by Matthew Modine and Kevin Anderson as his vulnerable captors.

Rest of cast: John Kellogg, Anthony Heald, Novella Nelson, Elizabeth Parrish, B. Constance Barry, Frank Ferrara, Clifford Fearl. Dir and Pro: Alan J. Pakula. Co-Pro: Susan Holt. Screenplay: Lyle Kessler, from his play. Ph: Donald McAlpine. Ed: Evan Lottman. Pro Des: George Jenkins. M: Michael Small. (Lorimar-Fox). Rel: floating; first shown London (Cannon Haymarket) 11 March 1988. 115 mins. Cert 15.

Albert Finney as the trussed-up gangster gives a friendly hug to one of his kidnappers (Kevin Anderson) in Lorimer/Fox's Orphans.

Shelley Long and Bette Midler persuade George Carlin to help them in their chase of their shared lover in Touchstone's Outrageous Fortune. Left: The birth of their unlikely friendship.

Outrageous Fortune. Good, old-fashioned Arthur Hiller comedy-thriller labelled by him as a 'female buddy action comedy', which just about sums it up. One of its greatest assets is the co-star casting of Shelley Long as the refined, prissy actress and Bette Midler as the loud-mouthed, street-wise go-getter. Their initial antipathy changes gradually to loving friendship as, following the discovery that they are sharing the same foreign-agent lover, they share some hair-raising adventures. The two stars' performances, some funny lines and some richly comic situations add up to 99 minutes of fast-moving, funny (and corny) movie.

Rest of cast: Peter Coyote, Robert Prosky, John Schuck, George Carlin, Anthony Heald, Ji-Tu Cumbuka, Florence Stanley, Jerry Zaks, John Di Santi, Diana Bellamy, Gary Morgan, Chris McDonald, J.W. Smith, Robert Pastorelli, Tony Epper, Bill Hart, Sally R. Brown, Carol Ann Susi, R.G. Clayton, Donald Ambabo, Paul Brooks, Barbara de Kins, Thomas Dillon, Sandra Eng, Robert Engstrom, Jose Garcia, Barney Garcia, James Espinoza, Mike Henry, Neil Hunt, Coral Kassel, Tom Lillard, James McIntire, Joan McMurtrey, Greg Mace, Bill Marcus, Phil Mead, J. Clell Miller, Lonna Montrose, Bob O'Connell, Steve Rotblatt, Johnny Sanchez, Pat Santino, Ade Small, Ebbe R. Smith, Bunny Summers, Anna Marie Wieder, Eyan Williams. Dir: Arthur Hiller. Pro: Ted Field and Robert Cort. Co-Pro: Peter V. Herald, Scott Kroopf and Martin Mickelson. Screenplay: Leslie Dixon. Ph: David M. Walsh. Ed: Tom Rolf. Pro Des: James D. Vance. M: Alan Silvestri. (Touchstone Pictures in assoc with Silver Screen Partners 11/Interscope Communications/UKFD). Rel: 11 September 1987. 99 mins. Cert 15.

Overboard. Predictable, sentimental, old-fashioned comedy about a rich bitch, Joanna Stayton (Goldie Hawn), who loses her memory and is taken in by low-life Dean Proffitt (Kurt Russell, Goldie's real-life beau). She hates him, he teaches her the ground rules for existence and so *The Taming of the Shrew* is re-enacted. You know what's going to happen, but because the stars are so engaging and the jokes above average, it's irresistible entertainment. Watch out for 7-year-old Joe Proffit (Jeffrey Wiseman), who thinks he's Pee Wee Herman.

Rest of cast: Edward Herrmann, Katherine Helmond, Roddy McDowall, Michael Hagerty, Jared Rushton, Brian Price, Jamie Wild, Frank Campanella, Harvey Alan Miller, Frank Buxton, Carol Williard, Doris Hess, Ed Cree, Mona Lyden, Lucinda Crosby, Bing Russell, Richard Stahl, Ray Combs, Marvin Braverman, Israel Juarbe, Lisa Hunter, Erin Grant, Paul Tinder, Scott Marshall, Don Thompson. Dir: Garry Marshall. Pro: Alexandra Rose and Anthea Sylbert. Ex Pro: Roddy McDowall. Screenplay: Leslie Dixon. Ph: John A. Alonzo. Ed: Dov Hoenig and Sonny Baskin. Art: James Shanahan and Jim Dultz. M: Alan Silvestri. (MGM-UIP). Rel: 10 June 1988. 112 mins. Cert PG.

Paltoquet. A Deville-ishly clever or pretentious (you decide which) French screen enigma: Michel Deville's highly original, stylish, near surrealistic whodunit in which the entire action – apart from the wilfully teasing final shot– takes place in a seedy, cavernous seaport bar ruled by owner Jeanne Moreau and her scruffy, mercurial and music-addicted waiter, the 'paltoquet' (good-for-nothing) of the title (Michel Piccoli). Who the killed, who the killer, why the killing? The answer put forward by director-scenarist Deville dips deep into the realms of dreams and reality and will leave at least some cinemagoers confused about where one starts and the other ends – and not sure if they care. Take along your thinking cap and a lot of patience for this one.

Rest of cast: Fanny Ardant, Daniel Auteuil, Richard Bohringer, Philippe Léotard, Claude Piéplu, Jean Yanne, Ann Luu, Sidy Dierra, Gérard Essomba, Gérard Dubois, Henri Bensoussan. Dir, adaptation and dialogue: Michel Deville; based on the Franz-Rudolf Falk novel *On a tué pendant l'escale*. Pro: Rosalinde Damamme. Ph: André Diot. Ed: Raymonde Guyot. Pro Des: Thierry Leproust. M: Dvořák and Janacek. (Elefilm/Erato Films with Soprofilms/TFI Films/Sofia/Sofima with participation of Centre National de la Cinematographie-Artificial Eye). Rel: floating; first shown London (Chelsea Cinema and Renoir) 3 July 1987. 92 mins. Cert 15.

Goldie Hawn learns something about life from her boyfriend Kurt Russell in MGM/UIP's Overboard.

Pee Wee's Big Adventure. With its main appeal to children, this red-favouring, TV-born, clownish character with the Norman Wisdom suit and cartoon voice appears in a nebulously plotted story about his search for his red bicycle, a thread that ties together some awful jokes, worse puns and a series of largely unrelated but sometimes amusing episodes, set in a world of childish wonder and naïvety.

Cast: Paul Reubens (Pee Wee Herman), Elizabeth Daily, Mark Holton, Diane Salin-

Pee Wee Herman and the red bicycle which plays a major role in the Mainline release Pee Wee's Big Adventure.

ger, Judd Omen, Jon Harris, Carmen Filpi, Tony Bill, James Brolin, Morgan Fairchild, Monte Landis, Damon Martin, Daryl Roach, Starletta DuPois, Ed Erlihy, Lou Cotell, Erica Yohn, Alice Nunn, Jan Hooks, Jason Hervey, Gilles Savard, Irving Hellman, David Glasser, Brown and Mark Everett, Bill Cable, Peter Looney, Prof. Toru Tanaka, Ralph Seymour, Raymond Martino, Bill Richmond, Ed Griffith, Simmy Bow, John Moody, John O'Neill, Alex Sharp, Chester Grimes, Luis Contreras, Lonnie Parkinson, Howard Hirdler, Cassandra Peterson, Bob McClurg, John Paragon, Susan Barnes, Zachary Hoffman, Lynne Stewart, George Sasiki, Richard Brose, Drew Seward, Brett Fellman, Bob Drew, John Gilgreen, Noreen Hennessy, Phil Hartman, Michael Varhol, David Rothenberg, Pat Cranshaw, Sunshine Barker. Dir: Tim Burton. Pro: Robert Shapiro and Richard Gilbert Abramson. Ex Pro: W.E. McEuen. Screenplay: Phil Hartman, Paul Reubens and Michael Varhol. Ph: Victor J.

TV's favourite Chinese detective David Yip plays a very different kind of role in Ping Pong, *an Anglo-Chinese comedy with a Soho background from Electric Pictures.*

Kemper. Ed: Billy Weber. Pro Des: David L. Snyder. M: Danny Elfman. (Aspen Film Soc/Robert Shapiro Pro-Mainline). Rel: floating; first shown London (Screen-on-the-Green and several Cannons) 14 August 1987. 92 mins. Cert U.

The Pied Piper (of Hamelin) – Krysar. This first feature film from a very gifted Czechoslovakian animation artist is a logically acceptable variation on the old German folk tale about the mysterious stranger who rids the town of Hamelin of its plague of rats by his music, only to be refused the promised reward by the townsfolk. He then inflicts a just revenge by ridding the town of them, too. A mixture of stylized carved wooden puppets and real rats, it is a remarkable and original achievement and a landmark in the area of animation.

Dir: Jiri Barta. Screenplay: Kamil Pixa. Ph: Vladimir Malik and Ivan Vit. Ed: Helena Lebduskova. Animation: Vlasta Pospilislova, Alfons Mensdorf-Pouilly, Jan Zach and Xenice Vanreckova. M: Michael Kobab. (Jiri Trnka Studio/TV 2000/Sudwestfunk Baden Baden-Contemporary). Rel: floating; first shown London (Everyman) 24 April 1988. 75 mins. Cert 15. (This feature is shown as a package with the same animator's equally remarkable short, a mixture of animation and live action, entitled *The Extinct World of Gloves*, written, designed and directed by Barta. 15 mins. Cert PG.

Ping Pong. Simple, pleasing and sometimes witty Anglo-Chinese film set in London's Chinatown, centred on Gerrard Street, Soho. The slim story is about a tyro girl lawyer who attempts to sort out the often odd bequests in the will of a Chinese restaurateur to his hardly close-knit family. It would have been even better with some shortening and tightening; nevertheless, a very refreshing Anglo-Chinese jump right out of the celluloid rut. Some excellent performances, notably from TV's detective hero David Yip and Lucy Sheen (though she could profitably do something about her voice) and some nicely judged moments of humour – the scene where some visiting Americans order a Chinese meal is a little gem.

Rest of cast: Robert Lee, Lam Fung, Victor Kan, Barbara Yu Ling, Ric Young, Victoria Wicks, Stephen Kuk, Rex Wei, Hi Ching, Won Hun Tse, Chad Lee, K.C. Leong, David Lyon, Karen Seacombe, Nigel Fan, Jonathan Elsom, Yee San Foo, Olivier Pierre, Eddie Yeoh, Lu San Wong, Susan Leong, Clive Panto, Jonathan Docker-Drysdale, Nicholas Pritchard, Errol Shaker, Juliet Hammond, Trevor Baxter, San Lee, Alan Wong, Philip Voon, Ryan Yap, Pat Starr, Kate Harper, Manning Redwood, Bruce Boa, Romolo Bruni, Kim Teoh, Linda Datsun, Stan Young, Vincent Wong, Diana Choy. Dir: Po Chih Leong. Pro: Malcolm Craddock and Michael Guest. Screenplay: Jerry Liu; based on an idea by Leong. Ph: Nick Knowland. Ed: David Spiers. Pro Des: Colin Pigott. M: Richard Harvey. (Picture Palace Films in assoc with Film Four International-Electric Pictures). Rel: floating; first shown London (Metro) 21 August 1987. 103 mins. Cert PG.

Pinocchio and the Emperor of the Night. By far the most expensive (it cost $8 million) animated feature in the 25-year history of Filmation, which, you may recall, made *Journey Back to Oz* with Liza Minnelli, Mickey Rooney and Milton Berle supplying the voices. It continues the story of the endearing little puppet which in the original *Pinocchio* – Disney's classic cartoon feature based on the Carlo Collodi story – became a real boy. In this follow-up the little lad succumbs to the temptations of the devil's carnival and almost loses his 'realness' for good.

With the voices of: Edward Asner, Lana Beeson, Tom Bosley, Linda Gary, Scott Grimes, Jonathan Harris, James Earl Jones, Rickie Lee Jones, Don Knotts, Frank Welker, William Windom. Dir: Hal Sutherland. Pro: Lou Scheimer. Screenplay: Robby London, Barry O'Brien and Dennis O'Flaherty; from an original story by O'Flaherty. M: Anthony Marinelli and Brian Banks. Songs: Will Jennings, Barry Mann and Steve Tyrell. (Filmation-Palace Pictures). Rel: 7 August 1987. 90 mins. Cert U.

P.I. Private Investigations. Bash-bang-wallop-chase thriller featuring crooked cops and a crusading editor, which sometimes looks much like a blown-up episode from a TV series. Amusingly incredible but with a – literally – cracking pace, a good quota of sometimes needless violence, plenty of excitement, paper-thin characters and a ruthless technical competence it is, admittedly, easily watchable.

Former puppet Pinocchio celebrates his first birthday as a real boy (with Alouette) in the first Filmation animated feature Pinocchio and the Emperor of the Night, *released by Palace Pictures.*

Cast: Clayton Rohner, Talia Balsam, Ray Sharkey, Vernon Wells, Martin Balsam, Anthony Zerbe, Anthony Geary, Paul LeMat, Robert Ito, Justin Lord, Phil Morris, Richard Cummings Jr, Desirée Boschetti, Andy Romano, Sydney Walsh, Jon St Elwood, Rex Ryon, Richard Kerkert, Frank

Ray Sharkey (right) as the crooked cop assassin in the Polygram/Blue Dolphin all-action movie P.I. Private Investigations. *Below: the innocent architect-prey (Clayton Rohner) with girlfriend Talia Balsam.*

John Candy (left) as the man most likely to stop Steve Martin keeping his promise to be home for Thanksgiving in Paramount-UIP's crazy comedy Planes, Trains and Automobiles.

Gangani, Big Yank, Nigel Dick, Robert Torti, Jean Claude, Dennis Phung, Sharon-lee MacLean, Michelle Seipp, Stan Yale, Hugh Slate, Del Zamora, Luis Manuel. Dir: Nigel Dick. Pro: Steve Golin and Sigurjon Sighvasson. Ex Pro: Michael Kuhn, David Hockman and Aart Dalhuisen. Screenplay: John Dahl and David Warfield. Ph: David Bridges. Ed: Scott Chestnut. Pro Des: Piers Plowden. Art: Nick Rafter. (Polygram Movies-Blue Dolphin). Rel: floating; first shown London (Odeon Kensington and several Cannons) 16 October 1987. 88 mins. Cert 18.

Planes, Trains and Automobiles. Everything that can go wrong does in this intermittently hilarious farce about an urbane advertising executive trying to get home for Thanksgiving. Steve Martin, arguably the funniest man in America, promises his wife (Laila Robbins) he'll be home for dinner by nine. The only problem is catching the six o'clock plane from New York to Chicago. However, Martin hadn't reckoned on

John Candy, a loud, obnoxious shower-curtain-ring salesman who dogs him across America as Thanksgiving becomes a more and more distant hope. Steven Martin plays his comedy straight, Candy plays his *fortissimo*, but you'll recognize a lot of truth in the duo's painful circumstances, based on director-writer John Hughes's own travelling experience.

Rest of cast: Michael McKean (as the State Trooper), Kevin Bacon, Dylan Baker, Carol Bruce, Olivia Burnette, Diana Douglas, William Windom, Martin Ferrero, Larry Hankin, Richard Herd, Susan Kellerman, Matthew Lawrence, Edie McClurg, George O. Petrie, Gary Riley, Charles Tyner. Dir, Pro and Screenplay: John Hughes. Ex Pro: Michael Chinich and Neil Machlis. Ph: Don Peterman. Ed: Paul Hirsch. Pro Des: John W. Corso. Art: Harold Michelson. M: Ira Newborn. (Paramount-UIP). Rel: 27 May 1988. 93 mins. Cert 15.

Playing Away. Periodically amusing British social comedy about the events leading up to a 'friendly' cricket match in Sneddington, Suffolk – conducted between the local hoorays and punks

against a visiting coachload of Brixton misfits. Horace Ové, who directed *Smile Orange* and should know better, throws in practically every black stereotype going, but does manage to touch a few raw nerves without applying a bludgeon. Also, a refreshing change of subject from other productions financed by Film Four and headed straight for television.

Cast: Norman Beaton, Robert Urquhart, Helen Lindsay, Nicholas Farrell, Brian Bovell, Gary Beadle, Suzette Llewellyn, Trevor Thomas, Stefan Kalipha, Bruce Purchase, Joseph Marcell, Sheila Ruskin, Mark Barratt, Valerie Buchanan, Jim Findley, Julian Granger, Ram John Holder, Patrick Holt, Elizabeth Anson, Juliet Waley, Ross Kemp, Gareth Kirkland, Archie Pool, Errol Shaker, Femi Taylor, Larry Dann, Neil Morrisey, Charles Pemberton, Roddy Maude-Roxby, Zulema Dene, Ian Cross, Jimmy Reddington, Lucita Lijerwood, Mary Tempest. Dir: Horace Ové. Pro: Brian Skilton and Vijay Amarnani. Assoc Pro: Christopher Sutton. Screenplay: Caryl Phillips. Ph: Nic Rowland. Ed: Graham Whitlock. Art: Pip Gardner. M: Simon Webb. (Insight Pro/Film Four-Electric Pictures). Rel: floating; first shown London (Cannon Tottenham Court Road and Brixton Ritzy) 6 November 1987. 97 mins. Cert 15.

Police Academy 4: Citizens on Patrol. Not exactly a critics' movie. But if you appreciated the tasteless fun of *PA*s 1 to 3 you may well enjoy the latest addition to the series, which digs even lower for its laughs as it ties a series of sight-and-sound gags together with an excuse for a story.

Cast: Steve Guttenberg, Bubba Smith, Michael Winslow, David Graf, Tim Kazurinsky, Sharon Stone, Leslie Easterbrook, Marion Ramsey, Lance Kinsey, G.W. Bailey, Bobcat Goldthwait, George Gaynes, Billie Bird, Derek McGrath, Scott Thomson, G.R. Robertson, Brian Tochi, Brian Backer, David Spade, Tab Thacker, Corinne Bohrer, Randall 'Tex' Cobb, Michael McManus, Colleen Camp, Andrew Paris, Arthur Batanides, Jackie Joseph, Arnie Hardt, Frank Canino, Bob Lem, Francois Klanfer. Dir: Jim Drake. Pro: Paul Maslansky. Assoc Pro: Donald West. Screenplay: Gene Quintano. Ph: Robert Saad. Ed: David Rawlins. Pro Des: Trevor Williams. Art: Rhiley Fuller. M: Robert Folk. (Warner). Rel: 2 October 1987. 87 mins. Cert PG.

Power. Slow-moving, complex and intelligent drama focusing on the US presidential elections. Richard Gere stars as a top media consultant who, for a considerable price, can transform an inarticulate greenhorn into a successful candidate for president. His success record may be extraordinary, but his scruples leave a lot to be desired. Only when Gere finds himself at the other end of a manipulating hand does he begin to question the morality of his own work. A challenging, mature piece of cinema.

Rest of cast: Julie Christie, Gene Hackman, Kate Capshaw, Denzel Washington, E.G. Marshall, Beatrice Straight, Fritz Weaver, Michael Learned, J.T. Walsh, E. Kathrine Kerr, Polly Rowles, Matt Salinger, Tom Mardirosian, Omar Torres, Ricardo Gallarzo, Jessica James, Glenn Kezer, Douglas Newell, Scott Harlan, Nick Flynn, Ed Van Nuys, Noel Harrison, Jackson Beck, Leila Danette, Kevin Hagen, Timothy Jecko, Margaret Barker, D.B. Sweeney, Linda DeNiro, Lynn Klugman, John Robert Evans, Elizabeth Kendrick, Robert Kruger. Dir: Sidney Lumet. Pro: Reene Schisgal and Mark Tarlov. Assoc Pro: Wolfgang Glattes and Kenneth Utt. Screenplay: David Himmelstein. Ph: Andrzej Bartkowiak. Ed: Andrew Mondshein. Pro Des: Peter Larkin. Art: William Barclay and Augustin Ytuarte. M: Cy Coleman. (Lorimar/Polar-Fox). Rel: floating; first shown London (Cannon Tottenham Court Road) 14 August 1987. 111 mins. Cert 15.

Richard Gere as the media consultant in Lorimar/Fox's political drama Power. *With him, his ex-wife, a journalist (Julie Christie).*

A Prayer for the Dying. An IRA gunman escapes to London and is forced by a local gangster to perform one last murder. An atmospheric, slow-moving drama notable for Mickey Rourke's convincing portrayal of a disillusioned Irishman and for Alan Bates's camp rendering of an East End hood. Surprisingly, the film was withdrawn from the 31st London Film Festival and, equally surprisingly, was disowned by its director for high-echelon meddling.

Mickey Rourke as the unhappy IRA killer in Guild's A Prayer for the Dying.

Strong-man expedition leader Arnold Schwarz-enegger, with fellow fighter Carl Weathers, stalked by a being from another world in the South American jungle in Fox's Predator.

Rest of cast: Bob Hoskins (miscast as a priest), Sammi Davis, Christopher Fulford, Liam Neeson, Alison Doody, Camille Coduri, Ian Bartholomew, Mark Lambert, Cliff Burnett, Anthony Head, David Lumsden, Lenny Termo and Ken Sharrock. Dir: Mike Hodges. Pro: Peter Snell. Screenplay: Edmund Ward and Martin Lynch; from the novel by Jack Higgins. Ph: Mike Garfath. Ed: Peter Boyle. Pro Des: Evan Hercules.

M: Bill Conti. (Sam Goldwyn Co.-Guild Film). Rel: 2 June 1988. 108 mins. Cert 15.

Predator. *Alien* meets *Commando* in this run-of-the-thrill sci-fi horror film, heavy on special effects and gore. Arnold Schwarzennegger heads a 'Magnificent Seven' commando unit sent into the jungles of Central America to retrieve MIAs, but encounters something completely different – a Thing from outer space out for the joy of the hunt. Of course, it hadn't reckoned on Arnold. Impressive stunts and an awe-

inspiring arsenal help alleviate the boredom created by too many close-ups, weak dialogue and a prodding, intrusive score.

Rest of cast: Carl Weathers, Elpidia Carrillo, Bill Duke, Jesse Ventura, Sonny Landham, Richard Chaves, R.G. Armstrong, Shane Black, and Kevin Peter Hall as It. Dir: John McTiernan. Pro: Lawrence Gordon, Joel Silver and John Davis. Assoc Pro: Beau E.L. Marks and John Vallone. Ex Pro: Laurence P. Pereira and Jim Thomas. Screenplay: Jim Thomas and John Thomas. Ph: Donald McAlpine. Ed: John F. Link and Mark Helfrich. Pro Des: John Vallone. M: Alan Silvestri. (Fox). Rel: 8 January 1988. 107 mins. Cert 18.

Prince of Darkness. Winner of the 1988 Critics' Prize at the International Festival of Fantasy at Avoriaz, John Carpenter's return journey to horror is a genuinely disturbing experience. A group of scientists and physics students are called on to analyse the source of a powerful energy field at an abandoned

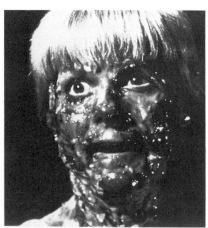

Donald Pleasence (far left) as the priest who has a devil of a time in the Guild release of John Carpenter's Prince of Darkness. *Left: Susan Blanchard as Satan's chosen host.*

The handsome Prince (Cary Elwes) defends his true love Buttercup (Robin Wright) in the fairy story told (right) by grandad Peter Falk to Fred Savage in Vestron's The Princess Bride.

church in downtown Los Angeles. To their (and our) growing alarm, the energy appears to defy all known natural phenomena. A clever script, pounding score and some hideous special effects help turn the screws of fear as a vision of pure evil is created. Both tasteless and blasphemous, the film's worst crime is its determined lack of humour.

Cast: Donald Pleasence, Victor Wong, Lisa Blount, Dennis Dun, Jameson Parker, Susan Blanchard, Anne Howard, Ann Yen, Ken Wright, Dirk Blocker, Jessie Lawrence Ferguson, Peter Jason, Robert Grasmere, Thom Bray, Joanna Merlin, Alice Cooper, Betty Ramey, Jessie Ferguson. Dir: John Carpenter. Pro: Larry Franco. Ex Pro: Shep Gordon and André Blay. Screenplay: Martin Quatermass. Ph: Gary B. Kibbe. Ed: Steve Mirkovich. Pro Des: Daniel Lomino. M: John Carpenter and Alan Howarth. (Alive-Guild). Rel: 13 May 1988. 101 mins. Cert 18.

The Princess Bride. At last – a real fairy tale for today's audience: a tale of true love, revenge, dastardly deeds, pirates, princesses and fire-breathing forests, set against a backdrop of sweeping scenery and magnificent castles. Although a thrilling, swashbuckling adventure in traditional vein, *The Princess Bride* doesn't take itself at all seriously and is consequently hilarious. A film for audiences of all ages.

Cast: Cary Elwes, Mandy Patinkin, Chris Sarandon, Christopher Guest, Wallace Shawn, Andre the Giant, Robin Wright, Peter Falk, Billy Crystal, Peter Cook, Mel Smith, Carol Kane, Willoughby Gray, Mal-

The Great American Dream is shattered again when the main characters, including Kiefer Sutherland and Meg Ryan, wake up to cold reality in Vestron's Promised Land.

colm Storry, Margery Mason, Betsy Brantley, Anne Dyson, Paul Badger. Dir: Rob Reiner. Pro: Andrew Scheinman and Rob Reiner. Ex Pro: Norman Lear. Screenplay: William Goldman; based upon his book. Ph: Adrian Biddle. Ed: Robert Leighton. Pro Des: Norman Garwood. M: Mark Knopfler. Costumes: Phyllis Dalton. (Vestron). Rel: 6 May 1988. 99 mins. Cert PG.

Prison. Well-made, straightforward thriller with enough horrors to keep the addicts happy. Welding the prison and supernatural genres into a tidy, spine-chilling whole, using some remarkable special effects and good camerawork, the Finnish director Renny Harlin makes a successful American debut. But he is, it should be stressed, catering for the hardened horror audience who can take it straight. The story? It's about the spirit of an executed innocent who returns to the jail to wreak bloody murder among the present inmates.

Cast: Viggo Mortensen, Chelsea Field, Lane Smith, Lincoln Kilpatrick, Tom Everett, Ivan Kane, André de Shields, Tom 'Tiny' Lister Jr, S.E. Kittle, Mickey Yablans, Larry Flash Jenkins, Arlen Dean Snyder, Hal Landon Jr, Matt Kanen, Rod Lockman, J.L. Deist, Kane Hodder, George D. Wallace, Luciana Capolozzi, Duke Spencer, Pat Noonan, Lyle D. Kelsey, Rob Brox, Larry Moore, John Hoke. Dir: Renny Harlin. Pro: Irwin Yablans. Ex Pro: Charles Band. Screenplay: C. Courtney Joyner; from a story by Irwin Yablans. Ph: Michael Ballhaus. Ed: Ray Lovejoy. Pro Des: Phillip Duffin. M: Richard Band and Christopher Stone. (Empire Pictures in assoc with Eden-Entertainment). Rel: floating; first shown London (Cannon Prince Charles). 17 June 1988. 103 mins. Cert 18.

Promised Land. Sincere retelling of the story of two boys from Idaho who grow up and apart as their idea of the American dream crumbles, ending in tragedy. Director Michael Hoffman (*Privileged, Restless Natives*) bases his first American screenplay on two boys he actually knew, boys who 'had been told that they could have it all . . .' Executive-produced by Robert Redford for the Sundance Institute, the film is

beautifully acted and photographed, but marred by fussy camerawork and dull pacing.

Cast: Kiefer Sutherland, Meg Ryan, Jason Gedrick, Tracy Pollan, Googy Gress, Deborah Richter, Oscar Rowland, Sondra Seacat, Jay Underwood, Herta Ware. Dir and Screenplay: Michael Hoffman. Pro: Rick Stevenson. Ex Pro: Robert Redford and Andrew Meyer. Ex in charge of Pro: M. Connold and Steven Reuther. Ph: Ueli Steiger and Alexander Gruszynski. Ed: David Spiers. Pro Des: Eugenio Zanetti. M: James Newton Howard. (Wildwood/Oxford Film Company-Vestron). Rel: floating; first shown London (Cannon Tottenham Court Road) 29 April 1988. 103 mins. Cert 15.

Raising Arizona. Basically this comedy is about an ex-con (Nicolas Cage) and a policewoman (the wonderful Holly Hunter) who kidnap a baby. But there's more, much more to it than that. From the brothers Joel and Ethan Coen (who brought us *Blood Simple*), this is a comedy of bad manners, a morality tale and every parent's nightmare; it's also one of the funniest and most original American films for years. Call it a cross between *Three Men and a*

Baby, *Easy Rider* and *True Stories*. Also, great photography and a great score.

Rest of cast: Trey Wilson, John Goodman, William Forsythe, Sam McMurray, Frances McDormand, Randall 'Tex' Cobb, T.J. Kuhn, Lynne Dumin Kitei, Peter Benedek, Charles 'Lew' Smith, Warren Keith, Henry Kendrick, Sidney Dawson, Richard Blake, Troy Nabors, Mary Seibel, John O'Donnal, Keith Jandacek, Warren Forsythe, Ruben Young, Dennis Sullivan, Dick Alexander, Rusty Lee, James Yeater, Bill Andres, Carver Barnes, Margaret H. McCormack, Bill Rocz, Mary F. Glenn, Jeremy Babendure, Bill Dobbins, Ralph Norton, Henry Tank, Frank Outlaw, Todd Michael Rogers, M. Emmet Walsh. Dir: Joel Coen. Pro: Ethan Coen. Co-Pro: Mark Silverman. Assoc Pro: Deborah Reinisch. Ex Pro: James Jacks. Screenplay: Ethan and Joel Coen. Ph: Barry Sonnenfeld. Ed: Michael R. Miller. Pro Des: Jane Musky. M: Carter Burwell. (Circle Films-Ted and Jim Pedas/Ben Barenholtz Pro-Fox). Rel: 10 July 1987. 94 mins. Cert 15.

Repentance – Monanieba. It took the new climate of *glasnost* to ensure a safe release of this mad Georgian mixture of drama and farce occasionally touched with surrealism (a court in which the judges wear traditional English wigs and the accused are in modern dress but are carted away in a tumbril-like wagon). Borrowing a bit from Hitchcock's *The Trouble with Harry*, it is about a dead dictator whose body is continually dug up by a woman bearing a grudge against him and exhibited in the town. Somewhere within all the words – and there are plenty – is a message that no individual, nor any regime, can permanently stamp out freedom.

Cast: Avtandil Makharadze, Iya Ninidze, Merab Ninisze, Zeynab Botsvadze, Ketevan Abuladze, Edisher Giorgobiani, Kakhi Kavsadze, Nato Otjigava, Dato Kemkhadze, etc. Dir: Tengiz Abuladze. Pro: Leomer Gugushvili. Screenplay: Abuladze, Rezo Kveselava and Nana Dzhanelidze. Ph: Mikhail Agranovitj. Ed: Guliko Omadze. Pro Des: Georgi Mikeladze. (Studio Gruzia, Tblisi/Sovexport-Cannon Rel). Rel: floating; first shown London (Cannon Premiere and Chelsea Cinema) 19 February 1988. 150 mins. Cert PG.

Retribution. Poor George, something nasty has taken over his soul and has transformed him into a cackling demon of death. Whenever this mild-mannered painter dozes off he sleep-

If you can't have, or can't adopt a baby, the last resort is to steal one – as do Ed (Holly Hunter) and 'Hi' (Nicolas Cage) in the Circle/Fox comedy Raising Arizona.

walks the streets of L.A. as a telekinetic nightmare, forcing unsuspecting citizens to do awful things to themselves. Despite yawning holes in the narrative, *Retribution* is a promising debut for TV director Guy Magar. Inventive casting, expedient editing and a chilling score all help to pile on suspense to almost unbearable level.

Cast: Dennis Lipscomb (as George), Leslie Wing, Suzanne Snyder, Jeff Pomerantz, George Murdock, Pamela Dunlap, Susan Peretz, Clare Peck, Chris Caputo, Hoyt Axton, Ralph Manza, Mario Roccuzzo, Harry Caesar, Jeffrey Josephson, Danny D. Daniels, Mike Muscat, Matthew Newmark, Brian Christian, Kenneth Gray, Guy Magar, Muriel Minot, Diane Robin. Dir, Pro and Ed: Guy Magar. Ex Pro: Scott Lavin and Brian Christian. Screenplay: Guy Magar and

Lee Wasserman. Ph: Gary Thieltges. Pro Des: Robb Wilson King. M: Alan Howarth. (Unicorn/Renegade-Medusa). Rel: 29 April 1988. 108 mins. Cert 18.

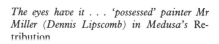

The eyes have it . . . 'possessed' painter Mr Miller (Dennis Lipscomb) in Medusa's Retribution.

Life in Bradford's lower-class suburbs, pictured in Mainline's Rita, Sue and Bob Too. *L. to r.: Patti Nicholls (Mum), Siobhan Finneran (Rita), Willie Ross (Dad), Michelle Holmes (Sue), Lesley Sharp (Michelle) and George Costigan (Bob).*

Rita, Sue and Bob Too. Crude British sex comedy, punctuated by four-letter words, and without a single likeable character. Two sexy schoolgirls are serviced in turn – and the continuing argument is about who gets the better deal by having him first – in the back of the car of a married man whose wife isn't at all keen on sex and for whom the girls babysit. Though overall the film paints a depressing picture of lower-working-class life in Bradford suburbia, it is often irrefutably funny on a very basic level.

Cast: Siobhan Finneran, Michelle Holmes, George Costigan, Lesley Sharp, Willie Ross, Patti Nicholls, Kulvinder Ghir, Danny O'Dea, David Britton, Mark Crompton, Stuart Goodwin, Max Jackman, Andrew Krauz, Simon Waring, Maureen Long, Joyce Pembroke, Jane Atkinson, Bryan Heeley, Paul Oldham, Joanna Steele, Jo-anne Barrow, Alison Goodman, Nancy Pute, Ken Hainsworth, Niall Costigan, Sinead Parkinson, Paul Hedges, Bernard Wrigley, Dennis Conlon, Charles Meek, Rachel Shepherd, Paula Jayne, Marie Jelliman, Laura Devon, Kailash Patel and Black Lace. Dir: Alan Clarke. Pro: Sandy Lieberson. Ex Pro: Oscar Lewenstein. Co-Pro: Patsy Pollock. Screenplay: Andrea Dunbar; based on her stage plays *The Arbour* and *Rita, Sue and Bob Too.* Ed: Stephen Singleton. Ph: Ivan Strasburg. Pro Des: Len Huntingford. M: Michael Kamen. (Film Four International/Umbrella Entertainment in assoc with British Screen-Mainline Pic-

tures). Rel: 11 September 1987. 93 mins. Cert 18.

River's Edge. A bleak, raw drama based on a true incident, indicting contemporary American youth. A group of teenagers in Northern California discovers that their friend John (Daniel Roebuck) has killed his girlfriend. None seems to be too moved by this, their emotions desensitized by the violence of cinema and TV. Ultimately, however, they are forced to confront the conflict of their loyalites. Moments of black humour alleviate the apathy and pessimism, and the young cast is mainly excellent, but otherwise it's a grim ride.

Crippled hermit and drugs supplier (Dennis Hopper, right) and client (Crispin Glover) – one of the 'outsiders' at the centre of the action in the Palace Pictures release River's Edge.

Rest of cast: Crispin Glover, Keanu Reeves, Ione Skye, Roxana Zal, Joshua Miller, Dennis Hopper, Josh Richman, Constance Forslund, Tammi Smith, Jim Metzler, Taylor Negron, Phil Brock, Leo Rossi, Tom Bower, Danyi Deats, Yuzo Nishihara, Chris Peters, Richard Richcreek, Maeve Odum, Frances de l'Etanche, Mike Hungerford, James Terry. Dir: Tim Hunter. Pro: Sarah Pillsbury and Midge Sanford. Co-Pro: David Streit. Ex Pro: John Daly and Derek Gibson. Screenplay: Neal Jimenz. Ph: Frederick Elmes. Ed: Howard Smith and Sonya Sonen. Pro Des: John Muto. M: Jurgen Knieper. (Hemdale-Palace). Rel: floating; first shown London (Curzon West End) 9 October 1987. 99 mins. Cert 18.

RoboCop. The posters screamed 'Part man. Part machine. All cop'. Audiences screamed, too, in equal bouts of laughter and fear as the Terminator of '87 strutted the streets of a decaying, futuristic Detroit, serving Truth, Justice and the Great American Way. But, in the tradition of every good twentieth-century fairy story, our indestructible humanoid remembers things past – indeed, he was once human, before being shot to shreds by a gang of frenzied psychos. Arguably the year's best sci-fi thriller, *RoboCop* is an ingenious, chilling piece of bravado film-making, as ruthlessly violent as it is tongue-in-cheek, backed up by excellent graphics and stunts. Surprisingly, for such a polished piece of cinema, the film was directed by Holland's Paul Verhoeven.

Cast: Peter Weller (RoboCop), Nancy Allen, Daniel O'Herlihy, Ronny Cox, Kurtwood Smith, Miguel Ferrer, Robert DoQui, Ray Wise, Felton Perry, Paul McCrane, Jesse Goins, Del Zamora, Calvin Jung, Rick Lieberman, Lee DeBroux, Mark Carlton,

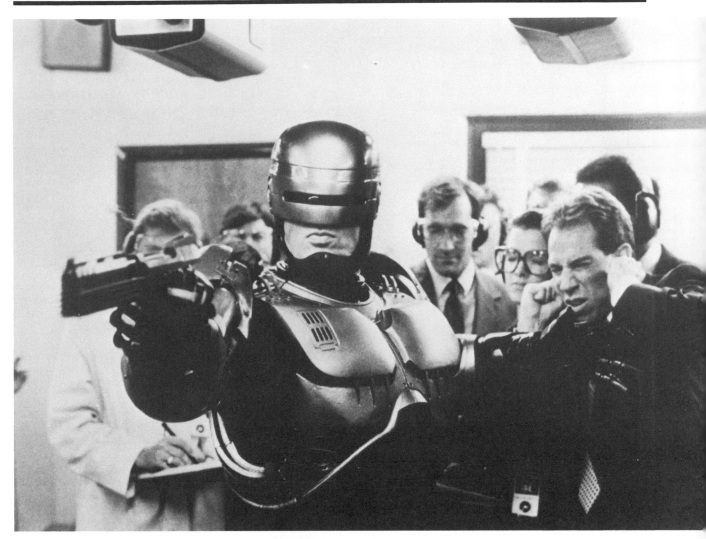

'Part man – part machine – all cop' – that's Peter Weller, shown demonstrating his prowess, in the Orion/Rank thriller RoboCop.

Edward Edwards, Michael Gregory, Fred Hice, Neil Summers, Gene Wolande, Gregory Poudevigne, Charles Carroll, Ken Page, Yolanda Williams, Tyress Allen, John Davies, Laird Stuart, Stephen Berrier, Sage Parker, Karen Radcliffe, Darryl Cox, Terry Haynes, Bill Shockley, Donna Livingstone, Joan Pirkle, Diane Robin, Adrianne Sachs, Maarten Goslins, Angie Bolling, Jason Levine, S.D. Nemeth, Bill Farmer, Michael Hunter, Spencer Prokop, Debra Zach, L.J. King, David Packer, Leeza Gibbons, Mario Machado. Dir: Paul Verhoeven. Pro: Arne Schmidt. Co-Pro: Edward Neumeier. Assoc Pro: Stephen Lim and Phil Tippett. Ex Pro: John Davison. Screenplay: Neumeier and Michael Miner. Ph: Jost Vacano. Ed: F.J. Urioste. Pro Des: William Sandell. Art: Gayle Simon. M: Basil Poledouris. (Orion-Rank). Rel: 12 February 1988. 103 mins. Cert 18.

Rouge Baiser. Paris, 1952. The story of a 15-year-old French girl (newcomer Charlotte Valandrey) torn between her love for Communism and a 'class enemy' photographer (Lambert Wilson). Sex, politics and history converge in this autobiographical drama, painstakingly made to recreate the Fascist Paris of the 'fifties. All the performances are admirable, but unfortunately the film is ultimately uninvolving and the pace sluggish. Perhaps director Véra Belmont was *too* close to her subject and needed an outsider to spirit her story along.

Rest of cast: Marthe Keller, Laurent Terzieff, Günter Lamprecht, Laurent Arnal, Audrey Lazzim, Elsa Lunghim, Yves Nadot, Riton Liebman, Isabelle Nanty, Corinne Juresco, Anne Dumas, Deborah Cohen, Jodi Pavlis, Georges Staquet, Lionel Rocheman. Dir, Pro and Screenplay (the last with Guy Konopnicki and David Milhaud): Véra Belmont. Ph: Raymond

Suarez. Sup Ed: Martine Giordano. M: Jean-Marie Senier. (Stephane Films/Films A2/Farena Films, Paris/C & H Films, West Berlin-The Other Cinema). Rel: floating; first shown London (Metro) 3 June 1988. 112 mins. Cert 15.

Roxanne. One of the year's funniest movies – a moving fantasy inspired by Rostand's *Cyrano de Bergerac*, adapted, updated and embodied by Steve Martin. A fire chief in a sleepy mountain town (Martin) falls in love with a beautiful astronomer (Daryl Hannah) who, in turn, falls for a younger, better-looking firefighter (Rick Rossovich). The fire chief, inhibited in his advances by his spectacularly long nose, ends up writing the florid love missives of his romantic rival. Steve Martin, probably the best actor in comedy films today, manages to be hilarious and pathetic at the same time, while creating a man of enormous charm, wit and intelligence

It's nose-go for fire chief Steve Martin when it comes to loving Roxanne *(Daryl Hannah) in Columbia's updated version of the Rostand classic* Cyrano de Bergerac.

(and believable, to boot). The film is also graced by a cracking good story, some top-notch photography (rare for a comedy), music and editing, and some excellent supporting performances (particularly Rossovich's), all guided with consummate skill by the Australian director Fred Schepisi. Wonderful, lunatic, first-class entertainment.

Rest of cast: Shelley Duvall, John Kapelos, Fred Willard, Max Alexander, Michael J. Pollard, Steve Mittleman, Damon Wayans, Matt Lattanzi, Shandra Beri, Blanche Rubin, Jane Campbell, Jean Sincere, Claire Caplan, Thom Curley, Ritch Shydner, Kevin Nealon, Brian George, Maureen Murphy, Jeffrey Joseph, Mike Glavas, Merrilyn Gann, Bernadette Sabath, Caroline Barclay, Heidi Sorenson. Dir: Fred Schepisi. Pro: Michael Rachmil and Daniel Melnick. Ex Pro and Screenplay: Steve Martin; from the play *Cyrano de Bergerac* by Edmond Rostand. Ph: Ian Baker. Ed: John Scott. Pro Des: Jack DeGovia. M: Bruce Smeaton. (Daniel Melnick Indieprod and L.A. Films-Columbia). Rel: 13 November 1987. 107 mins. Cert PG.

Salvation (US: *Salvation! Have You Said Your Prayers Today?*) 'The Dream', 'The Nightmare' and 'Salvation' are the three chapter headings of this bizarre look at commercial evangelism. Stephen McHattie stars as the TV preacher whose life is invaded by a gang of psychos who set about blackmailing him – for the unlikeliest of reasons. A high-octane, visually florid production, betraying the music-video roots of its director, Beth B.

Rest of cast: Dominique Davalos, Exene Cervenka, Viggo Mortensen, Rockets Redglare, Billy Bastiani. Dir: Beth B. Pro: Beth B. and Michael H. Shamberg. Ex Pro: Ned Richardson. Screenplay: Beth B. and Tom Robinson. Ph: Francis Kenny. Ed: Elizabeth Kling. Pro Des: Lester Cohen. M: New Order and Cabaret Voltaire. (Manipulator Co.-Recorded Releasing). Rel: floating; first shown London (Metro). 7 August 1987. 80 mins. Cert 18.

Sammy and Rosie Get Laid. From the team that made the highly successful *My Beautiful Laundrette* (writer, director, producer, editor and photographer are all the same), this film is something of a letdown. The story is more contrived and strained, the background sketchier and the characters with one exception are less convincing. That exception is Shashi Kapoor, who gives a brilliant performance as a former freedom-fighter, now under threat of death in Pakistan, who returns to the Britain he knew and lived in 30 years before and finds it seething with social unrest, with inner-city riots and clashes between police and populace. His efforts to pick up the threads of his British years end disastrously and he commits suicide. The film's underlying theme appears to be the impossibility of close human relationships or political balance, but all the edges are blurred and you could pick out other themes if you cared to see them. For all its shortcomings, full marks for attempting to be original.

Rest of cast: Claire Bloom, Ayub Khan Din, Frances Barber, Roland Gift, Wendy Gazelle, Suzette Llewellyn, Meera Syal, Badi Uzzaman, Tessa Wojtczak, Emer Gillespie, Lesley Manville, Mark Sproston, Cynthia Powell, Dennis Conlon, Megumi Shimanu-

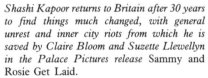

Shashi Kapoor returns to Britain after 30 years to find things much changed, with general unrest and inner city riots from which he is saved by Claire Bloom and Suzette Llewellyn in the Palace Pictures release Sammy and Rosie Get Laid.

ki, Buster Bloodvessle, Peter Kelly, Carol Frazer, Nicholas Pritchard, Valerie Buchanan, Allister Bain, Cleo Sylvestre, Freddie Brooks, Maurice D. Iley, Tariq Alibai, Patrick David, Paul Daley, Agnes Laye, Ade Supara, Gerard Horan, Anne Wood, Anne Hemery, Alan Adebisi, etc. Dir: Stephen Frears. Pro: Tim Bevan and Sarah Radclyffe. Screenplay: Hanif Kureishi. Ph: Oliver Stapleton. Ed: Mick Audsley. Pro Des: Hugo Luczyc Wyhowski. Art: David McHenry. M: Stanley Myers. (Nelson Entertainment with Working Title/Film Four International-Palace Pictures). Rel: 26 February 1988. 100 mins. Cert 18.

Sarraounia. Uppa Volta (now called Burkino Faso) – French co-production; an illuminating example of what Africa is promising for the cinematic future. It's about the warrior queen of the title who led the ultimately successful defence of her country when the French sent an invasion expedition in 1898. Firmly political – presenting the French invaders as a very nasty lot, which they almost certainly were; spectacular and visually gorgeous; overlong (it *has* been cut but not enough); very impressively directed; tartly satirical;

musically fascinating; and altogether a welcome glimpse of modern African cinema.

Cast includes: Ai Keita, Lynn Watts, Jean Roger Milo, Jean-Pierre Sentier, Feodor Atkin, Jean-Pierre Casteldi, Feodor Atkine, Aboubacar Traore, Tidjani Quedraogo. Dir, Pro and Screenplay (last with Abdul War; based on a story by Abdoulaye Mamani): Med Hondo. Ph: Guy Famechon. Ed: Marie-Thérèse Boiche. Pro Des: Jacques d'Ovidio. M: Pierre Akendengue. (Soleil Pro-ICA). Rel: floating; first shown London (ICA) 1 January 1979. 120 mins. Cert 15.

The Secret Policeman's Third Ball. Filmed highlights from the charity show in aid of Amnesty International – staged at the London Palladium in March 1987, with Joan Armatrading, Jackson Browne, Kate Bush, John Cleese, Robbie Coltrane, Duran Duran, Fry and Laurie, Peter Gabriel, Bob Geldof, Lenny Henry, Nik Kershaw, Lou Reed, Spitting Image etc.

Dir: Ken O'Neill. Pro: Neville Bolt and Tony Hollingsworth. (Elephant House Productions-Virgin Vision). Rel: floating; first shown London (Cannon Shaftesbury Ave) 25 September 1987. 93 mins. Cert 18.

Shattered Dreams – picking up the pieces. Obviously small-screen material, this openly polemical documentary about the Israeli-Arab conflict takes a new look at Israel which is very different from those sunny posters and inviting holiday commercials.

Dir, Pro (with Jenifer Millstone) and Screenplay: Victor Schonfeld. Various Ph credits. (Schonfeld Pro/Victor Pro in assoc with Channel 4 and assistance from Central Television). Rel: floating; first show London (Phoenix East Finchley) 27 November 1987. 173 mins. Cert 15.

Shy People. After nearly six years' holiday in the realms of reality Jill Clayburgh chose a somewhat odd vehicle for her return to the world of celluloid fantasy: the story of a New York journalist researching a magazine feature about her own family, living in the Louisiana bayou swamps, which provide a marvellously atmospheric background. Her investigations lead her to a crumbling wooden house where a domineering mother lives with her three dozy sons, all under the spell of the vanished, brutish 'Joe' (the journal-

Barbara Hershey and Jill Clayburgh share a stoop seat in Cannon's Shy People. *Inset, a closer view of the two stars.*

ist's own great-grandfather). Simmering passions lead up to a roaringly melodramatic climax in which the writer decides that her family's story is best left unwritten. It all adds up to a fascinating, flawed but compelling old-style movie.

Rest of cast: Barbara Hershey (superb), Martha Plimpton, Merritt Butrick, John Philbin, Don Swayze, Pruitt Taylor Vince, Mare Winningham, Michael Audley, Brad Leland, Tony Epper, Paul Landry, Warren Battiste, Edward Bunker, Vladimir Bibic, Dominic Barto, Dave Petitjean. Dir: Andrei Konchalovsky. Pro: Menahem Golan and Yoram Globus. Pro Ex: Rony Yacov. Screenplay: Gerard Brach, Marjorie David and Konchalovsky; from a story by Konchalovsky. Ph: Chris Menges. Ed: Alain Jakubowicz. Pro Des: Stephen Marsh. Art: Leslie McDonald. M: Tangerine Dream. (Cannon Films International-Cannon). Rel: floating; first shown London (Cannons Chelsea and Tottenham Court Road). 17 June 1988. 120 mins. Cert 15.

Siesta. A daredevil parachutist with amnesia struggles to unravel the mystery of why she's in Spain, on an airstrip and covered in blood. An unsettling, nonsensical film dotted with gratuitous cameos, *Siesta* is barely saved by a sensational performance from Ellen Barkin as the parachutist. Mary Lambert, fired from Prince's *Under the Cherry Moon*, makes her self-indulgent directorial debut.

Rest of cast: Gabriel Byrne, Julian Sands, Isabella Rossellini, Martin Sheen, Alexei Sayle, Grace Jones, Jodie Foster, Anastassia Stakis, Gary Cady, Graham Fletcher Cook, Santiago Alvarez, Daniel Martin, Fabian Conde, Pepe Canete, Susana Blazquez, Jose Teodoro, Paco Brana. Dir: Mary Lambert. Pro: Gary Kurfirst. Co-Pro: Chris Brown. Ex Pro: Nik Powell, Gary Kurfirst, Zalman King, Julio Caro and Anthony Rufus-Isaacs. Screenplay: Patricia Louisiana Knop, based on the novel by Patrice Chaplin. Ph: Bryan Loftus. Ed: Glen Morgan. Pro Des: John Beard. M: Miles Davis. (Lorimar/Siren-Palace). Rel: floating; first shown London (Chelsea Cinema) 27 May 1988. 100 mins. Cert 18.

Ellen Barkin gives a commendable performance as a daring parachutist in the Palace Pictures release Siesta.

Silent Voice (US *Amazing Grace and Chuck*). A delightful modern fairy story for adults about a minor-league boy baseball star who is so disturbed by a conducted tour of an atomic rocket launch site, featuring a commentary extolling its destruction potential, that he vows he'll never play again until all atomic threat is past. He is quickly joined in his protest by one of America's black major-league stars, and together these two see their rebellion spread, first throughout America and then to the USSR, until the American President and the Soviet leader are forced into an agreement to destroy their respective nuclear armaments. A pleasing, natural debut performance by leading baseball player Alex English, but a less appealing one by the boy. How good, too, to see Gregory Peck back on the big screen after six years away from it, showing (as the US President) what fine acting is all about.

Rest of cast: Dean Alexander, Jim Allen, Jim Antonio, Red Auerbach, Alan Autry, Michael Bond, Steven Bothun, Michael Bowen, Frances Conroy, James Cotterell, Jamie Lee Curtis, Clarence Felder, Lynne

(L. to r.) Michael Bowen, Alex English, Joshua Zuehlke and Alan Autry as the baseball players who start an ultimately successful anti-nuclear crusade in Tri-Star/Columbia's Silent Voice. *Gregory Peck (right) returned to the screen after years away from it to play the US President.*

Turner Fitzgerald, Brian R. Hager, Robert Harper, James Lindley Hathaway, A.J. Kallan, Matt Kerns, Cortney Kutner, Dennis Lipscomb, Harvey Martin, Johnny Most, Natalie Oliver, Kurt Olsson, Gwen Petersen, Maite Petersen, William L. Petersen, Lee Richardson, John Russell, Joe Sabatini, Robert Schenkkan, Vasek C. Simek, Harris Smithe, Rudolf Svehla, Manfred Sypold, Robert Tilson, James Tuomey, Cara Wilder, Joshua Zuehlke. Dir: Mike Newell. Pro and Screenplay. David Field. Ex Pro: Roger M. Rothstein. Ph: Robert Elswit. Ed: Peter Hollywood. Pro Des: Dena Roth. M: Elmer Bernstein. Art: John Myhre. (Tri-Star-ML/Delphi Premier Pro-Columbia). Rel: floating; first shown London (Cannon Panton St) 19 February 1988. 115 mins. Cert PG.

Sitting in Limbo. Out-of-the-ordinary Canadian production about some English-speaking blacks in French-speaking Montreal who are finding

their teenage existence in the city pretty hard-going, partly owing to their own failings. A semi-documentary with non-professional players, it presents a real-life peek into a little-known world.

Cast: Pat Dillon, Fabian Gibbs, Sylvie Clarke, Debbie Grant, Compton McLean, Millicent Dillon, Ronald Lang, Milton Poltash, Sally Bochner, André Bélanger, Bernard St Pierre, Peter Klym, Allan Walker, Lionel Gormandy, Cécile Zaleski, Robert Ludvick, James Durant, Gaston Bélanger, Charles Husbands, Robert Dyers, Anthony McRae, Lance Jerome Clarke, Nathan Grant. Dir: John N. Smith. Pro and Screen-

play: Smith and David Wilson. Ph: Barry Perles and Andreas Poulsson. Ed: Wilson. M Ed: Julian Olson. (National Film Board of Canada-Other Cinema). Rel: floating; first shown London (Metro) 11 December 1987. 96 mins. No cert.

Slam Dance. Made sketchily in the currently popular style, skating with cheerful aplomb over the general untidiness of the script and finally leaving a number of loose ends flapping miserably, this English-backed, American-set whodunit is for those who can enjoy a slick, fast-paced and eye-catching glossy surface and not be concerned about its ramshackle foundations. Tom (Mozart in *Amadeus*) Hulce plays an untidy, unshaven, and somewhat unsavoury 'underground' cartoonist who becomes the victim of a plot to pin on him the murder of a beautiful woman with whom he has had an instant liaison, forcing him into flight from just about everything and everyone including the – guilty – cops.

Rest of cast: Mary Elizabeth Mastrantonio, Adam Ant, Judith Barsi, Rosalind Chao, Sasha Delgado, Joshua Caceras, Don Opper, John Doe, Marty Levy, John C. Slade, Julian Deyer, Dennis Hayden, Harry Dean Stanton, Robert Beltran, Virginia Madsen, Herta Ware, Marc Anthony

The pretty pick-up (Virginia Madsen) who leads cartoonist Drood (Tom Hulce) into having to flee from a murder charge in the Palace Pictures release Slam Dance. *Right: Harry Dean Stanton as the cop with a guilty conscience.*

Thompson, Lin Shaye, Michael Ennis, Lisa Niemi, Jerris L. Poindexter, Christopher Keene, Millie Perkins, Laura Campbell, Philip Granger, John Fleck, Buckley Norris, Frazer Smith. Dir: Wayne Wang. Pro: Rupert Harvey and Barry Opper. Ex Pro: Cary Brokaw. Screenplay: Don Opper. Ph: Amir Mokri. Ed: Lee Percy and Sandy Nervig. Pro Des: Eugenie Zanetti. Art: Philip Dean Foreman. M: Mitchell Froom. (Sho Films Pro-Zenith Pro/Island Pictures-Palace Pictures). Rel: 13 November 1987. 100 mins. Cert 15.

Slate, Wyn and Me. Two young brothers kidnap an attractive schoolteacher after she has witnessed them rob a bank and kill a cop. On the run, Slate and Wyn Jackson force their unwilling captive into the heart of the Outback where she slowly, and deliberately, turns them against each other. Entertaining enough, the film moves along at a reasonable pace, making the most of the Australian scenery, and proves a strong showcase for its three leading players – if not much else.

Cast: Sigrid Thornton, Simon Burke, Martin Sacks, Tommy Lewis, Lesley Baker, Harold Baigent, Michelle Torres, Murray Fahey, Taya Straton, Julia MacDougall, Peter Cummins, Reg Gorman, Warren Owens, Eric McPhan, Simon Westaway, Kurt von Schneider. Dir and Screenplay: Don McLennan; from the novel *Slate and Me and Blanche McBride* by Georgia Savage. Pro: Tom Burstall. Line Pro: Brian D. Burgess. Ex Pro: Antony I. Ginnane and William Fayman. Ph: David Connell. Ed: Peter Friedrich. Pro Des: Patrick Reardon. (Hemdale/Palace). Rel: floating; first shown London (Cannon Oxford St) 3 July 1987. 90 mins. Cert 18.

Someone to Watch Over Me. Infinitely stylish, impeccably photographed romantic thriller with a good story, outstanding performances and a handful of moral dilemmas to chew over. Tom Berenger (*Platoon, The Big Chill*) stars as a happily married cop from Queens assigned to protect a rich Manhattan socialite (Mimi Rogers), a sole murder witness. The killer (Andreas Katsulas) turns himself in and then gets himself released on a technicality. He wants the socialite dead, Berenger wants her in bed, Manhattan's 21st Precinct wants Berenger off the streets. The plot thickens, congeals and then slides to a heart-pounding, if familiar climax. An interesting portrayal of New York class distinction and of police ethics, two issues that save this from looking like a virtual copy of *Fatal Attraction*, although this film was in fact scripted first, in 1982.

Rest of cast: Lorraine Bracco (excellent, as Berenger's wife), Jerry Orbach, John Rubinstein, Tony DiBenedetto, James Moriarty, Mark Moses, Daniel Hugh Kelly, Harley Cross, Joanne Baron, Anthony Bishop, David Berman, Sharon Brecke, Peter Carew, Christopher Cass, Jim Paul Eilers, Susi Gilder, Mary Gillis, Billy Kane, Helen Lambros, Jack McGee, Meg Mundy, Jeff Neilsen, Harlan Cary Poe, Marilyn Rockafellow, Helen Tran, Harvey Vernon, Mark Voland. Dir and Ex Pro: Ridley Scott. Pro: Thierry de Ganay and Harold Schneider. Assoc Pro: Mimi Polk. Screenplay: Howard Franklin. Ph: Steven Poster. Ed: Claire Simpson. Pro Des: Jim Bissell. M: Michael Kamen. (Columbia). Rel: 8 April 1988. 106 mins. Cert 15.

Martin Sacks (left) as Slate and Simon Burke as brother Wyn with their kidnapped schoolteacher Blanche (Sigrid Thornton) in the Palace Pictures release Slate, Wyn and Me.

Tom Berenger as the cop assigned to protect a murder witness (Mimi Rogers) under threat, in Columbia's Someone to Watch Over Me.

Wall Street square Jeff Daniels and wilful wildcat Melanie Griffith as the unlikely couple who manage to make their romance a success in the Rank release Something Wild.

Something Wild. Not so much a tale of boy meets girl, as of girl traps boy and boy changes his spots. Lulu (Melanie Griffith) is a wildcat; Charlie (Jeff Daniels) is a Wall Street square. But all Charlie needs is the right girl to turn him into the animal that is hiding under the collar and tie – except that Lulu's craziness is merely a façade, a ploy for running away from the quieter side of herself. Director Jonathan Demme, master of the American road movie (*Citizen's Band, Melvin and Howard*) returns to home asphalt and delivers an engaging, meandering story with as many twists and turns as a spaghetti junction. It's all very contrived, but the steady flow of eccentric detail keeps up the interest.

Rest of cast: Ray Liotta, Margaret Colin, Tracey Walter, George Schwartz, Leib Lensky, Maggie T., Patricia Falkenhain, Sandy McLeod, Robert Ridgely, Buzz Kilman, Kenneth Utt, Adelle Lutz, Charles Napier, Jim Roche, John Sayles, John Wa-ters, The Texas Kid, Byron D. Hutcherson, Eleana Hutcherson, Thomas Cavano, Dorothy Demme, Emma Byrne, Dana Preu, Mary Ardella Drew, Joseph Lee Davis, Edward Saxon, The Feelies, James Hurd, Joanna Kitchen-Hurd, Jack Gilpin, Su Tissue, Gary Goetzman, Chloe Amateau, Dung Chau, The Crew, Steve Scales, John Mont-gomery, Kristin Olsen, Heather Shaw, Vic Blair, D. Stanton-Miranda, Johnny Marrs, George Henry Wyche Jr, Marilee K. Smith, Jeffrey R. Rioux, Jeff Herig, Gil Lazier, Anna Levine, 'Sister Carol' East, Debbi Ellis, John Robotham, George Marshall Ruge, Billy Anagnos. Dir: Jonathan Demme. Pro: Jonathan Demme and Kenneth Utt. Exec Pro: Edward Saxon. Screenplay: E. Max Frye. Ph: Tak Fujimoto. Ed: Craig McKay. Pro Des: Norma Moriceau. Art: Steve Lineweaver. M: John Cale and Laurie Anderson. Opening song by David Byrne. (Religioso Primitiva-Orion/Rank). Rel: 17 July 1987. 113 mins. Cert 18.

Spaceballs. Mel Brooks's spoof of *Star Wars*, a visual film reference book packed with hilarious, average and terrible gags. A beautiful princess (Daphne Zuniga) is captured by the loathsome and short Dark Helmet (Rick Moranis) and it's up to space cowboy Lone Star (Bill Pullman) to save her. A big budget, fine special effects and spasms of invention keep the interest going, while Dom DeLuise steals the film as a human pizza – Pizza the Hutt.

Rest of cast: Mel Brooks, John Candy, Dick Van Patten, George Wyner, Michael Winslow, Joan Rivers, Lorene Yarnell, John Hurt (as John Hurt), Sal Viscuso, Ronny Graham, Jim J. Bullock, Leslie Bevis, Jim

Winona Ryder as the teenager about to leave her chicken-farming grandad (Jason Robards) and grow up fast in Enterprise's Square Dance.

Yogurt (Mel Brooks) explains the mysterious 'Schwartz' Force to Bill Pullman (left) in UIP's Brooks comedy Spaceballs.

Jackman, Michael Pniewski, Sandy Helberg, Stephen Tobolowsky, Jeff MacGregor, Henry Kaiser, Denise Gallup, Gail Barle, Dey Young, Rhonda Shear, Robert Prescott, Jack Riley, Tom Dreesen, Rudy DeLuca, Tony Griffin, Rick Ducommun, Ken Olfson, Bryan O'Bryne, Wayne Wilson, Ira Miller, Earl Finn, Mitchell Bock, Tommy Swerdlow, Tim Russ, Deanna Booher, Johnny Silver, Brenda Strong. Dir: Mel Brooks. Pro: Mel Brooks. Co-Pro: Ezra Swerdlow. Screenplay: Mel Brooks, Thomas Meehan and Ronny Graham. Ph: Nick McLean. Ed: Conrad Buff IV. Pro Des: Terence Marsh. M: John Morris; with songs from The Spinners, Kim Carnes, Jeffrey Osborne, Berlin, Van Halen, Bon Jovi, The Pointer Sisters, Ladyfire. (MGM/UA-UIP). Rel: 11 December 1987. 97 mins. Cert PG.

Square Dance. Texas, 1987. Thirteen-year-old Gemma (Winona Ryder) grows up fast when she deserts her cantankerous old grandfather (Jason Robards) and his chicken farm to live with her sexually promiscuous mother (Jane Alexander) in the Big City, where she meets – and falls in love with – a retarded 21-year-old (Rob Lowe). A small, sincere drama that serves as a superlative showcase for its four stars, but is undermined by some slapdash editing and an intrusive musical score.

Rest of cast: Deborah Richter, Guich Kooch, Elbert Lewis, Charlotte Stanton, J. David Moeller, Dixie Taylor, Irma P. Hall, Barbara Britt, Brad Leland, Dee Pyland, Gwen Little, Jim Bynum, Linda Nye, Newt Davis, Harlan Jordan, Dennis Letts, Annabelle Weenick, Liz Williams. Dir and Pro: Daniel Petrie. Ex Pro: Charles Haid and Jane Alexander. Screenplay: Alan Hines. Ph: Jacek Laskus. Ed: Bruce Green. Pro Des: Jan Scott. M: Bruce Broughton. (Island-Enterprise). Rel: floating; first shown London (Cannon Haymarket) 13 November 1987. 112 mins. Cert 15.

The Squeeze. Engaging, light-hearted comedy about a New York conman (Michael Keaton, amiable) involved in the alternate attainment and loss of a mysterious black box apparently worth $56 million. A briskly-paced, colourful caper with a wonderful turn from Meat Loaf as a perspiring villain. N.B. This film is not to be confused with either the Stacy Keach or Lee Van Cleef features of the same name.

Rest of cast: Rae Dawn Chong, Joe Pantoliano, John Davidson, Liane Langland, Ric Abernathy, Danny Aiello III, Bobby Bass, Leslie Bevis, Jophrey Brown, Lou Criscoulo, Ray Gabriel, George Gerdes, Ronald Guttman, Paul Herman, Richard E. Huhn, John Dennis Johnston, Jeffrey Josephson, Diana Lewis, Frank Lugo, Pat MacNamara, Andrew Magarian, Mick Muldoon, Jack Murray. Dir: Roger Young. Pro: Rupert Hitzig and Michael Tannen. Screenplay: Daniel Taplitz. Ph: Arthur Albert. Ed: Harry Keramidas. Pro Des: Simon Waters. M: Miles Goodman. (Tri-Star-Col-EMI-Warner). Rel: floating; first shown London (Cannons Panton St and Edgware Rd) 5 February 1988. 102 mins. Cert 15.

Stakeout. Richard Dreyfuss and Emilio Estevez star as a couple of unlikely, lovable cops staking out the house of a cop killer's girlfriend. The trouble is, Dreyfuss falls for the girl and becomes a target of the killer *and* the police, while Estevez looks on (through binoculars), wise-cracking. Dreyfuss gives a first-rate performance, as always, and newcomer Madeleine Stowe is gorgeous as everybody's trophy. John Badham directs with a flawless eye for the commerciality of his product and pips Spielberg to the post. He's given

Rae Dawn Chong and Michael Keaton (as a New York based con-man) in Columbia's caper comedy, The Squeeze. *Right: Meat Loaf as the villain,* Titus.

Cops Emilio Estevez and Richard Dreyfuss investigate the murder of one of their associates in Warner's Stakeout. *Inset: Madeleine Stowe is not aware that Dreyfuss is staking out her apartment when she begins to fall in love with him.*

Jim Kouf. Ph: Peter McLennan. Ed: Tom Rolf and Michael Ripps. Pro Des: Philip Harrison. M: Arthur B. Rubinstein. (Touchstone-Warner). Rel: 4 March 1988. 117 mins. Cert 15.

Below: the psychotic killer (Terry O'Quinn) in the credible, honest and carefully made Virgin thriller The Stepfather.

us an engaging love story, a funny comedy, a muscular thriller and a good story – all in one.

Rest of cast: Aidan Quinn (excellent, as the killer), Dan Lauria, Forest Whitaker, Ian Tracey, Earl Billings, Jackson Davies, J.J. Makaro, Scott Andersen, Tony Pantages, Beatrice Boepple, Kyle Woida, Jan Speck, Kim Kondrashoff, Gary Heatherington, Don Mackay, Don S. Davis, Roger Dean, David Brass, Elizabeth Bracco, Denny Williams, Norma Matheson, Blu Mankuma, Lossen Chambers, Lloyd Berry. Dir and Ex Pro: John Badham. Pro: Jim Kouf and Cathleen Summers. Sup Pro: Gregg Champion. Assoc Pro: Dana Satley. Screenplay:

The Stepfather. Most thrillers take liberties with credibility but this one doesn't: it drops the clues and leaves you to pick them up . . . or not. It's about a psychotic killer who has murdered his entire family and has started a new life for himself, his young wife and her teenage daughter. Will he get away with it? Gradually the net closes . . . Very refreshing and very creditable as well as credible.

Cast: Terry O'Quinn (the killer), Jill Schoelen, Shelley Hack, Stephen Shellen, Charles Lanyer, Stephen E. Miller, Robyn Stevan, Jeff Schultz, Lindsay Bourne, Anna Hagan, Gillian Barber, Blu Mankuma, Jackson Davies, Sandra Head, Gabrielle Rose,

Richard Sargent, Margot Pindivic, Rochelle Greenwood, Don S. Williams, Don Mac-Kay, Dale Wilson, Gary Hetherington, Andrew Snider, Marie Stillin, Paul Batten, Sheila Patterson. Dir: Joseph Ruben. Pro: Jay Benson. Pro Ex: Dennis A. Brown.

They're flying again tonight . . . Superman Christopher Reeve uses his unique gifts once more to save his fellow men and women in Cannon's Superman IV. *Left: two of those fellow men, Gene Hackman and Jon Cryer.*

Screenplay: Donald E. Westlake; from a story by him, Carolyn Lefcourt and Brian Garfield. Ph: J.W. Lindley. Ed: George Bowers. Pro Des: James Newport. Art: David Willson. M: Patrick Moraz. (ITC Pro-Virgin). Rel: 22 January 1988. 98 mins. Cert 18.

The Strike. Minor British, TV-destined film about a young Welshman who writes a film script about the miners' strike and is lucky enough to sell it to a film company, which immediately changes it into a first feature with big stars ('Robert De Niro' and 'Meryl Streep') and nothing left of the original story. When the embittered young wri-

ter returns to the valleys he gets it in the neck from his former friends who feel he has sold them out for cash. A typical Comic Strip caper.

Cast: Alexei Sayle, Keith Allen, Robbie Coltrane, Adrian Edmondson, Dawn French, Rik Mayall, Nigel Planer, Peter Richardson, Jennifer Saunders, Keith Allen, Ronald Allen, Kevin Allen, Katrina Mansoor, Derren Nesbitt, Steven O'Donnell, Daniel Peacock, Peter Richens. Dir and Screenplay: Peter Richardson. Pro: Chris Brown. Ph: John Metcalfe. Ed: Geoff Hogg. Pro Des: John Ebden. M: Richard Niles. (Comic Strip for Channel 4-Palace Pictures). Rel: floating; first shown London (with *The Yob* as a double bill) (Scala) 8 January 1988. 53 mins. No cert.

Strikebound. Richard (*Dogs in Space*) Lowenstein's first (1984) professional Australian feature film; a grittily realistic account of a coal strike which brought into being the first Communist trade union in Gippsland, Victoria in 1927. Filmed in the actual coalmine which was the centre of the strife, with no attempt to disguise Lowenstein's own political sympathies.

Cast: Chris Haywood, Carol Burns, Hugh Keays-Byrne, Rob Steele, David Kendall, Declan Affley, John Flaus, John Howard, Tony Hawkins, Marion Edward, Nik Forster. Dir and Screenplay: Richard Lowenstein; based on Wendy Lowenstein's book *Dead Men Don't Dig Coal*. Pro: Miranda Bain and Timothy White. Ph: Andrew de Groot. Ed: Jill Bilcock. Pro Des: Tracy Watt. M: Declan Affley. (TRM in assoc with Film Victoria-ICA). Rel: floating; first shown London (ICA) 4 June 1988. 100 mins. Cert PG.

Superman IV – The Quest for Peace. You'll believe a man has wires! Superman returns yet again, this time to save the world from nuclear threat and, in particular, Lex Luthor's latest creation, Nuclear Man. The special effects may be third-class, and some of the locations dubious (Milton Keynes doubling for

Metropolis, the London Underground a poor substitute for New York's Subway), but the spirit of the original is intact, and it's a good deal more endurable than *Superman III*. Forget the inconsistencies (Lois Lane has forgotten who Clark Kent is!) and enjoy yourself.

Cast: Christopher Reeve (as Superman/Clark Kent), Gene Hackman (Lex Luthor), Jackie Cooper, Marc McClure, Jon Cryer, Sam Wanamaker, Mark Pillow (as Nuclear Man), Mariel Hemingway, Margot Kidder (Lois Lane), Clive Mantle, Damian McLawhorn, William Hootkins, Jim Broadbent, Stanley Lebor, Don Fellows, Robert Beatty, Bradley Lavelle, Mac McDonald, Czeslaw Grocholski, Steve Plytas, John Hollis, William Armstrong, Elizabeth Richardson, Bob Sherman, Eiji Kusuhara, Yuri Borienko, Boris Isarov, Dorota Zienska, Jiri Stanislav, Jayne Brook, Kevin Elyot, Ron Travis, Matthew Freeman, Indira Joshi, Mark Caven, Esmond Knight, Eugene Lipinski, Barbara Rosenblat, Bernard Spear, Rex Robinson, Kerry Shale and the voice of Susannah York. Dir: Sidney J. Furie. Pro: Menahem Golan and Yoram Globus. Assoc Pro: Michael Kagan and Graham Easton. Screenplay: Lawrence Kohner and Mark Rosenthal; from a story by Christopher Reeve, Kohner and Rosenthal. Ph: Ernest Day. Pro Des: John Graysmark. Art Dir: Leslie Tomkins. M: John Williams. (Cannon-Warner). Rel: 24 July 1987. 90 mins. Cert PG.

Surrender. Agreeable, lightweight comedy starring Michael Caine as a successful novelist committed to enormous alimony and palimony payments. So disillusioned by the opposite sex that he erects a 'no women' sign outside his Beverly Hills estate, Caine accidentally bumps into Sally Field, a struggling artist. Against his better instincts he falls in love with her, apparently the first woman not interested in his wealth. Or is she? A witty script, likeable performances and a decent story make this one of the more engaging comedies set on the battlefield of the sexes.

Rest of cast: Steve Guttenberg, Peter Boyle, Jackie Cooper, Iman, Julie Kavner, Louise Lasser, Michael Andrews, Jerry Lazarus, Tony Borgia, Frank Dicopoulos, Charley Noland, Dominic Messina, Paddy Edwards, Bill McIntyre, Bruce French, Steven Rotblatt, Mark Pilon, Stan Roth, Lee Ryan, Ted Lehmann, Christian Clemenson, Channing Chase, Joan McMurtrey, F.J. Oneil, Donald Grant, Karen Huie, David Hess, Timothy Jecko, Ann Walker, Selwyn Emerson, Duke Mooskian, Robert Nadder, Bunny Kacher, Dan Navratil, Frank Lugo, Eduardo Ricard, Yacub Salih, Julie Silliman, Jim Van Wyck. Dir and Screenplay: Jerry Belson. Pro: Aaron Spelling and Allan Greisman. Ex Pro: Menahem Golan and Yoram Globus. Ph: Juan Ruiz Anchia. Ed:

Michael Caine and Sally Field are held at gunpoint by a thief in the Cannon comedy Surrender.

Cher, as the defence attorney with her deaf mute client (Liam Neeson) in the Tri-Star/Columbia release Suspect.

Wendy Greene Bricmont. Pro Des: Lilly Kilbert. M: Michel Colombier. (Cannon). Rel: 20 November 1987. 95 mins. Cert PG.

Suspect. A staff member of the Justice Department in Washington is murdered, a tramp is found at the scene of the crime with the victim's wallet; Cher, as public defender, is called in to rest the case. More intrigue in high places in this tense, gripping and intelligent thriller produced with first-rate professional know-how. Cher is surprisingly good as the attorney, Dennis Quaid as charistmatic as ever as her illegal aid and Liam Neeson strong and silent as the tramp.

Rest of cast: John Mahoney, Joe Mantegna, Philip Bosco, E. Katherine Kerr, Fred Melamed, Lisbeth Bartlett, Paul D'Amato, Bernie McInerney, Thomas Barbour, Katie O'Hare, Rosemary Knower, Aaron Schwartz, Lloyd White, Myra Taylor, Bill Cobbs, Sam Gray, Richard Gant, Billy Williams, Sandra Bowie, Darryl Palmer. Dir: Peter Yates. Pro: Daniel A. Sherkow. Ex Pro: John Veitch. Assoc Pro: Jennifer Ogden. Screenplay: Eric Roth. Ph: Billy Williams. Ed: Ray Lovejoy. Pro Des: Stuart

Wurtzel. M: Michael Kamen. (Tri-Star-Columbia). Rel: floating; first shown London (Cannon Group) 3 June 1988. 121 mins. Cert 15.

Swan Song – Jue Xiang. Another impressive example of the new and more liberated Chinese cinema, this time the initial production from a young director of 34. This is admittedly a pretty depressing story, of 30 years (covering the period of the Cultural Revolution) in the life of a Cantonese composer whose music is attacked and derided, whose wife leaves him and son cheats him. Even after his death the sad story continues, with his music being mutilated into a Western-style mess. The film is finely directed, professionally acted and technically first-class.

Cast: Kung Zianzhu, Chen Rui, Feng Diqing, Mo Shaoying etc. Dir and Screenplay: Zhang Zeming; based on the novel by Kung Jiesheng. Ph: Zheng Kangzhen and Zhao Xiaoshi. M: Zhao Xiaoyuan. (Pearl River Film Studios – Youth Section Pro-ICA). Rel: floating; first shown London (ICA) 20 May 1988. 100 mins. No cert.

Sweet Lorraine. Leisurely – perhaps 'slow-paced' would be a more apt description – but quite charming movie

about a long-established hotel retreat in the Catskill mountains which is slowly going downhill because it would be too costly to bring it up to scratch. This summer season is expected to be its last, until the son of the matron (Maureen Stapleton) turns up unexpectedly in search of a job. No excitement here, but a most pleasant 90 minutes of relaxing cinema.

Rest of cast: Trini Alvarado, Lee Richardson, John Bedford Lloyd, Freddie Roman, etc. Dir and Pro: Steve Gomer. Ex Pro: Angelika Saleh and Joseph Saleh. Line Pro: Iain Paterson. Screenplay: Michael Zettler and Shelly Altman; from their story written with George Malko. Ph: Rene Ohashi. Ed: Laurence Solomon. Pro Des: David Gropman. Art: Karen Schulz. M: Richard Robbins. (Autumn Pictures-NFT). Rel: floating. 91 mins. Cert PG.

Swimming to Cambodia. Without any attempt to hide the film's stage origins, set against a painted background and negligible props, Spalding Gray (who had a small role in *The Killing Fields*) relates with humour, irony and wit his experiences in Thailand during the making of that film there. It's very uncinematic but quite a watchable *tour de force*.

Dir: Jonathan Demme. Pro: R.A. Shafransky. Ex Pro: Lewis Allen and Peter Newman. Co-Ex Pro: Amir Malin and Ira Deutchman. Screenplay: Spalding Gray. Ph: John Bailey. Ed: Carol Littleton. Pro Des: Sandy McLeod. M: Laurie Anderson. (Demme-Mainline). Rel: floating; first shown London (Screen-on-the-Hill) 21 August 1987. 87 mins. Cert 18.

Take It Easy. Gold medallist Mitch Gaylord stars as the pouting hero in this inoffensive, corny story of the poor boy who dreams of becoming an international gymnast. Albert Magnoli, who steered Prince through *Purple Rain*, directs his second film as if it were a commercial.

Rest of cast: Janet Jones, Michelle Phillips, Tiny Wells, Michael Pataki, Patrice Donnelly, R.J. Williams, John Aprea, Katherine Gosney, Stacy Maloney, Peter Tramm, Maria Anz, Jenny Ester, Andrew M. White, Dick McGarvin, Mark Oates, Jan Claire, Megan Marsden, Li Yuejiu, Bruce Burns, Lisa Marie Campos, Bob Gauthier, Lisa Green, Tim Darling, Chris Riser, Lyn Schmitt, Kent Weaver, Steve Elliott, Matt Arnot, Scot Barclay, Mike Bowers, Philippe Chartand, Glen Cooper, John Eccelston, Mark Ewers, Brett Finch, Doug Foersch, Steve Friedman, Rick Hall, Paul Hartman, Celeste Kelty, Tom Kennedy, Jeff Knepper, John Levy, Wcs Lewis, Gerald Martin, Bert Mathieson, Brian Meeker, Wally Miller, Magic Moore, Peter Morgan, Jim Muenz, Jeff Nasby, Brad Peters, Becky Rashoff, Jody Raymond, Jeff Richards, Frank Rosch, Tony Russo, Mike Sims, Scott Wilbanks, Steve Yasukawa. Dir: Albert Magnoli. Pro: Robert Schaffel and Doug Chapin. Assoc Pro: Tony Wade. Ex Pro: Freddie Fields. Screenplay: Evan Archerd and Jeff Benjamin; from a story by Archerd, Benjamin and Susan Williams. Ph: Donald E. Thorin. Ed: James Oliver. Pro Des: Ward Preston. M: Alan Silvestri. (Lorimar-Fox). Rel: floating; first shown London (Odeon Kensington) 17 July 1987. 101 mins. Cert PG.

Tampopo – Dandelion. Following in the illustrious footsteps of French (*La Grande Bouffe*) and Danish (*Babette's Feast*) forerunners, Japan's director/writer/actor Juzo Itami devotes his entire two-hour film to the subject of food: the preparation and serving of the perfect bowl of noodle soup. But during that somewhat self-indulgent, lengthy lesson Itami makes dozens of hilarious side-steps, many witty, some satirical, one stomach-churning (preparing a live turtle for the soup), but all (with that exception) quite deliciously entertaining. The cast – headed by Itami's delightful wife Nobuko Miyamoto – contains many of Japan's most popular screen stars. Here is a natural comic talent who will bring a breath of fresh and funny air to the screen.

Rest of cast: Tsutomu, Yamazaki, Koji Yakusho, Shuji Otaki, Fukumi Kuroda, Mariko Okado, Yoriko Doguchi, Ken Watanabe, Izumi Hara, Toshimune Kati, etc. Dir and Screenplay: Juzo Itami. Pro: Yasushi Tamaoki and Seigo Hosogoe. Ph: Masaki Tamura. Ed: Akira Suzuki. Art: Takeo Kimura. M: Western classics arr. Kunihiko Murai. And not forgetting a Food Design credit to Ozumi Ishimori. (Itami-Contemporary Films/Electric Pictures). Rel: floating; first shown London (Screen-on-the-Hill and Metro) 6 May 1988. 117 mins. Cert 18.

Teen Wolf Too. Vacuous, computer-programmed sequel to the mild Michael J. Fox hit about a friendly, over-achieving werewolf. This time there's no Fox, but Jason Bateman (TV's *It's Your Move, Valerie's Family*) as the wolf whose lupine talents in the boxing ring make him too big for his paws. *Rocky* with fangs – but without the bite.

Rest of cast: Kim Darby, John Astin, Paul Sand, James Hampton, Mark Holton, Estee Chandler, Stuart Fratkin, Robert Neary, Beth Ann Miller, Rachel Sharp, David Burton, William H. Burton, Kathleen Freeman, Eric Matthew, Kevin Kaye. Dir: Christopher Leitch. Pro: Kent Bateman (father of Jason). Ex Pro: Thomas Coleman and Michael Rosenblatt. Screenplay: R. Timothy Kring; from a story by Joseph Loeb III and Matthew Weisman, based on characters by Joseph Loeb III and Matthew Weisman. Ph: Jules Brenner. Ed: Steven Polivka, Kim Secrist, Harvey Rosenstock and Raja Gosnell. Art: Peg McClellan. M: Mark Goldenberg. (Atlantic Entertainment). Rel: 12 February 1988. 94 mins. Cert PG.

Terminus. This somewhat unhappy example of French-German collaboration features a weird hybrid sporting event of the future, in which a computer-programmed truck driven by the heroine (Karen Allen, who doesn't help matters by expiring a mere third of the way through the movie) and her

Janet Jones and Olympic-medal-holding gymnast Mitch Gaylord making his screen debut in Lorimar-Fox's Take It Easy.

replacement (Johnny Hallyday) is obliged to struggle against both intended and accidental hazards towards the winner's rostrum. It's all a bit too involved for its own good, with some pretentious trimmings.

Rest of cast: Jürgen Prochnow, Gabriel Damon, Julie Glenn, Louise Vincent, Dieter Schidor, Janos Kulka, Dominique

Stuart Franklin looks on enviously as Teen Wolf Jason Bateman gets a sexy clinch from an admirer in Entertainment's Teen Wolf Too.

Ben Kingsley plays Russian composer Dmitri Shostakovich in Tony Palmer's highly individual Enterprise release Testimony.

Valera, Jean-Luc Montama, Ray Montama, Bruno Ciarrochi, David Jalil, André Nocquet. Dir: Pierre-William Glenn. Pro: Anne François. Ex Pro: Glenn and François. Screenplay: Glenn and Patrice Duvic; from a story by Alain Gillot. Ph: Jean-Claude Vicquery. Ed: Thierry Derocles. Art: Alain Challier. M: David Cunningham (songs by Stan Ridgway). (CAT Pro/Films du Cheval de Fer/Initial Groupe/CLB Films West Berlin/Films A2 Paris-Fox). Rel: floating; first shown London (Cannon Tottenham Court Road) 12 February 1988. 83 mins. Cert 15.

Testimony. Endless, self-indulgent, repetitive, infuriating, sporadically brilliant 'life and times' of Russian composer Dmitri Shostakovich. *Testimony* is, in fact, three films: a black-and-white biography; a concert of the works of the composer (in colour); and a montage of newsreel footage of Russia in the twentieth century. Ben Kingsley is brilliant, as always; the photography is stunning and the music alternately intrusive and inspiring. The English

locations are for the most part pretty well disguised.
Rest of cast: Sherry Baines (as Nina Shostakovich), Magdalen Asquith, Mark Asquith, Terence Rigby (as Stalin), Ronald Pickup, John Shrapnel, Robert Reynolds, Vernon Dobtcheff, Colin Hurst, Joyce Grundy, Mark Thrippleton, Liza Goddard, Peter Woodthorpe, Robert Stephens, William Squire (as Khatchaturyan), Murry Melvin, Robert Urquhart, Christopher Bramwell, Brook Williams (as H.G. Wells), Marita Phillips, Frank Carson, Chris Barrie, Mitzi Mueller, Tracey Spence, Dorota Rae, Bronco McLoughlin, Ed Bishop. Dir, Pro, Co-Screenplay, Pro Des, Ed: Tony Palmer. Ex Pro: Michael Kustow, Grahame Jennings and Michael Henry. Co-Screenplay: David Rudkin. Ph: Nic Knowland. Costumes: John Hibbs. M: Dmitri Shostakovich. Singers: John Shirley-Quirk and Felicity Palmer. (Isolde Films/Mandemar Group/Film Four-Enterprise). Rel: floating; first shown London (Curzon Shaftesbury Ave) 13 May 1988. 157 mins. Cert PG.

Three Men and a Baby. Amusing remake of the 1985 French hit *Three Men and a Cradle*, with Tom Selleck, Steve Guttenberg and Ted Danson as three swinging Manhattan bachelors caught

holding the baby. Fairly faithful to the original, the Americanization misses some of the charm and eccentricity, but is well compensated by Selleck's touching rendition of a hunk coming to terms with his vulnerability in the face of innocence. Leonard Nimoy directs with spirit and candy floss, having taken over from the French film-maker Coline Serreau four weeks before the start of filming.

Rest of cast: Nancy Travis, Margaret Colin, Philip Bosco, Lisa Blair and Michelle Blair, Celeste Holm, Paul Guilfoyle, Cynthia Harris, Derek de Lint. Dir: Leonard Nimoy. Pro: Ted Field and Robert W. Cort. Ex Pro: Jean-François Lepetit. Co-Pro: Edward Teets. Screenplay: James Orr and Jim Cruickshank; based on the French screenplay *Trois Hommes et un couffin*, by Coline Serreau. Ph: Adam Greenberg. Ed: Michael A. Stevenson. Pro Des: Peter Larkin. M: Marvin Hamlisch. (Buena Vista-Touchstone-Disney-Warner). Rel: 29 April 1988. 102 mins. Cert PG.

Throw Momma from the Train. Danny DeVito meets Alfred Hitchcock in this farcical homage to *Strangers on a Train*. Larry (Billy Crystal), a teacher

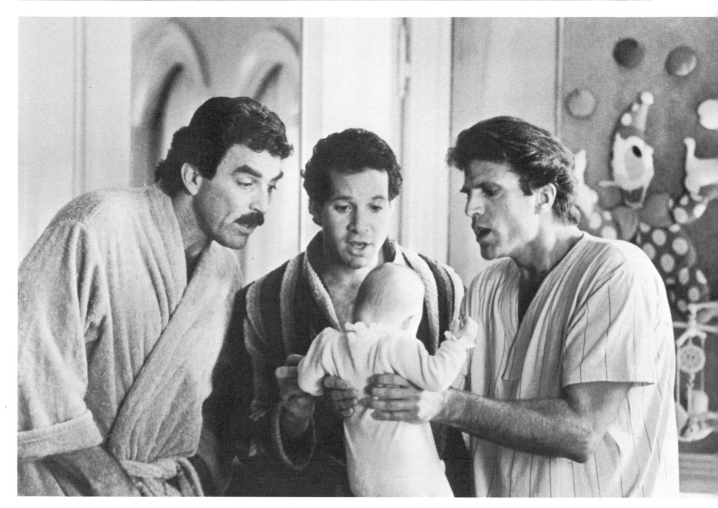

Tom Selleck, Steve Guttenberg and Ted Danson as a trio of unprepared dads in the Disney remake of the great French comedy success Three Men and a Baby.

of creative writing, has his novel stolen by his ex-wife; student Owen (DeVito) is persecuted by a gorgon – his mother. Owen kills Larry's ex-wife for a favour – except Larry knows nothing about the deal. Over-the-top, black, slapstick comedy express ride, over-directed by DeVito.

Rest of cast: Kim Greist, the late Anne Ramsey (as Momma), Kate Mulgrew, Branford Marsalis, Rob Reiner, Bruce Kirby, Joey DePinto, Annie Ross, Raye Birk, Oprah Winfrey, Olivia Brown, Philip Perlman, Stu Silver, J. Alan Thomas, Randall Miller, André 'Rosey' Brown, Tony Ciccone, William Ray Watson, Larry McCormick, Peter Brocco, Hettie Lynne Hurtes, Fred Scialla, Karen J. Westerfield, Myra Worrell, Stanley L. Gonsales, Fred Gephart. Dir: Danny DeVito. Pro: Larry Brezner. Ex Pro: Arne L. Schmidt. Co-Pro: Kristine Johnson. Screenplay: Stu Silver.

Ph: Barry Sonnenfeld. Ed: Michael Jablow. Pro Des: Ida Random. M: David Newman. (Orion-Rank). Rel: floating; first shown London (Odeon Leicester Square) 24 June 1988. 87 mins. Cert 15.

A Tiger's Tale. Texas, 1987. Boy meets girl, boy loses girl, boy gets girl's

mother. 'That way,' remarks 20-year-old C. Thomas Howell to 47-year-old

Ma (Anne Ramsey) rightly guesses that her son Owen (Danny DeVito) is trying to bring about her demise in DeVito's first stab at cinema direction, Orion-Rank's comedy Throw Momma from the Train.

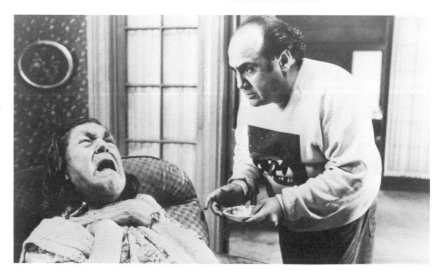

Ann-Margret, 'we're both at our sexual peaks.' In fact, nothing peaks in this turgid, old-fashioned comedy. The tiger – that Howell keeps at his father's gas station – has the best lines.

Rest of cast: Charles Durning, Kelly Preston, William Zabka, Ann Wedgeworth, James Noble, Tim Thomerson, Steven Kampmann, Traci Lin, Angel Tompkins, Linda Rae Favila, Steve Farrell, David Denney, Jo Perkins, Valentino as himself (the tiger). Dir, Pro, Screenplay: Peter Douglas; based on the book *Love and Other Natural Disasters* by Allen Hanney III. Ph: Tony Pierce-Roberts. Ed: David Campling. Pro Des: Shay Austin. M: Lee Holdridge. Costumes: Elizabeth Palmer. (Atlantic-Entertainment). Rel: floating; first shown London (Cannon Panton St) 27 May 1988. 97 mins. Cert 15.

Time to Die – Tiempo de Morir.
Columbian/Cuban film about a killer (in a duel) who comes home after eighteen years in jail to find everyone anxious that he should get out of town before the murdered man's sons take their revenge on him. He stays, but

Ann-Margret and C. Thomas Howell as the incompatible couple in Entertainment's A Tiger's Tale.

when he finally does decide to move on he is waylaid and forced into killing again. It's a sort of South American western in the classic manner and, despite some weaknesses, well worth watching.

Cast: Gustavo Angarita, Sebastian Ospina, Jorge Emilio Salazar, Maria Eugenia Davila, Lina Botero, Enrique Almirante, Carlos Barbosa, Monica Silva, Hector Rivas, Luis Chiape, Rodolfo Miravalles, Lucy Martinez, Edgardo Roman, Nelly Moreno, Patricia Bonilla, Alicia De Rojas, Berta Catano, Giovanni Vargas, Bizcocho, Cesar Ambalena. Dir: Jorge Ali Triana. Pro and Screenplay: Gabriel Garcia Marquez. Ex Pro: Gloria Zea. Ph: Mario Garcia Joyo. Ed: Nelson Rodiquez. Pro Des: Patricia Bonilla. M: Leo Brower and Nafer Duran. (Focine, Bogota/ICIAC, Havana-Artificial Eye). Rel: floating; first shown London (ICA) 19 February 1988. 94 mins. Cert 15.

The Time to Live and the Time to Die – Tong bien Wang shi.
(In the US the articles became indefinite.) From the director of that charming modern Chinese classic *Summer at Grandpa's* comes this equally, if not more, winning collection of boyhood memories, nostalgically recollected and told at a leisurely pace with such beautiful camerawork that at times one might be watching a series of classic paintings. The period is the closing stages of the Chinese Revolution and the establishment of Taiwan as a political and commercial entity divorced from the mainland. It was a turbulent period of history and no less turbulent a period in the boy's life as, dismissed from school, he becomes involved with delinquent gangs before reaching mental and physical maturity.

Cast (as children): Chang Ning, Luo Tse-chung, Luo Ch'eng-ye etc.; (as adults): T'ien Feng, Mei Fang, T'ang Ju-yun, Hsiao Ai etc. Dir: Hou Hsiao-hsien. Pro: Ling Teng-Fei. Screenplay: Chou Tien-wen and Hsiao-Hsien. Ed: Wang Chi-yang. Ph: Li Ping-Pin. M: Wu Ch'u-ch'u. (Central Motion Picture Co.-ICA). Rel: floating; first shown London (ICA) 8 April 1988. 137 mins. No cert.

Tin Men.
About that title: it refers to a special breed of door-to-door salesmen who made big business in Baltimore in the 1960s out of flogging, by fair means and (mostly it seems) foul, enamelled aluminium strips to householders to embellish the wooden or shingled houses common to the region. A feud develops between two rival super-

Left: the clash of cars which triggers the subsequent feud between Tin Men *Richard Dreyfuss (top) and Danny DeVito (bottom) in the Touchstone/Fox comedy of that title. Above: Dreyfuss and Barbara Hershey in a weird and wet marriage proposal scene.*

salesmen, starting with an accidental clash of cars and leading to deliberate sabotage and one salesman stealing the other's wife. Some amusing – and some pretty coarse – dialogue, plenty of comic action and a trio of sharply etched performances (by Richard Dreyfuss, Danny DeVito and Barbara Hershey) add up to a pretty consistently chuckly movie.

Rest of cast: John Mahoney, Jackie Gayle, Stanley Brock, Seymour Cassel, Bruno Kirby, J.T. Walsh, Richard Portnow, Matt Craven, Alan Blumenfeld, Brad Sullivan, Michael Tucker, Deidre O'Connell, Sheila McCauley, Michael S. Willis, Penny Nichols, Susan Duvall, David DeBoy, Florence Moody, Myron Citrenbaum, Ralph Tabakin, Norma Posner. Dir and Screenplay: Barry Levinson. Pro: Mark Johnson. Assoc Pro: Kim Kurumada. Ph: Peter Sova. Ed: Stu Linder. Pro Des: Peter Jamison. M: David Steele and Andy Cox. (Touchstone Pictures, in assoc with Silver Screen Partners 2-UK Film Dist.). Rel: floating; first shown London (Warner) 31 July 1987. 112 mins. Cert 15.

Tough Guys Don't Dance. American novelist Norman Mailer (*The Naked and the Dead*) directs the screen version

John Bedford Lloyd pulls a gun on Ryan O'Neal in Norman Mailer's directing debut, Tough Guys Don't Dance (a Cannon release), adapted by Mailer from his own novel.

of his own 1984 novel, an intriguing experiment that misfires hilariously. Ryan O'Neal, (mis)cast as a New Englander framed for murder, revered the script, saying, 'The lines are very natural, very easy to say.' For example, 'We could hear our thoughts so clearly, it was as if we were drawing from the same well' . . . and worse. If the truth be told, the dialogue is among the worst you'll ever hear, but there are corpses and crazy characters galore and picturesque coastal views.

Rest of the cast: Isabella Rossellini (briefly), Debra Sandlund, Wings Hauser, John Bedford Lloyd, Lawrence Tierney, Penn Jillette, Frances Fisher, R. Patrick Sullivan, John Snyder, Stephan Morrow, Clarence Williams III, Kathryn Sanders, Ira Lewis, Ed Setrakian, Faith Cahn, Edward Bonetti, Joel Meyerowitz, Greg Hodal, Katrina Mar-

Leo McKern in ecstatic musical mood in Recorded Releasing's Australian import, Travelling North.

shall and the voices of Sally Moffett and Carol Stevens. Dir and Screenplay: Norman Mailer; based on his own novel. Pro: Menahem Golan and Yoram Globus. Ex Pro: Francis Coppola and Tom Luddy. Ph: Michael Moyer. Add Ph: Danny Dukovny. Ed: Debra McDermott. Pro Des: Armin Ganz. M: Angelo Badalamenti. (Cannon). Rel: 15 January 1988. 108 mins. Cert 18.

Travelling North. The retirement and romance of a gruff, arrogant 70-year-old civil engineer in Australia may not sound like the stuff of great drama, but this film is not to be missed. Australian actor Leo McKern, in his native debut, won his country's top award for best actor in a role that seems tailor-made. He plays Frank, former Communist candidate for Tourac, ex-bullying husband and soft-hearted father, who spirits the serene, beautiful Frances (Julia Blake) off to a tropical paradise in northern Queensland. There, the neighbours ogle Frances, and he ignores her, while his heart complaints take up all his interest. Brusquely unsentimental, David Williamson's literate script sparkles with wit, observation and compassion, is frequently hilarious and often painful. The entire cast is

superb, particularly Henri Szeps as Frank's brow-beaten, finally submissive, ulcer-ridden doctor. The soundtrack of classical music, lush lighting and unobtrusive camerawork complete the perfection of this moving, memorable masterwork.

Rest of cast: Graham Kennedy, Michele Fawdon, Diane Craig, Andrea Moor, Drew Forsythe, John Gregg. Dir: Carl Schultz. Pro: Ben Gannon. Screenplay: David Williamson. Ph: Julian Penney. Ed: Henry Dangar. Pro Des: Owen Paterson. M: Alan John. (View Films/Cel Film Dist.-Recorded Releasing). Rel: floating; first shown London (several Cannons) 13 May 1988. 95 mins. Cert 15.

Twenty Days Without War – Dvadtsat dnei bez voini. Twelve years after it was started (two years in the making followed by ten shelf years owing to Soviet disapproval of its content) this splendid film gets a general, approved release. A war correspondent spends twenty days' leave from the Stalingrad front in Tashkent, his home town. There he finds a film company making a movie based on his own stories of the war and, though he is asked to help

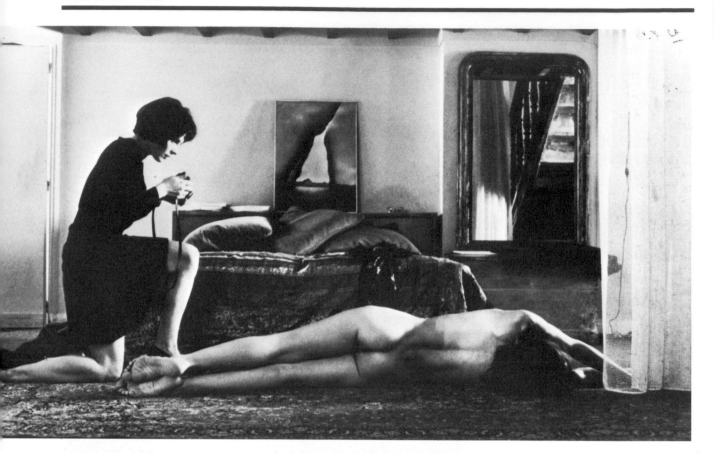

The remarkable and erotic scene where Tereza (Juliette Binoche) and Sabina (Lena Olin) hold a nude photographic session in UIP's The Unbearable Lightness of Being. *Left: Tereza with husband (Daniel Day-Lewis) and Karenin, their beloved pet dog.*

The Unbearable Lightness of Being. One of the most unusual movies, in terms of mind-teasing depth and tasteful eroticism, to come out of America (though with such European ingredients as a French co-scriptwriter, English, Swedish and French players, a Swedish cameraman and French and Swiss backgrounds) in several blue moons. *The Unbearable Lightness of Being* is based on the acclaimed novel by the Czech writer Milan Kundera. It tackles the problems posed by the difference between sexual appetite and love, against the background of the Soviet invasion of Czechoslovakia in 1968 and its chilling aftermath. A quite remarkable achievement in terms of maintaining the atmosphere and integrity of its source, it is also a very brave film in its makers' refusal to compromise – even in terms of the

with accuracy, his suggestions are ignored. The film also touches on reactions to the infidelity of soldiers' wives; the contrast between patriotic illusion and brutal reality; and the futility of war.

Cast: Yuri Nikulin, Liudmila Gurchenko, R. Sadykov, A. Petrenko, A. Stepanova, M. Kononov, E. Vasilyeva, N. Grinko, P. Ovchinnikova, D. Bessonov, D. Zarubin, Z. Vinogradova, G. Diudyaev, L. Zaitseva, D. Zarubin, I. Makeyev, V. Mishanin, N. Mikheyev, V. Pechnikov, M. Ryabtseva, Yu Solovyev, V. Suborov. Dir: Alexei Gherman. Ex Pro: F. Eskin. Screenplay: Konstantin Simonov. Ph: Valery Fedosov. Ed: E. Makhankovoi. Pro Des: Yevgeny Gukov. M: V. Lavrov. (Lenfilm-The Other Cinema). Rel: floating; first shown London (Metro) 25 September 1987. 100 mins. No cert.

difficult and (to some) off-putting title – for the promise of box-office returns. In three never-palling hours the three main characters play out – with touches of humour – a drama of existence and growth to maturity.

Cast: Daniel Day-Lewis, Juliette Binoche, Lena Olin, Derek de Lint, Erland Josephson, Pavel Landovsky, Donald Moffat, Daniel Olbrychski, Stellan Skarsgard, Tomek Bork, Bruce Myers, Pavel Slaby, Pascale Kalensky, Jacques Ciron, Anne Lonnberg, Laszlo Szabo, Vladimir Valenta, Clovis Cornillac, Leon Lissek, Consuelo de Haviland. Dir: Philip Kaufman. Pro: Saul Zaentz. Ex Pro: Bertil Ohlsson. Assoc Pro: Paul Zaentz. Screenplay: Philip Kaufman and Jean-Claude Carriere; based on the novel by Milan Kundera. Ph: Sven Nykvist. Sup. Ed: Walter Murch. Pro Des: Pierre Guffroy. M: Mark Adler and Ernie Fosselius. (Saul Zaentz Co-UIP). Rel: 6 May 1988. 172 mins. Cert 18.

Uncommon Senses (US: *Plain Talk and Common Sense*). Another of the prolific John Jost's one-man-band, personal movies. Here he looks at America from a somewhat odd angle. Its importers, ICA, say it's 'Uncompromising and fascinating. Maybe it's a masterpiece.' Maybe . . .

Dir, Pro, Screenplay, Ed and Ph: John Jost. (Jost-ICA). Rel: floating; first shown London (ICA) 28 March 1988. 117 mins. No cert.

Under Satan's Sun – Sous le soleil de Satan. Heavy-handed drama with Gérard Depardieu as an earnest country priest haunted by the growing presence of Satan. Well-written, acted and photographed, the film won the Palme d'Or at the 1987 Cannes Film Festival – which stunned everybody.

Rest of cast: Sandrine Bonnaire, Maurice Pialat, Alain Artur, Yann Dedet, Brigitte Legendre, Jean-Claude Bourlat, Jean-Christophe Bouvet, Philippe Pallut, Marcel Anselin. Dir: Maurice Pialat. Ex Pro: Daniel Toscan du Plantier. Screenplay: Sylvie Danton; based on the novel by Georges Bernanos; adaptation/dialogue: Sylvie Danton and Maurice Pialat. Ph: Willy Kurant. Ed: Yann Dedet. Art: Katia Vischkof. M: Henri Dutilleux. (Erato Films/Films A2/Action Films-Cannon). Rel: floating; first shown London (Cannon Premiere) 6 May 1988. 98 mins. Cert 15.

The Untouchables. In spite of some convoluted reviews by a few critics anxious to prove the movie's hidden depths and their own psychological insight and literary brilliance, this is just a straightforward, technically first-class and otherwise pretty outstanding commercial gangster thriller set in mob-ruled, Prohibition-era Chicago, which

The Untouchables, *an odd quartet of law enforcers (Andy Garcia, Sean Connery, Kevin Costner and Charles Martin Smith), prepare to do battle with Al Capone's mob in the Paramount/UIP release.*

relates the downfall of bootlegger king Al Capone. It has plenty of the bloody violence inseparable from the period and genre, with an outstanding performance by Sean Connery as the honest cop, a good one (in fact his best for several movies) by a carefully bloated De Niro as Capone and an impressive one by comparative newcomer Kevin Costner as the US Treasury Department's special, gun-toting investigator. Fine support, tight writing and direction (too tight for complete clarity in one out-of-city raid sequence) by Brian de Palma, who proves his mastery of the medium with several superb scenes including one classically Hitchcockian

A big business baddie-teacher Michael Douglas (who won an Oscar for this performance) and well-taught pupil Charlie Sheen (right) in confrontation in Fox's Wall Street.

sequence concerning a baby in a pram caught in a shoot-out. In short, a superb example of professional cinema.

Rest of cast: Charles Martin Smith, Andy Garcia, Richard Bradford, Jack Kehoe, Brad Sullivan, Billy Drago, Patricia Clarkson, Vito D'Ambrosio, Steven Goldstein, Peter Aylward, Don Harvey, Robert Swan, John J. Walsh, Del Close, Colleen Bade, Greg Noonan, Sean Grennan, Larry Viveirto Sr, Kevin Michael Doyle, Mike Bacarella, Michael P. Byrne, Kaitlin Montgomery, Aditra Kohl, Charles Keller Watson, Larry Brandenburg, Chelcie Ross, Tim Gamble, Sam Smiley, Pat Billingsley, John Bracci, Jennifer Anglin, Eddie Minasian, Tony Mockus Sr, Will Zahrn, Louis Lanciloti, Vince Viverto, Valentine Cimo, Joe Greco, Clem Caserta, Bob Martana, Joe Scianablo, George S. Spataro, Melody Rae, Robert Miranda, Jock Guthrie, Basil Reale. Dir: Brian de Palma. Pro: Art Linson. Assoc Pro: Ray Hartwick. Screenplay: David Mamet. Ph: Stephen H. Burum. Ed: Jerry Greenberg and Bill Pankow. Art: William

Elliott. M: Ennio Morricone. (Paramount-UIP). Rel: 25 September 1987. 120 mins. Cert 15.

Wall Street. Comic-book look at the giddy world of high finance and insider training, released in the US at the time of the Ivan Boesky trial. A young broker (Charlie Sheen) sells his morals to team up with an evil money baron (Michael Douglas) and becomes embroiled in manipulation, greed and illegal practice. A slick, fast-paced and engrossing – if somewhat confusing – drama, with Michael Douglas giving his best performance to date – it won him the Best Actor Oscar – as the demonic prince of Wall Street.

Rest of cast: Daryl Hannah, Martin Sheen, Hal Holbrook, Terence Stamp, Sean Young, Sylvia Miles, Richard Dysart, Saul Rubinek, Annie McEnroe, James Spader, James Karen, John C. McGinley, Franklin

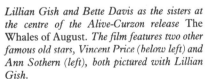

Lillian Gish and Bette Davis as the sisters at the centre of the Alive-Curzon release The Whales of August. *The film features two other famous old stars, Vincent Price (below left) and Ann Sothern (left), both pictured with Lillian Gish.*

Cover, Josh Mostel, Millie Perkins, Monique van Vooven, etc. Dir: Oliver Stone. Pro: Edward R. Pressman. Co-Pro: A. Kitman Ho. Screenplay: Stanley Weiser and Stone. Ph: Robert Richardson. Ed: Claire Simpson. Pro Des: Stephen Hendrickson. Art: J.J. Moore. M: Stewart Copeland. (Fox). Rel: 13 May 1988. 126 mins. Cert 15.

The Wannsee Conference – Die Wannseekonferenz. A careful reconstruction of one of the less publicized and therefore generally little-known but very important events of the Second World War: a gathering of fifteen leading Nazis at which the decision was taken to implement Hitler's plan for the 'final solution of the Jewish question'. The terrible decision was reached in 85 mins (the film lasts two more minutes than that) and the only arguments arose from the subject of half-Jews and others with only some Jewish blood in them. It is all quite incredible, yet is meticulously based on fact.

Cast: Robert Artzorn, Friedrich Beckhaus, Gerd Bockmann, Jochen Busse, Hans W. Bussinger, Harald Dietl, Peter Fitz, Reinhard Glemnitz, Dieter Groest, Martin Luttge, Anita Mally, Dietrich Mattausch, Gerd Rigauer, Franz Rudnick, Gunter Sporrle, Rainer Steffen. Dir: Heinz Schirk. Pro: Manfred Korytowski. Ex Pro: Siegfried B. Gloker. Screenplay: Paul Mommertz. Ph: Horst Schier. Ed: Ursula Mollinger. Art: Robert Hofer-Ach and Barbara Siebner. (Infafilm GmbH, Munich/Manfred Korytowski/Austrian TV/Orf/Bavarian Broadcasting Co.-NFT). Rel: floating; first shown London (NFT) 17 March 1988. 87 mins. No cert.

The Whales of August. A sympathetically and sensitively directed and superbly acted study of old age in the *Golden Pond* tradition. Bette Davis's acerbic voice is a vivid reminder of her screen-scorching prime, while dear old nonogenarian Lillian Gish gives a subtle performance. With deft and polished

Sir 'Jock' Delves Broughton (Joss Ackland) teaches his wife (Greta Scacchi) how to shoot while his friend Soames (the late Trevor Howard) looks on in Columbia's White Mischief. *Left: members of the Muthaiga Club, including Charles Dance, Greta Scacchi, Geraldine Chaplin, Sarah Miles (with a hat over her eyes) and John Hurt (helmeted).*

What Happened to Kerouac? And why? Those are the questions this documentary puts to its audience. Why did this increasingly successful American cult author, poet and voice of the Beat Generation drink himself to an early death? Answers are suggested by some of his friends, relatives and others, some more interesting than others, and the film is a complex tapestry – with a few threadbare patches – of interviews old and new(er), home movies, TV appearances and other materials originally assembled into a 55-minute video and later extended to a 96-minute cinema movie with colour and black-and-white footage. With Kerouac, Neal Cassady, William Burroughs, Gregory Corso, Lawrence Ferlinghetti, Allan Ginsberg, Charles Parker etc.

playing by Vincent Price, the film offers a trio of gems. The simple story, with serious undertones, concerns two aged sisters living together in less than perfect harmony in their summer cottage on the coast of Maine.

Rest of cast: Harry Carey Jr, Ann Sothern (so delightful to see her back on the screen), Frank Grimes, Frank Pitkin, Mike Bush, Margaret Ladd, Tisha Sterling, Mary Steenburgen. Dir: Lindsay Anderson. Pro: Carolyn Pfeiffer and Mike Kaplan. Pro Ex: Victoria Lee Pearman. Assoc Pro: Stuart Beser. Ex Pro: Shep Gordon. Screenplay: David Berry; based on his stage play. Ph: Mike Fash. Pro Des: Jocelyn Herbert. M: Alan Price. (Alive Films with Circle Associated Ltd/Nelson Entertainment-Curzon Film Dist.). Rel: floating; first shown London (Curzon Mayfair) 27 May 1988. 91 mins. Cert U.

Dir: Lerner and Lewis MacAdams. Co-Pro: by them and Nathaniel Dorsky and Malcolm Hart. Ph: Lerner and Dorsky etc. Assoc Pro: Eve Levy. Ed: Dorsky and Robert Estrin. M: Thelonius Monk. (Blue Dolphin). Rel: floating; first shown London (ICA) 9 October 1987. 96 mins. Cert 15.

White Mischief. Technically polished, impressive and generally assured British film set in Kenya during the last war and recording the debauched, uncaring and decadent lifestyle of white society in their 'Happy Valley'. Based on a true story – considerably twisted for dramatic effect – about the murder of the philandering marshal Earl Erroll (Charles Dance), who has seduced the lovely young wife (Greta Scacchi) of the newly arrived, middle-aged Sir 'Jock' Broughton (Joss Ackland – surely his best screen performance yet). After this dramatic high-point the rest is somewhat anti-climactic and adds too many needless minutes. But the film is finely acted, carefully directed and altogether another production of which Britain can rightly be proud.

Rest of cast: Sarah Miles, John Hurt, Susan Fleetwood, Alan Dobie, Hugh Grant, Jacqueline Pearce, Catherine Neilson, Murray Head, Gregor Fisher, Ray McAnally, Geraldine Chaplin, Trevor Howard, Tristram Jellinek, Tim Myers, Sean Mathias, Ron Donachie, Douglas Chege, Wensley Pithey, Stephan Chase, Clare Travers-Deacon, Seipal Ngojine, Pilip Saitoti, Amanda Parkin, Louis Mahoney, Ilario Bisi-Pedro, David Quilter, John Rees, Olivier Pierre, Anthony Benson, Nigel Levaillant, Basil Whybray, John Darrell, Bill Moody, Susannah Harker, Gary Beadle, Edwin Mahinda. Dir: Michael Radford. Pro: Simon Perry. Ex Pro: Michael White. Assoc Pro: Simon Bosanquet. Screenplay: Radford and Jonathan Gems; from the book by James Fox. Ph: Roger Deakins. Ed: Tom Priestley. Pro Des: Roger Hall. M: George Fenton. (Nelson Entertainment and Goldcrest Films/Michael White Umbrella Films in assoc. with Power Tower Investments, Kenya and BBC-Columbia). Rel: 4 March 1988. 105 mins. Cert 18.

Who's That Girl? Boy meets girl, boy wishes he had never set eyes on her, boy falls in love. The cartoon sequence that accompanies the opening credits of this hectic, untidy New York farce sets the tone for what is to come: cartoon fantasy (or cartoon nightmare, depending on your outlook), with every bloated cliché in the book. There are camp sales assistants, gay detectives, a dotty English millionaire (Sir John Mills, begging for laughs), a ruthless, domineering father-in-law and a bride so sweet you could dissolve her in tea. Any film that stoops to showing people snoring for comic effect *has* to be desperate. Griffin Dunne (*After Hours*) is the boy, Madonna the girl. Boy, does she pick 'em!

Rest of cast: Haviland Morris, John McMartin, Bibi Besch, Robert Swan, Drew Pillsbury, Coati Mundi, Dennis Burkley, Jim Dietz, Cecile Callan, Karen Baldwin, Kimberlin Brown, Crystal Carson, Elaine Wilkes, Tony La Fortezza, Thomas Pinnock, Alvin Hammer, Sean Sullivan, Helen Lloyd Breed, Dalton Dearborn, Robert E. Weil, Robert Cornthwaite, Albert Popwell, Alice Nunn, Gary Basaraba, Ron Taylor, Stanley Tucci etc. Dir: James Foley. Pro: Rosilyn Heller and Bernard Williams. Ex Pro: Peter Guber, Jon Peters and Roger Birnbaum. Screenplay: Andrew Smith and Ken Finkleman; from a story by Andrew Smith. Ph: Jan DeBont. Ed: Pembroke Herring. Pro Des: Ida Random. M: Stephen Bray. (Warner). Rel: floating; first shown London (Warner) 23 October 1987. 92 mins. Cert 15.

Wings of Desire. Extraordinary, poetic film, shot predominantly in black-and-white, about a band of angels who visit

Madonna, with John Mills and Griffin Dunne, in Warner's Who's That Girl?

Berlin. One angel, Damiel (Bruno Ganz), who cannot stand the deprivation of human feeling (taste, cold, pain), befriends Peter Falk (as himself, a fallen angel) and falls in love with a trapeze artist (Solveig Dommartin). Self-indulgent to a fault, Wim Wenders's return to his roots is not easily forgotten. Winner of the Best Director award at Cannes (1987).

Rest of cast: Otto Sander, Curt Bois, Hans Martin Stier, Elmar Wilms, Sigurd Rachman, Beatrice Manowski, Lajos Kovacs, Bruno Rosaz, Laurent Petitgand, Dominique Rojo, Otto Kuhnle, Christoph Merg, Peter Werner, Jerry Barrish, Jeanette Pollak, David Crome. Dir, Co-Pro and Co-Screenplay: Wim Wenders. Co-Pro: Anatole Dauman. Ex Pro: Ingrid Windisch. Co-Screenplay: Peter Handke. Ph: Henri Alekan. Ed: Peter Przygodda. M: Jurgen Knieper and Laurent Petitgand. (Argos Films/Road Movies/Westdeutscher Rundfunk-Recorded Releasing). Rel: 24 June 1988. 127 mins. Cert 15.

Wish You Were Here. An uneven British comedy, in turn hilariously funny and dullish, tinged with bitterness, and sometimes cruelty as it relates the story of a motherless teenager growing up in a typical small British seaside town. Promiscuous, and using the most foul language for both fun and fury, a cause of her losing job after job, the girl finally cocks a snook at local society with her bright yellow dress and her bonny illegitimate baby. Tyro actress Emily Lloyd gives a marvellous performance and lifts the whole film many

notches above where it would otherwise have been, while writer-director David Leland, in his film debut, shows he has a lot to offer the cinema.

Rest of cast: Trudy Cavanagh, Clare Clifford, Barbara Durkin, Geoffrey Hutchings, Charlotte Barker, Tom Bell, Chloe Leland, Susan Skipper, Geoffrey Durham, Sheila Kelley, Neville Smith, Pat Heywood, Charlotte Ball, Marjorie Sudell, Lee Whitlock, Jesse Birdsall, Frederick Hall, Bob Flag, Heathcote Williams, William Lawford, Pamela Duncan, David Hatton, Ben Daniels, Val McLane, Kim McDermott, Barrie Houghton, Jim Dowdall, Danielle Phelps, George (the dog), Brendan Donnison (voice only). Dir and Screenplay: David Leland. Pro: Sarah Radclyffe. Ph: Ian Wilson. Ed: George Akers. Pro Des: Caroline Amies. Art: Nigel Phelps. M: Stanley Myers. (Zenith Films in assoc with Working Title/Film Four International-Palace Pictures). Rel: 22 January 1988. 92 mins. Cert 15.

The Witches of Eastwick. Jack Nicholson out-*Shining* himself as the ambiguously devilish, oddly attired, randy male newcomer to the big house in the small New England town of the title, where he proceeds to seduce three

Talented newcomer Emily Lloyd as the terrible teenager on the brink of losing yet another job in Palace Pictures' British comedy Wish You Were Here.

attractive local witches by playing, literally, in one case, on their desires and needs. But when fulfilled the trio turns on him because of his continued demands, and destroys him in a whizbang, farcical, very funny finale, leaving them in peaceful domesticity with their three obviously devilish babies. All this serves to illustrate, yet again, the battle of the sexes. Though uneven, the film is full of good things, including Nicholson's over-the-top performance, and he is ably assisted by his three loves: Susan Sarandon, Cher and Michelle Pfeiffer.

Rest of cast: Veronica Cartwright, Richard Jenkins, Keith Jochim, Carel Struycken, Helen Lloyd Breed, Caroline Struzik, Michele and Nicol Sincavage, Heather Coleman, Carolyn, Cynthia and Christine Ditmars, Craig Burket, Abraham Mishkind, Christopher Verrette, Becca Lish, Ruth Maynard, Lansdale Chatfield, Carole Ita White, Babbie Green, Jane A. Johnston,

Merrily Horowitz, Harriet Medin, Margot Dionne, James T. Boyle, John Blood, Ron Campbell, Eugene Boles, Corey Carrier, Kate Barret, Dan Edson, Anthony Falco, Kevin Goodwin, Tara Halfpenny, David Hazel, Melanie Hewitt, Matt Kane, Anne Lingren, Jessica Macdonald, Corinna Minnar, Scott Nickerson, Stephen Oakes, Ann Senechal, James Staunton, Amy Warner. Dir: George Miller. Pro: Neil Canton, Peter Guber and Jon Peters. Ex Pro: Rob Cohen and Don Devlin. Screenplay: Michael Cristofer; based on the novel by John Updike. Ph: Vilmos Zsigmond. Ed: Richard Francis-Bruce, Hubert C. de la Bouillerie and Howard Stein. Pro Des: Polly Platt. M: John Williams. (Warner Bros/Guber-Peters Co/Kennedy Miller-Warner). Rel: 13 November 1987. 118 mins. Cert 18.

Withnail and I. Fond, semi-autobiographical backward glance at London in the 'sixties (Camden Town, 1969), beautifully written, superbly acted and very witty. Erstwhile actor Bruce Robinson (*Romeo and Juliet, The Story of Adele H*) directs his second screenplay with biting confidence, following the ramshackle lives of two out-of-work actors trying to come to terms with England and themselves.

Cast: Richard E. Grant (as Withnail), Paul McGann (as I), Richard Griffiths, Ralph Brown, Michael Elphick, Daragh O'Malley, Michael Wardle, Una Brandon-Jones, Noel Johnson, Irene Sutcliffe, Llewellyn Rees, Robert Oates, Anthony Wise, Eddie Tagoe. Dir and Screenplay: Bruce Robinson. Pro: Paul M. Heller. Ex Pro: George Harrison and Denis O'Brien. Co-Pro: David Wimbury. Ph: Peter Hannan. Ed: Alan Strachan. Pro Des: Michael Pickwoad. M: David Dundas and Rick Wentworth. (HandMade-Recorded Releasing). Rel: 8 April 1988. 102 mins. Cert 15.

The Woo Woo Kid. A comedy – said to be based on fact – about a very precocious 14-year-old who elopes with an older man's wife. He is caught, the marriage is annulled, and he is placed in his Californian uncle's care. But he is soon sexually involved again, this time with an absent seaman's wife. Caught again, and imprisoned, he escapes, then falls for the charms of a cinema usherette nearer his own age, whom he marries. All charges against him are dropped, making way for a happy-ever-after ending. It all proves considerably more amusing than you might expect from this outline (or the ghastly title), thanks largely to a good script, some witty lines and nice period (1944) background.

Cast: Patrick Dempsey, Talia Balsam, Beverly D'Angelo, Michael Constantine, Betty Jinnette, Kathleen Freeman, Peter Hobbs, Tony Longo, Douglas Rowe, Ernie Brown, Kim Myers, Brian McNamara, Dana Short, Josh Cadman, Nan Woods, Tom Breznahan, Gillian Grant, Lisanne Falk, Barbara Wint, Burt Middleton, Jarad Chandler, Edith Fellows, Tom Tarpey, Crane Jackson, Neil Elliot, Mae Williams, Janet Rotblatt, Harvey J. Goldenberg, Tom Maier, Putter Smith, Lenore Woodward, Lee Garlington, Charles Stevenson, Carl Parker, Wayne Grice, J.A. Chandler, Robert Gould, Jordan Myers, Rick Salassi, Thomas Ryan, Walter Zeri, Nitche Vo Miller, Laura Bastianelli, Ted Noose, Charlie Holliday, Valeria Reynolds, Rocky Giordani, Darwin Swalve, W.T. Zacha, Kitty Swink, Steve Whittaker, T.A. Clay, Tony Monaco, Terry Camilleri, Mike Darrell, David Schermerhorn, John Zarchen, Cletus Young, Bert Conway, Ana Helena Berenguer, Jay Varela, etc. Dir: Phil Alden Robinson. Pro: Gary Adelson and Karen Mack. Assoc Pro: Brian Frankish. Pro Co-Ord: Ronnie Kramer. Screenplay: Phil Alden Robinson; from a story by Bob Kosberg, David Simon and Robinson. Ph: John Lindley. Ed: Patrick Kennedy. Pro Des: Dennis Gassner. Art: Dins Danielson.

M: Ralph Burns. (Lorimar/Kings Rd. Entertainment-Guild). Rel: 8 January 1988. 100 mins. Cert PG.

The Yob. Minor British film (designed and destined for TV) from the Comic Strip company about the switching of personalities of two contrasting characters, one from the lower strata of society and the other from near the top.

Cast: Keith Allen, Gary Olsen, Lia Williams, Linda Henry, Betsy Brantley, Adrian

Mysterious stranger Jack Nicholson (top) faces the very devil of a blow in Warner's The Witches of Eastwick. *Above, l. to r.: the three witches of the title, Susan Sarandon, Michelle Pfeiffer and Cher.*

Edmondson, Peter Wyngarde, etc. Dir: Ian Emes. Screenplay: Keith Allen and Daniel Peacock. (Comic Strip in assoc with Channel 4-Palace Pictures). Rel: floating; first shown London (Scala) – with *The Strike* as a double bill. 8 January 1988. 53 mins. No cert.

The Foreign Language Film

For full details of the films illustrated in this section, see 'Releases of the Year'

Bernard Giraudeau as the drunken Paris flic in Edouard Niermans's Angel Dust – Poussière d'ange (a Palace Pictures release). Only his second film, a full five years after his first, Angel Dust has a quality and class which raises it well above most of its Gallic film noir kind. The drunken detective becomes involved with an . attractive, mysterious teenager (impressive Fanny Bastien, left) progressively sobering up as he uncovers the girl's secret activities. Niermans is a Paris-born Frenchman who was educated in a Jesuit school, which gave him the theme and background for his debut movie Anthracite.

To celebrate the 80th birthday (in September 1987) of Robert Bresson, one of France's most distinguished moviemakers, London's Everyman Cinema (Electric Pictures) revived his first feature film, Les Anges du péché, showing it in a new 35mm print taken from the original negative. Made in 1943 but impressive even by today's standards, the film is about an order of Dominican nuns called Béthanie (which gave the film its original title) devoted to the rehabilitation of female ex-criminals. It was not shown in full in France until revived there in 1987 and had never previously been released in Britain in any form.

Extremely popular in France and elsewhere across Europe and beyond, the Asterix comic strip cartoons have not so far made as much of an impact on the British, something which the producers of the second Asterix feature film, Asterix in Britain – Astérix chez les Bretons, hoped to alter. Certainly there's fun to be had from this animated movie about Asterix coming to Britain with his coterie in order to help his English cousin defeat the invading Roman legions.

Stéphane Audran, as a formerly famous French chef, now exiled and living as the servant-cook to two sisters in a bleak Danish seaside village, leads the way up the beach with the supplies from France. She has spent her entire lottery win on luxury food, with which she prepares Babette's Feast – Babettes Gaestebud, an epicurean masterpiece which has a profound effect on the normally meagre-living villagers. Remarkably and lovingly detailed, the feast in this brilliantly directed (by Gabriel Axel) and beautifully acted Danish film provides the mouth-watering climax to an original and memorable movie, which richly deserved the Best Foreign Film Oscar it won for 1987–8.

Theodorus Angelopoulos's The Beekeeper – O
Melissokomos *(Artificial Eye) offered Marcello Mastroianni a further opportunity for one of
his masterly character studies, this time of an
elderly, retired school teacher whose hobby is
keeping beehives at various well dispersed sites.
On one of his regular tours to these hives he
picks up a young girl (Nadia Mourouzi), whose
casual lifestyle initially intrigues him but eventually brings him to violent despair. The combination of the acting and sensitive direction –
by a director previously known for politically
inspired films – produces a minor but memorable movie.*

*Jean Delannoy, the once prestigious French
director who in the 'fifties suffered vicious
verbal attacks from the 'New Wavers', has not
made a cinema movie since 1972 and his* Pas
folle la guêpe, *devoting all his time to television
work. Ironically, that is where his new film, the
Cannon-France release* Bernadette, *is likely to
find its largest audience. With its cold, formal,
somehow old-fashioned style, this true story of
the peasant girl whose visions of the Virgin
Mary established Lourdes as a place of international pilgrimage remains remote and uninvolving. Bernadette is played by a young American
actress (dubbed), Sydney Penny, with sincerity
but without passion. With her in this scene,
Jean-Marc Bory as the Holy Father.*

*Made in 1983 and having apparently enjoyed a
successful season in Paris, writer-director Leos
Carax's Metro release* Boy Meets Girl *turned
up in Britain in mid-July 1987 with the reputation of having reached 'cult' status. It certainly
proved to have limited appeal, with its strange,
almost surrealistic story about youthful liaisons
in a shadowy, unfamiliar night-time Paris.
Mireille Perrier (with dark glasses, below)
plays the girl whose lover prefers to make love to
her when she is asleep so that he can pretend she
is dead. All very odd, and not a little pretentious. (An Other Cinema release.)*

The Valery Ogorodnikov Russian film The Burglar – Vzlomshchik *is about a Soviet heavy metal band with a 'difficult' young leader. Although he becomes more socially acceptable before the end it is still a most extraordinarily 'liberal' film to come out of the USSR and could certainly not have been made or released there a few years back. The two leads, suitably if surprisingly attired, are played by Konstantin Kinchev and Oleg Yelykomov. (An Other Cinema import.)*

Klaus Kinski was an apt choice for the leading role in Werner Herzog's Palace Pictures release Cobra Verde. *It tells the story of a Brazilian whose wildly adventurous career starts with gold prospecting, but who becomes a murderer when swindled out of his gains, and then turns to banditry and slave trading before leading an Amazonian army to victory against a jungle dictator. But everything eventually falls apart for him and he becomes a hunted fugitive. The film is based on Bruce Chatwin's book* The Viceroy of Ouidah.

While not all critics seem to have considered writer-director Erik Clausen's The Dark Side of the Moon – Manden I Manen *worth the eight awards and Oscar nomination that it has garnered since its unveiling, there is no denying the mesmeric quality of this stylish and imaginatively told story of a man who murders for love, killing his wife rather than losing her to another man. Gloomily Germanic in atmosphere, leisurely paced, sometimes ambiguous in its story of the murderer's reactions to the strange, foreign world into which he is eventually released and with which he has to cope. Not the least of the film's numerous assets is the debut performance of Peter Thiel as the murderer (seen about to start his prison sentence).*

Myriam Mezières reveals her all to co-star Benoit Regent in A Flame in My Heart – Une flamme dans mon coeur, *a Swiss–French co-production made in black-and-white, released in the UK by Mainline. In addition to contributing her feminine charms, Mezières shares the credit of writing this verbose movie with director Alain Tanner, Switzerland's best-known and most talented writer–director, who once worked for the British Film Institute. Politically conscious in a leftwards way, like all Tanner's films, this is a dense and rather indigestible, but always fascinating work, and very, very sexual.*

Contrasting town and country girls Jöelle Mi-quel and Jessica Forde become friends in Eric Rohmer's four-part film Four Adventures of Reinette and Mirabelle – Quatre Aventures de Reinette et Mirabelle, *a curiously casual movie. Full of effortless charm, the story is based on the personal experiences of Jöelle, which she related to Rohmer during the making of his* Le Rayon vert *and was made, according to some sources, on a shoestring budget wholly for the director's personal pleasure. If so, that pleasure is reflected in the film. (Artificial Eye release.)*

Gérard Depardieu (as Jean) with screen (and actual) wife Elisabeth, and Ernestine Mazur-owna (as the daughter) in Claude Berri's Jean de Florette *(a Cannon release). Made simultaneously with the sequel (*Manon des sources) *on location in the arid, hostile terrain of Haute Provence, this adaptation of one of Marcel Pagnol's classic stories of Provence and the Provençals (which in turn was based on a previous Pagnol movie) turned out to be one of the most expensive – as well as one of the best – movies in the history of the French film; the actual cost of the two films is reputed to be in the region of £12 million. The source material for book and films was a true story about a cruel plot, in the film by a grasping old village patriarch and his dimwit nephew, to gain* possession of a parcel of land for a carnation-growing project, and then to steal the spring water from an adjoining property in order to make the plan viable. The duped neighbour (a *former town-dweller struggling to make a living from the poor and parched earth) dies as a result of the plot. Inset: the two villains, marvellously played by Daniel Auteuil and Yves Montand.*

The family of women in Let's Hope It's a Girl
– Speriamo che sia femmina *(the Countess –
Liv Ullmann, above left; her town-tired sister –
Catherine Deneuve, driving; the essential
home-help – Athina Cenci; and two of the
children) decide, after all the traumas caused by
their unsatisfactory menfolk, that the only happy way ahead lies in an all-female co-operative
running of the Countess's old Tuscan farmhouse. Below: the last few minutes in the life of*
*the charming but hopelessly impractical Count
(Philippe Noiret) before he obeys the casual
directions of the vague old uncle (Bernard
Blier) and reverses his car over the edge of the
abyss. Set against the lusciously photographed
Tuscan countryside, beautifully acted, this
ambling Italian comedy by Mario Monicelli is
as good a tonic as a lazy afternoon spent
relaxing in the Tuscan sunshine. An Artificial
Eye import.*

*Tseshang Rigzin (above) in the title role in
China's* Horse Thief – Daoma Zei, *shown in
Britain by ICA Projects. An example of China's new, liberated attitude, the film still met
some official opposition and only eventually
won a limited release in the country of origin
with cuts and, so it is said, after a change of
period from the late 1980s to the early 'twenties.
The film's message seems to be that even the
traumas of the Cultural Revolution could not
bring some of China's far-flung provinces into
political line.*

The story of corruption in high places, Bo Widerberg's The Man from Majorca – Mannen fran Mallorca (a Cannon/Gala release) is about two detectives (played by Sven Wollter and Tomas von Bromssen, below) whose increasingly successful investigation into a post office robbery and two subsequent – at first apparently unrelated – murders is suddenly stopped on orders from above. The story was written by angry criminologist Leif Persson, a former Swedish Police Board officer who was himself forced into resignation after a scandal involving a Cabinet minister and drew upon his own bitter experience for the film's story.

Rolan Bykov (above) in the leading role as a Nobel prize-winning professor in Letters from a Dead Man – Pisma Myortvovo Cheloveka, a Soviet film (distributed in this country by Artificial Eye) about the aftermath of an atomic 'accident' which, made long before the Chernobyl disaster, proved strangely prophetic. Dull and sincere, its pessimistic effect is enhanced by sepia-toned photography.

Following on the events of Jean de Florette comes the second of Claude Berri's masterly interpretations of the Marcel Pagnol novel, Manon of the Spring – Manon des sources (also a Cannon release). Set some years later, the sequel continues the story of the human tragedy centred on the stolen spring which alone makes cultivation possible in the arid hills of Provence. Now the lovely young Manon, – beautifully played by Emmanuelle Beart (below right) – learning the truth, takes a bitter revenge on the man who caused her father's death; neither of them knows that he is in fact her grandfather. Below: as the stone-hearted old 'fox', Yves Montand (right) gives another Oscar-worthy performance, and Daniel Auteuil (left), as the nephew, is even more impressive in this film than in its predecessor.

Michael Sarrazin plays a chief inspector who appears to spend more time committing than solving crimes in the somewhat pretentious French/Dutch/Belgian co-production Mascara *(a Cannon import). Shown above: the inspector with 'Pepper', played by Eva Robbins, who gives the film its most dramatic moment when the lovely 'girl' turns to the camera and reveals 'her' male attributes.*

Julie Christie (below) as Miss Mary, *the prim governess employed by an Argentinian cattle-ranching family just before the Second World War. Told by sometimes rather erratic flashbacks, the story rises to a climax during one stormy night of melodramatic passion when the governess and her male pupil make love together, a lapse of control that causes one of her female charges to enter into an unhappy marriage, the other to go insane, and the governess's own dismissal. All this personal trauma is seen against the turbulent Argentinian politics of the period, which were leading to Perón's seizure of power. A New World, Entertainment release.*

Having switched partners, firm friends Blanche (Emmanuelle Chaulet) and Lea (Sophie Renoir) find they had no real cause for their guilty feelings in Eric Rohmer's My Girlfriend's Boyfriend – L'Ami de mon amie, *the very different young men being played by Eric Vieillard (top, with blonde Emmanuelle) and François-Eric Gendron (with brunette Sophie).*

As befits a film made by a professor of literature, it is all delightfully literate; more so, and more polished, than the last couple of movies in Rohmer's long-running series labelled 'Comedies and Proverbs', of which he is said to have declared that the present film will be the last. If so, the series ends on a very high note. An Artificial Eye Release.

The doctor (Rudolf Hrusinsky) and his nurse get a new angle on the situation in Jiri Menzel's delightful Czechoslovakian comedy (released in Britain by Cannon) My Sweet Little Village – Vesnicko má Středisková. *Menzel (who won an Oscar for his 1966 black comedy classic* Closely Observed Trains) *has seldom been heard of since the Soviet invasion of his country, but here he shows that during the hiatus he has lost none of his shrewd sense of irony or his cinematic flair.*

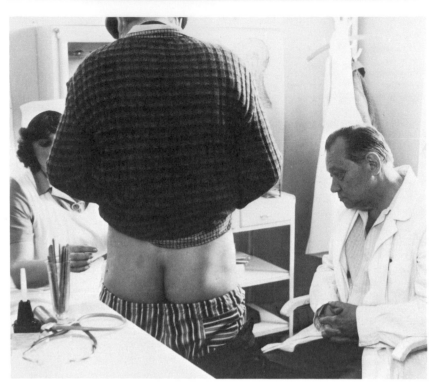

Juliette Binoche (whom we first saw in Godard's controversial Hail Mary *and who has since been kept busy by her roles in seven subsequent films) and Michel Piccoli plan to steal, for financial gain, a valuable new medical culture, in the Artificial Eye import* The Night is Young – Mauvais Sang. *Twenty-seven-year-old writer-director Leos Carax, whose previous (first) film was* Boy Meets Girl, *makes no concessions to his audience in either of his films, which are equally intricate and confusing, individualistic and surrealistic, though both show considerable promise of less pretentious and better things to come.*

Grazyna Szapolowska (below) in the Polish, Artificial Eye release No End – Bez Konca. *Shown in Poland in 1984, it was originally refused an export licence by the authorities, who were worried by its political implications. Even when the ban was lifted two years later, it took a further two years to reach Britain. Superficially it's about a wife's efforts to come to terms with her lawyer husband's demise, while he keeps popping up from time to time to watch her trying to cope and to see how the case he was preparing (the political angle) is progressing in the courts. But it is all pretty grey and grim and a far cry from those vintage Polish comedies.*

After four years away from the film studios Jeanne Moreau (right) returns to play the owner of a gloomy bar in a seaport town where it rains every day at precisely 5 p.m. Dreams and reality merge to such an extent that it is virtually impossible to guess where one ends and the other begins in this very odd Michel Deville produc- tion, entitled Paltoquet (which means the good- for-nothing). Bottom (l. to r.): Jean Yanne (the detective) and his suspects, Daniel Auteuil (the journalist), Richard Bohringer (the doctor), and Claude Piéplu (the professor), all view the body of the murdered man, together with Fanny Ardant, also pictured below in a hammock.

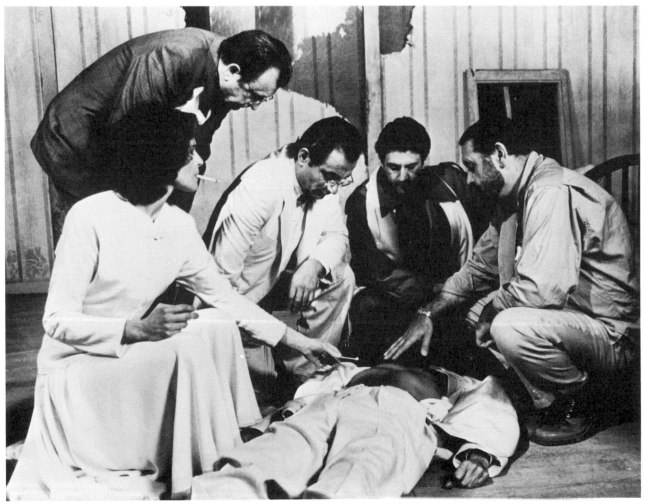

The piper in the remarkable Czech animated feature The Pied Piper – Krysar is, like the other Gothic-styled wooden puppets, carved in walnut. These bizarre characters are mixed with the live members of the cast, the rats, to extraordinary effect. The first feature movie (following four shorts, of which at least one, The Extinct World of Gloves, was wholly original) to be made by 40-year-old Czech artist Jiri Barta, who studied film and television graphics at Prague University, The Pied Piper is unlike any other animated film you may have seen. First glimpsed at the 1987 London Film Festival, it was the always-adventurous Everyman cinema which saved it from subsequent oblivion.

Edisher Giorgobiani as the artist arrested by the mayor of a small Georgian community, along with his wife (Ketevan Abuladze) and small daughter, from whom he is separated and whom he never sees again. When this much respected mayor dies and his body is continually dug up, his true character is revealed in the court case which results. Carrying a message of social and political criticism, Repentance – Monanieba (a Cannon import) was written in 1981, made in 1984 and shelved by censorship until 1986, when the new political climate allowed it to be screened in the USSR.

Lambert Wilson and Charlotte Valandrey (above) in the French/West German Rouge Baiser, in which director-writer-producer Vera Belmont shows love and politics can be bedfellows, albeit uneasy ones. Apparently based on her own experiences, and set in Paris of the early 1950s, this, her second film (the first was Prisoner of Mao) follows her heroine's disillusionment with the Communist beliefs that she has inherited from her parents and equal disappointment when her photographer lover volunteers for army service in Indo-China as an alternative to facing a statutory charge of rape. An Other Cinema release.

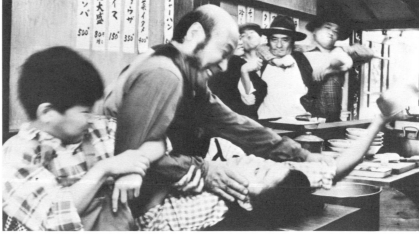

A gangster and a girl (Koji Yakusho and Fukumi Kuroda, left) make a shared egg yolk a memorable erotic experience in Tampopo – Dandelion. Above, a rival restaurateur shows his displeasure at the efforts of the widow Dandelion (Nobuko Miyamato) to prepare and present the best noodle soup in Japan. The director of this Good Food classic, Juzo Itami, is a man of many parts. As an actor he has won a number of major awards for his performances; as an author he has sold a million-plus books; he is a family man and a gourmet cook; and as a film director his latest production has won him nine Japanese Academy Awards. In Tampopo he certainly shows an individual and original talent for screen comedy.

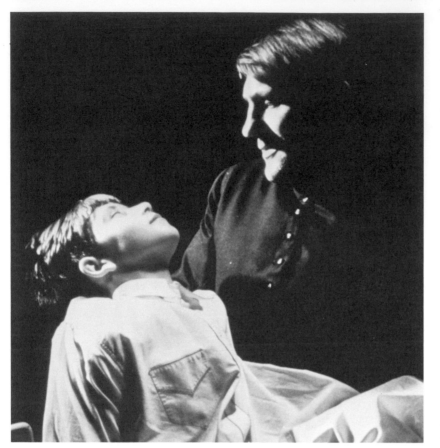

The final tragedy which convinces the intensely dedicated, simple rural priest (Gérard Depardieu) that the devil is supreme in Maurice Pialat's controversial and very Catholic Under Satan's Sun – Sous le Soleil de Satan, which met a lot of opposition when it was awarded the Cannes Film Festival's premier prize in 1987. After a long night of argument trying to save the soul of a 16-year-old pregnant wanton (Sandrine Bonnaire) the priest finds he has driven her to the cardinal sin of suicide.

Daniel (Bruno Ganz) takes heed of what Peter Falk is saying during their meeting at a Berlin coffee-stall in Wim Wenders's Wings of Desire – Der Himmel über Berlin (alternative English title The Sky Over Berlin), a story about angels on earth. Wenders's return to his native soil after excursions abroad takes the form of a movie which one critic has labelled 'a sublimely beautiful, deeply romantic film for our times'; and others seem more or less to concur. There is more than a little significance in Wenders's dedicating his film to Ozu and Truffaut. Released in the UK by Recorded Releasing.

Letter From Hollywood

ANTHONY SLIDE

There is much that is comic about Hollywood and so it is perhaps appropriate to begin this overview of the Hollywood year with the presentation of the first American Comedy Awards in May 1987. The Awards were the brainchild of ABC-TV, which broadcast them and solicited nominations in some fourteen categories from various producers, writers, executives, etc. The winners were voted by 700 comedy performers. The big winners were Robin Williams – who was not present at the Awards – and Bette Midler, who was, and who commented upon being presented with the Lifetime Achievement Award, 'Hey, I'm only 29. I'm not through yet.'

The comedy continued in Hollywood with Paramount's celebration of its 75th anniversary in 1987, despite its not having been founded until 1914-15; and despite the fact that Adolph Zukor's Famous Players Company, which *was* founded 75 years ago, was not the parent company of Paramount. Anyway, why should Paramount care? It garnered considerable publicity for itself and was the subject of a mammoth retrospective tribute by the Los Angeles County Museum of Art and the UCLA Film and Television Archive, towards the cost of which it contributed not one penny.

Further comedy was provided by Hollywood itself, which celebrated its 100th birthday this year, despite its not having become a city until 1903 and its then having remained one for only seven years until it was annexed by Los Angeles. ABC was also involved in this event through a television spectacle en-

The famous Bronson Gate in Hollywood, as seen in Sunset Boulevard *(1950).*

titled *Happy Birthday, Hollywood*, which was presented at the Shrine Auditorium on 26 April 1987. Naturally there were one hundred stars present, including June Allyson, Lucille Ball, Leslie Caron, Cyd Charisse, Alice Faye, Lillian Gish, Bob Hope, Ruby Keeler, Dorothy Lamour, Gregory Peck, Luise Rainer, Ginger Rogers, Lana Turner and Esther Williams.

There were a number of other silly things going on in connection with Hollywood's birthday. A new McDonald's opened on Hollywood Boulevard, with the announcement from the Hollywood Chamber of Commerce that it would 'capture the essence of Hollywood in its glamorous past while projecting the spirit of its exciting future'. The Hollywood Brown Derby, which had closed a couple of years previously, reopened at a new site, at the corner of Hollywood and Vine. The 1,500 movie-star caricatures, which were well known to tourists at the old location, are on the walls of the new restaurant.

Cesar Romero is rapidly becoming the male counterpart of Jane Withers in his willingness to appear at any event, no matter how insignificant. He was present in March 1988 to launch a project to restore some of the damaged stars on Hollywood's 'Walk of Fame'. Romero's time would have been better spent in promoting the addition of those stars who still remain unhonoured, despite their importance to Hollywood's past.

Perhaps the silliest Hollywood event was the dedication of a Marilyn Monroe time capsule, which will be opened in 75 years' time. Among the 'celebrities' participating in this non-event were Monroe's make-up man, Allan Schneider, who deposited the lipstick with which he made up the star; James Hall, the ambulance man who drove her body to the hospital after her death; Bob Slatzer, who claims to have been married to Monroe; and her stand-in, Evelyn Moriarty. A day after this major event, it was announced that Bill Mack, who had designed the time capsule, would sculpt a life-size bronze statue of the actress in her 1955 feature, *The Seven Year Itch*.

The American Film Institute presented its sixteenth annual Life Achievement Award to Jack Lemmon on 10 March 1988. The star-studded event, hosted by Julie Andrews, included appearances by Walter Matthau,

Billy Wilder, Shirley MacLaine, Roddy McDowall, Janet Leigh, Blake Edwards, Garson Kanin, Neil Simon and Michael Douglas.

The award to Jack Lemmon brings these AFI tributes into the post-war era and, while it is well deserved, the question must arise as to why the award is going to someone whose career is far from over. Surely there are many personalities from an earlier era still deserving of the tribute, such as Bob Hope, Lucille Ball, Lana Turner, Jean Arthur and Irene Dunne? (Katharine Hepburn has turned the AFI down.) Yes, we know the AFI Life Achievement Award is primarily a television special and ratings are more important than the recipient's life achievement, but this is not the way it should be.

There was a comic aspect to Pope John Paul II's visit to Hollywood in September 1987, which drew bigger crowds than recent British royal visitors. He addressed a Hollywood film community gathering, primarily of the Jewish faith, on the subjects of 'values, morality and conscience' in the communications industry. According to *Daily Variety* the following day, the Pope's comments got 'mixed reviews'. The president of Atlantic Records called the Pope's message 'dated material. He's got to come into the twentieth century. Certainly morality is necessary, but you can no longer ignore such issues as divorce, birth control, homosexuality and abortion. He's just not in touch.' The manager of casting for NBC-TV noted that 'the millions of dollars spent on the visit could have been spent on AIDS research, the homeless'. The actress Marlo Thomas regretted she could not have had a dialogue with the Pontiff about 'women priests, married priests and birth control'. All in all, it was agreed that the audience of 1,600 was there not because of the Pope, but because Lou Wasserman, the equivalent of a secular papal head of Hollywood, had invited them to be there.

There were other anniversaries celebrated in Hollywood. It has been ten years since the release of *Star Wars*, 25 years since the release of the first James Bond movie, and 50 years since the release of *Snow White and the Seven Dwarfs*. A year-long celebration for the last of these included the inevitable television special, a star on the Hollywood Walk of Fame, and the reissue of

the feature in brand-new prints, made from a new master generated by the Burbank-based YCM company, which specializes in colour restoration. It has worked closely with the UCLA Film and Television Archive in the preservation of *Becky Sharp*, *Toll of the Sea*, *She Wore a Yellow Ribbon*, *A Star Is Born* and other features, and is currently working with Turner Entertainment on the creation of new master elements for *Gone with the Wind*.

The Academy of Motion Picture Arts and Sciences celebrated its 60th anniversary with an Oscar presentation which was as tedious as most of the previous ones of recent memory. There were a few highlights, notably Robin Williams's irreverent introduction to the Best Direction Awards – describing *The Last Emperor* as Ronald Reagan's favourite film – and the animated Mickey Mouse sequence, well conceived and executed. (It was also Mickey's 60th birthday.)

As part of its celebration, the Academy had invited celebrities associated with the previous 59 Best Picture winners to participate in a production number. However, the number had to be cancelled because many of the participants were stuck in a traffic jam *en route* to the Shrine Auditorium (the new home for the Awards), and failed to arrive in time. Some were also in disagreeable moods. Joan Fontaine checked into the hotel booked for her by the Academy only to find she was on the same floor as her estranged sister, Olivia de Havilland!

The Academy president, Robert Wise, announced an interesting development, the proposed move of the Academy's Margaret Herrick Library – arguably the largest film-related library in the world – to a new location in a 61-year-old building belonging to the City of Beverly Hills. The plan is that the new building will permit the Academy to house all of its collections under one roof, whereas at present much of its archival holdings is in storage.

Among the tributes for 1987/8, the most moving and emotionally sincere was to John Huston, who died on 30 August 1987. Some two weeks later, the Directors' Guild hosted a programme of film clips and commentary by Lauren Bacall, Richard Brooks, Jack Nicholson, costume designer Dorothy Jeakins, Jack Haley Jr, Harry

Dean Stanton, agent Paul Kohner, and Huston's daughter Anjelica. The first speaker, Robert Mitchum, summed up Huston's career with the remark, 'He'd done just about everything he ever wanted to attempt, and he did it with grace and some triumph.' The programme ended with Walter Huston's recording of 'September Song'.

An event which seems to attract a host of celebrities is the American Cinema Awards ceremony. In February 1988, it was the turn of Gene Kelly, Shirley Temple and the music video star Janet Jackson to be honoured. On hand to honour Kelly were Georges Guetary, Donald O'Connor, Rosemary Clooney, Debbie Reynolds and Leslie Caron, who flew in from Paris to present the American Cinema Award to her co-star in *An American in Paris*. She commented, 'You taught me everything. You set a degree of excellence in films that was hard to touch. You were prince among dancers. Your vitality, your *joie de vivre* were very catching. You made millions of people happy around the world. And you made rain fashionable.'

Among those paying tribute to Shirley Temple were Buddy Ebsen, Tony Martin and Alice Faye. Ebsen, who co-starred with Temple in *Captain January*, praised her 'mature professionalism'.

Leslie Caron was in town for Gene Kelly, but whenever she visits Los Angeles she is always available to see Dido Renoir, the remarkable widow of director Jean Renoir. Dido celebrated her 80th birthday last year, and it was an honour to be a member of the small gathering at her house of friends, who included Caron, Norman Lloyd and Dorothy Maguire. I first got to know Dido when UCLA's Robert Gitt and I would visit Jean most weekends and screen films for him during the last three years of his life, when incapacity prevented his going out, and when Norman and Peggy Lloyd, Ingrid Bergman, Leslie Caron and François Truffaut were among his visitors.

Two major film music events took place during the last year in Los Angeles. In November 1987, André Previn conducted the Los Angeles Philharmonic Orchestra and the Los Angeles Master Choral in a live presentation of the score by Sergei Prokofiev for Eisenstein's *Alexander Nevsky*, which was shown with dialogue and sound effects only. Previn did a magnificent job of synchronization, and brought to life a score which had sounded lacklustre on the film's soundtrack.

The last event was held to raise money for the Los Angeles Philharmonic Musicians' Pension Fund and the American Film Institute's National Center for Film and Video Preservation. A second musical event held to raise funds for the preservation of film music was 'A Night of Great Movie Music', hosted in March 1988 at UCLA by Robert Redford's Sundance Institute. Celebrities on hand included Charlton Heston, who acted as master of ceremonies, Robert Redford, Tippi Hedren and Kathleen Turner. David Newman conducted a 90-piece orchestra through selections from scores by Erich Wolfgang Korngold, Miklos Rozsa, Alex North, Jerry Goldsmith, Franz Waxman, John Barry and Max Steiner. The event helped to put into perspective the problem of preserving film music, which often does not survive in the form of original scores (simply because studios have neither the space nor the interest to keep such material).

With the demise of Filmex, Ken Wlaschin, the former head of the London Film Festival, now directs the American Film Institute International Film Festival, held during April and May 1988 in Century City. Some 90 films from 43 countries were screened. The event was dedicated to screenwriters – surely not because the Writers' Guild of America was on strike? – and special events included a salute to women screenwriters, new writers talking about how to break into Hollywood, and Academy Award-winning screenwriters discussing their work.

In September 1987 the Academy of Motion Picture Arts and Sciences organized a tribute to Fredric March, hosted by Norman Corwin. His widow, Florence Eldridge, was in the audience, although she did not speak. Those who had reminiscences to share included three of March's leading ladies, Martha Scott, Teresa Wright and Shelley Winters, together with the actor Earl Holliman, the writers Jerome Lawrence and Robert E. Lee, and that man-of-many-professions John Houseman. Most spoke of March's political concerns and acting ability, with only Shelley Winters providing a lighter note by describing the actor as 'the sexiest man who ever lived'.

Two other major Academy tributes were to Boris Karloff (in celebration of the 100th anniversary of his birth) and Noël Coward. The latter, held in February 1988, included reminiscences from Roddy McDowall, Lynn Redgrave, Ronald Neame, Michael York and Coward's biographer, Sheridan Morley.

The Noël Coward tribute was part of a major cultural event entitled *UK/LA 88*, which included film screenings, music and dance events, and a poorly received adaptation of *The Mikado*, directed by Jonathan Miller and starring Dudley Moore (both of whom were proud to boast of never having seen a Gilbert and Sullivan operetta). In connection with *UK/LA 88*, the Academy also presented a photographic exhibit on 'The British and the Oscar'.

Despite banners all over town, the festival did not seem to have much of an impact on the average citizen of Los Angeles. The visit by Prince Andrew and 'Fergie', tied in with the Festival, generated a considerable amount of space in local newspapers. It also generated a number of negative comments as to why public money was spent hosting members of the British royal family, along with unpleasant pro-IRA remarks from habitués of the many Irish pubs in Los Angeles. Both of the city's major newspapers tend to adopt a pro-IRA stance, and the visit by the royal couple simply fuelled the continuing support for IRA terrorism, which has unfortunately become the norm in many areas of the United States.

One unusual aspect of the *UK/LA* event was a visit by Martin Jenkins, senior director of recording for the BBC, who directed two radio programmes for the local station KCRW. The productions, heard on 10 and 17 April, were Arthur Miller's *The Crucible* and Eric Bentley's *Are You Now or Have You Ever Been?*, and among the stars participating were Edward Asner, Richard Dreyfuss, Harry Hamlin, Carol Kane, Stacy Keach, James Whitmore, Michael York and Fionnula Flanagan. The last, who is frequently seen on the guest lists of parties at the British Consulate, recently gave an interview with the *L.A. Times* in which she announced support for the IRA and stated that if she lived in Ireland she would be toting a gun.

Gustav von Seyfferitz and Cuester Morris in the recently restored film, The Bat Whispers *(1930).*

The English host of a popular programme on KCRW, Ian Whitcomb, was probably the last attraction at the Variety Arts Center in downtown Los Angeles, which houses a magnificent collection of materials relating to the history of popular entertainment. The organization has been under severe financial pressure, and on Easter Sunday it held what may have been its last event – a dance, at which Ian Whitcomb sang period songs and led a ten-piece orchestra.

Another British-related event was the closing of the most famous of English restaurant-pubs in Los Angeles, the Cock'n'Bull on Sunset Strip. Opened in 1939 by Anglophile Jack Morgan, the Cock'n'Bull was a favourite meeting place for celebrities including Rod Stewart, Somerset Maugham and Richard Burton. It was here that a popular drink known as the Moscow Mule was first concocted. The Cock'n'Bull closed on 22 August 1987.

Of the many organizations which claim to be concerned with film preservation, it is the UCLA Film and Television Archive which has gained an international reputation for its work. The Preservation Supervisor, Robert Gitt, is responsible for an impressive programme which has brought new life to films as varied as *Becky Sharp*, Orson Welles's *Macbeth* and *For Whom the Bell Tolls*.

In the spring of this year, UCLA organized what was billed as the first annual Festival of Preservation. Some nineteen features were screened as well as a number of shorts.

UCLA Film and Television Archive is particularly proud of its effort to restore films to their original status. *My Man Godfrey* had previously been seen only in poor-quality prints but is now available in a pristine 35mm version. The same can be said for *One Hour with You*, *A Star Is Born* (1937), Jean Renoir's *The Southerner* and other features. Roland West's *The Bat Whispers* (1930) is now preserved in a widescreen version. Some early Vitaphone

shorts, including George Burns and Gracie Allen in *Lamb Chops*, are now preserved thanks to UCLA, as are the Spanish-language versions of their comedies made by Laurel and Hardy. The Boys are not dubbed, but are actually speaking in Spanish!

Hollywood is not exactly known for a concern with its past. Most studios had little interest in preserving their early films. All this is changing, thanks in no small part to the efforts of the UCLA Film and Television Archive. Warner Brothers turned over its collection of Vitaphone discs, which enabled many of these early sound shorts to be preserved. MCA/Universal co-operates with UCLA in the preservation of the Paramount features which it owns, and the Turner Organization is very supportive of UCLA's work in preserving MGM, Warner Brothers and RKO features which it controls. There is comedy and tragedy in Hollywood, but there is also dedication and serious attention to business, as the work of the UCLA Film and Television Archive indicates.

The Ten Most Promising Faces of 1988

JAMES CAMERON-WILSON

Ellen Barkin was every film buff's favourite supporting actress. At least, she was a year ago; maybe two. She was a wise talent in some cult movies: *Diner, Tender Mercies*, Jim Jarmusch's *Down By Law*. Then she became a star – and about time, too. The actress has the presence of a Meryl Streep, the sex appeal of a goddess on heat and the daring of a De Niro. Yet Barkin's looks belie her power: the face is frying-pan flat, the eyes are too wide apart, the mouth slopes precipitously, the nose is knob-like. But the body is flawless – and Ellen Barkin knows how to use it.

Born 34 years ago in the Bronx, New York, Barkin trained at the High School of Performing Arts before playing Daniel Stern's ignored spouse in *Diner*. The film was rightly praised and put some promising young men on the map: Steve Guttenberg, Mickey Rourke and Kevin Bacon for starters, but Barkin was obscured in the male camaraderie. She was Timothy Hutton's bitter wife in *Daniel*, and played a young mother in the omnibus picture *Enormous Changes at the Last Minute*, her favourite performance to date. She was Robert Duvall's mutinous daughter in *Tender Mercies*, another strong cameo, and then Robby Benson's prospective girlfriend in *Harry and Son*, directed by Paul Newman.

Lead roles were not forthcoming, but only the best directors were casting her: Barry Levinson in *Diner*, Sidney Lumet in *Daniel*, Bruce Beresford in *Tender Mercies*, Paul Newman in *Harry and Son*.

There was a hiccup with *The Adventures of Buckaroo Banzai Across the 8th Dimension*, but she was sensational as the bottle-swilling heroine, and then there was the well-reviewed but little-seen *Desert Bloom*, with Jon Voight.

Her cameo as a raucous prostitute in Alan Rudolph's *Made in Heaven* was memorable, but the film was not, and she was unbilled – by request.

Then came *The Big Easy*, the film that hurled Ms Barkin into the limelight. As an emotionally aloof DA in New Orleans, she was all women to all men: strong, intelligent, vulnerable,

Ellen Barkin was the saving grace in the otherwise forgettable Siesta.

romantic, stubborn, funny and disturbingly sexy. The film garnered an enormous following and Hollywood woke up. Next, she bared all in *Siesta*, and received solo billing above the title; while the likes of Gabriel Byrne, Isabella Rossellini, Martin Sheen and Jodie Foster played second fiddle. The film was awful, Barkin unforgettable. She'll next be seen in Jerry Schatzberg's *Blood Money*, with Andy Garcia, and opposite Al Pacino in Harold Becker's *Sea of Love*.

Pierce Brosnan as the smooth KGB killer in The Fourth Protocol.

Pierce Brosnan. With his chiselled jaw line, mocking eyebrows and Mediterranean good looks, Pierce Brosnan looks the perfect mate for *Dynasty*'s Alexis Carrington. It is surprising then to learn that Brosnan was born in Ireland and made his film debut as an IRA terrorist in *The Long Good Friday*.

His rise to fame was slow and unglamorous. He was, however, announced as the 'new' James Bond on a number of occasions. At the time he was starring in the American spy series *Remington Steele*, and the show's producers refused to release him from his contract. 'I was looking forward to playing Bond,' the actor confessed, 'and I was deeply frustrated when I couldn't. But it was out of my control.'

Born in Drogheda 35 years ago, Brosnan was deserted by his father at the age of one, lived with his grand-parents for a while, and then left Ire-land to join his mother in London at the age of eleven. There, after studying at the London Drama Centre, he scram-bled to stay in work for years, barely able to pay his milk bill. His first real break came with a leading role in TV's *The Manions of America*, and while he was promoting the series in Los Angeles he landed the pilot for *Remington Steele*, playing the title role. He signed a seven-year contract.

'Unheard of in England,' he admits. 'I didn't want to sign it, but it was that or nothing. I wasn't doing too well financially in London, and I did have a family to support.'

He is married to actress Cassandra Harris (Lisl in *For Your Eyes Only*), and has two stepchildren as well as their own son, Sean. During the seven years and 110 episodes of *Remington Steele*, the actor also managed to star in a dreary thriller, *Nomads*, with Lesley-Anne Down, and won a Golden Globe nomination for his appearance in the BBC's *Nancy Astor*. Since then he has starred opposite Michael Caine in Frederick Forsyth's exciting thriller *The Fourth Protocol*, playing a smooth KGB killer, and then essayed 'an Irish Clint Eastwood' in *Taffin*, the story of one man's fight to stop unscrupulous businessmen from building a chemical plant on the outskirts of a Southern Ireland town. He also headed an international star cast in *Noble House*, the TV mini-series based on the James Clavell bestseller. Next, Brosnan will be seen in the Merchant-Ivory thriller *The Deceivers*, as an English officer who unearths a nefarious cult in 1824 India.

Robert Downey Jr shot to fame in The Pick-Up Artist.

Robert Downey Jr, the son of film-maker Robert Downey, sprang into the public gaze with his dynamic performance of a likeable skirt-chaser in the Warren Beatty-produced film *The Pick-Up Artist*. Molly Ringwald was the star, but Downey hogged the viewer's attention. Although the film was not the stuff of which hits are made, enough of the right people saw it to ensure Downey a workload fit to short-circuit a robot.

Previously best known for his role as Keith Gordon's crazy friend in *Back to School* (which *was* a hit), Downey also appeared in his father's *Greaser's Palace* (in 1972, aged five), John Sayles's *Baby, It's You, Firstborn, Tuff Turf* and *Weird Science*.

Now that he's in demand, Downey is a regular on *Saturday Night Live*, and has appeared in his father's forthcoming *Rented Lips*; the Ernest Thompson-scripted-and-directed *1969* – with Kiefer Sutherland; the Yuppie drug drama *Less Than Zero*; the unfortunate *Johnny Be Good*; and he is due soon in *True Believer*, opposite James Woods.

Perhaps the greatest honour afforded the actor yet is his inclusion on the roster of names picked to read the letters on the soundtrack of *Dear America*, a documentary reliving the hell of Vietnam through a combination of news footage, period music and genuine correspondence from the soldiers to their loved ones. The stars chosen to narrate this impressive document include Robert De Niro, Robin Williams, Kathleen Turner, Michael J. Fox, Ellen Burstyn, Martin Sheen, Tom Berenger, Sean Penn and Downey, their services contributed gratis.

To date, the films of Robert Downey Jr have not amounted to a great deal, but the actor has squeezed some memorable performances from a lot of weak material and sooner or later he is going to hit home base. *Dear America* and *True Believer*, at least, should see to that.

He will be seen next in *Life After Life* with Cybill Shepherd and Ryan O'Neal.

Holly Hunter. For her role as Jane Craig in *Broadcast News* Holly Hunter was voted Best Actress by the New York Film Critics, the Los Angeles Film Critics and the National Board of Review, and was nominated for an

Holly Hunter won an Oscar nomination for her part in Broadcast News.

Oscar. Previously, she had only starred in one movie – *Raising Arizona* – but strolled away with the picture anyway as a Southern policewoman in dire need of motherhood.

When Ms Hunter auditioned for *Broadcast News*, the writer-producer-director James L. Brooks hadn't heard of her. He had considered Sigourney Weaver, Christine Lahti, Judy Davis and Elizabeth McGovern for the role, but none of them had seemed quite right. He had written it with Debra Winger in mind, but *she* had got pregnant. Holly Hunter, to be honest, was a last-ditch hope. But then the magic happened. 'Five lines into the reading,' he said, 'I knew she was the one.' William Hurt, the star of the movie, could not contain himself. 'We've found her, we've found her,' he blurted out, adding: 'and she's an actress – not a movie star!'

Holly Hunter was born in Georgia 30 years ago, the youngest of seven children. Raised on a 250-acre cattle-and-hay farmstead, she was a genuine hayseed tomboy, learning to drive a tractor at a tender age – against her father's wishes.

Holly's acting career sprung up in New York, in a series of plays by Beth Henley, but her film roles were small. There was a bit in an appalling horror opus, *The Burning*, and assorted parts in the TV movies *An Uncommon Love, Intent to Kill* and *A Gathering of Old Men*. On the large screen she was featured in *Swing Shift, Animal Behaviour* and *End of the Line*, none of which made it to British cinemas.

Now, with an Oscar nomination behind her, Holly's stardom is assured. She is not about to take her career lightly.

'I'm spoiled now,' she says, 'and I'm going to stay that way. If that means not working very often, OK. I'll do whatever exciting script comes along – I don't care if it's a big movie or a play on 49th Street.'

She'll next be seen in the film version of Beth Henley's *The Miss Firecracker Contest*, with Mary Steenburgen.

Emily Lloyd making a promising screen debut as the rebellious teenager in Wish You Were Here.

Emily Lloyd. The cheek of it. Fifteen-year-old Emily Lloyd walked out of school and into the lead of a low-budget British classic. Her innocent incantation of 'Up yer bum' in *Wish You Were Here* became something of a catch-phrase in the great tradition of popular British entertainment. Asked by an American reporter if she was *virgo intacta*, young Emily answered with a salutatory 'Up yer bum'. It was all part of the act. Or was it?

The queen of English cheek was soon being courted by Hollywood. She was on Johnny Carson, going bowling with Charlie Sheen and being dated by Matt Dillon. Movie executives were queueing up to meet her; Spielberg dropped in to give his approval; the National Board of Review of America voted her best actress of 1987.

The British film industry, stirred by all this attention, boldly announced two forthcoming films with Our Emily: *Loser Takes All*, also starring Robert Lindsay (fresh from winning a Tony on Broadway); and *Scandal*, with John

Hurt. Neither project showed signs of lift-off when Emily was reputedly given a million dollars to star in Norman Jewison's *In Country* – in California. Before then, the actress teamed up with Peter Falk in Susan Seidelman's *Cookie*, as – of all things – a streetwise Brooklyn urchin. To prepare for the role the English actress had to learn to talk New York, to smoke, drive and to chew gum. Her co-stars included Jerry Lewis and Dianne Wiest.

Brought up in Islington, North London, Emily is the product of a broken home and eight schools. Her parents divorced when she was two, but she has a good relationship with her father, the actor Roger Lloyd Pack.

In her auspicious film début, in *Wish You Were Here*, she played Lynda, the insolent, rebellious teenager modelled on the early Cynthia Payne. *Wish You Were Here* first caught the attention of the French at Cannes, then opened in New York to sensational reviews. A long time later the film opened in London, by which time Emily Lloyd was a celebrity.

To all intents and purposes, Emily Lloyd *is* the film. She holds it together with spit and vim, transforming a grim,

low-budget item into a star vehicle. Emily Lloyd made us believe she was *born* to play Lynda. It will be interesting to see her play something else.

Gary Oldman. For a while, Gary Oldman was known exclusively as the kid who played Sid Vicious. In Alex Cox's brilliant, anarchic *Sid and Nancy*, Oldman was the very embodiment of impropriety, with barely a shred of humanity in sight. So total was the actor's portrayal of the repellent, tragic bass player of the Sex Pistols, that he became associated with that very breed of social vermin. In *Prick Up Your Ears*, the repellent, tragic (but often very funny) story of playwright Joe Orton, Oldman played another social misfit.

'I always look for neuroses in the characters I play,' the actor explained; 'I like the ones who are on the edge.' *Ears* was a less effective slice of docudrama than *Sid and Nancy*, but was more widely praised, at least in Britain; helped, no doubt, by the supportive presence of such respected actors as Vanessa Redgrave, Julie Walters and Wallace Shawn. Anyway, Oldman had two hits in a row on his CV and was a certified star.

America beckoned, and Oldman found himself starring opposite Theresa Russell (as her son) in Nicolas Roeg's *very* strange *Track 29*, and immediately afterwards teamed with Kevin Bacon in *Criminal Law*, as a successful Boston lawyer. After that, the actor returned to England for a supporting role, as Alan Bates's ex-lover in Colin Gregg's *We Think the World of You*, from a screenplay by Hugh Stoddart. Six years earlier the star had made his screen debut, in a smallish part, in the Stoddart-Gregg *Remembrance*, for Channel 4.

The son of a welder from South London, Oldman, born in 1959, left comprehensive school to work in a sports shop in Peckham and dreamed of being a pianist. The film *If . . .* changed his mind.

'I suppose it all started with Malcolm McDowell,' he said. 'I would love to have machine-gunned my teachers. Then I saw McDowell again, in *Raging Moon*, and decided I had to have a go at acting.'

He graduated with a BA honours degree from the Rose Bruford College and plunged himself into regional theatre. He was offered a role in the film *The Bounty*, with Anthony Hopkins, but turned it down to continue his theatre work. In 1985 *Drama* magazine named him and Anthony Hopkins as best actor in a tie-win.

Meg Ryan was a relative latecomer to acting. Journalism had been her forte, or so she thought. Following her parents' divorce when she was fifteen, she shut herself off, but a year later watched a TV movie about marital break-up that opened her eyes – not to her parents' dilemma, but to acting as a career.

Her début was a small role, obtained by her mother, a casting agent, as Candice Bergen's daughter in *Rich and Famous*. A night course in journalism at New York University followed, which she financed by appearing in the daytime soap *As the World Turns*. So effective was her performance that she was retained for two years, during which time her character (Betsy) suffered a kidnapping, a pregnancy, a marriage to a psychotic paraplegic and finally a devastating car smash. In 1984 Ms

Gary Oldman.

Meg Ryan (right) in Promised Land.

Ryan toured Europe, returned to college, and appeared in a shortlived Disney series, *Wildside*. The movies returned with a small role in *Amityville 3-D*, and then the part of Anthony Edwards's wife in *Top Gun*. Suddenly, producers across the US were taking notice.

She won the female lead in the Steven Spielberg-produced *Innerspace*, and turned in a feisty performance as the journalist mismatched with Martin Short, both of whom are in search of her true love, Dennis Quaid, accidentally miniaturized and injected into Short's bloodstream. The film was not the success it should have been, but was a pronounced step up for Miss Ryan and an introduction to Quaid, her real-life beau.

She gave another glitzy performance as a troubled, kooky tearaway in *Promised Land*, produced by Robert Redford, and then teamed up with Quaid in the remake of the 1949 thriller *D.O.A.*

'Brat Pack' favourite, Kiefer Sutherland.

Again, she was irresistible – as an infatuated teenage student – and then starred opposite Sean Connery and Mark Harmon in *The Presidio*, a murder mystery in which she plays Connery's daughter and Harmon's lover, a 'hot vixen, siren' role, she says. She was due to team up with Dustin Hoffman and Tom Cruise in *Rainman*, but the film was delayed, and when Steven Spielberg took over as director he cast newcomer Madeleine Stowe in Ryan's role. In the event, Spielberg also left the production and was replaced by Barry Levinson.

Next, the 27-year-old actress will be seen in Rob Reiner's *Boy Meets Girl*, with Billy Crystal.

Kiefer Sutherland. While Tom Cruise and Michael J. Fox were fighting to prove themselves as actors, Kiefer Sutherland sneaked in the side door as *the* talent to watch. He was simultaneously the critics' darling and a cult favourite among young audiences, equally at home as the snarling villain of *The Lost Boys* and *Stand By Me* and as the gauche hero of *Promised Land* and *The Bay Boy*.

Kiefer left home at fifteen, quitting boarding school in Ottawa to head for Toronto, leaving his mother and a twin sister behind. He rarely saw his father, the actor Donald Sutherland, anyway.

In Toronto Kiefer waited on tables and landed the title role in Daniel Petrie's autobiographical film *The Bay Boy* – opposite Liv Ullmann – for which he was nominated for a Canadian Genie Award. After that – nothing.

'I had no money; I couldn't get a job to save my life,' he said. So he drove to Los Angeles, dossed down on the beach and won the lead in a TV movie, *Trapped in Silence*, as a self-imposed mute. He went up for the boy lead in *The Emerald Forest*, but, according to director John Boorman, although impressive, he was too 'strange and quirky'.

His billing faltered with *Stand By Me*, but as Ace Merrill, the rooster-crowned public menace, he was strikingly memorable. The film was a hit and Kiefer was in demand.

There followed an avalanche of work: Tim in *At Close Range*; an episode of Spielberg's *Amazing Stories* (released for the big screen in an omnibus compilation); the florid vampire of *The Lost Boys*; a psycho in *The Killing Time*; the disillusioned Danny in *Promised Land*; a would-be hippy in Ernest Thompson's *1969*; and a coke fiend in James Bridges's *Bright Lights, Big City*. The fashionable media couldn't get enough of him.

On the set of *The Killing Time*, Kiefer met actress Camelia Kath, fourteen years his senior, and a year later they were married. Now, Kiefer is the proud stepfather of a 12-year-old beauty and is also a brand new dad. He is 22.

The young actor will next be seen in *Young Guns*, an offbeat Brat Pack western, with Charlie Sheen, Lou Diamond Phillips and, as Billy the Kid, Emilio Estevez.

Joanne Whalley. With eyes you could drown in, Joanne Whalley has seduced the British armchair public since the age of twelve. She had announced her intent to act before leaving her Stockport primary school and, together with two mates, created a dreadful act called the Dolly Sisters. At twelve she had an Equity card and was soon appearing regularly on Granada and Yorkshire TV. Her breakthrough was a lead role in Stan Barstow's *A Kind of Loving*, which prompted the actress to move to London in search of stage work. There, she worked at the Royal Court and at the National Theatre, and secured her best TV role to date as Bob Peck's daughter in the BBC's acclaimed *Edge of Darkness*. She returned North, to Liverpool, to co-star in Alan Bleasdale's scabrous, chilling screenplay *No Surrender* (her film debut), and then played Anthony Hopkins's mistress in Mike Newell's stunning *The Good Father*. Joanne's big-screen break came with the female lead – Sorsha – in the epic, high-budget *Willow*, a children's fantasy in which she starred opposite her American husband Val Kilmer. This was followed by another lead, opposite Christopher Lambert, in the French-American *To Kill a Priest*, and then the role of Christine Keeler in *Scandal*, with John Hurt.

As an actress, Joanne Whalley is a rare find, a beauty with talent, a child actress who has made it to adult roles, a British performer who is scoring points in Hollywood. She has all the makings of stardom, and could, just could, pull it off. There are plenty of British actresses emerging in films – Amanda Pays, Natasha Richardson, Janet McTeer, Imogen Stubbs, Amanda Donohoe – but Joanne has my vote. On television, perhaps her most important role was that of Nurse Mills in Dennis Potter's fearsome, award-laden musical series *The Singing Detective*.

Bruce Willis. Whether marrying Demi Moore or dating Don Johnson, Bruce Willis could not keep his name out of the media. He was everybody's favourite bad boy.

In very little time he had leapt from obscurity to snatch the lead in a hit TV series, to release a hit record and to star in a hit film. At the time of going to press he was reportedly demanding – and getting – $5 million per movie. Ironically, he has been wary of interviews, but the publicity keeps coming.

Eleven years ago Willis was a security guard in New Jersey, pulling in $4 an hour. Acting lessons secured him a small part in an off-Broadway play, *Heaven and Earth*, and other plays began trickling his way. There were stretches of unemployment, the occasional commercial and periodic bar work, until Willis began popping up in some decent New York-based movies, including Sidney Lumet's *The Verdict* and *Prince of the City* and the Frank Sinatra potboiler *The First Deadly Sin*.

Things really started hotting up when the actor moved to Los Angeles. He lost the part of Madonna's boyfriend in *Desperately Seeking Susan* but was offered the role of David Addison in a TV sitcom called *Moonlighting*.

'It took me about a week after I'd been offered the part to really make up my mind that I wanted it,' he confessed, expressing his fear of the life

sentence of a TV contract. He accepted the part and the series went through the roof.

Unlike other TV stars with such ambitions, Willis also made a success of his recording career. His first album, *The Return of Bruno*, spawned two hit singles: *Respect Yourself* and *Under the Boardwalk*.

Willis's first starring role in a film, *Blind Date*, was likewise a hit, in which he played a career-muzzled klutz besieged by a *femme fatale* (Kim Basinger). The director was Blake Edwards, who next cast Willis as Tom Mix in *Sunset*, with James Garner as Wyatt Earp. Neither thriller nor comedy, the film suffered disastrously at the hands of the critics and public alike, so Willis opted for all-action on his next enterprise, *Die Hard*. In this 'explosive' thriller Willis plays a tough New York cop (opposed to a *weak* New York cop), in the first of what is hoped will be a series. *Die Hard* will be followed by a part in Norman Jewison's *In Country*.

Joanne Whalley in the children's epic fantasy Willow.

TV superstar Bruce Willis played Tom Mix in Sunset.

A Survey of
the Australian Year

JAMES CAMERON-WILSON

Without a Paul Hogan or Mel Gibson in sight, the Australian film industry suffered badly in the late '87–early '88 drought. While Gibson was raking in the bucks overseas with *Lethal Weapon* and Hogan preparing '*Crocodile*' *Dundee II*, not a single home-grown production made the Australian top ten.

Overseas, the picture was equally bleak. In Britain, *Slate, Wyn and Me*, *The Good Wife* and *Bliss* played fleetingly, in spite of the Australian Oscars heaped on the last named. A quirky black comedy that looked as if it had been directed by Paul Cox in a bad mood, *Bliss* won excellent reviews all over the world but had a mixed reception in Britain. Indeed, the film is brimful of mixed blessings. It is slow, meandering and ponderous, but it is also frantically original, occasionally inspired and disturbingly memorable. Ultimately, though, it is self-indulgent to a fault, and was a surprising choice for Best Film at the 1985 Australian Film Institute Awards.

The story of a successful, happily-married advertising executive (Barry Otto) who dies, is revived and then sees his life for what it really is, *Bliss* also won accolades for Best Director (Ray Lawrence) and for Best Screen Adaptation (Lawrence and Peter Carey, from the latter's novel). It just shows what a sorry state the Australian film industry is in.

The Good Wife, known as *The Umbrella Woman* down under, was no better. In spite of some exceptional photography and a well-propelled climax, there was a lot of narrative flab. With the potential for being a stirring *menage à trois* drama, the film dragged its feet through the period (1939) detail and only picked up when Sam Neill did his impression of an antipodean Rhett

Butler. Nevertheless, Rachel Ward – our lady from Chipping Norton – won a prize for Best Actress at the Tokyo Film Festival, while her husband (in both the film and real life), Bryan Brown, was nominated for an Australian Oscar. Young Steven Vidler, who played the good wife's infatuated brother-in-law, was also nominated, in the supporting category. Sam Neill has since landed the juiciest role of the year: playing Michael Chamberlain to Meryl Streep's Lindy in *Evil Angels*, directed by Fred Schepisi.

Slate, Wyn and Me was better, but not much. Of course, anything with Sigrid Thornton in it can't be *all* bad. She played a fiery schoolmistress kidnapped by two muddled youths (Simon Burke, Martin Sacks) after she has witnessed them kill a policeman. Far from being their subservient hostage she turns them against each other as they fall hopelessly under her hot-headed charm. The Outback scenery was beautifully caught, as were the undoubted attractions of Ms Thornton, making up for the asinine behaviour of the brothers Wyn and Slate. Again, the film was a mixed bag, showing promise, but decidedly ponderous in its direction.

All the good directors were abroad making plenty of money. George Miller, of *Mad Max* fame, directed *The Witches of Eastwick*, and watched it make more money than either *Lethal Weapon* or *Dirty Dancing*. In Australia the film was equally successful, grossing $A2,073,000 from 83 screens. Fred Schepisi (*The Chant of Jimmie Blacksmith*) likewise had a success with *Roxanne*, which won Steve Martin a handful of awards for his perfectly judged portrayal of a modern Cyrano de Bergèrac in love with Daryl Hannah.

Beautiful to look at, human and very, very funny, *Roxanne* was probably the best comedy of the year. It was also a financial success.

Graeme Clifford, Australian editor turned director (with *Frances*, 1982), tackled two foreign productions: *Gleaming the Cube* for 20th Century-Fox and *Water Dance*, for New World, about long-distance female swimmers.

Less felicitous were the foreign efforts of directors Bruce Beresford, Russell Mulcahy and Carl Schultz. Beresford, very much in demand after *Crimes of the Heart*, invested enormous amounts of energy and time preparing for his next project, the big-budget sci-fi movie *Total Recall*. This was to be Dino De Laurentiis's first production for his Australian arm, De Laurentiis Entertainment Ltd (DEL), and at various stages both Dennis Quaid and Patrick Swayze were tipped to star. However, when the budget came in at $A28 million, the film was taken under the wing of the American-based De Laurentiis Entertainment Group, that sort of money being far more than DEL could afford. Then DEG collapsed, thanks to such resounding American turkeys as *The Million Dollar Mystery* and *King Kong Lives*, and with DEG went *Total Recall*. But Beresford, in as much demand as ever, was snatched up by Warner Brothers to direct Tom Selleck in *Her Alibi*.

Russell Mulcahy, the flashy director of *Razorback* and *Highlander*, was to direct Sylvester Stallone in *Rambo III*, but thanks to an unending series of delays disappeared from the project. When the film *did* go – in August, 1987 – camera operator Peter MacDonald was in control. However, there is now talk of a sequel to *Highlander*.

Carl Schultz, who won the Australian

Real-life husband and wife Rachel Ward and Bryan Brown as screen couple the Hills, in Entertainment's The Good Wife. *Sam Neill (right) plays the dashing city boy who comes between them.*

Oscar in 1983 for his direction of *Careful, He Might Hear You*, made his first American film, *The Seventh Sign*. Starring Demi Moore and Michael Biehn, it was an uneven affair about the coming of the apocalypse, provoked by Ms Moore giving birth to a child without a soul. The film, intended to frighten the socks off us, was about as scary as a snooker match. The American critics were not kind.

Back home, Schultz had more luck with the modest romantic comedy *Travelling North*, a tender, captivating tale of a peppery old engineer who returns to the subtropical Far North with his mistress. The film was a huge critical success, winning its star, Leo McKern, best actor nods from the Montreal and Houston Film Festivals and the Australian Film Institute. It was also cited best film by the Sydney Film Critics' Circle and won an Australian Oscar for best adapted screenplay,

while English-born Julia Blake – as Leo's lady-love – received a nomination as Best Actress. *Travelling North*, adapted by David Williamson from his own play, was also a well-deserved popular triumph.

Without doubt, however, the film of the year was John Duigan's *The Year My Voice Broke*, sweeping up all the major 1987 awards (best film, direction, screenplay, etc.). A low-budget tale of young love in a backwater town in the early 'sixties, the film had no stars, no special effects and no commercial prospects. It was, however, a good film which was not afraid to be Australian and was a critical and popular success.

As the future of government assistance to cinema became more and more uncertain, producers deserted the small-scale, high-quality product of yesteryear (*Caddie*, *The Devil's Playground*) and concentrated on more obviously commercial material.

One good idea was to re-team the director (Gillian Armstrong) and star (Judy Davis) of *My Brilliant Career*. The result, *High Tide*, would surely be a box office winner. Not so: this tale of

a young mother who meets up with the daughter she abandoned ten years previously was unfortunately savaged by certain critics, who put the public off. It would appear, then, that more Australian cinemagoers read newspapers than their British and American counterparts.

Other disappointments of 1987 were Simon Wincer's epic *The Lighthorsemen*, possibly the most expensive Australian film ever made, and the feature-length Barry Humphries AIDS commercial, *Les Patterson Saves the World*. The former was just not good enough – although the climactic charge will be remembered – while the latter proved too distasteful even for Outback ockers. *The Lighthorsemen* made money, but nowhere near enough to justify its $A10½ million budget. Barry Humphries, it seems, is more popular in Blighty.

Other commercial projects – the aforementioned *Slate, Wyn and Me*, the comedy-thriller *Running From the Guns*, horror item *Frenchman's Farm* and the expensive *Time Guardian* – flopped at the box office, which all goes to show that Australian audiences are not interested in local facsimiles of American genres. Hollywood, with all its money and experience, can do these things so much better.

True to form, it was Hollywood that filled the cinemas in 1987. *Beverly Hills Cop II*, *Platoon* and *Lethal Weapon* were all predictable smash-hits. *Children of a Lesser God*, less predictably, did substantial business (which proves that Australian cinemagoers are more discerning than . . . etc.), as did *The Witches of Eastwick*, *The Color of Money*, *La Bamba*, *The Untouchables* and *Mannequin*.

The Lighthorsemen was the local winner, and became the 330th biggest money-making film in Australian history (for the record, *'Crocodile' Dundee* is the all-time champ).

At the time of going to press *Return to Snowy River Part II* was going great guns, but could not shake *Three Men and a Baby* from the top spot. Nevertheless, in its third week it had taken more money than *The Lighthorsemen* made in a year. Other local 'performers' of 1988 included the Steve Jodrell-directed *Shame*, the story of the impact of a rape on a small isolated town, and Mike Thornhill's *The Everlasting Secret Family*, about the infrastructure of an

Sigrid Thornton as the kidnapped teacher Blanche in Palace's Slate, Wyn and Me.

arcane society. Neither film broke any records, but the fact that they were making *any* money is worth recording. *Warm Nights on a Slow-Moving Train* opened even better, thanks, no doubt, to some excellent reviews and to the fact that Wendy Hughes won the best actress prize at the Rio de Janeiro Film Festival. As always the actress was excellent, this time playing an upmarket prostitute who plies her trade on the overnight train between Sydney and Melbourne. Beautifully photographed, intelligently written and sensitively made, this was only the second film by its director, Bob Ellis, following the low-budget *Unfinished Business*. This time he made sure he had an excellent (though expensive) cast, which included Norman Kaye (from *Man of Flowers*), Rod Zuanic, Lewis Fitzgerald, Chris Haywood and the ubiquitous Colin Friels (also seen in *High Tide*).

Friels popped up again, and was nominated for an 'Ozcar', for his role in

the 1987 *Ground Zero*, as a photographer investigating the suspicious death of his father. In spite of favourable reviews and a good cast (Jack Thompson and Donald Pleasence also starred), the public was (presumably) put off by the film's nuclear theme. Nevertheless, it was an elegant thriller with an articulate and pertinent voice.

The other real quality feature of 1987 was Paul Cox's *Vincent – the Life and Death of Vincent Van Gogh*. Part documentary, part dramatization, the film was a moving, intelligent tribute to the great Dutch painter, with whom Cox has a birthplace in common. The director constructed his picture using letters, read off-camera by John Hurt, written by Van Gogh to his brother Theo, and filling the screen with images of Holland: the trees, fields, plants, sunflowers and, of course, the paintings of the master himself. In documentary terms, the film was a popular success with the public.

Although no homegrown production did phenomenal business in 1987, there are some crumbs of optimism to be found. The tax incentive scheme of yore (that government contrivance that

sent shivers into the very marrow of the treasury), which included a 133 per cent tax write-off, was to be abolished on the last day of June 1988. Investors cried shy and film production all but ground to a halt. But the rumours were good: word had it that from 1 July a government-backed film finance corporation would handle an investment fund of \$A75–120 million. However, this is still possum-feed compared to the annual \$A180 million-worth of production generated under the previous arrangement. Still, with current levels of investment put at a paltry \$A39 million, the new scheme should wake up a few wallets. We can only hope that producers will recognize the *commerical* need for genuine Australian films, rather than pale imitations of American gloss and dross – and that includes the importation of foreign stars.

Lately, we've seen American singer Laura Branigan in the catastrophic comedy *Backstage*, Dee Wallace Stone (*Critters*) in George Miller's *Bushfire Moon*, Warren Mitchell in Ted Robinson's *Kokoda Crescent* (a.k.a. *Mission Impractical*), Tom Conti in Robinson's *Two Brothers Running*, the American actor Jeff Fahey in *Outback*, Brian Dennehy in *The Return to Snowy River Part II*, Carrie Fisher and Dean Stockwell in *The Time Guardian* and, of course, Meryl Streep in *Evil Angels*, an act of superstar casting that caused a rumpus with Australian Equity and delayed the film's production by weeks.

But the British actor Shane Briant took the biscuit. He appeared in no less than *five* Australian features, namely *Grievous Bodily Harm*, *Cassandra*, *The Lighthorsemen*, *Out of the Body* and *Outback*.

The busiest local actor, as always, was Chris Haywood, who clocked up five Australian features, the Anglo-Yugoslav *Manifesto* and a New Zealand picture, *The Navigator* (in between TV work). The other most active actors around were Bruno Lawrence, Arthur Dignam, Bill Hunter, Gary Sweet and John Waters.

Besides the healthy, upwardly mobile business of *The Return to Snowy River Part II* (a crazy title, incidentally), the future should light up with such films as Mark Joffe's exciting Sydney-set crime thriller *Grievous Bodily Harm*, with Colin Friels and John Waters; John Laing's wry political thriller *Body Politic*; the film version of David Williamson's excellent play *Emerald City*; the Western Australian *Boundaries of the Heart*, with Wendy Hughes and John Hargreaves; the $A8 million *Honor Bright*, New World Pictures' first Australian production with, one hopes, many more to come; *Evil Angels*, the controversial, true story of Lindy Chamberlain and that dingo; and, for a laugh, Philippe Mora's *Howling III – The Marsupials*, starring Barry Otto, with Barry Humphries in a supporting role.

Mora, better known for his Australian films *Mad Dog Morgan* and *Death of a Soldier* than for such American schlock as *The Beast Within* and *A Breed Apart*, returned to the States to take on the esteemed duty of directing the film of Whitley Strieber's controversial, autobiographical bestseller *Communion*. The story of the author's meetings with unknown visitors from an alternative dimension made compulsive reading and could be a sensational film. Christopher Walken stars.

Another Antipodean who headed Stateside was John Duigan, fresh from the success of *The Year My Voice Broke*. Also known for his direction of *The*

Winter of Our Dreams and *Far East*, the film-maker made his American début with *Romero*, shot in Mexico with Raul Julia and Richard Jordan heading the cast. Five days earlier, Phillip Noyce (*Newsfront*, *Heatwave*) had started filming in Texas, directing Tim Matheson and Rutger Hauer in the dubiously-named *Blind Fury*.

For the record, that divinely moulded, silent spokesman for the Australian way, Mel Gibson, was back in the US filming a Warren Beatty reject, *Tequila Sunrise*, an epic production co-starring Kurt Russell, Michelle Pfeiffer and Raul Julia. Plans to team up with Judy Davis down under in Gillian Armstrong's *Clean Straw for Nothing* appear to have evaporated.

This leaves *'Crocodile' Dundee II*. Although its critical reception was decidedly mixed, in June '88 the continuing adventures of the amiable Ocker opened to sensational business in the United States, grossing $29,215,731 in only six days. In Australia the film dismantled every record going. In the same six days Mick Dundee picked up $3,207,600 at 103 cinemas. There's nothing like an old friend to bail you out of trouble.

Australia's Twenty Top-grossing Films

1. *'Crocodile' Dundee*
2. *The Man from Snowy River*
3. *Gallipoli*
4. *Mad Max II*
5. *Phar Lap*
6. *Mad Max – Beyond Thunderdrome*
7. *Mad Max*
8. *Picnic at Hanging Rock*
9. *Alvin Purple*
10. *Breaker Morant*
11. *Puberty Blues*
12. *Malcolm*
13. *We of the Never Never*
14. *My Brilliant Career*
15. *Storm Boy*
16. *Caddie*
17. *They're a Weird Mob*
18. *The Year of Living Dangerously*
19. *The Hostage*
20. *Careful, He Might Hear You*

Next year's list will, of course, include *'Crocodile' Dundee II* and *The Return to Snowy River Part II*.

Leo McKern gives a marvellous performance in Recorded Releasing's Travelling North.

TV Feature Films of the Year

In this section you will find all the made-for-television movies shown on BBC1 and BBC2, ITV and Channel 4 during the period covered by this edition of *Film Review*. The date given in brackets after each title is the year the movie was made.

Films reviewed in previous editions of *Film Review* are listed at the end of the feature, with dates of both the repeat and the original showings together with the edition of *Film Review* in which the detailed note was included.

And I Alone Survived (1978). The truth-based story of a girl who of all the passengers of a crashed airplane emerges alive to struggle across the inhospitable Sierra Nevada mountains to safety. Blair Brown, Vera Miles, David Ackroyd. Dir: W.A. Graham. Screenplay: Lane Slate. BBC1, 9 March 1988.

Angel on my Shoulder (1980). A TV re-make of the 1946 cinema feature, with Peter Strauss in the old Paul Muni role of the murderer sent back to earth by Satan to do some devil's work. Barbara Hershey, Janis Paige. Dir: John Berry. Screenplay: George Kirgo; based on the original script by Roland Kibbee and Harry Segal. Channel 4, 13 June 1988.

Arthur's Hallowed Ground (1983). Old-time comic Jimmy Jewell giving a superb, heartwarming performance in a lovely little film about a cricket groundsman beset by problems. Dir: Freddy Young. Screenplay: Peter Gibbs. Channel 4, 27 August 1987.

Attack on Fear (1984). A true story feature about a couple of investigative hacks who delve into nasty rumours about a local cult. Paul Michael Glaser, Linda Kelsey etc. Dir: Mel Damski. Screenplay: T.S. Cook. BBC2, 20 June 1988.

Badge of the Assassin (1985). Based-on-fact feature about the murder of two New York cops by Black Liberation terrorists and the sequel two years later. Tense and fascinating. James Woods, Yaphet Kotto etc. Dir: Mel Damski. Screenplay: Lawrence Roman; based on the book by R.K. Tannenbaum. ITV, 11 April 1988.

Because He's My Friend (1978). Another good, sensitively directed and acted movie from down under, this time about the trials of parents with a retarded youngster. Karen Black, Keir Dullea, Jack Thompson. Dir: Ralph Nelson. Screenplay: Peter Schreck. BBC1, 27 April 1988.

Between Friends (1983). Elizabeth Taylor and Carol Burnett, both recently divorced and finding adjustment not all that easy and a testing period for their friendship. Some very nice acting. Dir: Lou Antonio. Screenplay: Jonathan Estrin and Shelley List; based on the book *Nobody Makes Me Cry* by the latter. BBC2, 16 May 1988.

Beyond the Bermuda Triangle – formerly **Beyond This Place There Be Dragons** (1975). Routine treatment of a splendidly intriguing subject: vanishing ships, aeroplanes and people in this mysterious area of the Caribbean. Fred MacMurray, Donna Mills. Dir: William Graham. Screenplay: Charles McDaniel. ITV, 12 September 1987.

Birds of Prey (1973). Though made for American TV, this pretty good aerial thriller was first shown in the UK as a cinema film (released 14 October 1973) and was fully reviewed as such in the 1973–4 *Film Review*. ITV, 17 December 1987.

Bitter Harvest (1981). Rather long-drawn-out social-theme story of a farmer fighting red tape when his cattle are stricken by a mysterious illness. Derived from frightening fact. Art Carney, Ron Howard. Dir: Roger Young. Screenplay: Richard Friedenberg; from the book by Frederic and Sandra Halbert. Channel 4, 6 June 1988.

Bogie (1979). Sadly inadequate bio-pic about Bogart, even if it does have its moments of interest. Kevin O'Connor plays the title role; also Kathryn Harrold (Bacall) and numerous look-alikes. Dir: Vincent Sherman. Screenplay: Daniel Taradash; based on Joe Hyams's book *Bogie*. BBC1, 2 December 1987.

Border (1987). The dangerous crossing to freedom from Czechoslovakia, attempted in 1952 by some brave, bedevilled citizens, provides the plot for an exciting historical thriller. Shaun Scott, Catherine Schell and Edita Brychta are among those heading a quite enormous cast. Dir: Misha Williams. Screenplay: Tim Rose Price; based on a story by Jiri Stanislav. BBC2, 7 February 1988.

Born of Fire (1987). Professional flautist Peter Firth is nearly driven nuts by mysterious music coming from . . . well, somewhere 'out there'. Taking a female astrologer's advice, he goes to Turkey to face the devil's music. Very odd and eerie. Stefan Kalipha, Suzan Crowley etc. Dir: Jamil Dehlavi. Screenplay: Raficq Abdulla. Channel 4, 14 April 1988.

The Burning Bed (1984). Farrah Fawcett excellent as the battered wife who is driven by her brute of a husband to take the wrong way out of her dilemma. Pretty grim watching. Paul Le Mat. Dir: Robert Greenwald. Screenplay: Rose Leiman Goldemberg. ITV, 12 March 1988.

Burning Patience (1983). Chilean TV film about the romance of the village postman and a waitress at the local bar and how it is helped along by a Chilean poet-statesman. Pretty slow to unwind but finally rewarding. Oscar Castro, Roberta Parado etc. Dir: Antonio Skarmeta. Screenplay: Ulla Zieman. Channel 4, 2 July 1987.

Callie and Son (1981). Two-part super-soap about the upwardly mobile career of a determined young lady (Lindsay Wagner) from the wrong side of the social tracks. If you can stomach *Dallas* and all those other US familiars you'll probably enjoy the struggle. Also Jameson Parker, Dabney Coleman etc. Dir: Waris Hussein. Screenplay: Thomas Thompson. BBC1, 3 and 4 September 1987.

Camille (1984). After numerous silent and sound large-screen movies based on the Dumas classic, TV tries to go one better and certainly doesn't skimp on the cost of the players, with Ben Kingsley, John Gielgud, Billie Whitelaw, Denholm Elliott, Colin Firth, Ronald Pickup and Greta Scacchi (in the title role). You must decide if the old warhorse was worth dragging out of the stable again. Dir: Desmond Davis. Screenplay: Blanche Hanalig. Channel 4, 26 January 1988.

Cannon (1971). The original pilot feature which was followed by the successful series about the fat and food-loving private eye, played by William Conrad. Here he is investigating an old pal's death and uncovering small-town corruption. Like the series, routine but very watchable. Also Vera Miles, Barry Sullivan, Keenan Wynn and J.D. Cannon etc. Dir: George McCowan. Screenplay: Edward Hume. BBC1, 5 March 1988.

Carpool. (1983). Wacky comedy, which increases pace and possibility as it progresses, about four car-sharing commuters who suddenly find themselves in possession of a million dollars dropped off the back of a van (actually an armoured car). Harvey Korman. Peter Scolari, Ernest Borgnine etc. Dir: E.W. Swackhamer. Screenplay: Stanley and Carole Cherry. ITV, 18 August 1987.

The Cartier Affair (1984). Weak soap-opera send-up which would be pretty diabolical if it weren't for the fun to be had from seeing Joan Collins parodying herself and the no-holds-barred performances by baddies Telly Savalas and Ed Lauter. Dir: Rod Holcomb. Screenplay: Brad Buckner and Eugenie Ross Leming. ITV, 1 February 1988.

Casebusters (1986). Normally a maker of bloodbath thrillers, Wes Craven took time off to do this 'family fare' Disney film about two teenage amateur crime investigators amusingly assisted by their dear old grandfather. Virginia Keehne, Noah Hathaway and Pat Hingle etc. Dir: Wes Craven. Screenplay: G.A. Bloom and D.P. Roos. ITV, 20 March 1988.

A Case of Deadly Force (1986). Well crafted and played crime and court thriller about a black woman trying to clear the name of her husband, who was gunned down by the cops. Was it self-defence or murder? Richard Crenna, John Shea, Dylan Baker etc. Dir: Michael Miller. Screenplay: Dennis Nemac. BBC1, 25 March 1988.

A Case of Libel (1983). Reconstruction of the historical trial in which famous US war correspondent Quentin Reynolds was sued for libel over a book review. Absorbing stuff, with Gordon Pinsent as Reynolds and Edward Asner as counsel Louis Nizer. Dir: Eric Till. Screenplay: Henry Denker. Channel 4, 23 May 1988.

Child's Cry (1985). Sincere addition to the topical subject of child abuse, with Lindsay Wagner as the worried social worker and Peter Coyote as the suspect parent. Dir: Gilbert Cates. Screenplay: Jon B. Bontels Jr. Channel 4, 9 May 1988.

China Hand (1987). David Soul having a pretty tough time in a rollicking series of adventures as he searches for lost gold in the Orient, while the cops and the crooks think he's already got it. Fast fun stuff. David Hemmings, Mike Preston etc. Dir: Jerry London. Screenplay: R.A. Simmons. ITV, 26 April 1988.

Christmas Eve (1986). An updated variation on the old Scrooge story with a New York big-business background. Some pleasant performances by a vintage cast including Loretta Young and Trevor Howard. Dir: Stuart Cooper. Screenplay: Blanche Hanalis. ITV, 24 December 1987.

The Christmas Gift (1986). Odd little seasonal film about Kris Kringle (alias Father Christmas) in a small Colorado town which still believes in him. John Denver, Jane Kaczmarek. Dir: Michael Pressman. Screenplay: Jeb Rosebrook and Christopher Grabenstein. ITV, 23 December 1987.

Crazy Like a Fox – The Movie (1986). Jack Warden, as American private eye Harry Fox, finds his London holiday no fun when Scotland Yard accuses him of murdering a much-respected member of the British aristocracy. A neatly assembled whodunit. John Rubinstein, Penny Peyser etc. Dir: Paul Krasny. Screenplay: George Schenk and Frank Cardea. ITV, 29 August 1987.

Crazy Times (1981). Astonishingly, it was apparently expected that this mediocre stuff about warring youngsters in 1955 New York would pave the way for a series about them. Ray Liotta, David Caruso etc. Dir: Lee Philips. Screenplay: George Reeves. BBC1, 26 February 1988.

Crime of Innocence (1985). Dramatically overdone story

about two silly youngsters sent to jail by a judge who has his own stern ideas about justice. Was he right or wrong? Andy Griffith, Ralph Waite, Shawnee Smith. Dir: Michael Miller. No writing credit. BBC1, 16 April 1988.

Criminal Conversation (1980). Irish film about an – not *the* – Irish problem: infidelity in a country which refuses to acknowledge divorce. Emmet Bergin, Deirdre Donnelly, Peter Caffrey and Leslie Lalor as the quartet revealing the truth beneath the shining surface. Dir: Kieran Hickey. Screenplay: Hickey with Philip Davison. Channel 4, 20 September 1987.

Crisis at Central High (1981). Overlong but interesting and finely acted story of the enforced integration at an American Girls' High School in the 'fifties. Based on the writer's experiences. Joanne Woodward, Charles Durning etc. Dir: Lamont Johnson. Screenplay: Richard Levinson and William Link; based on the book by Elizabeth P. Huckaby. Channel 4, 29 March 1988.

The Day the Bubble Burst (1982). Rather dull feature about an exciting historical event: the great US stock market crash of 1929, more relevant since the crash of '87. Richard Crenna, Robert Vaughn. Dir: Joseph Hardy. Screenplay: Stanley Greenberg; based on a book by Gordon Thomas and Max Morgan-Witts. Channel 4, 5 September 1987.

Dead Lucky (1987). Not all pools winners find the cash brings happiness and in the case of Martin Urban (Nicholas Farrell) it brings something *very* different. A well-crafted thriller. Also Philip Davis, Harriet Bagnall etc. Dir: Barbara Rennie, who also adapted the Ruth Rendell novel *Lake of Darkness*. BBC2, 17 January 1988.

A Deadly Business (1986). The always good Alan Arkin as a gangster whose conscience gets the better of him so that he turns FBI informer – all apparently based on fact. Worth seeing, with Armand Assante as a wonderful 'nasty'. Dir: John Korty. Screenplay: Al Ramus. BBC2, 9 May 1988.

The Deadly Dream (1971). Swedish actor turned TV director (in America) Alf Kjellin must have had an off-day when he made this weird but not wonderful science-fiction story of a scientist trying to ensure all children are born with a uniform mental ability. Lloyd Bridges, Janet Leigh, Leif Erickson. Dir: Kjellin. Screenplay: Barry Oringer. ITV, 5 September 1987.

Dead Man on the Run (1975). Government agent Peter Graves is given a Mission Incredible, if not Impossible, when he is sent to New Orleans (a fascinating background) to try to solve the killing of his predecessor. Murders come thick and heavy before 'whodunit' becomes 'hedidit' and Peter can get back to his series success. Also Katherine Justice, Pernell Roberts etc. Dir: Bruce Bilson. Screenplay: Ken Pettus. ITV, 10 October 1987.

A Death of Innocence (1971). With such veterans as Shelley Winters, Arthur Kennedy and Ann Sothern pulling out most of the stops, and Tisha Sterling (*could* she have done it?) not too hesitant either, this story of a loyal

suburban mum beginning to doubt her daughter in the latter's trial for murder makes watchable entertainment. Dir: John Wendkos. Screenplay: Joseph Stafano. ITV, 24 February 1988.

The Death of Ocean View Park (1980). Competent, routine addition to the 'disaster' cycle: this time something like a typhoon hits an amusement park and sparks off fire and fear. Mike Connors, Martin Landau etc. Dir: E.W. Swackhamer. Screenplay: J. Furia Jr and B. Oringer. ITV, 28 July 1987.

Death Sentence (1974). How would you feel if you were serving on a jury and came to realize that the man in the dock was innocent and that it was your husband, or wife, that should be there? That's the dilemma faced by Cloris Leachman in this thriller, which has good performances by her, Laurence Luckinbill and Nick Nolte. Dir: E.W. Swackhamer. Screenplay: John Neufeld; based on the novel by Eric Roman. ITV, 3 October 1987.

The Desperate Miles (1975). Somewhat dreary story about another Vietnam veteran, this time a wheelchair case who wheels himself 130 miles to prove his independence – and test the audience's stamina. Tony Musante, Joanna Pettet, Jeanette Nolan. Dir: Dan Haller. Screenplay: Chris Wicking. ITV, 18 May 1988.

The Disappearance of Flight 412 (1975). Chasing a supposed UFO, two aeroplanes vanish. Suspicious US Air Force officer Glenn Ford investigates . . . A routine suspense thriller. Also Bradford Dillman, Guy Stockwell and David Soul etc. Dir: Jud Taylor. Screenplay: George Simpson and Neal Burger. ITV, 6 September 1987.

Disaster on the Coastliner (1979). Commendably well-made old-style thriller about two express trains approaching each other on the same track . . . Will they? Won't they? Whew! Those facing death include Raymond Burr, Lloyd Bridges, Yvette Mimieux and William Shatner. Dir: Richard C. Sarafian. Screenplay: David Ambrose. ITV, 24 November 1987.

Dixie: Changing Habits (1983). Farcical tale about a New Orleans brothel keeper (Suzanne Pleshette) sent to a convent for a three-month rehabilitation course. It's all made worthwhile by Cloris Leachman's mother superior. Dir: George Englund. Screenplay: John Considine. BBC1, 23 March 1988.

Double Agent (1987). A Disney 'family film': a spy spoof with all the usual dependable ingredients in the way of slapstick fun. A quiet-living vet is suddenly forced to step into the shoes of his secret agent twin . . . and doesn't find them a very good fit. Michael McKean, Lloyd Bochner, Susan Walden. Dir: Mike Vejar. Screenplay: Bill Walsh and Don DaGradi; based on a novel by Ben Stahl. ITV, 21 February (Part 1) and 28 February (Part 2) 1988.

Earth II (1971). Very expensive sci-fi feature about friction on an international space station when China launches a nuclear bomb at the Soviet Union. A good basic idea, spoilt by lacklustre writing. Gary Lockwood, Tony Franciosa, Lew Ayres, Scott Hylands. Dir: Tom Gries. Screenplay: William R. Woodfield and Alan Balter. ITV, 26 January 1988.

Eleanor, First Lady of the World (1982). Jean Stapleton gives a good performance in a careful bio-pic about the later life of Eleanor Roosevelt. Dir: John Erman. Screenplay: Caryl Ledner and Cynthia Mandelberg. Channel 4, 4 August 1987.

Etude in Black (1972). Peter Falk as TV's familiar Lieutenant Columbo sorting out the murder suspects in Hollywood musical circles. The starry cast includes Myrna Loy, John Cassavetes, Anjanette Comer, Blythe Danner etc. Dir: Nick Colosanto. Screenplay: Steven Boshco. ITV, 21 November 1987.

Experience Preferred – But Not Essential (1982). Gently amusing, soundly made British comedy with nothing very much happening, but most of it funny. It follows the affairs of the members of the staff in a Welsh seaside hotel; more especially the romance of the student waitress and the chef. Elizabeth Edmonds, Sue Wallace, Ron Bain etc. Dir: Peter Duffell. Screenplay: June Roberts. Channel 4, 30 July 1987.

The Face of Fear (1971). Familiar thriller about a woman (Elizabeth Ashley) who pays a killer to kill her and then changes her mind – but the killer doesn't take no for an answer. Jack Warden, Ricardo Montalban. Dir: George McCowan. Screenplay: Edward Hume. ITV, 20 June 1988.

The Fifth Missile (1986). Suspense deep down when a US submarine involved in a dubious exercise looks like letting go of her atomic arsenal. It is uncomfortably realistic and possible. Could it really happen like this? Good performances by the three gold-capped members of the crew: David Soul, Robert Conrad and Sam Waterston. Dir: Larry Peerce. Screenplay: Eric Bercovici. ITV, 4 October 1987.

The First Kangaroos (1987). This story about Rugby League in general, and one of its foremost founder players – Albert Goldthorpe (Dennis Waterman) – in particular, and his legendary game against the first Australian XV visitors, is a must for all rugby fans; enjoyable for non-fans too. Also Chris Haywood, Dominic Sweeney etc. Dir: Frank Cvitanovich. Screenplay: Nigel Williams. Channel 4, 21 April 1988.

Florence Nightingale (1985). Let's face it, the Lady with the Lamp never looked as lovely as Jaclyn (*Charlie's Angels*) Smith who took her role in this sumptuous bio-pic. The excellent star-studded cast includes Claire Bloom, Jeremy Brett, Timothy Dalton etc. Solidly entertaining. Dir: Daryl Duke. Screenplay: Ivan Moffat and Rose Goldenberg. ITV, 8 May 1988.

Found Money (1983). Nice to see veterans Dick Van Dyke and Sid Cesar together in a mildly amusing story about a retired bank teller who sets himself up as a sort of Robin Hood, diverting the boss's cash to the needy until a suspicious bank calls in the cops. Dir: Bill Persky. Screenplay: Michael and Richard Sanders. BBC1, 26 March 1988.

A Friend In Deed (1975). Scruffy-looking sleuth Columbo (Peter Falk) smashing a carefully concocted alibi and pinning the killing on the culprit. Apparently this is the only cinema or TV feature ever directed by Falk's pal Ben Gazzara. Screenplay: Peter S. Fischer. ITV, 3 April 1988.

Friendly Fire (1979). Then, as now, the Vietnam war and its ramifications filled a lot of American large- and small-screen time; this is a small-screen feature about parents investigating their son's death, caused officially by 'friendly fire' and unofficially by something else. Carol Burnett, Ned Beatty, Sam Waterston etc. Dir: David Greene. Screenplay: Fay Kamin; based on a book by C.D. Bryan. BBC1, 11 September 1987.

The Fun Seekers (1988). The Comic Strip company – whose product is variable to say the least – goes to Ibiza to manufacture the fun, with numerous echoes of the classic 'Carry On Abroad' movies. Nigel Planer, Peter Richardson, Liz Crowther etc. Dir: Baz Taylor. Screenplay: Nigel Planer and Doug Lucie. Channel 4, 26 March 1988.

A Gathering of Old Men (1987). An unusually good TV feature with highly professional and finely polished work from all concerned. It's nice to see Richard Widmark back on the screen, playing a sheriff who when about to arrest a black suspect for the murder of a white man finds eighteen fellow blacks anxious to admit to the killing. A rare not-to-be-missed TV movie. Louis Gossett Jr, Holly Hunter, Woody Strode. Dir: Volker Schlondorff. Screenplay: Charles Fuller; based on a novel by E.J. Gaines. Channel 4, 19 May 1988.

The Grizzly and the Treasure (1976). Gold, grizzlies and the harsh winter of the Klondike at the end of the 1800s are some of the ingredients of this fight-for-survival story. A nice family film. Dan Haggerty, John Dehner etc. Dir: Richard Friendenberg. No screenplay credit. ITV, 7 November 1987.

The Haunting Passion (1983). Jane Seymour as the ex-football-star's wife who dreams about another man and then finds him on the doorstep. Millie Perkins. G. McRaney etc. Dir: John Korty. Screenplay: M. Berk and D. Schwartz. ITV, 21 June 1988.

Heart of Steel (1983). Social problems abound when an American steel mill closes and the employees become redundant . . . and it has plenty of British echoes. A good script allied to some good performances. Peter Strauss, Pamela Reed, John Doucette. Dir: Donald Wrye. Screenplay: Gary DeVore. Channel 4, 28 July 1987.

Help Wanted: Kids (1986). Real-life partners Bill Hudson and Cindy Williams playing a New York couple who need an instant family to please their boss. It sounds silly but it works surprisingly well in this mild Disney comedy. Dir: David Greenwalt. Screenplay: Stephen Black and Harry Stern. ITV, 31 January (Part 1) and 7 February (Part 2) 1988.

145

High Country (1984). An Australian western about a cattleman, his speedy horse and the crooks who would do anything to get hold of it. A routine story, with gorgeous backgrounds. John Waters, Terry Serio etc. Dir: Bill Hughes. Screenplay: Graham Farmer. BBC1, 25 July 1987.

High Risk (1976). Familiar story about a group of specialists (in this case from a circus) who come together to make the impossible theft, in spite of every device the US State Department can dream up to prevent them. Victor Buono, Don Stroud, Joseph Sirolo etc. Dir: Sam O'Steen. Screenplay: Robert Carrington. ITV, 11 March 1988.

Hit and Run (1982). *What* a coincidence! The third time that taxi driver Paul Perri takes a gorgeous passenger to a house in Connecticut, he finds the body of the hit-and-run driver who killed his wife. Minor-league mystery. Also Claudia Cron and Will Lee. Dir: Charles Braverman. Screenplay: Don Enright; based on the Lucille Fletcher novel *Eighty Dollars to Stamford*. BBC2, 27 September 1987.

Hostage Flight (1985). An all-too-familiar story of aerial thuggery. Ned Beatty, Dee Wallace Stone, Barbara Bosson etc. Dir: Steven Hilliard Stern. Screenplay: Felix Culver and Stephen Zito. ITV, 22 June 1988.

The Hostage Heart (1977). Poorly scripted if highly original story of a new kind of ransom demand, centred on an operating theatre. Bradford Dillman, Vic Morrow, Cameron Mitchell etc. Dir: Bernard McEveety. Screenplay: Eric Kaldor, Charles Sailor and Andrew Fenady. ITV, 25 April 1988.

Hot Rod (1980). Another unremarkable youth movie about a young hot-rod car racer on the road to California to enter his jalopy in the national drag races there. Gregg Henry, Robert Culp, Ed Begley Jr etc. Dir and Screenplay: George Armitage. ITV, 19 January 1988.

The House (1984). Stretch your imagination – a lot – and picture a Britain landlocked between Latvia and Russia having gone to war against Latvia *circa* 1884 in order to secure an outlet to the oceans of the world. And now, supposing Russia came in to support Latvia. What would you have? A fantasy from writer-director Mike Figgis, who certainly has a highly developed imagination. Cast includes Stephen Rea, Diana Hardcastle, Nigel Hawthorne and many familiar players. Channel 4, 23 August 1987.

I Know Why the Caged Bird Sings (1978). Screen version of black writer Maya Angelou's book about her childhood in America's Deep South in the 1930s. Diahann Carroll, Constance Good (as Maya). Dir: Fielder Cook. Screenplay: Leonora Thuna and Maya Angelou; based on the latter's book. Channel 4, 14 July 1987.

In Broad Daylight (1971). Familiar theme with a new twist: the one about the man – in this case a blind actor – who plans to murder his unfaithful wife and her lover. But old hat or not, Richard Boone, Suzanne Pleshette, Fred Beir and Stella Stevens make it very watchable. Dir: Robert Day. Screenplay: Larry Cohen. ITV, 17 October 1987.

International Airport (1985). After a quartet of cinema *Airports*, TV comes up with its own. George Kennedy still holds the joy stick and may have a bomb on board. All very familiar thriller stuff. Gil Gerard, Vera Miles, Robert Vaughn etc. Dir: Don Chaffey and C.S. Dubin. Screenplay: Robert McCullough. ITV, 2 May 1988.

Isabel's Choice (1981). Problems, problems. Should ultra-efficient secretary Isabel (Jean Stapleton) follow her long-term boss into semi-retirement or should she switch loyalty to his dynamic successor? The National Commission of Working Women voted Miss Stapleton an award for her playing of the role. Richard Kiley, Peter Coyote, Betsy Palmer etc. Dir: Guy Green. Screenplay: Oliver Hailey. BBC1, 20 January 1988.

I Want to Live (1983). Why *do* they do it? A poor remake of the 1983 cinema movie in which Susan Hayward (role now taken by Lindsay Wagner) won an Oscar for her part of a prostitute who is questionably sentenced to death for murder. Martin Balsam, Harry Dean Stanton. Dir: David Lowell Rich. Screenplay: D. M. Mankiewicz and Gordon Cotler. BBC2, 23 May 1988.

Jessie (1984). 'Bionic Woman' Lindsay Wagner as a psychiatrist working for the police department, in a routine rape and murder investigation. This is the feature introduction to a 3-year-old series now brought across the Atlantic by ITV. The biggest mystery is why, if the writer was Eric Bercovici (as the *TV Times* says), that credit is given to a certain Felix Culver. Dir: Richard Michaels. ITV, 30 September 1987.

Johnny Belinda (1982). A TV remake of the 1948 cinema success which starred Jane Wyman as the deaf-mute maiden raped by the local villain. Good old-fashioned melodrama, with Rosanna Arquette doing pretty well in the Wyman part. Also Richard Thomas, Dennis Quaid, etc. BBC2, 19 January 1988.

Kenny Rogers as the Gambler (1980). A western woven around popular singer Rogers, based on one of his songs. According to the *Radio Times* this feature had the largest ever TV audience in the US. Also Christine Belford, Bruce Bixleitner, Lee Purcell, Clu Gulager etc. Dir: Dick Lowry. Screenplay: Jim Byrnes. BBC1, 4 November 1987.

The Key to Rebecca (1985). Condensation to feature length of the TV mini-series of some years back: a story of Second World War spies and counter-spies against a Tunis background. Cliff Robertson, David Soul, Anthony Quayle, David Hemmings and other familiar faces. Dir: David Hemmings. Screenplay: Sam Harris; based on the novel by Ken Follett. ITV, 9 April 1988.

The Killer Who Wouldn't Die (1976). Wan introductory feature for a hoped-for follow-on series: widowed detective (his wife killed in the bomb blast meant for him), now resigned and 'messing about with boats', is drawn into a friend's plight and an assassination plot. Mike Connors, Samantha Eggar, Clu Gulager etc. Dir: William Hale. Screenplay: Cliff Gould. ITV, 5 December 1987.

Knight Rider – The Movie (1982). The pilot feature which launched the successful series of the same name and of which a fantasy car – popular with the kids – is the real star. Vince Edwards, David Hasselhoff, Richard Basehart etc. Dir: Dan Haller. Screenplay: G.A. Larson. ITV, 1 April 1988.

Kojak – The Belarus File (1985). Curious cop Kojak cuts through the red tape intended to entangle him, to uncover a horrid plot by Nazis in New York to murder Russian émigrés. As always when Telly Savalas is involved, all very watchable. Also Max von Sydow and Suzanne Pleshette etc. Dir: Robert Markowitz. Screenplay: Albert Ruben. ITV, 31 August 1987.

The Last Days of Patton (1986). George C. Scott back in the role which brought him his 1970 Oscar: the last chapter in the life of the 'blood-and-guts' general. Eva Marie Saint. Dir: Delbert Mann. Screenplay: W. Luce. ITV, 12 June 1988.

The Last Electric Knight (1986). One of Disney's harmless family films, this features a mysterious little oriental lad who turns up at a New York cop's door and says he has been 'willed' to look after him. Competent comedy. Gil Gerard, Ernie Reyes Jr, Keye Luke. Dir: James Fargo. Screenplay: Dan Gordon. ITV, 14 February 1988.

The Last Ninja (1983). Apparently the pilot feature for a proposed kung fu series (which doesn't seem to have materialized) about a young martial arts exponent fighting lots of San Francisco baddies. Michael Beck, Nancy Kwan. Dir: W.A. Graham. Screenplay: Ed Speilman. ITV, 28 March 1988.

Living Apart Together (1982). Glaswegian writer-director Charles Gormley's amusing examination of the stresses that a showbiz marriage encounters. With B.A. Robertson, Barbara Kellerman, Jimmy Logan etc. Channel 4, 7 May 1988.

Little Lord Fauntleroy (1980). Though made as a TV feature, this film was released in the cinema on 12 April 1982 and fully reviewed as such in the 1981–2 *Film Review*. BBC2, 30 December 1987.

Lovebirds (1987). A mixture of race relations and maternity-ward friendships, plus a comedy conclusion. Paul Bhattacharjee, Jane Gurnett, Linda Henry etc. Dir: Stephen Whittaker. Screenplay: Harry Collins. BBC2, 6 March 1988.

Lucky Sunil (1988). Rather unexciting record of a young Pakistani's adventures in London, with his ambitions always at risk from girls and bad guys. Kulvinder Ghir, Tariq Yunus etc. Dir: Michael Caton-Jones. Screenplay: Andrew Davies, based on a story by Tariq Yunus. BBC2, 17 April 1988.

MacGruder and Loud (1985). Neatly crafted cop crime thriller. A husband-and-wife team investigates MacGruder's ex-partner's murder . . . and they soon realize husband Mac

may be next on the killer's list. John Getz, Kathryn Harrold. Dir: Jerry London. Screenplay: Lane Slate. ITV, 8 April 1988.

Magee and the Lady (1977). You *must* have seen that movie classic *The African Queen*? Well, here's a lesser-quality sort of re-vamp with Australia substituting for Africa and Tony Lo Bianco and Sally Kellerman standing in for Bogart and Hepburn (and the *Cobargo* taking the place of the *Queen*). Dir: Gene Levitt. Screenplay: Colin Free. BBC1, 21 October 1987.

The Magnificent Magical Magnet of Santa Mesa (1977). A naïve if brilliant young scientist invents a revolutionary new magnet which he reckons will help mankind, while his baddie boss wants to use it for his own benefit. Michael Burns, Jane Connell etc. Dir: Hy Averback. Screenplay: Dee Caruso and Gerald Gardner. ITV, 30 December 1987.

Maschenka (1987). John Mortimer's script is based on a Vladimir Nabokov love story set in a seedy boarding house in 1920s Berlin, the refuge of various exiles. Cary Elwes, Irina Brook, Freddie Jones etc. Dir: John Goldschmidt. Channel 4, 31 March 1988.

A Masterpiece of Murder (1986). A whodunit worth seeing for the stars alone (there's not much else to enthuse over). They include Bob Hope, Don Ameche, Yvonne de Carlo and Stella Stevens, with some laughable lines. Dir: C.S. Dubin. Screenplay: Terry Nation and Andrew Fenady. ITV, 24 December 1987.

Midnight Lace (1981). Sadly unsuccessful effort to remake the 1960 Doris Day–Rex Harrison movie, which itself was far from being a screen classic. Mary Crosby now struggles to create the threatened housewife who hears voices. Dir: Ivan Nagy. Screenplay: Jerry Ludwig. ITV, 27 October 1987.

Miss All-American Beauty (1982). Small-screen look at the Beauty Contest business in the US; a follow-up to the more successfully managed large-screen *Smile* (1975) . . . but those Fort Worth and Dallas backgrounds *are* interesting. Diane Lane, Cloris Leachman, Jayne Meadows. Dir: Gus Trikonis. Screenplay: Penny Fraser, Betty Quin, Sally Webb, Bill Searle and Christine Schofield. BBC1, 17 February 1988.

Mongo's Back in Town (1971). He's a cold, ruthless, professional hit-man (Joe Don Baker) whose return to his home town puts the local cops' nerves on edge. For what (or whom), has he come back? Big-name cast includes Sally Field, Telly Savalas, Anne Francis and Martin Sheen. Dir: Marvin Chomsky. Screenplay: Herman Miller; from the book by E. Richard Johnson. BBC1, 14 August 1987.

Mr Boogedy (1986). He's the spectral ex-owner of the 'haunted' old house purchased by a salesmen of joke gimmicks, and as it's from Disney the concentration is on family-suited comedy. Richard Masur, Mimi Kennedy etc. Dir: Oz Scott. Screenplay: Michael Janover. ITV, 27 March 1988.

Mr Corbett's Ghost (1986). Danny directs his (now late) dad John Huston and a star-studded cast including Paul Scofield, Burgess Meredith, Alexei Sayle and Mark Farmer in an eerie little piece about an old man who collects souls. It all takes place in Gospel Oak on New Year's Eve 1767. Quite a promising directorial debut. Dir: D. Huston. Screenplay: Gerry Wilson; from a story by Leon Garfield. ITV, 29 December 1987.

Mrs Delafield Wants to Marry (1986). A made-to-measure (for Katharine Hepburn) movie about a wealthy old widow who upsets her New England class-conscious family by announcing she is going to marry a Jewish doctor. Denholm Elliott, Harold Gould etc. Dir: George Schaffer. Screenplay: James Pridaux. BBC2, 6 June 1988.

Murder – By Reason of Insanity (1985). A borrowed-from-life story about a Polish couple who have defected to America and find the switch so difficult that the husband becomes increasingly violent to his wife, whose life before and after divorce is fraught with fear. All pretty grim. Candice Bergen (very good) and Jurgen Prochnow. Dir: Anthony Page. Screenplay: Scott Swanton. Channel 4, 18 August and repeated on same channel on 10 September 1987.

Murder on Flight 502 (1975). Solidly entertaining suspense material about a killer on board a transatlantic jet. Whodunit in the air, with a starry passenger list: Robert Stack, Ralph Bellamy, Polly Bergen, Theodore Bikel, Dane Clark, Farrah Fawcett-Majors, Hugh O'Brian, Walter Pidgeon, to name just some of them. Dir: George McCowan. Screenplay: David Harmon. ITV, 22 February 1988.

My Wicked, Wicked Ways – The Legend of Errol Flynn (1985). A look at the wild life and career of 'wicked' Errol Flynn, culled from his own autobiography. Duncan Regeher (Flynn), Barbara Hershey, Lee Purcell etc. Dir: Don Taylor. Screenplay: Jill Trump, Doris Keating, James Lee and Taylor. ITV, 29 December 1987.

Nazi Hunter – The Search for Klaus Barbie (1986). Topical stuff (true, too) about a young German woman (Farrah Fawcett, most impressive) and her mission to bring Barbie and his Nazi ilk to justice, ending in the Lyon show trial in the summer of 1987. Highly dramatic. Also Tom Conti, Geraldine Page etc. Dir: Michael Lindsay-Hogg. Screenplay: Frederic Hunter. ITV, 12 August 1987.

Night Partners (1983). Aggrieved housewives Diana Canova and Yvette Mimieux patrol the streets in their battered old car ready to help crime victims like themselves and find it a sometimes dangerous business. Also M. Emmet Walsh etc. Dir: Noel Nosseck. Screenplay: Judy Merl and Paul Eric Myers. ITV, 19 March 1988.

Night Slaves (1970). Superior direction by veteran Ted Post lifts this SF thriller about a man who wakes up in a small western town to find his wife has been abducted by the aliens who have taken over. James Franciscus, Lee Grant etc. Screenplay: R. Specht and Everett Chambers. ITV, 13 May 1988.

Die Niklashauser (1970). One of Rainer Werner Fassbinder's TV features, based on a true fifteenth-century case of a man who claimed that the Virgin Mary was guiding him in his efforts to inspire dramatic social reforms. Hanna Schygulla, Fassbinder, Michael Konig etc. Dir and Screenplay (latter with Michael Fengler): Fassbinder. Channel 4, 23 July 1987.

No Place to Hide (1981). Involved – and quite involving – thriller from Jimmy Sangster's pen about a girl terrorized by a man in dark glasses who follows her. But she can't make anyone take the threat to her seriously. Mariette Hartley, Kathleen Beller, Keir Dullea etc. Dir: J. L. Moxey. Screenplay: J. Sangster. ITV, 22 December 1987.

Not in Front of the Children (1982). Husband and wife no longer, they take their battle for their children's custody into the courts. Linda Gray, John Getz. Dir: Joseph Hardy. Screenplay: Cynthia Mandelberg. Channel 4, 21 July 1987.

One Hour to Doomsday (1970). Made for TV but first released in the UK as a cinema film on 16 April 1972 and fully reviewed as such in the 1971–2 *Film Review*. BBC2, 14 December 1978.

Operation Heartbeat (1986) This was the pilot feature for the successful series, *Medical Center*, that was to follow. It must have been the players rather than the material that impressed. Edward G. Robinson, James Daly, Maurice Evans, Kim Stanley etc. Dir: Boris Sagal. Screenplay: Al C. Ward. ITV, 2 February 1988.

Packin' It In (1983). The well-worn plot about an urban family, disgusted with town troubles, trying the country, only to find there are plenty of problems there, too. A hard-working cast is headed by Richard Benjamin and Paula Prentiss. Dir: Jud Taylor. Screenplay: Donald Reiker and Patricia Jones. BBC1, 30 March 1988.

Panic on the 5.22 (1974). Routine suspenser about a trio of hoodlums who hold up the Club Car passengers on a New York train. Ina Balin, Dana Elcar, Linden Chiles etc. Dir: Harvey Hart. Screenplay: Eugene Price. ITV, 10 March 1988.

Parent Trap II (1987). Interestingly, this Disney TV feature brings back Hayley Mills in the role – in fact roles, as she plays twins – she first played 26 years ago in the original *PT*. But apart from this there's not much to enthuse over. Dir: R.F. Maxwell. Screenplay: Stuart Krieger. ITV, 17 (Part 1) and 24 (Part 2) January 1988.

Passions (1984). Yet another film in which Joanne Woodward's shining performance lifts what would otherwise be undistinguished soapstuff into very watchable melodrama. She plays the wife who learns about the other woman only on her husband's death. Lindsay Wagner, Richard Crenna, Viveca Lindfors. Dir: Sandor Stern. Screenplay: Stern, Janet Greek and Robin Maxwell. ITV, 3 November 1987.

Peace is our Profession (1972). The famous canine star Lassie chalks up another quite incredible good deed. BBC2, 29 December 1987.

Perry Mason – The Case of the Lost Love (1987). Another in the short new series of Mason cases; this time he becomes involved in the defence of an ex-girlfriend's husband accused of murder. Raymond Burr, Barbara Hale, Jean Simmons, William Katt. Dir: Ron Satlof. Screenplay: Anne Collins. BBC1, 4 April 1988.

Perry Mason – The Case of the Notorious Nun (1986). Another feature spin-off from the outstanding old series, with Raymond Burr in complete control, defending Sister Margaret from a charge of murder. Grand old-style courtroom stuff. Also Barbara Hale, William Katt, Timothy Bottoms etc. Dir: Ron Satlof. Screenplay: Joel Steiger. BBC1, 30 August 1987.

Perry Mason – The Case of the Shooting Star (1986). A popular TV chat show personality is shot down and apparently killed by the film star he is interviewing. Raymond Burr then goes into court to try to prove that 40 million viewers should not believe their eyes. Lovely stuff. Barbara Hale, William Katt etc. Dir: Ron Satloff. Screenplay: Anne Collins. BBC1, 27 December 1987.

Peyton Place – The Next Generation (1985). Maybe *Return to P.P.* would have been a better title, for that's what it is, with all the nasty people still doing the same nasty things. Bits and pieces from the old TV series of the 'sixties are stitched in as flashbacks, which makes it all the more bitty. You'll have to be a real P.P. fan to enjoy it. Dorothy Malone, Barbara Parkins, Ed Nelson. Dir: Larry Elikann. Screenplay: Rita Lakin, ITV, 29 September 1987.

The President's Plane Is Missing (1973). Political thriller which – with such a fine cast (Buddy Ebsen, Peter Graves, Raymond Massey, Mercedes Cambridge, Rip Torn, Arthur Kennedy etc.) and a good if unlikely story about the apparent crash in the desert of the US president's airplane with him and his staff on board – promises far more than it delivers. Dir: Daryl Duke. Screenplay: Mark Carliner and Ernest Kinoy; based on the novel by R.J. Serling. BBC1, 14 October 1987.

Probe (1972). Fascinating feature introduction to the series about the way that detectives will work in the future . . . maybe. A wired-up Hugh O'Brian seeks the solution to the mystery of the missing jewels. Starry support includes John Gielgud, Elke Sommer, Burgess Meredith, Angel Tompkins etc. Dir: Russ Mayberry. Screenplay: Leslie Stevens. ITV, 1 September 1987.

Professor Poopsnagle's Steam Zeppelin – The Last Mineral (1986). The last of a series of six Australian comedies made for the kids. Ken Talbot, Justine Clark etc. Dir: Howard Rubie and Russell Webb. ITV, 2 April 1988.

Professor Poopsnaggle's Steam Zeppelin – Lost in the Desert (1986). Another in this pleasant series of six films from Australia appealing to junior. Ken Talbot, Gerry Duggan. Dir: Howard Rubie and Russell Webb. ITV, 12 July 1987.

Professor Poopsnagle's Steam Zeppelin – A Race to the Finish (1986). The fifth of the 'Pro Poop' kids films to be shown at intervals over a period. Nice good-*v.*-evil story with a high moral tone. Fun, too. Dir: Howard Rubie and Russell Webb. ITV, 26 December 1987.

Pursuit (1972). Well-crafted thriller about a millionaire terrorist who chooses a political convention attended by the US President to announce his possession of a deadly new nerve gas and his intention to use it. Will he do it or will he be thwarted at the last tingling minute? Dir: Michael Crichton. Screenplay: Robert Dozier; based on Crichton's novel *Binary* (though he wrote it under the name of John Lange). BBC1, 27 October 1987.

Ransom for a Dead Man (1971). Made as a TV pilot for what was to become a popular detection series (*Columbo*), this movie made its debut on this side of the Atlantic in 1974 as a cinema release and was reviewed as such in the 1973–4 *Film Review*. A wife's plan to murder her husband is ruined by the shabby detective Peter Falk. Dir: Richard Irving. Screenplay: Dean Hargrove; from a story by Richard Levinson and William Link. ITV, 24 October 1987.

Raspberry Ripple (1987). Odd little movie about a home for the disabled lorded (should it be ladied?) over by Faye Dunaway, uncomfortably cast as matron. Easily missable. John Gordon-Sinclair etc. Dir: Nigel Finch. Screenplay: Rupert Haselden. BBC1, 31 March 1988.

Reasonable Force (1987). Unfortunately very topical, a very professional TV feature about police problems; illustrated by the story of a demonstrator killed in a riot, and the aftermath. Tough and convincing. Jeremy Kemp, Adrian Dunbar, Warren Clarke etc. Dir: Jim Goddard. Screenplay: P.G. Duggan. BBC2, 27 March 1988.

The Return of the Beverly Hillbillies (1981). A comedy about old granny's special 'mixture' which if developed commercially might just revolutionize the world! An amusing spin-off feature from the very successful comedy series of the 'sixties. Buddy Ebsen, Nancy Culp, Imogene Coca etc. Dir: Robert Leeds. Screenplay: Paul Henning. ITV, 26 December 1987.

Rio das Mortes (River of the Dead) (1970). Rainer Werner Fassbinder directed this West German TV film – and a pretty poor effort it is, too – about a treasure hunt in Peru. Hanna Schygulla etc. Dir and Screenplay: Fassbinder. Channel 4, 16 July 1987.

Rita Hayworth – The Love Goddess (1983). Bio-pic thin on facts but thick with frills, and interesting in the light it sheds on other aspects of Hollywood. Lynda Carter (of *Wonder Woman* fame), Michael Lerner, John Considine, Alejandro Rey etc. Dir: James Goldstone. Screenplay: F.A. Kean; based on the book by John Kobal. ITV, 10 February 1988.

Run for the Lifeboat (1988). Strangely colourless movie about a Welsh coastal village where life centres on the local lifeboat, one of the crew of which the colourless heroine marries for the sake of her fatherless child. Stacey Tendeter, David Burke, John Pickard. Dir and Screenplay: Douglas Livingstone. BBC2, 24 April 1988.

Sadgati (1981). A perfect little gem from India's movie-master Satyajit Ray, subtly examining human behaviour in a simple story set in a small village. Om Puri, Mohan Agashe. Dir and Screenplay: Satyajit Ray. Channel 4, 24 April 1988.

Secrets (1983). Four nice schoolgirls giving nice perform-ances as a quartet of curious youngsters getting involved in Masonic mysteries. Helen Lindsay, Anna Campbell Jones, Daisy Cockburn, Rebecca Johnson etc. Dir: Gavin Millar. Screenplay: Noella Smith. (And, a recommendation, a David Puttnam film.) Channel 4, 16 July 1987.

The Secret War of Jackie's Girls (1980). A very unlikely yarn about a group of American girl pilots who with their helicopters did a lot to help the RAF win the Second World War in the skies – or so the makers claim. Mariette Hartley, Lee Purcell, Ann Dusenberry etc. Dir: Gordon Hessler. Screenplay: T. Jonas and D. Guthrie. ITV, 15 December 1987.

Shadow on the Earth (1987). Slight comedy from the director of *Letter to Brezhnev*, about a 7-year-old lad who decides that the mysterious neighbour must be an alien. Billy Hickman, Sheila Grier etc. Dir: Chris Bernard. Screenplay: David Kane. BBC2, 13 March 1988.

Sharma and Beyond (1984). Romance between a young teacher obsessed with science-fiction and the daughter of his favourite sci-fi author. Michael Maloney, Suzanne Burden. Dir and Screenplay: Brian Gilbert. Channel 4, 6 August 1987.

She Cried Murder (1973). Telly 'Kojak' Savalas changes hats and becomes the baddy cop sent to interview the only person who witnessed him pushing a girl under a New York subway train. Good or bad, he's always worth watching. Also Lynda Day George, Mike Farrell, Kate Reid etc. Dir: Herschel Daugherty. Screenplay: Merwin Gerard. ITV, 2 April 1988.

The Silent Twins (1985). Journalist Marjorie Wallace did a top-class job with this real-life story about identical twins – now in Broadmoor – whose strange behaviour is pinned down to their macabre love-hate relationship. An odd and fascinating story. Shirley and Sharon Parker etc. Dir: John Amiel. Screenplay: M. Wallace. BBC2, 20 March 1988.

Single Bars, Single Women (1984). They are both comic and tragic, the customers who come to Bandini's bar seeking solace, sex, romance or just a good time. They are portrayed by some interesting players, like Paul Michael Glaser, Christine Lahti, Shelley Hack, etc. Dir: Harry Winer. Screenplay: Michael Bortman. Channel 4, 23 February 1988.

Snowbeast (1977). That Abominable Snowman walks again, in a snow-bound Colorado Rockies resort, and puts a damper on preparations for the winter carnival. A neat combination of stars and thrills. Clint Walker, Yvette Mimieux, Bo Svenson etc. Dir: Herb Wallerstein. Screen-play: Joseph Stefano. ITV, 7 August 1987.

Something Evil (1972). It's in the farmhouse that Sandy Dennis and her husband buy in Pennsylvania, and she becomes convinced it's trying to possess her. Early, interest-ing Spielberg. Dir: Steven Spielberg. Screenplay: Robert Clouse. Channel 4, 9 January 1988.

Something So Right (1982). Bright little blond star (well, he's not quite so little these days, with several major roles behind him) Ricky Schroder plays the problem child of a broken marriage, who is brought to see the light by his big brother, nightclub boss James Farentino (an intriguing performance). Also Patty Duke Astin etc. Dir: Lou Anto-nio. Screenplay: Shelley List and Jonathan Estrin. Channel 4, 25 August 1987.

Special People (1984). First-class, documentary-style, fact-based, fictionally-trimmed story about Canada's Famous People Players, a puppet group formed by some mentally handicapped youngsters, moulded to success by their gifted teacher. Brooke Adams, Susan Roman etc. Dir: Marc Daniels. Screenplay: Corey Blechman. Channel 4, 1 September 1987.

The Spy Killer (1969). Ex-Hammer horror writer Jimmy Sangster wrote this complicated espionage yarn in which an ex-spy, now private eye, is blackmailed into taking up the search for a mysterious missing notebook. Robert Horton, Sebastian Cabot, Eleanor Summerfield etc. Dir: Roy Ward Baker. Screenplay: J. Sangster. ITV, 7 November 1987.

Standing Tall (1978). Little *v.* big: small rancher *v.* the big landgrabber. A familiar enough theme on big or small screen, but always heart-warming stuff. Robert Forster as the little-man hero (Linda Evans as helpmate wife) and Chuck Connors as his powerful tycoon opponent. Dir: Harvey Hart. Screenplay: Franklin Thompson. Channel 4, 14 August 1987.

Stanley (1987). Bio-pic about that most controversial of Cookham's residents, brilliant, scandalous painter Stanley Spencer, whose riverside 'Resurrection' was among the best of his output. Interesting; with Anton Lesser as Stanley. Also Juliet Stevenson, Sarah Berger etc. Dir: Anna Benson Gyles. Screenplay: Elaine Morgan. BBC2, 31 January 1988.

Stark (1985). Hopefully made as the first episode in a new crime series that in fact never got further than this, this is the story of a cop who uncovers the Mafia under the Las Vegas carpet of crime. Nicolas Surovy, Marilu Henner, Dennis Hopper. Dir: Rod Holcomb. Screenplay: Ernest Tidyman and Bill Stratton. BBC1, 11 January 1988.

Staying Together (1984). Yet another based-on-truth tear-jerking story about a boy who tries to keep the family together while embarking on a songwriting career. Lee H.

Montgomery, Jill Schoelen etc. Dir: Jerry Thorpe. Screenplay: Chris Beaument. BBC2, 27 June 1988.

The Stranger Within (1974). An unborn child begins to take over its worried bearer, who knows that no human being has impregnated her. This kind of theme has had better treatment on the large screen. Barbara Eden, Nehemiah Persoff, George Grizzard etc. Dir: Lee Philips. Screenplay: Richard Matheson; based on his own story. BBC1, 10 October 1987.

The Streets of San Francisco (1972). The feature film that introduced the successful, still-running cops-and-crime series. Karl Malden, Robert Wagner, Michael Douglas. Dir: Walter Grauman. Screenplay: Ed Hume. ITV, 21 July 1987.

Striker's Mountain (1973). Familiar villainy (a mountain lodge threatened by redevelopment villain Leslie Nielsen) against superbly unfamiliar Canadian Rockies background; a treat for the eyes if not the mind. Mimi Kuzyk, Bruce Greenwood. Dir: Alan Simmonds. Screenplay: Pete White. BBC1, 24 February 1988.

Svengali (1983). Yet another screen version of and variation on the famous du Maurier classic. This one is below par; the only good reason for watching it is Peter O'Toole's bravura – to say the least – performance, with Jodie Foster as the victim-pupil. Dir: Anthony Harvey. Screenplay: Frank Cucci. Channel 4, 2 February 1988.

Sweet As You Are (1987). Topical AIDS scarer about a college professor, his pupil-mistress and his wife – and the ruination of a hitherto happy marriage. Liam Neeson, Miranda Richardson, Alex Pakenham. Dir: Angela Pope. Screenplay: William Nicholson. BBC2, 24 January 1988.

Take Your Best Shot (1982). Comedy, with Robert Urich as the unsuccessful actor trying to keep career and marriage off the rocks. Meredith Baxter Birney. Dir: David Greene. Screenplay: Richard Levinson and William Link. BBC2, 13 June 1988.

The Temptation of Eileen Hughes (1988). Novelist Brian Moore's own adaptation of his story about a young Irish shop girl who accepts the McAuley family's invitation to spend a holiday in London with them and finds more than she bargained for. Angharad Rees, Jim Norton, Ethna Ruddy etc. Dir: Tristram Powell. BBC2, 2 April 1988.

Terror at London Bridge (1985). The bridge of the title is the one that was transported from the Thames to Arizona some years ago, and this highly imaginative thriller tells how the ghost of Jack the Ripper was exported along with it. Swallow that one . . . David Hasselhoff, Stephanie Kramer, Clu Gulager etc. Dir: E.W. Swackhamer. Screenplay: W.F. Nolan. ITV, 6 April 1988.

This Man is Dangerous (1985). The pilot feature for the *Stingray* series with adventurer Stingray (Nick Mancuso) agreeing to the pretty Deputy DA's (Robyn Douglass) plea that he help her track down and free her kidnapped boss. It

turns out to be a pretty rough, tough assignment. Dir: Richard A. Colla. Screenplay: S.J. Cannell. ITV, 31 July 1987.

Thompson's Last Run (1986). Things look black for detective Red (Wilford Brimley) when his old safe-cracker mate (Robert Mitchum) escapes while in his custody. He *knows* he's innocent, but can he prove it? The pair are always worth watching, regardless of their material. Dir: Jerrold Freedman. Screenplay: John Carlen. BBC1, 3 October 1987.

Tomorrow's Child (1981). Competent, routine test-tube baby drama. Stephanie Zimbalist, William Atherton, Dir: Joseph Sargent. Screenplay: Jerry McNeely. ITV, 8 February 1988.

Tumbledown (1988). Based on the true story of Lieutenant Robert Lawrence (Colin Firth) who fought in the Falklands conflict and had to cope in the aftermath with the fact that 40 per cent of his brain had been shot away. A lavish TV film with an enormous cast. Dir: Richard Eyre. Screenplay: Charles Wood. BBC1, 31 May 1988.

The Ultimate Impostor (1979). Pretty silly SF story about an American secret agent who can link his brain to a computer for a mission. The snag is that the link wears thin after 72 hours, so speed is a matter of life or death. Joseph Hacker, Keith Andes etc. Dir: Paul Stanley. Screenplay: Lionel Siegel. ITV, 25 August 1987.

The Untouchables (1960). The very popular TV crime series was brought back by bundling up several episodes into a number of feature films; but this one started out as a two-part movie called *The Big Train*, which was about Al Capone. Robert Stack, Neville Brand etc. Dir: John Tayser. Screenplay: William Spier. BBC1, 18 September 1987.

The Vision (1987). Dirk Bogarde stars in a topical and well-contrived story about the struggle to achieve supremacy in the increasingly important world of satellite TV. Also Lee Remick, Eileen Atkins, Helena Bonham Carter etc. Dir: Norman Stone. Screenplay: William Nicholson. BBC2, 10 January 1988.

We're Fighting Back (1981). Regrettably relevant to Britain today, a timely drama about thugs terrorizing travellers on the Underground and how young New Yorkers set about dealing with the problem in their city. The pilot feature for another series that never was. Kevin Mahon, Paul McCrane, Ellen Barkin etc. Dir: Lou Antonio. Screenplay: T.S. Cook. BBC1, 27 February 1988.

Where the Ladies Go (1980). A bunch of 'ladies' regularly visits Buck's (Earl Holliman) Bar to talk and flirt and pass the time. Just that. Karen Black, Candy Clark etc. Dir: Theo Flicker. Screenplay: Carol Sobieski. ITV, 8 December 1987.

Who Is the Black Dahlia? (1975). This is the story of one of the murders which the Los Angeles cops failed to solve: the 1947 killing of a woman in her twenties. So it is all a bit inconclusive. Lucie Arnaz, Efrem Zimbalist Jr, Macdonald Carey, Gloria DeHaven etc. Dir: Joseph Pevney. Screenplay: R.W. Lenski. ITV, 31 October 1987.

Who Killed Miss USA? (1970). Remember the 1968 Clint Eastwood film *Coogan's Bluff*? Here's a sort of remake for TV, presented as a pilot for what was to become a pretty popular series, *McCloud*, with Dennis Weaver now the hick cop in the Big City (New York) and finding things a bit different from his home territory. Dir: R.A. Colla. Screenplay: Stanford Whitmore, Richard Levinson and William Link. ITV, 14 November 1987.

Winner Take All (1975). Having ruined her first marriage by her compulsive gambling, housewife Shirley Jones seems all set to smash her second when her husband discovers she has lost the nest egg he had put by for starting a new business venture. Laurence Luckinbill, Sam Groom etc. Dir: Paul Bogart. Screenplay: Caryl Ledner. BBC1, 3 February 1988.

Witness for the Prosecution (1982). Small-screen remake of the 1957 large-screen Agatha Christie whodunit success, based on her famous thriller play. A superb cast includes Sir Ralph Richardson, Deborah Kerr, Wendy Hiller, Peter

Sallis, Diana Rigg and many more. Dir: Alan Gibson. Screenplay: John Gay. BBC1, 23 August 1987.

The Woman Hunter (1972). A wealthy lady (Barbara Eden) on a lush holiday with her husband stumbles on the uncomfortable truth that she is being tracked down by a killer. But it's all rather flat. Robert Vaughn, Stuart Whitman. Dir: Bernard Kowalski. Screenplay: Brian Clemens and Tony Williamson. ITV, 23 March 1988.

Women of San Quentin (1984). Yaphet Kotto dominates this otherwise routine and sometimes hysterical story about the female warders looking after 3000 male convicts in California's San Quentin jail. Stella Stevens, Debbie Allen etc. Dir: W.A. Graham. Screenplay: Mark Rodgers. ITV, 21 April 1988.

Zuma Beach (1978). Zuma Beach is where pop star Bonnie Kate (Suzanne Somers) grew up, and where she returns in order to sort herself out and plan a comeback. Familiar teenager fare but with an interesting cast including Michael Biehn, Rosanna Arquette, Tanya Roberts and others. Dir: Lee H. Katzin. Screenplay: William Schwartz. ITV, 9 February 1988.

The following is a list of TV feature films shown during the year which have been previously televised and have been duly noted in past editions of *Film Review*. For the record, they are listed here with date of repeat showing, together with date of previous showing and the edition of *Film Review* in which they were described more fully. The following abbreviations apply: Rev for Reviewed; C4 for Channel 4; *FR* for *Film Review*.

Acceptable Levels (1983). C4 28 Jan and 18 Feb 1988 (C4 30 Apr 1984 – 1984–5 *FR*).
After Pilkington (1986). BBC1 3 Nov 1987 (BBC2 25 Jan 1987 – 1987–8 *FR*).
The A-Team (1986). ITV 29 Aug 1987 (ITV 22 July 1983 – 1984–5 *FR*).
Attica – The Story of a Prison Riot (1980). ITV 12 Jan 1988 (ITV 15 June 1985 – 1985–6 *FR*).
Best Little Girl in the World (1981). C4 16 May 1988 (C4 5 July 1983 – 1984–5 *FR*).
The Biggest Bank Robbery (1980). ITV 24 July 1987 (ITV 25 Aug 1983 – 1984–5 *FR*).
Billion Dollar Threat (1979). ITV 9 Sept 1987 (ITV 23 Aug 1983 – 1984–5 *FR*).
Blue Knight (1975). ITV 21 May 1988 (BBC2 11 June 1984 – 1984–5 *FR*).
The Calendar Girl Murders (1984). ITV 19 Sept 1987 (C4 18 Nov 1987 – 1987–8 *FR*).
The Capture of Grizzly Adams (1981). ITV 25 July 1987 (ITV 25 Dec 1983 – 1984–5 *FR*).
China Rose (1983). BBC1 20 Apr 1988 (BBC1 30 Sept 1984 – 1985–6 *FR*).

A Christmas Without Snow (1980). C4 30 May 1988 (C4 18 Dec 1984 – 1985–6 *FR*).
City Killers (1984). ITV 22 Sept 1987 (ITV 5 Jan 1986 – 1986–7 *FR*).
Climb an Angry Mountain (1980). ITV 17 Nov 1987 (BBC2 16 May 1986 – 1986–7 *FR*).
Counting Sheep (1982). BBC2 18 Sept 1987 (BBC2 5 Apr 1986 – 1986–7 *FR*).
The Country Girls (1983). C4 23 Apr 1988 (C4 20 June 1985 – 1985–6 *FR*).
Crisis in Mid-Air (1979). ITV 13 Oct 1987 (BBC1 4 Oct 1986 1987–8 *FR*).
Crowhaven Farm (1970). ITV 19 Sept 1987 (ITV 7 Nov 1985 – 1986–7 *FR*).
The Dark Mirror (1984). ITV 10 Nov 1987 (BBC1 13 Feb 1985 – 1985–6 *FR*).
Deadly Message (1985). ITV 4 Aug 1987 (ITV 15 Sept 1985 – 1986–7 *FR*).
(Agatha Christie's) *Dead Man's Folly* (1986). ITV, 12 June 1988 (ITV 25 Dec 1986 – 1987–8 *FR*).
Death Cruise (1974). ITV 26 Sept 1987 (ITV 3 June 1986 – 1986–7 *FR*).
Death Stalks (1975). ITV 16 Feb 1988 (ITV 28 Nov 1985 – 1986–7 *FR*).
Detour to Terror (1980). ITV 26 Mar 1988 (26 Aug 1986 – 1987–8 *FR*).
The Disappearance of Aimee (1976). C4 27 June 1988 (C4 6 Nov 1984 – 1985–6 *FR*).
Escape (1980). BBC1 6 Feb 1988 (BBC1 15 Oct 1984 – 1985–6 *FR*).
Every Move She Makes (1974). ITV 8 Mar 1988 (ITV 21 Apr 1986 – 1986–7 *FR*).

The Eyes of Birds (1982). C4 9 May 1988 (C4 13 Mar 1986 – 1986–7 *FR*).

Flight to Holocaust (1976). ITV 30 Nov 1987 (ITV 5 Jan 1985 – 1985–6 *FR*).

Her Life as a Man (1984). BBC1 2 Mar 1988 (BBC1 19 Apr 1986 – 1986–7 *FR*).

Horror at 37,000 Feet (1972). ITV 25 Jan 1988 (BBC1 12 Sept 1984 – 1985–6 *FR*).

The Invisible Man (1985). ITV 22 Aug 1987 (ITV 30 Dec 1983 – 1984–5 *FR*).

Killdozer (1974). ITV 2 May 1988 (ITV 28 May 1984 – 1984–5 *FR*).

Kim (1984). ITV 28 Dec 1987 (ITV 26 Dec 1984 – 1985–6 *FR*).

Marathon (1980). C4 20 June 1988 (C4 15 May 1984 – 1984–5 *FR*).

The Mask of Death (1984). C4 22 Oct 1987 (C4 23 Dec 1984 – 1985–6 *FR*).

Massarati and the Brain (1985). ITV 29 Sept 1987 (ITV 27 Dec 1983 – 1984–5 *FR*).

Murder by the Book (1972). ITV 3 June 1988 (ITV 26 Aug 1984 – 1985–6 *FR*).

Nelly's Version (1983). C4 4 June 1988 (C4 21 Nov 1985 – 1986–7 *FR*).

Nightmare (1973). ITV 18 Mar 1988 (ITV 5 Dec 1985 – 1986–7 *FR*).

Nightmare in Badham County (1976). ITV 15 Sept 1987 (ITV 23 June 1987 – 1987–8 *FR*).

Northstar (1985). ITV 6 Apr 1988 (ITV 27 Dec 1985 – 1986–7 *FR*).

Nurse (1980). C4 1 Mar 1988 (C4 1 May 1984 – 1984–5 *FR*).

OHMS (1980). ITV 14 Aug 1987 (C4 17 July 1984 – 1985–6 *FR*).

The Other Woman (1983). ITV 9 Feb 1988 (C4 23 Apr 1985 – 1985–6 *FR*).

Out of the Darkness (1985). ITV 14 July 1987 (ITV 22 Feb 1986 – 1986–7 *FR*).

A Perfect Match (1980). BBC1 18 Nov 1987 (BBC2 2 Oct 1985 – 1986–7 *FR*).

Praying Mantis (1982). Part 1 C4 26 May 1988 (C4 7 and 8 Nov 1984 – 1985–6 *FR*).

Prisoner Without a Name, Cell Without a Number (1983). BBC1 12 Mar 1988 (BBC2 9 Oct 1985 – 1986–7 *FR*).

Reunion at Fairborough (1985). ITV 11 Sept 1987 (ITV 23 Mar 1986 – 1986–7 *FR*).

Revenge of the Stepford Wives (1980). BBC1 16 Sept 1987 (BBC 6 Nov 1983 – 1984–5 *FR*).

The Scarlet and the Black (1983). ITV 30 Aug 1987 (ITV 28 May 1985 – 1985–6 *FR*).

The Scarlet Pimpernel (1982). C4 20 Dec 1987 (ITV 27 Dec 1983 – 1984–5 *FR*).

Shadow Rider (1982). BBC1 25 May 1988 (BBC1 2 June 1987 and BBC1 14 Oct 1983 – 1984–5 *FR*).

Skyway to Death (1974). ITV 28 May 1988 (ITV 29 Aug 1986 – 1987–8 *FR*).

The Snowman (1982). C4 25 Dec 1987 (C4 24 Dec 1985 – 1986–7 *FR*).

Sparkling Cyanide (1983). ITV 31 Dec 1987 (ITV 26 Apr 1984 – 1984–5 *FR*).

Special Bulletin (1983). ITV 3 Apr 1988 (ITV 4 Dec 1985 – 1986–7 *FR*).

Starflight One (1982). ITV 5 Jan 1988 (ITV 29 Dec 1985 – 1986–7 *FR*).

Studio Murders (1981). BBC1 18 Jan 1988 (BBC 18 Dec 1983 – 1984–5 *FR*).

They Call It Murder (1981). ITV 21 June 1988 (ITV 30 July 1984 – 1985–6 *FR*).

Thirteen at Dinner (1985). ITV 16 Dec 1987 (ITV 8 June 1986 – 1986–7 *FR*).

Trackdown: Finding the Goodbar Killer (1983). ITV 13 Oct 1987 (ITV 29 Sept 1985 – 1986–7 *FR*).

A Very Missing Person (1972). ITV 28 Nov 1987 (ITV 23 Aug 1984 – 1985–6 *FR*).

Winter Flight (1984). C4 23 July 1987 (C4 20 Dec 1984 – 1985–6 *FR*).

Video Releases

ANTHONY HAYWARD

Christmas 1987 was no gift for British video shops, which had hoped to rent out a record number of cassettes to keep everyone entertained during the holiday. Some owners blamed the strong line-up of films on television for their disappointing trade, but they also had to reflect on a year that saw a fall in the average number of tapes rented by the public.

One tape that did attract people to video shops was the feature film *'Crocodile' Dundee*, the most popular rental cassette in the run-up to Christmas – just as it was the top cinema film of 1987 in Britain.

The success of 'sell-through' tapes at budget prices is one reason for the change in rental habits. This market is booming, although few feature films are among the biggest-selling videos. Pop music, children's television programmes and workout tapes are the most popular. *Grease*, the 1978 film starring John Travolta and Olivia Newton-John, was the only 'sell-through' feature – itself a rock musical – among 1987's twenty bestsellers, although *Beverly Hills Cop* and *Ghost Busters* were big Christmas successes.

The slight gloom in the rental market was relieved by a boom in early 1988: business for the first quarter was up twenty per cent on the same period of the previous year.

As in the USA, more than half of all households in Britain now own video recorders, of which 70 per cent belong to 25- to 34-year-olds.

Watching videos at home is the seventh most popular leisure activity, according to a Crown survey published in early 1988 (the favourite is watching television). It seems that people are finding more of their entertainment at home, perhaps because of sophisticated hi-fi systems, central heating and increasingly large households.

The British Videogram Association believes that 25 to 28 million people watch videos each week and claims that 40 per cent of a feature film's gross profit is generated by video.

But video piracy is still a problem in Britain. The country's industry-funded Federation Against Copyright Theft estimated that piracy had fallen to about one in five tapes available by the end of 1987 – compared with three in five in 1983 – but illegal copying appears to be increasing again. *Beverly Hills Cop II* was already available illegally in late 1987, before its official release the following May.

The Action Hunter (Pace) August 1987
L'Addition (Rank) April 1988
The African Run (Atlas) March 1988
Against All Odds (RCA/Columbia) January 1988
Airplane 2 – The Sequel (CIC) March 1988
Aladdin (Rank) June 1988
The Alamo – 13 Days to Glory (Virgin/PVG, two tapes) October 1987
Alien Terror (Cineplex) January 1988
Allan Quartermain and the Lost City of Gold (Rank) May 1988
The Allnighter (CIC) April 1988
Almost You (CBS/Fox) February 1988
Alpha City (Colourbox) April 1988
Amazonia (Avatar) September 1987
Amazon Women on the Moon (CIC) March 1988
The Ambush Murders (IVS) October 1987
American Anthem (Guild) December 1987
American Ninja 2 – The Confrontation (Rank) June 1988
America 3000 (MGM/UA) June 1988
And Then You Die (Screen Entertainment) June 1988
Angel Heart (Guild) April 1988

April Fool's Day (CIC) April 1988
The Armour of God (VPD) December 1987
Asphalt Warriors (Hi-Pressure) September 1987
Assassination (Rank) March 1988
The Assault (MGM/UA) October 1987
Assault on Precinct 13 (Palace/PVG) January 1988
Avenging Force (MGM/UA) March 1988

Back to School (RCA/Columbia) September 1987
Back to the Beach (CIC) May 1988
Bad Timing (Video Collection) February 1988
The Ballad of Cable Hogue (Warner) August 1987
The Baltimore Bullet (Video Collection) February 1988
Band of the Hand (RCA/Columbia) February 1988
Bandwagon (MGM/UA) March 1988
Barbarian Revenge (Barbarian Theatre) November 1987

Bates Motel (CIC) January 1988
Beauty of the Barbarian (Barbarian Theatre) November 1987
Behind Convent Walls (VPD) July 1987
The Belly of an Architect (Palace Premiere/PVG) February 1988
The Berk (IVS) March 1988
Berserker (Video Movie Company) November 1987
The Best Little Whorehouse in Texas (CIC) June 1988
Best Seller (RCA/Columbia) June 1988
Best Shot (RCA/Columbia) November 1987
Betrayed by Innocence (CIC) October 1987
Better Off Dead (CBS/Fox) July 1987
Betty Blue (CBS/Fox) July 1987
Beverly Hills Cop (CIC) November 1987
Beverly Hills Cop II (CIC) May 1988
Beyond Therapy (New World) May 1988
Big Bad Mama 2 (MGM/UA) June 1988
The Big Bang (EV) September 1987
The Big Bet (American Imperial) October 1987
The Big Easy (RCA/Columbia) March 1988
Bigfoot (Walt Disney) April 1988
Big Shots (Guild) June 1988

The Big Town (Rand) May 1988
Big Trouble (RCA/Columbia) May 1988
The Bikini Shop (Channel 5) June 1988
Birds of Prey (Hi-Pressure) July 1987
The Black Cobra (VPD) June 1988
Blade in Hong Kong (Virgin/PVG) September 1987
Blades of Steel (Screen Entertainment) April 1988
Blind Date (RCA/Columbia) February 1988
Blindside (Sheer Entertainment) June 1988
Blonde Venus (CIC) February 1988
Blood Vows (Virgin/PVG) August 1987
Bloody New Year (Braveworld/IVS) September 1987
Blue Hotel (CIC) June 1988
Blue Movies (IVS) May 1988
Blue Sunshine (Video Movie Company) April 1988
Blue Velvet (CBS/Fox) March 1988
Boot Hill (Action Channel) October 1987
Bound for Glory (Warner) August 1987
The Bourne Identity (Warner) June 1988
The Brain (CIC) October 1987
Brain Damage (Palace Premiere/PVG) March 1988
Brainkill (Cougar) January 1988
Bride of Boogedy (Walt Disney) March 1988
Bride of Frankenstein/Frankenstein (CIC, two films on one tape) June 1988
Brighton Beach Memoirs (CIC) January 1988
Brother Sun, Sister Moon (CIC) March 1988
Bulletproof (Virgin/PVG) January 1988
Bullies (Sheer Entertainment) January 1988
Burglar (Warner) January 1988
Business as Usual (Warner) April 1988
The Butterfly Revolution (CBS/Fox) October 1987

Cactus (PolyGram) August 1987
Cactus Jack (RCA/Columbia) June 1988
California Bulls (Mogul) May 1988
Camorra (Rank) July 1987
Campus Man (Vestron) May 1988
Canon Operation (Falcon) December 1987
Can You Feel Me Dancing? (New Dimension) March 1988
Caribe (Vestron) May 1988
The Carrier (Medusa) June 1988
Case Closed (CBS/Fox) April 1988
Cassandra (Virgin/PVG) March 1988
Catch-22 (CIC) March 1988
Cat o' Nine Tails (Warner) September 1987
Cellar Dweller (EV) April 1988
Centrefold Screen Test (Rogue) August 1987
Certain Heat (Artic) July 1987
A Certain Sacrifice (True Blue) July 1987
Child of Glass (Walt Disney) November 1987
Children of a Lesser God (CIC) February 1988
China Girl (Vestron) April 1988
The Chinese Typewriter (CIC) January 1988
Chopping Mall (First Choice/Vestron) November 1987
Chrome and Hot Leather (Orion) July 1987
Circleman (Medusa) June 1988
City Beneath the Sea (Warner) July 1987

The City's Edge (MGM/UA) July 1987
Cobra Against Ninja (Ninja Theatre) November 1987
Cocaine Wars (Medusa) August 1987
Cold Steel (New Dimension) March 1988
Colonel Redl (Rank) November 1987
The Color of Money (Touchstone) October 1987
Combat Academy (New World) November 1987
Combat Zone (IVS) August 1987
The Comeback Kid (IVS) February 1988
Comet Quest (EV) July 1987
The Coming (VPD) July 1987
Commander Lawin (Trans-Global) October 1987
Command in Hell (Futuristic Entertainment) June 1988
Confidential (RCA/Columbia) January 1988
The Conflict (Screen Indoors) March 1988
Control (Braveworld) June 1988
Courage (New World) September 1987
The Courier (Palace/PVG) June 1988
The Cowboys (Warner) August 1987
The Crack Connection (Guild) August 1987
Crackdown (Nova/PVG) October 1987
Crazy Legs (Trans-Global) October 1987
The Creeper (AVR) July 1987
Creepozoids (Colourbox) May 1988
Creepshow 2 (New World) April 1988
Crimes of the Heart (CBS/Fox) March 1988
Crime Story (New World) July 1987
Crime Story 2 – The Mafia War (New World) November 1987
Crime Story 3 – Blood Feud (New World) November 1987
Critical Condition (CIC) June 1988
Critters (RCA/Columbia) July 1987
'Crocodile' Dundee (CBS/Fox) September 1987
Crystal Heart (New World) February 1988
Cujo (Video Collection) March 1988
Cult of the Dead (Cineplex) January 1988
The Curse of the Black Widow (IVS) February 1988
Cyclone (EV) July 1987

Dance of Death (Cineplex) January 1988
Dancing in the Dark (New World) September 1987
Dangerous Affection (New World) May 1988
Dark Age (Nelson) March 1988
Dead Even (Pace) September 1987
Dead Heat (RCA/Columbia) June 1988
Deadline – Madrid (CIC) February 1988
Deadly Care (CIC) November 1987
Deadly Deception (CBS/Fox) October 1987
Deadly Friend (Warner) August 1987
The Dead of Night (Medusa) April 1988
Dead of Winter (MGM/UA) May 1988
Deadtime Stories (Braveworld/IVS) July 1987
Death Before Dishonour (New World) August 1987
Death Flash (New Dimension) July 1987
Death Games (Sony) April 1988
Death Mask (Trans-Global) October 1987
Death of a Salesman (Warner) August 1987
Death of a Soldier (Vestron) July 1987

Deathstalker 2 (New Dimension) September 1987
The Decline of the American Empire (New World) October 1987
Defence Play (Virgin/PVG) January 1988
The Delos File (Braveworld/IVS) January 1988
Demon of Paradise (New Dimension) September 1987
Demons 2 (Avatar) November 1987
Desert Bloom (RCA/Columbia) January 1988
Desperado (CIC) March 1988
Detective School Drop-Outs (Rank) October 1987
Devil in the Flesh (Mogul Plus) February 1988
Devils of Monza (Mauve) December 1987
The Devil's Paradise (Guild) May 1988
Dirty Dancing (Vestron) March 1988
Dirty Laundry (American Imperial) November 1987
Disorderlies (Warner) June 1988
Distortions (Virgin Premiere/PVG) April 1988
The Doctor and the Devils (CBS/Fox) August 1987
The Dog That Stopped the War (New World) January 1988
Dolls (Vestron) January 1988
Don't Panic (Colourbox) February 1988
Door to Door (Pace) September 1987
Double Switch (Walt Disney) December 1987
Double Target (Avatar) August 1987
Downpayment on Murder (CBS/Fox) March 1988
Down the Long Hills (Walt Disney) October 1987
Downtwisted (Warner) December 1987
Dragnet (CIC) March 1988
Dragon Fighter (VPD) July 1987
Dragons (ShowChannel) December 1987
Dream No Evil/Thirsty Dead (AVR, two tapes) November 1987
Dream to Believe (Rank) June 1988
Driving Academy (Virgin/PVG) May 1988
Duel (CIC) March 1988
Duet for One (Guild) October 1987
Dutch Treat (Rank) January 1988

Earthquake (CIC) November 1987
Earth Star Voyager (Buena Vista) June 1988
Eat and Run (New World) July 1987
Eat the Rich (CBS/Fox) June 1988
Echoes in the Darkness (Medusa, two volumes) April 1988
The Edge of Hell (IVS) August 1987
The Education of Allison Tate (Medusa) January 1988
The Education of Sonny Carson (IVS) October 1987
The Eight Masters/Jaws of the Dragon (Turbophase, two tapes) November 1987
Eight Million Ways to Die (CBS/Fox) June 1988
84 Charing Cross Road (RCA/Columbia) November 1987
11 Days, 11 Nights (Avatar) July 1987

The Eleventh Commandment (Concord) October 1987
Emmanuelle in America (Rogue) March 1988
Empire State (Virgin/PVG) November 1987
Enemy Territory (EV) October 1987
Enforcer 2 (Cougar) January 1988
Epitaph (Castle/IVS) August 1987
Ernest Goes to Camp (Touchstone) April 1988
Escalier C (Rank) May 1988
Escape From Sobibor (Sony) December 1987
Eternal Evil (First Choice) June 1988
Every Time We Say Goodbye (Vestron) June 1988
Evil Dead 2 (Palace/PVG) September 1987
Evil Senses (Avatar) September 1987
Evil Town (Mogul Plus) September 1987
Executioners From Shaolin (Warner) October 1987
Extreme Prejudice (Guild) December 1987
Eye of the Eagle (CBS/Fox) November 1987
Eye of the Tiger (Medusa) February 1988

Fame (MGM/UA) November 1987
Fate of the Hunter (MGM/UA) May 1988
Fat Guy Goes Nutzoid (AVR) August 1987
A Father's Revenge – The Terrorists (Braveworld/IVS) April 1988
Ferris Bueller's Day Off (CIC) September 1987
Field of Honour (Rank) March 1988
52 Pick-Up (Rank) December 1987
A Fight for Jenny (Apollo Entertainment) January 1988
Final Cut (Pace) September 1987
Firehouse (Academy) October 1987
Firewalker (Rank) February 1988
Flesh Gordon (EV, reissue) May 1988
Flight of the Navigator (CBS/Fox) May 1988
Florida Straits (Orion) January 1988
The Fly (CBS/Fox) March 1988
Footloose (CIC) March 1988
Force of Evil (Academy) October 1987
Ford – The Man and the Machine (Cineplex, two volumes) April 1988
Foreign Body (RCA/Columbia) April 1988
Forever Lulu (Vestron) May 1988
For Love and Honour (MGM/UA) January 1988
Fortune Dane (Sony) September 1987
The Fourth Protocol (Rank) November 1987
Frankenstein/Bride of Frankenstein (CIC, two films on one tape) June 1988
Fraternity Vacation (Channel 5) June 1988
The Freeway Killings (MGM/UA) December 1987
The French Conspiracy (Turbophase) August 1987
Frenchman's Farm (Avatar) July 1987
Friday's Curse (CIC) May 1988
Friday the 13th – The Final Chapter (CIC) August 1987
Friday the 13th – The Legacy (CIC) March 1988
Friday the 13th Part 5 – A New Beginning (CIC) December 1987
From Beyond (Vestron) November 1987
From Noon Till Three (Warner) August 1987

Full Metal Jacket (Warner) May 1988
Funeral in Berlin (CIC) February 1988

Game of Death 2 (Rank) March 1988
Gangland – The Verne Miller Story (EV) February 1988
The Garbage Pail Kids Movie (EV) January 1988
Garden of Death (AVR) July 1987
The Gate (Medusa) November 1987
Geek (Sheer Entertainment) August 1987
Ghetto Warriors (AVR) August 1987
Ghosthouse (Colourbox) March 1988
Ghost of a Chance (Guild) August 1987
The Ghost of Cypress Swamp (Walt Disney) July 1987
Ghostriders (Castle/IVS) November 1987
The Ghosts of Buxley Hall (Walt Disney) June 1988
Ghoulies 2 (EV) October 1987
The Girl (Hi-Pressure) July 1987
Girls in the Street (Atlas) October 1987
The Gladiator (New World) October 1987
The Gods Must Wait (Screen Indoors) March 1988
The Golden Child (CIC) November 1987
Good Morning Babylon (Palace/PVG) January 1988
The Good Wife (EV) November 1987
Gor (Warner) March 1988
Gothic (Virgin/PVG) September 1987
Graveyard Disturbance (Avatar) January 1988
The Great Caruso (MGM/UA) November 1987
Gremloids (ShowChannel) July 1987
Gunbus (EV) March 1988
Gung Ho (CIC) January 1988
Gunslinger (Orion) July 1987
Gunsmoke – Return to Dodge (CBS/Fox) March 1988

Half Moon Street (Embassy/Nelson) October 1987
Hammerhead Jones – Death Match (VPD) September 1987
Hands of a Stranger (CBS/Fox, two volumes) February 1988
Hannah and Her Sisters (Orion) October 1987
Hard Choices (Medusa) July 1987
Harem (Rank) August 1987
Harper Valley PTA (Studio International) January 1988
Haunted (Screen Indoors) October 1987
Haunted Honeymoon (RCA/Columbia) February 1988
A Hazard of Hearts (MGM/UA) April 1988
Headin' for Broadway (Motion Pictures On Video) October 1987
Heart (New World) June 1988
Heartbreak Ridge (Warner) October 1987
Heartburn (CIC) August 1987
Hearts of Fire (Guild) April 1988
Heavenly Kid (Orion) July 1987
Hellraiser (New World) February 1988
Heroes of Telemark (Video Collection) February 1988

Heroes Two (Warner) October 1987
He's My Girl (Medusa) April 1988
Hidden Fear (PolyGram) November 1987
Hide and Shriek (Virgin/PVG) February 1988
High Season (Virgin/PVG) December 1987
High Stakes (Sheer Entertainment) September 1987
Hijack to Hell (CIC) July 1987
The Hit Man (Motion Pictures On Video) November 1987
A Hobo's Christmas (New World) December 1987
Hollywood Air Force (New Dimension) October 1987
Hollywood Sex Slaves (Motion Pictures On Video) November 1987
Hollywood Zap (AVR) July 1987
Home Sweet Home (Academy) October 1987
Honeymoon (Vestron) October 1987
Horror Convention (Imperial) July 1987
Hostage (First Choice) May 1988
Hot Paint (MGM/UA) April 1988
Hot Splash (Hi-Pressure) December 1987
Hour of the Assassin (MGM/UA) September 1987
Housekeeping (RCA/Columbia) June 1988
House 2 – The Second Story (EV) September 1987
The House Where Hell Froze Over (Clockwork) September 1987
The Howards of Virginia (RCA/Columbia) September 1987
The Human Factor (Video Collection) March 1988
The Hunger (MGM/UA) November 1987
Hunk (Vestron) January 1988

If It's Tuesday It Still Must Be Belgium (MGM/UA) March 1988
If Looks Could Kill (Nova/PVG) September 1987
I Live With My Dad (CBS/Fox) November 1987
The Impossible Spy (MGM/UA) March 1988
Impure Thoughts (Futuristic Entertainment) May 1988
Inferno Thunderbolt (Galaxy) October 1987
Initiation (Avatar) October 1987
Inner Space (Warner) June 1988
In the Custody of Strangers (New Generation) September 1987
The Intruder (Video Movie Company) April 1988
Iron Warrior (Orion) September 1987
Ishtar (RCA/Columbia) May 1988
The Italian Job (CIC) March 1988
It's Not Easy Bein' Me (Orion) May 1988

Jail Bird (Motion Pictures On Video) March 1988
Jaws (CIC) November 1987
Jaws of the Dragon/TheEight Masters (Turbophase, two tapes) November 1987
Jaws – The Revenge (CIC) April 1988
Jaws 2 (CIC) March 1988
The Jerk (CIC) April 1988
Jocks (Warner) November 1987

Journey to the Centre of the Earth (Rank) June 1988

Jumpin' Jack Flash (CBS/Fox) March 1988

Junior (previously released as *Hot Water*) (Video Flyers) November 1987

Just Between Friends (RCA/Columbia) September 1987

Kandyland (New World) May 1988

Kangaroo (Vestron) April 1988

Kidnapped (1971) (Video Collection) March 1988

Kidnapped (1986) (Virgin/PVG) July 1987

The Kidnapping of Baby John (Chrome) October 1987

The Kids Who Knew Too Much (Walt Disney) August 1987

Killer Instinct (Vestron) March 1988

The Killer Meteors (Trans-Global) February 1988

The Kindred (EV) August 1987

King of Love (MGM/UA) May 1988

Kismet (MGM/UA) March 1988

The Kitchen Toto (Warner) May 1988

Knightriders (Warner) September 1987

Knights and Emeralds (Warner) August 1987

La Bamba (RCA/Columbia) March 1988

Labyrinth (Nelson) October 1987

Lady Avenger (Palace/PVG) January 1988

Lady Beware (Medusa) March 1988

Lady Truckers (IVS) March 1988

The Lady Vanishes (Video Collection) February 1988

The Lamp (Braveworld/IVS) November 1987

Land of the Giants (Mogul Plus) July 1987

Last Chance (Pace) October 1987

The Last Innocent Man (Guild) September 1987, reissued February 1988

The Last Radio Station (CIC) September 1987

Last Restort (Vestron) July 1987

The Last Winter (RCA/Columbia) January 1988

Latino (CBS/Fox) July 1987

Leader of the Band (CBS/Fox) June 1988

Legacy of Blood (Screen Indoors) October 1987

Legal Eagles (CIC) September 1987

The Legend of Black Thunder Mountain (IVS) February 1988

The Legend of the Golden Pearl (EV) February 1988

The Legend of Lobo (Walt Disney) May 1988

The Legend of Wolf Lodge (Vestron) June 1988

Lethal Weapon (Warner) January 1988

Let's Get Harry (RCA/Columbia) December 1987

The Liberators (Walt Disney) January 1988

The Light in the Forest (Walt Disney) September 1987

Line of Duty (Buena Vista) May 1988

The Lion of Africa (Guild) January 1988

Little Shop of Horrors (1969) (Vestron) July 1987

Little Shop of Horrors (1986) (Warner) November 1987

Little Sweetheart (Nelson) June 1988

The Living Daylights (Warner) March 1988

Logan (Mogul Plus) August 1987

Long Journey Home (Guild) June 1988

The Long Shot (RCA/Columbia) June 1988

The Loveless (Palace/PVG) May 1988

The Lover (Rank) November 1987

Made in Heaven (Guild) February 1988

The Magic Toyshop (Palace/PVG) November 1987

A Man and a Woman – 20 Years Later (Warner) July 1987

Manaos (Motion Pictures On Video) October 1987

Mannequin (Warner) November 1987

Mascara (Warner) April 1988

Master Ninja 5 (Ninja Theatre) July 1987

Master Ninja 6 (Ninja Theatre) September 1987

Master Ninja 7 (Ninja Theatre) December 1987

Maxie (Orion) July 1987

Maximum Security (New World) February 1988

Meatballs (CIC) June 1988

Meatballs 3 – Summer Job (Braveworld/IVS) September 1987

Melba (Screen Entertainment) March 1988

Menace on the Mountain (Walt Disney) August 1987

Men from the Monastery (Warner) October 1987

Mercy or Murder? (MGM/UA) November 1987

Messenger of Death (VPD) September 1987

Midnight Offerings (CIC) May 1988

Million Dollar Madness (Rank) February 1988

Mind Killer (Mauve) February 1988

Mind Over Murder (CIC) May 1988

The Mines of Kilimanjaro (American Imperial) April 1988

Mirrors (Castle/IVS) August 1987

Miss Mary (New World) March 1988

Modern Girls (EV) January 1988

Moon Pilot (Walt Disney) July 1987

The Morning After (Guild) November 1987

The Mosquito Coast (CBS/Fox) August 1987

Movers and Shakers (Warner) January 1988

Mrs vs Mistress (Rank) July 1987

Murder Ordained (Sheer Entertainment, two tapes) May 1988

Murders in the Rue Morgue (Chrome) December 1987

The Naked Cage (Rank) September 1987

The Naked Country (Pace) September 1987

The Name of the Rose (Nelson) November 1987

Near Dark (EV) March 1988

News at Eleven (Panther) November 1987

Nice Girls Don't Explode (New World) June 1988

Night of the Creeps (CBS/Fox) May 1988

Night of the Demons (Palace Premiere/PVG) April 1988

Night Force (First Choice) September 1987

The Night of the Grizzly (CIC) November 1987

Nightmare City (Medusa) November 1987

Nightmare on Alcatraz (Pace) July 1987

A Nightmare on Elm Street 3 – Dream Warriors (Warner) April 1988

Night Mother (CIC) March 1988

Night Screams (Braveworld/IVS) December 1987

Nightside (CIC) December 1987

Nights in White Satin (Mauve) June 1988

1941 (CIC) June 1988

Ninja and the Warriors of Fire (Falcon) October 1987

Ninja Commandments (Ninja Theatre) January 1988

Ninja in the Killing Field (Ariel) July 1987

Nobody's Fool (Sony) October 1987

No Mercy (CBS/Fox) April 1988

No Safe Haven (Medusa) March 1988

No Sweat (Mogul Plus) February 1988

Nothing in Common (RCA/Columbia) October 1987

Notorious/Spellbound (Video Collection, two films on one tape) February 1988

Not Quite Human (Walt Disney) May 1988

Nowhere to Hide (Guild) October 1987

Number One with a Bullet (Rank) December 1987

The Nutcracker – The Motion Picture (EV) November 1987

Off Beat (Touchstone) September 1987

Omega Syndrome (New World) January 1988

Omen of Evil (ShowChannel/PVG) February 1988

The One and Only Genuine Original Family Band (Walt Disney) July 1987

One By One (IVS) August 1987

One Crazy Summer (Warner) July 1987

One Night Stand (Vestron) November 1987

One Summer Love (Orion) July 1987

On Wings of Eagles (Heron) April 1988

Open House (Heron) June 1988

Order of the Black Eagle (CBS/Fox) March 1988

Ordinary Heroes (Vestron) November 1987

Ordinary People (CIC) March 1988

Outback Vampires (Guild) June 1988

Outlaw Force (Nova) January 1988

Outlaws (CIC) September 1987

Outrageous Fortune (Touchstone) March 1988

Outrageous Party (IVS) March 1988

Overkill (Hi-Pressure) September 1987

Over the Top (Rank) October 1987

Pack of Lies (Futuristic Entertainment) January 1988

Pals (Futuristic Entertainment) October 1987

Paradise Motel (Channel 5) June 1988

Party Camp (Vestron) September 1987

The Peanut Butter Solution (New World) August 1987

Pee Wee's Big Adventure (Warner) March 1988

157

Peggy Sue Got Married (CBS/Fox) November 1987

Penalty Phase (New World) October 1987

Penitentiary 3 (Warner) May 1988

Perfect Timing (First Choice/Vestron) January 1988

Personal Services (Virgin Premiere/PVG) October 1987

The Pink Chiquitas (Hi-Pressure) August 1987

Pinocchio (Walt Disney) October 1987

P.I. Private Investigations (Castle) June 1988

Pirates (Warner) July 1987

The Pit and the Pendulum (Video Gems) February 1988

Platoon (RCA/Columbia) January 1988

Pleasure Vacation (Cassex) November 1987

Poker Alice (New World) November 1987

Police Academy 4 (Warner) January 1988

Police Assassins (Screen Entertainment/PVG) July 1987

Police Girls' Academy (VPD) February 1988

Poltergeist (MGM/UA) November 1987

Poor Little Rich Girl (Concord, two volumes) February 1988

Positive I.D. (CIC) June 1988

Possessed (Warner) September 1987

P.O.W. – The Escape (MGM/UA) July 1987

Pretty Kill (Guild) July 1987

Pretty Smart (New World) October 1987

Prick Up Your Ears (Virgin Premiere/PVG) March 1988

Prince of Bel Air (Castle/IVS) October 1987

Prison Ship Star Slammer (Sheer Entertainment) February 1988

Private Investigations (Cassex/AVR) September 1987

Project A (American Imperial) January 1988

Project X (CBS/Fox) February 1988

A Promise Made (Walt Disney) November 1987

Prom Night 2 – Hello Mary Lou (Sheer Entertainment) April 1988

Psycho II (CIC) May 1988

Psycho 3 (CIC) July 1987

Quest (CIC) September 1987

The Quick and the Dead (Guild) July 1987

Radio Days (RCA/Columbia) April 1988

Raging Fury (PolyGram) October 1987

Rags to Riches (New World) December 1987

Raiders in Action (Warner) June 1988

Raiders of the Lost Code (AVR) September 1987

Raid on Entebbe (Video Movie Company) September 1987

Raising Arizona (CBS/Fox) April 1988

Ratboy (Warner) January 1988

The Rats (Video Collection) March 1988

Raw Deal (CBS/Fox) February 1988

Rawhead Rex (First Choice) March 1988

Rear Window (CIC) April 1988

Red-Headed Stranger (Nelson) April 1988

The Reluctant Dragon (Walt Disney) July 1987

Remote Control (CBS/Fox) March 1988

Rent-a-Cop (Vestron) June 1988

Rest in Pieces (Chrome) October 1987

Retaliator (Imperial Entertainment) August 1987

The Return of Josey Wales (ABC) July 1987

The Return of Sherlock Holmes (CBS/Fox) August 1987

Return of the Big Cat (Walt Disney) June 1988

The Return of the Six Million Dollar Man and the Bionic Woman (CIC) January 1988

Return to Horror High (New World) September 1987

Revenge of the Dragons (Clockwork) September 1987

Revenge of the Iron Fist Maiden (Pace/PVG) July 1987

Rich Bitch (Cassex/AVR) September 1987

Right to Die (Sheer Entertainment) June 1988

Rita, Sue and Bob Too (Virgin Premiere/PVG) June 1988

River's Edge (Palace Premiere/PVG) December 1987

Road to Morocco (CIC) February 1988

Rolling Vengeance (Medusa) May 1988

The Room Upstairs (Futuristic Entertainment) November 1987

Rose Marie (MGM/UA) November 1987

Rotor (RCA/Columbia) June 1988

Round Midnight (Warner) October 1987

Roxanne (RCA/Columbia) April 1988

Rude Boy (Hendring/PVG) August 1987

Runaway Passion (Cassex) November 1987

Running Scared (MGM/UA) November 1987

The Rutherford County Line (CIC) April 1988

Saigon Commandos (Medusa) March 1988

Salvador (Vestron) September 1987

Sammy and Rosie Get Laid (Nelson) May 1988

Savage Streets (Medusa) September 1987

Saving Grace (Embassy) July 1987

Say Yes (Medusa) November 1987

Scalps (Ariel) January 1988

Scared Stiff (CBS/Fox) January 1988

Scorpion (Warner) December 1987

The Sea Wolves (Video Collection) March 1988

Secret Executioners (VPD) November 1987

Secret Ninja, Roaring Tiger (VPD) September 1987

The Secret of My Success (CIC) March 1988

Secret of the Sahara (Braveworld/IVS) March 1988

Secrets of the Bermuda Triangle (Warner) July 1987

Secrets of the Pirates' Inn (Walt Disney) September 1987

Seven Minutes in Heaven (Warner) July 1987

Shadow Dream (Nelson) March 1988

Shallow Grave (Embassy) September 1987

Shape-Up (Hi-Pressure) December 1987

Sharks' Paradise (Vestron) July 1987

Shattered Innocence (Guild) April 1988

She's Gotta Have It (Palace Premiere/PVG) September 1987

Short Circuit (CBS/Fox) December 1987

Silver Dragon Ninja (Ninja Theatre) August 1987

Six Against the Rock (Vestron) February 1988

Skeleton Coast (Sheer Entertainment) March 1988

Slamdance (Palace Premiere/PVG) January 1988

Slammer Girls (Vestron) October 1987

Slash (Trans-Global) October 1987

Slate, Wyn and Me (Palace Premiere/PVG) August 1987

Slaughter High (Vestron) August 1987

Slaughterhouse (Braveworld/IVS) May 1988

Sleeping Beauty (Warner) December 1987

Smith (Walt Disney) June 1988

Smokey and the Bandit (CIC) June 1988

Solarwarriors (MGM/UA) December 1987

Soldier Warriors (Falcon) December 1987

Something Wild (RCA/Columbia) June 1988

Sorority House Massacre (Medusa) August 1987

Spacerage (Vestron) October 1987

Specters (Avatar) December 1987

Spellbound/Notorious (Video Collection, two films on one tape) February 1988

Space Camp (CBS/Fox) January 1988

Space Island (Braveworld/IVS) January 1988

Square Dance (Sony) February 1988

Sssnake (CIC) August 1987

Stand By Me (RCA/Columbia) October 1987

Starcrash (Video Gems) February 1988

Star Knight (Vestron) August 1987

Star Trek 4: The Voyage Home (CIC) December 1987

Star Trek – The Motion Picture (CIC) November 1987

A State of Emergency (Trans-Global) October 1987

Staying Alive (CIC) February 1988

Steel Arena (Vestron) September 1987

Steel Dawn (Virgin/PVG) April 1988

Steele Justice (EV) October 1987

The Stepfather (Virgin/PVG) May 1988

The Stepford Children (Screen Entertainment) January 1988

Stewardess School (RCA/Columbia) July 1987

Still Watch (Sheer Entertainment) November 1987

Stogies (Guild) July 1987

Stormquest (Palace/PVG) January 1988

Straight to Hell (Nelson) January 1988

A Stranger Waits (Guild) September 1987

Street Justice (Guild) January 1988

Streets of Gold (Vestron) October 1987

Strike of Mantis Fist (VPD) December 1987

Striking Chance (RCA/Columbia) February 1988

Stripped to Kill (MGM/UA) October 1987

Stronghold (Rank) August 1987

Stuck On You (Channel 5) June 1988

Summer Camp (IVS) August 1987

Summer Heat (EV) June 1988

Summer Holiday (Warner) June 1988

Summer Magic (Walt Disney) August 1987

Summer School (CIC) June 1988

Sunday Drive (Walt Disney) October 1987

Supercarrier (Cineplex) June 1988
Superman 4 – The Quest for Peace (Warner) February 1988
The Sure Thing (Channel 5) June 1988
Surf Nazis (Cineplex) March 1988
Surrender (Warner) June 1988
Survivor (New Dimension) February 1988
Sweet Revenge (First Choice/Vestron) December 1987
Sweet Sixteen (VPD) July 1987
Sworn to Silence (Braveworld/IVS) April 1988
Symphony of Evil (Academy) December 1987

Take Me High (Warner) June 1988
Take Two (Nova/PVG) November 1987
The Talk of the Town (RCA/Columbia) September 1987
Tarka the Otter (Video Collection)
Teddy (Nova/PVG) March 1988
Teenwolf Too (EV) April 1988
10 to Midnight (Video Collection) April 1988
Terminal Entry (Braveworld/IVS) January 1988
Terror at Ten Killer (Castle/IVS) December 1987
Thirsty Dead/Dream No Evil (AVR, two tapes) November 1987
This Island Earth (CIC) February 1988
Thrashin' (CBS/Fox) July 1987
The Three Amigos (RCA/Columbia) December 1987
Three for the Road (CBS/Fox) June 1988
Thunder 2 (Medusa) September 1987
A Tiger's Tale (EV) June 1988
Tim (ShowChannel/PVG) April 1988
Time Games (Apollo) June 1988
Timestalkers (CBS/Fox) November 1987
Tin Men (Touchstone) February 1988
Tongs (IVS) December 1987
Too Much (Warner) June 1988

Top Gun (CIC) October 1987
The Torture Zone (Cineplex) January 1988
Touch and Go (First Choice) February 1988
Tough Guys (Touchstone) November 1987
Tough Ninja the Shadow Warrior (Ninja Theatre) February 1988
Tour of Duty (New World) March 1988
Tour of Duty – Under Siege (New World) June 1988
Trading Places (CIC) April 1988
Trapped (CIC) May 1988
Tropical Fruit (Screen Indoors) August 1987
Trouble in the City of Angels (Guild) March 1988
True Stories (Warner) September 1987
Turnaround (Guild) July 1987
Tusks (Guild) April 1988

Undercover (Warner) March 1988
Under Cover (IVS) July 1987
Up the World (Atlas) October 1987

Valley Girls (AVR) July 1987
Vampire at Midnight (Palace Premiere/PVG) April 1988
Vasectomy (Castle/IVS) November 1987
Victims (Warner) January 1988
The Video Dead (Medusa) January 1988
Violent Rage (Atlas) March 1988

Walk Like a Man (MGM/UA) January 1988
The Warriors (CIC) April 1988
War Zone (Guild) September 1987
Welcome to 18 (Vestron) January 1988
Werewolf (EV) May 1988
Westward Ho, The Wagons (Walt Disney) January 1988
What Comes Around (Avatar) December 1987
Wheels of Terror (Medusa) October 1987
When the Wind Blows (CBS/Fox) October 1987

When You're in Love (RCA/Columbia) September 1987
Where Eagles Dare (MGM/UA) March 1988
Where the River Runs Black (MGM/UA) September 1987
Whiffs (Wildcat) December 1987
The Whistle Blower (Nelson) February 1988
White of the Eye (Warner) February 1988
White Ghost (Virgin/PVG) June 1988
White Phantom (Medusa) February 1988
The Whoopee Boys (CIC) October 1987
Whoops Apocalypse (Virgin/PVG) July 1987
Who's That Girl (Warner) December 1987
Wild Thing (EV) December 1987
Willy Milly (Medusa) December 1987
Wimps (Vestron) February 1988
Windmills of the Gods (CBS/Fox) June 1988
Wisdom (Warner) March 1988
Wiseguy (EV) June 1988
Wish You Were Here (Palace Premiere/PVG) May 1988
Witchboard (Guild) August 1987
Witchfinder General (Imperial) July 1987
The Wizard of Oz (Apollo) November 1987
Wolf at the Door (RCA/Columbia) May 1988
The Women's Club (Sony) November 1987
Wonderful Life (Warner) June 1988
The Woo Woo Kid (Guild) May 1988
Working Girls (Palace Premiere/PVG) July 1987

Yellow Submarine (Warner) August 1987
Young Harry Houdini (Walt Disney) February 1988
The Young Ones (Warner) June 1988
You Ruined My Life (Walt Disney) January 1988

Zombie Aftermath (Trans-Global) October 1987
Zombie High (Vestron) April 1988

In Memoriam

A list of the stars, directors and producers who have died during the year, with biographical details and, in many cases, a tribute to their contribution to the cinema.

Edgar Anstey, whose real name was Harold Macfarlane Anstey, from Watford, Herts, died at the age of 80 on 26 September 1987. He was one of John Grierson's famous élite group of British documentary moviemakers who led the world in this genre in the 'thirties and 'forties. Anstey was with the Empire Marketing Board's film unit from 1930 to 1934, later organizing the Shell Film Unit before accepting the position of London producer/director for the *March of Time* series. He then went to New York to become foreign editor of the films. After producing a number of factual films for the British government during the war, in 1949 Anstey set up the British Transport Film Unit. For five years, starting in 1941, he wrote the *Spectator*'s weekly film column and from 1946 to 1949 he was the BBC's film critic. In 1948 his book *The Development of Film Technique in Great Britain* was published. He served as chairman of the British Film Academy in 1956, became president of the International Scientific Film Association between 1959 and 1962, was made a governor of the British Film Institute in 1964 and was elected chairman of the Society of Film and Television Arts in 1967. His film output, comparatively small, included *Uncharted Waters, Eskimo Village, Housing Problems* and *Enough to Eat* in the 'thirties and, later, *Journey into Spring, Between the Tides, Under Night Skies, Terminus* (which won the Best Short prize at the 1961 Venice Film Festival) and *Wild Wings*, which brought him the 1966 Oscar for the year's Best Non-Fiction Short.

The son of an Austrian emigrant father, who built up a successful brewery business in Omaha, USA, and a schoolteacher mother, Frederic Austerlitz – better known as **Fred Astaire** – died on 22 June 1987 in the arms of his second wife after a common cold had turned into pneumonia. He was 88. Considered by many critics and others to be the greatest popular dancer of all time,

Fred Astaire.

he was also greatly respected in the world of ballet for his inspired choreography, nimble-footedness and perfect sense of style. Astaire began taking dancing lessons, with his sister (and later stage partner) Adele, before he was five. While still very young, the pair were signed up for a four-month vaudeville tour, after which they settled down to some serious schooling. But when Fred was fifteen he and Adele were back on the boards and were soon earning rave notices for their spot in the Broadway musical *Over the Top*. After a successful eighteen-month season in

London, the pair returned to New York to make a hit in *Lady Be Good*. After another success in *The Band Wagon* in 1931, Adele, now married to Lord Charles Cavendish, decided to retire, leaving Fred professionally alone for the first time. Watched with interest by the critics, Fred took the change in his nimble stride. His screen debut came in 1933 with the offer of a small role in *Dancing Lady*, with Joan Crawford, and then, in the same year, a single number with his pretty new partner Ginger Rogers in *Flying Down to Rio* rocketed the pair to stardom. They went on to make ten more films together, including such classics as *Roberta* in 1935, *Top Hat* in the same year, *Follow the Fleet* in 1936 and *The Story of Vernon and Irene Castle* in 1939. After a ten-year interval they teamed up again for their last film together, *The Barkleys of Broadway*. Fred's partners during those ten years included Eleanor Powell (*Broadway Melody of 1940*), Rita Hayworth (*You'll Never Get Rich* in 1941 and *You Were Never Lovelier* in 1942) and Ann Miller (in *Easter Parade* in 1948). In 1959 Astaire neatly side-stepped into dramatic roles with his character performance in *On the Beach* and continued to play similar parts in non-musical films such as *The Towering Inferno* in 1974. But in 1968, at the age of 68, Astaire did make a one-off return to dancing on screen, in *Finian's Rainbow*. During these later years he did a great deal of TV work. Though Astaire never won an Oscar for a film role, he was given a special Academy Award in 1949. Always a perfectionist, he put his partners through endless rehearsals during which he was a very hard taskmaster (Fred once described himself as being 'bad-tempered, impatient and hard to please'); but he never worked them harder than he worked himself. Not much of a singer, he had a style perfectly suited to his range; not handsome, he had a wry smile and considerable charm; it all added up to a great, popular and much loved personality who won countless fans. He was unique; a great artist. As one critic said, there'll never be anyone quite like or as good as Fred Astaire.

Lucille Vasconcellos Langhanke, or **Mary Astor** as the film world knew her, died on 25 September 1987 at the age of 81. The famous star, who chalked up well over 100 films in her

Mary Astor (with Humphrey Bogart).

long career, had been in poor health since the mid-'seventies and in hospital since the beginning of 1986. From Quincy, Illinois, the daughter of a German immigrant father who persuaded his daughter to enter a beauty contest when she was only fourteen, Miss Astor started to make films the following year, if somewhat inauspiciously – her role in her first film, *Sentimental Tommy*, ended up on the cutting-room floor and her second film, *Bullets or Ballots*, was completed but never released. But things improved and she had bit parts in a number of silents, culminating in her being selected by John Barrymore to play opposite him in *Beau Brummel* when she was just eighteen. Her career peaked in the 'thirties and 'forties with films like *Dodsworth*, *The Prisoner of Zenda*, *Brigham Young*, *The Great Lie*, *The Palm Beach Story*, *Meet Me in St Louis*, *Little Women* and, possibly her greatest success, *The Maltese Falcon* (1941). The transition from silent to sound movies had not been easy for Mary, and it was only after a year's

absence that she was invited back to the studios. Meanwhile Miss Astor's private life often made the Hollywood headlines: following her tempestuous affair with John Barrymore during the making of *Beau Brummel*, she married the first of her four husbands; there was a court case over the custody of her daughter; the release of pages (some of which she claimed had been faked) from her scandalous diary; her parents' demand for financial support; her hospitalization for alcoholism; and her overdose of sleeping pills – which she said was an accident. After completing *Any Number Can Play* in 1949 Miss Astor did not go before a camera again until 1956, when she made *A Kiss Before Dying*. Her final three films were *Return to Peyton Place* in 1961, *Youngblood Hawke* in 1964 and *Hush, Hush, Sweet Charlotte* in 1965. Despite her many fine performances Miss Astor won only one Oscar, for Best Supporting Performance in *The Great Lie* (1941). She had a weekly radio show at one time and also appeared on television and on stage in California and New York. Apart from her autobiography *My Story* (published in 1959) and *A Life on Film* (1967), she had five published novels to her credit.

Alfie Bass, who died in his birthplace, London, on 15 July 1987, at the age of 66, will always be remembered for his Cockney characters, but he had quite a considerable range, including Shakespeare. Perhaps moviegoers will best recall him for his *tour de force* in the 1955 film of his stage success *The Bespoke Overcoat*. In all, Alfie appeared in some 30 films, starting with Ealing Studio's *Johnny Frenchman* in 1945. Later appearances included those in *The Lavender Hill Mob* (1951), *It Always Rains on Sunday* (1947), *A Tale of Two Cities* (1958), the Beatles' film

Alfie Bass.

Help! (1965), *Alfie* (1966) and *Up the Junction* (1968). His final screen performance was in *Dick Turpin* (1980). A graduate from the old Unity Theatre, Alfie's professional debut was in that playhouse's 1939 production of *Plant in the Sun*, starring Paul Robeson. Later he was successfully to succeed Topol in *Fiddler on the Roof*, appear in the musical *Finian's Rainbow* and play roles in *Hamlet*, *The Taming of the Shrew* and other Shakespeare plays. On the small screen his greatest success was in the series *Bootsie and Snudge*.

Known in Hollywood as 'The Serial King', **Spencer Gordon Bennet** died, aged 94, in Santa Monica on 8 October 1987. Creator on screen of such popular characters as the first Superman, Batman and Robin and Captain Video, Bennet made more than a hundred films, including a classic collection of serials. Starting as a daring stuntman in the early days of the industry, he graduated to feature direction and became famous in Hollywood for being able to bring modest features in on time and within modest budgets, a reputation which pushed him into a B-movie rut from which he undeservedly never escaped. His last productions were both for Embassy Pictures in 1965: *Requiem for a Gunfighter* and *The Bounty Killer*.

Somewhat surprisingly omitted from even some British film 'who's who' publications, **Ballard Berkeley** died, aged 83, on 16 January 1988. He made his screen debut in 1930 in *The Chinese Bungalow* and subsequent screen credits include *In Which We Serve*, *See How They Run*, *The Outsider* and *They Made Me a Fugitive*. Most people will now recall him most readily in the role of an eccentric guest in the TV series *Fawlty Towers*.

When he died on 17 August 1987, aged 97, **Clarence Brown** was not only the longest-living of Hollywood film directors but also one of the most successful and distinguished. Although he made some all-time greats and earned six nominations, Brown never won an Oscar, though several of his films richly deserved that accolade. The son of a Southern cotton manufacturer, Clarence Brown achieved two Engineering degrees at the University of Tennessee and his first jobs were in the automobile industry, before he switched to his other passion, motion pictures. Visiting the studios, he managed to persuade Maurice Tourneur, then recently moved from France to Hollywood, to take him on as his assistant and during the next few years he became the great man's assistant director, editor and Second Unit director before co-directing with him. Brown was later to admit that it was to the Frenchman's training and help that he owed his successful career and he often said, 'I owe everything I've got in the world to him.' Certainly there was something of Tourneur in all of Brown's films: the European style, the pictorial quality and the polished romantic sophistication that were the maestro's trade marks. Most of the great Hollywood stars of that period appeared in the 50-odd films that Brown directed, most notably Greta Garbo, who produced her finest performances for him in silent films such as *The Flesh and the Devil* (1927) and *A Woman of Affairs* (the following year) and in the talkies *Anna Christie, Romance* (both 1930) and *Inspiration* (1931). Other classics (with Brown sometimes doubling up as producer as well as director) included *Anna Karenina* (1935) and *Marie Waleska/ Conquest* (1937). Further notable films in the list, which started with his co-direction with Tourneur of *The Last of the Mohicans* and *The Foolish Matrons* (in 1920), were *The Light in the Dark* with Lon Chaney in 1922, *The Eagle*, starring Valentino – Brown's first really big success (1925), *A Free Soul* with Norma Shearer in 1931, *Night Flight* (1933, starring Lionel and John Barrymore, Clark Gable and Helen Hayes), *Ah Wilderness* (1935), *The Gorgeous Hussy* (1936), *Idiot's Delight* and *The Rains Came* (1939), *The Human Comedy* (1943) and *The White Cliffs of Dover* (1944). Two of his greatest popular successes were *National Velvet* (starring Mickey Rooney and introducing the 12-year-old Elizabeth Taylor) in 1945 and *The Yearling* (with Gregory Peck and Jane Wyman and introducing another youthful discovery in the Oscar-winning Claude Jarman Junior) in 1947. Brown's personal favourites from among his large output were *Intruder in the Dust* in 1950 and *Song of Love*, made three years previously. In 1952, Brown produced (but did not direct) *Never Let Me Go*, at the conclusion of which he walked out of the film studios for ever, spending the next 25 years happily employed in his hobbies of hunting, flying and motor cars, and dabbling successfully in the real-estate deals which considerably enhanced his reputation for being one of the richest men in American showbiz. During his long motion-picture career Clarence Brown almost miraculously managed to keep up a very high standard and, looking through the 50 or so movies with which he was concerned in one way or another, it is impossible to recall a real dud – a very remarkable achievement.

Madeleine Carroll died in Marbella, Spain, where she had lived for many years, on 2 October 1987 at the age of 81 after a long illness. For British moviegoers of the 'thirties, she will always be associated with two of Alfred Hitchcock's vintage thrillers, *The 39 Steps* and *The Secret Agent*. Born Marie-Madeleine Bernadette O'Carroll in West Bromwich, she completed her education by winning a BA (with Honours) in French at Birmingham University. She taught that language at a Brighton girls' school for one term then, with £20 in her pocket, went to London determined to be an actress. She almost starved before she got a part with a touring company, and she modelled hats to supplement her income. But screen success followed her London stage debut in 1927, when she was picked from 150 hopefuls to play a role in the film *The Guns of Loos*, followed by two more screen roles the same year, in *The First Born* and *What Money Can Buy*. Her subsequent busy schedule (in all she made 23 films in Britain, eighteen in America, plus one in France) included *Atlantic* (1929), *Young Woodley* (1930), *I Was a Spy* (1933), *The World Moves On* (1934) and *The Dictator* in 1935, the year she had her greatest success, *The 39 Steps*. Hitchcock used her again the following year in another winner, *The Secret Agent*. These led to Hollywood offers and Miss Carroll crossed the Atlantic that same year to make a trio of moves (*The Case Against Mrs Ames*, *The General Died at Dawn* and *Lloyds of London*. There followed *The Prisoner of Zenda* (1937), *Café Society* (1939), *My Son, My Son* and *North-West Mounted Police* in 1940 and *My Favorite Blonde* in 1942, co-starring with Bob Hope. During the war Miss Carroll served with the Red Cross in France for four years and her services were acknowledged with membership of the Légion d'Honneur. After the war she made one British and two American films: *White Cradle Inn* (alternative title, *High Fury*) in 1946, *An Innocent Affair* (alternative title *Don't Trust Your Husband*) in 1948 and, her final screen appearance, *The Fan* in 1949. Subsequently, apart from a few TV, radio and stage appearances, most of her time was spent working for UNESCO.

Primarily a man of the theatre, Sir **John Clements** – who died at the age of 77 on 6 April 1988 – contributed some sterling performances to the movies; notably in *The Four Feathers* (1939), *Ships*

Madeleine Carroll.

with Wings (1941), *South Riding* (1938), *Knight Without Armour* (1937), *Rembrandt* (1936), *Oh! What a Lovely War* (1969) and, his final appearance, *Gandhi* (1983). His one film directing credit was *Call of the Blood*, which he also wrote and produced in 1948. Clements's career began on the West End stage in 1930 and it was not so long before he was directing his own company at the famous old Intimate Theatre at Palmer's Green. He played Macbeth at the Old Vic and appeared in *St Joan* in New York. More recently he ran the Chichester Drama Festival for seven years. Despite 50 successful years in the theatre, and his knighthood in 1966 for his services to the profession, for some reason – maybe his personality was not quite strong enough – he never achieved the popularity and acclaim which many felt was his due; he was always one step behind the Oliviers, Richardsons and Gielguds of this world.

The name of **Nat** (Nathaniel) **Cohen** may not mean much to moviegoers, but for many years it has meant a great deal to the people who make and show movies. Son of a London butcher, he built up a small chain of cinemas before turning to film production. He joined with Stuart Levy to form Anglo-Amalgamated Films, which in turn became ABC. Cohen's last film, as executive producer, was the John Cleese comedy *Clockwise*, one of many successes with which his name is associated. In both public and private life he avoided the limelight and was known to some as the 'Quiet Man'. A racehorse owner of note, he was, with Levy, co-owner of two Grand National winners. He had reached the age of 82 when he died in a London hospital on 10 February 1988, after 50 years in the film business.

Patience Collier, whose role of Mrs Poulteney in *The French Lieutenant's Woman* was her last and almost certainly her most impressive screen performance, died, aged 76, in London on 13 July 1987. Rene Ritcher, to give her real name, was a veteran stage actress whose professional debut was made in 1932. After the usual round of touring companies and repertory Miss Collier graduated to the British National Theatre and the Royal Shakespeare Company, and had been associated with the latter for the past twenty years. Her comparatively few screen roles included those in *Decline and Fall*, *Every Home Should Have One*, *Countess Dracula* and *Fiddler on the Roof*.

For most people, the name of **Andrew Cruickshank** conjures up a picture of the crusty old GP who shared a Scottish rural practice with Dr Finlay in the long-running TV series *Dr Finlay's*

Andrew Cruickshank.

Casebook. But Cruickshank, who was born in Aberdeen on Christmas Day 1907, and died on 29 April 1988, had a distinguished theatrical career and was no stranger to the film studios. A trained engineer, he decided on an acting career after appearing with the Aberdeen Lyric Opera Company and moved across to touring and repertory company productions, ending up in London in 1930 in *Othello* with Paul Robeson. New York and London productions followed, as did Old Vic tours of Europe and Eygpt. He made his first film, *Auld Lang Syne*, in 1938 and, after service in the Army from 1940 to 1945,

he resumed his acting career and made his second, *Idol of Paris*, in 1948. A number of other film roles followed but Cruickshank always remained by choice primarily a stage actor. He was the author of two performed plays, *Lysistrata* and *Adults Only*. His films included *El Cid*, *Kidnapped*, *The Cruel Sea* and *Richard III*.

Though his name is missing from most film reference books, **Allan Cuthbertson**, who died, aged 67, on 8 February 1988, had appeared in more than 40 films, including *The Guns of Navarone*, *Tunes of Glory*, *Room at the Top* and *Law and Disorder*. He made his screen debut as a shifty army officer in the 1954 film *Carrington VC*, a role he subsequently played in the stage and television versions of the drama. Cuthbertson began his career in radio and theatre in his native Australia, but came to Britain in 1947 and stayed on. He appeared in many stage productions and was frequently to be seen on television. He may be best recalled in that medium as one of the characters in the classic comedy series *Fawlty Towers*.

Silent star **Priscilla Dean** was 91 when a fall precipitated her demise in Las Vegas on 27 December 1987. Born in New York to theatrical parents, she started working with them as a small child, and was already a polished and assured performer by the time she had reached her tenth birthday. She made her screen debut at the age of fourteen, appearing in a Biograph one-reeler and she reached stardom in the 1917 serial *The Gray Ghost*. Between then and her last film role – in *Behind Stone Walls* (1922), made after a five-year retirement – she appeared in more than 30 films, including *The Virgin of Stamboul* (1920) and *Under Two Flags* (1922).

For many years Billy Wilder's favourite scenarist and associate producer, **I.A.L. Diamond** (real name Itek Dommnici – he was born in Rumania) died, aged 67, on 21 April 1988. He contributed a great deal to many of Wilder's classic successes, such as *Love in the Afternoon* (1957), *Some Like it Hot* (1959), *The Front Page* (1947) and *The Apartment* (1960), which brought him a screen-writing Oscar, shared with Wilder.

With some 50 screen appearances to her credit in her 40-year career in films and TV series, **Jeff Donnell** (real name Jean Marie Donnell) died, aged 66, in Hollywood on 11 April 1988. Starting off as a teenager in Columbia films, she graduated to main supporting player and, occasionally, the lead in minor movies, winding up by playing more mature, matronly roles. Her first screen appearance was in *My Sister Eileen* in 1942; other titles included *The Fuller Brush Girl* (1950), *The Blue Gardenia* (1953), *My Man Godfrey* (1957), *Tora! Tora! Tora!* (1970) and *Stand Up and Be Counted* (1972). She also appeared in a number of American TV series, more recently as the housekeeper in *General Hospital*.

Rugged **Richard Egan**, who died in Santa Monica on 20 July 1987 at the age of 65, was both a BA (San Francisco) and an MA (Stamford). At the former

Richard Egan.

he taught public speaking until joining the US Army, where he taught judo before seeing active service in the Philippines. Demobilized as Captain Egan, he returned to Stamford, where he taught theatrical history and dramatic literature and appeared in a number of the university dramatic society's plays. It was in one of these that he was noticed by a visiting Warner Brothers talent scout and invited to Hollywood. Within the year, 1949, he had appeared in his first two films: *The Damned Don't Cry* and *Undercover Girl*. He was to make more than 30 films over the next 30 years, including *Violent Saturday*

(1955), *Love Me Tender* (1956), *A Summer Place* (1959), *Pollyanna* (1960), *Valley of Mystery* (1967), *The Big Cube* (1969), *The Sweet Creek County War* (1979) and *The Amsterdam Kill* (1978).

The American-Chinese actor and restaurateur **Benson Fong** died of a stroke at the age of 70 on 1 August 1987. He made his screen debut in 1943 and went on to play Chinese, Japanese and other assorted Oriental characters, mostly villains, in 30 films, including *Charlie Chan in the Secret Service, Keys of the Kingdom, Dark Alibi, The Peking Express, His Majesty O'Keefe, Our Man Flint, The Love Bug, The Strongest Man in the World* and *Oliver's Story*. It was Gregory Peck, when they were working together on *Keys of the Kingdom*, who suggested that Fong open a restaurant in Hollywood; at one time he owned four in the celluloid city. His was also a familiar face on American TV.

It is of some significance that the passing of **Bob Fosse** at the age of 60 was recorded in the 'legitimate' (theatrical) pages of *Variety* rather than in the film section. Fosse, who died of a heart attack while walking in a Washington street (after rehearsing a revival of *Sweet Charity*) on 23 September 1987, was the son of a vaudeville-performer-father and first trod the boards as a dancer at an early age. In touring companies of shows like *Call Me Mister*, he made his Broadway debut in the flop *Dance Me a Song* (35 performances). This persuaded him to try Hollywood, where in 1953 he appeared in three musicals, including *Kiss Me Kate*. Two years and one rung up the ladder later, Fosse choreographed as well as appeared in Columbia's *My Sister Eileen*, repeating that double-act with the films of two other stage shows, *The Pajama Game* and *Damn Yankees*. Back in the theatre, his reputation increased with every show he did and in 1958 he was handed *Redhead* to direct on Broadway. After a whole string of theatrical successes as director, leading player and choreographer, he returned to Hollywood to direct his first film, *Cabaret*, which won him a 1973 Oscar. He was nominated for another Academy Award with his second film, the bio-pic *Lenny*, about the controversial cabaret performer Lenny Bruce. Fosse choreographed and performed in the charming film *The Little Prince* (also

released in the UK in 1976–7). His next film as director was the Oscar-laden (nine nominations, four awards) autobiographical *All That Jazz*, the 1980 release about an actor-director who works himself into a heart attack – as did Fosse in his next film, the 1983–4 release *Star 80*. This was to be his last film, for he then returned to the theatre to produce the only flop among his thirteen Broadway shows, *Big Deal*, which he had adapted from an Italian film comedy *Big Deal on Madonna Street*. This disaster was somewhat mitigated by the concurrent triumphal success of his revival of *Sweet Charity*. *Variety*'s epitaph was: 'one of the master creators of the Broadway musical.'

Co-founder (with his friend Henri Langlois) of the prestigious Cinémathèque Française in 1937, **Georges Franju** died, aged 75, on 5 November 1987. After working in the decor departments of the *Folies Bergère* and the Casino de Paris, Franju made a short film in 1934 with Langlois (whose family loaned the two men the cash to get the project off the ground) called *Le Métro* and at the same time started an unsuccessful film magazine – it lasted just two issues – and also opened a club, 'Le Cercle du Cinéma'. It was the last of those projects which two years later was to result in their starting Cinémathèque Française, leading a year after that to Franju's election as executive secretary of the International Federation of Film Archives. In 1949 Franju made the first of the thirteen documentaries which were to establish him as one of France's most outstanding moviemakers. This was *Le Sang des bêtes*, a mixture of poetry and bloody, brutal realism shot in the Paris abattoirs. It was not until 1959 that Franju made the first of his very limited output of feature films, *The Keepers – La Tête contre les murs*, a film about the horrors of mental asylums. Later titles included *Spotlight on Murder – Pleins Feux sur l'assassin, Thérèse, Thomas the Imposter – Thomas l'imposteur, Judex* (generally accepted as his most popular feature), *Shadowman – L'Homme sans visage* (also shown as *Les Nuits rouges*) and *The Shadow Line*, which he made for TV in 1974 and which was to be his final production. Essentially individual in style and content, most of Franju's fictional work was in the world of nihi-

listic horror and fantasy. It was with his non-fiction films that he made the greatest impact and ensured himself a place in film history.

Just a year after winning the Laurence Olivier award for his performance in a revival of Priestley's *When We Are Married*, north-of-the-border actor **Bill Fraser** died, at the age of 79, from the effects of emphysema on 5 September 1987. A keen amateur actor in his teens, Fraser began his professional career at the age of twenty with his own repertory company at Worthing. He made his West End debut in 1939 in the revue *New Faces*. On demobilization from the RAF, Fraser appeared, after the war, with the Royal Shakespeare, British National, Chichester and other companies; he also toured Australia and appeared in the Canadian George Bernard Shaw Festival. He was a great favourite on TV, with big successes in

Bill Fraser.

The Army Game, Bootsie and Snudge and *Rumpole of the Bailey* series. He also appeared in and co-wrote six episodes of the John Buchan *John MacNab* series. Though primarily a stage and small-screen actor, Fraser chalked up appearances in some 30 films including *The Corn Is Green, Doctor at Large, Captain Nemo and the Underwater City, Masquerade* and *A Home of Your Own*.

Best known in the States for his considerable and very popular television work in such series as *The Honeymooners, Cavalcade of Stars, Life of Riley* and

The Jackie Gleason Show, plump and jovial **Jackie Gleason** will always be associated in the UK with his Oscar-nominated role of 'Minnesota Fats' in the 1961 classic movie *The Hustler*, and with his part as the sheriff in *Smokey and the Bandit*. He died at the age of 71 on 24 June 1987 (notification came too late for last year's 'In Memoriam'). Herbert John Gleason was born in Brooklyn and spent much of his early life in local pool halls (which is probably why he was good as the ace pool player in *The Hustler*), but after winning an amateur talent contest when he was fifteen he embarked on a showbiz career, playing in carnivals, night-clubs, music halls and anywhere he could get a booking. In 1940 he won his first film contract but it was on television that he began to make his mark, though he did appear in a number of Broadway stage successes including *Hellzapoppin'* in 1938 and *Take Me Along* in 1959 – a show that brought him a Tony Award. His large-screen debut was made in *Navy Blues* in 1941, the first of about a score of films which included *Orchestra Wives* (1942), *Desert Hawk* (1950), *Gigot* (1963, for which he wrote the story), *Skidoo* (1968), *Smokey and the Bandit* (1977), *The Sting 2* (1983), *The Toy* (1983) and his final film *Nothing in Common* in 1987. An interesting and little-known facet of his talent was his considerable output of musical compositions: though he always maintained that he could neither play an instrument nor read music, with the Jackie Gleason Orchestra, he recorded enough numbers to fill 35 albums.

Jackie Gleason.

Lorne Greene.

Lorne Greene, who died on 11 August 1987, aged 72, was best known for his role of Ben Cartwright in the long-running TV series *Bonanza*, but he did appear in some dozen movies, including the originally made-for-TV *Battleship Galactica* in 1979. Canadian, born in Ottawa, Lorne began his career as one of that country's most popular television newsreaders, and it was in the early 'fifties that he moved to America and began his stage and screen career. His first film was *The Silver Chalice* in 1954 and he subsequently appeared in (among others) *Peyton Place* (1957), *The Buccaneer* (1958), *Earthquake* (1974) and *Klondike Fever* (1979). He also made a movie in Japan, *Tidal Wave*, in 1975.

It was not until she was in her thirties and her mother had passed on that **Irene Handl** – who died in London, the city of her birth, at the age of 85 on 29 November 1987 – decided to make acting her future. She made an instant impression – but not the one she had hoped for! Having enrolled in the old Swiss Cottage Theatre's Embassy drama school, she was sacked within a few weeks; according to Patrick Ide, an Embassy actor at that time, the school's manager, Eileen (sister of Dame Sybil) Thorndike, told her that nobody as eccentric as Miss Handl could ever succeed on the stage. How very wrong she was later proved to be: Miss Handl made almost 100 films, sometimes at the rate of six a year (one year, indeed, she had roles in ten productions). She also appeared in a large number of plays

and became one of TV's favourite comediennes. Although best known for her inimitable comedy performances, Miss Handl appeared in many classics: for instance, as Wilde's Lady Bracknell, Sheridan's Mrs Malaprop and Coward's Madame Arcati. In fact it was not until 1961 that Irene created her famous Cockney character with her playing of the charlady in *Goodnight Mrs Puffin*, which ran for two years. Irene Handl made her film debut in 1938 in *Missing, Believed Married*; and among the titles that followed were *George and Margaret* (1940), *Dear Octopus* and *Millions Like Us* (1943), *Brief Encounter* (1946), *The Shop at Sly Corner* (1947), *The History of Mr Polly* (1949), *Belles of St Trinians* (1954), *Carry On Nurse* (1959), *School for Scoundrels* (1960), *The Italian Job* (1969), *The Private Life of Sherlock Holmes* (1970), *Adventures of a Private Eye* (1977), *The Hound of the Baskervilles* (1978) and scores of other films, all enriched by her special kind of humour. She added her extra dimension to such TV series as *Hancock's Half-Hour*, *You Must Be Joking*, *The Rag Trade* and the recent series *Never Say Die*. It was only recently that Miss Handl, who never married, said she would not retire until her audiences asked her to do so . . . and never in a million years would they have done that.

Best known for her editing of classic films by Jean Renoir and Jacques Becker, including *La Grande Illusion* and *Casque d'or*, **Marguerite Houllé-Renoir** died in Paris in July 1987, aged 82. Having started her career at fifteen (hand-colouring silent films), she also edited films for Buñuel, Carné and Mocky.

The quintessentially British actor **Trevor Howard** died, aged 80, on 7 January 1988. Born in Margate and educated at Clifton College, Howard made his professional debut in 1934, while still at RADA, at the Gate Theatre, an odd little playhouse underneath the Charing Cross railway arches, in *Revolt in a Reformatory*. From then until the war interrupted his career Howard appeared in some sixteen other plays, both old and modern classics. An officer in the Paratroopers, Howard won the Military Cross for bravery but

Trevor Howard.

was invalided out of the Army after being wounded and in due course returned to acting. After a small screen part in *The Way Ahead* in 1944, he won a role in *The Way to the Stars* (1945) and in that same year achieved major success with his sensitive playing opposite Celia Johnson in Coward's *Brief Encounter*. From then on it was success all the way, with a string of films that included *Green for Danger* (1946), *The Passionate Friends* (1948), *The Third Man* (1949), *The Clouded Yellow* (1950) and *Cockleshell Heroes* (1955). When Howard went to Hollywood his success continued in films like *Mutiny on the Bounty* (as Bligh in 1962), *Father Goose* (1964) and *Von Ryan's Express* (1965). He had important roles in *The Battle of Britain* (1969), *Ryan's Daughter* (1970), *Pope Joan* (1972), *Ludwig* (as Wagner, 1973), *Conduct Unbecoming* (1975), *Aces High* (1976), *Stevie* (1978), *Sir Henry at Rawlinson End* (1980), *Gandhi* (1983) and the not-yet-released *The Unholy*. In all, Trevor Howard appeared in some 70 films, including the occasional French, German, Italian and Australian production. Inexplicably, his only Oscar nomination was for his performance in *Sons and Lovers* in 1960 (he did not win) but he was given the British Film Academy's Best Actor award for his part in John Huston's *The Roots of Heaven*. Howard also appeared in a large number of TV productions and periodically returned to the theatre, generally in the classics. Extremely versatile, he moved with ease from romantic hero roles to self-contained military types and varied character roles. Notoriously a hard drinker and former hell

raiser, Howard never let his private life interfere with his professional career. A fellow actor once said that Howard never once gave a bad or even a careless performance and by all accounts this judgement was true. During his entire career he lived by the ethic that he owed his audiences nothing less than his best.

Outstanding as writer, director, actor and larger-than-life personality, **John Huston** died in his sleep at the age of 81 on 28 August 1987. He was still working: having only recently completed *The Dead* (which he directed, with his son Tony as screenwriter and daughter Anjelica starring), he was already at work on *Mr North*, of which he was co-writer, executive producer and in which he was supposed to play a role (because he felt ill, he had passed the part on to Robert Mitchum). Son of the famous actor Walter Huston (remember him singing 'September Song' in John's film *The Treasure of the Sierra Madre*?), John spent most of his childhood travelling around with the family, first with both his parents and then, after they split up, with one or the other alternately. A sickly child, at the age of

John Huston.

twelve he spent time in hospital with an enlarged heart and kidney trouble, but within two years had recovered enough to become the amateur lightweight boxing champion of California. At nineteen he was playing in off-Broadway stage productions, and had married, but he soon grew tired of both the theatre and marriage and went off to become a cavalry officer in the Mexican army. In his spare time he wrote a play called *Frankie and Johnny* which was staged as a puppet production in 1929 and published in book form the following year. After small roles in several William Wyler films he became a New York reporter, but was soon sacked for putting too much imagination into his reports. After a spell of screenwriting and writing dialogue for other people's scripts, he suddenly left Hollywood in 1932 to go to Paris (where he sketched tourists to earn enough francs to eat) and London (where he sang in the gutter for pennies and lived rough in Hyde Park). Back in New York, he worked briefly as a magazine editor and then went to Chicago to play the title role in a production of *Abraham Lincoln* (a character previously portrayed by his father in a different play). In 1937 a somewhat sobered Huston, now remarried, returned to Hollywood to take up his old job of screenwriting, successfully enough this time, for it led to his being offered his first chance of feature directing, with *The Maltese Falcon*. After directing a couple more films and some stage productions, Huston joined the US Army in 1942 and while in uniform made three of the best American documentaries to emerge from the Second World War. These brought him promotion to Major and a medal for his courageous filming while under fire in both the European and Pacific areas of the conflict. Back in Hollywood in 1945, he divorced his second wife and married his third, actress Evelyn Keyes (the marriage lasted for five years), and, after critical success and commercial failure with his staging of Sartre's *No Exit* on Broadway, he made his first post-war movie, *The Treasure of the Sierra Madre*, which (apart from bringing his father the Best Actor Oscar) earned him Oscars for direction and writing. Then came the magnificent gangster film *The Asphalt Jungle*, the critically acclaimed box-office disaster *The Red Badge of Courage*, and his great popular success *The African Queen*. In 1952 he left Hollywood to live in Ireland and work in Europe and it was twenty years before he returned, this time to make another outstanding film about boxing, *Fat City*. John Huston made 37 films and fourteen of them earned at least Oscar nominations, including his recent *Prizzi's Honour*. Among those 37, some are established classics of the screen but others, especially those he made in latter years, did not measure up. Apart from the films already mentioned some of his best work was in *Key Largo, Moulin Rouge, Beat the Devil, Moby Dick, The Misfits, Freud, The Man Who Would Be King* and *Wise Blood*. His autobiography, *An Open Book*, appeared in 1980. Not in the best of health for the past few years, he had recently been suffering from emphysema. Because there were admittedly some failures (by his standards) among his films, Huston has often been undervalued. He did however produce some screen classics and the cinema would have been much poorer without him; for that he should be honoured.

India's most popular actor of the 'forties, and fairly familiar to British movie buffs, **Raj Kapoor** died in New Delhi on 2 June 1988 at the age of 64, He also directed and produced many of the films in which he starred and stunned

Indian audiences – and angered the censor – by introducing nudity to the normally strictly moral Indian movies. His father was a silent star and his three sons and two brothers are all actors; of the brothers Western audiences are most familiar with Shashi, who has made several films outside his own country.

Alf Kjellin, the Swedish actor/director with an international reputation on both counts, died in Los Angeles, aged 68, on 5 April 1988. After appearing in a number of Swedish movies he had a big success opposite Mai Zetterling in Alf Sjoberg's 1944 film, written by Ingmar Bergman, *Frenzy* (*Torment* in the USA). But thereafter he appeared in a succession of routine Swedish, American and British movies until, in the early 'fifties, he returned to Sweden to direct the first of a number of films including the Bergman/Erland Josephson-scripted *Pleasure Garden*. Returning to Hollywood in 1959, he was kept busy acting and directing TV features and series episodes. The last couple of films he made were *Midas Run* in 1969 and *The McMasters* the following year. He had suffered from acute arthritis for many years.

Jesse Lasky Jr, son of the famous pioneer moviemaker with the same name, died in London, where he had lived since 1962, on 11 April 1988 at the age of 77. He did a considerable amount of scriptwriting and for some years collaborated with Cecil B. DeMille on a number of his spectacular productions such as *Union Pacific, North West Mounted Police* and *The Ten Commandments*. In addition Lasky was author of many novels and volumes of poetry and, with his wife Pat Silver, worked on a number of BBC and ITV series, notably *The Saint, Secret Agent* and *The Avengers*.

Director and/or producer of many classic movies, **Mervyn LeRoy**, who died on 13 September 1987, was concerned in one way or another with the production of as many movies as the years of his life – he would have celebrated his 87th birthday in October '87. Born in San Francisco, at the age of six he experienced the great earthquake and fire which nearly wiped out the city; it certainly wiped out the family business.

So at the age of ten Mervyn began his working life as a street-corner newsboy and his stage debut came about two years later when a regular customer, an actor, offered him the role of newsboy in a new play. This experience gave the youngster a taste for a footlights career and he subsequently appeared in vaudeville with an act called 'The Singing Newsboy'. Armed with a letter of introduction from his cousin Jesse L. Lasky, LeRoy went to Hollywood, where he obtained a job in the wardrobe department of the Famous Players studio; subsequently branching out in a series of jobs there, including assistant cameraman and small-part player, leading in 1927 to his being offered his first chance of feature direction with *No Place to Go*. Extremely versatile, he tackled with considerable success everything from gangster films (like the classic *Little Caesar* in 1931) to big musicals (such as *Golddiggers of 1933*), from comedies (like *Tugboat Annie*, also 1933) to gigantic spectacles (such as *Quo Vadis* in 1951), and even films with a political message (*I Am a Fugitive from a Chain Gang*, in 1932). As a producer one of his greatest successes was 1939's *The Wizard of Oz*. Other films which LeRoy directed – and in some cases also produced – included *Anthony Adverse* (1936), *The King and the Chorus Girl* (1937), *They Won't Forget* (1937), *Waterloo Bridge* (1940), *Johnny Eager* (1942), *Random Harvest* (1942), *Madame Curie* (1943), *Little Women* (1949), *Rose Marie* (1954), *The Bad Seed* (1956), *The FBI Story* (1959) and, his last film, *Moment to Moment* (1966). In 1945 LeRoy was awarded a special Oscar for a short film starring Frank Sinatra (*The House I Live In*) and he was also awarded the Academy's Irving G. Thalberg Memorial award in 1975 for his long-standing and numerous contributions to motion pictures. Incidentally, it was LeRoy who introduced his friend Ronald Reagan to Nancy. His autobiography, *Mervyn LeRoy: Take One*, was published in 1939.

One of the cinema's greatest showmen, as producer, cinema owner, distributor, publicist and financial backer (he once boasted he had a hand in the production of some 500 movies), **Joseph E. Levine** died, aged 81, in Greenwich, Connecticut on 31 July 1987. The son of a Russian-Jewish immigrant, Levine started making money by delivering newspapers and shining shoes, leaving school when he was fourteen to work in a tailor's. He was a café manager before buying his local cinema (at one time he owned seven cinemas) and eventually becoming a distributor. In 1956 he bought *Attila* from the Italians for $100,000, spent $600,000 on publicity and walked away with a $2 million fortune, the first of a long line of such deals. When Warner Brothers asked him to publicize their Italian buy, *Hercules*, with the then little-known Steve Reeves, Levine insisted they spend a million dollars *more* than they had paid for the rights ($120,000) on dubbing and publicity, and then vindicated his methods when the film took nearly $4¾ million at the box-office. To continue the Levine (and his Embassy Pictures) story in any detail would take pages. However, it is impossible to omit mention of his collaboration with Carlo Ponti; this resulted in *The Women*, which won Sophia Loren her Oscar; he also helped to finance Fellini's *8½* and backed many other Italian winners, including *Marriage Italian Style* and *Boccaccio '70*. Levine was also responsible for importing a number of British films into the US including John Schlesinger's *Darling*, the ballet film *Romeo and Juliet* and *The Spy with a Cold Nose*. He built two new cinemas in New York; was a major shareholder in, and became a producer for, Paramount. He paid author Harold Robbins nearly $1 million for the screen rights to three of his novels. He was executive producer of, and was very closely involved with, the $50 million success *The Graduate*, and it was he who signed Mel Brooks to make another memorable comedy, *The Producers*. Perhaps surprisingly, his own favourite production was the critical success and Oscar-winning classic *The Lion in Winter* and he spent more than two years in producing the impressive, Attenborough-directed war epic *A Bridge Too Far*. His last two films were both more critically interesting than financially successful: *Magic* in 1978 and *Tattoo* in 1981. Right up to his death Levine was full of plans for future productions, including an Anthony Shaffer adaptation of the thriller *The Glow*. According to *Variety*, he was known to be a loyal friend and a good employer. He held no less than six honorary university degrees and was

Harvard's first 'Man of the Year' in 1978. In recording his passing *Variety* said of this short, tubby and talented fellow: 'He was perhaps the last of the major film tycoons to be based in New York.'

To the still large number of moviegoers who remain loyal fans of the good old western, especially the classic B-movies, the news of the demise of **Robert Livingstone** on 7 March 1988 at the age of 83 will come as a sad reminder of the passing of an era. Son

Robert Livingstone.

of a newspaper columnist and himself at one time a reporter on a Californian paper, Robert E. Randall (his real name: he changed it so as not to be confused with his actor brother Addison 'Jack' Randall) switched to acting in the late 1920s, learning the business at the Pasadena Playhouse. After appearing in plays there and elsewhere and making a few short films, Livingstone was signed up by MGM, but getting nowhere there he changed to the old Republic Studios and for the next twenty years was one of their B-western stars, appearing in some 50 movies in addition to such popular series as *The Lone Ranger Rides Again* and *The Three Mesquiters*. The more familiar of his films include *Renfrew of the Royal Mounted* (1937), *Pistol Packin' Mama* (1943), *Beneath Western Skies* (1944), *Dakota* (1945), *Night Train to Galveston* (1952), *The Three Godfathers* (1936), *The Laramie Trail* (1944), *Mule Train* (1950) and *The Winning of the West* (1953). In contrast to some other

old stars of the western, Livingstone also appeared in quite a large number of other movies such as *Murder in the Fleet* (1935), *Storm Over Lisbon* (1944) and *Daredevil of the Clouds* (1948). The recurrence of an old leg injury (he was accidentally shot in the knee while filming some years previously) during the making of *Once Upon a Horse* in 1958 brought about his retirement, but he did make a brief return to the studios in 1974 to appear in a trio of films of which the titles say all: *Girls for Rent*, *The Naughty Stewardesses* and *Blazing Stewardesses*. Livingstone was presented with the Golden Boot Award for Cowboy Stars in 1987 by the Motion Picture and Television Fund.

Though his output of films was comparatively small – sixteen features in all – **Rouben Mamoulian**, who died, aged 90, on 4 December 1987, with his innovative mind and experimental methods earns a well-deserved place in the cinema's history. Born in Tiflis, in the Caucasus, of Armenian descent, Mamoulian spent his childhood in Paris and later went back to Moscow University to study criminology. He then joined the Moscow Arts Theatre, subsequently opening his own drama school in Tiflis. In 1920 he toured England with the Russian Repertory Theatre and two years later directed his first play in London. In 1923 he went to America, at the invitation of George Eastman, and there staged musicals, operettas and operas for the next three years. He directed his first film, *Applause*, in 1929 and in it introduced new technology to the sound film by moving the camera around and using new sound techniques. He carried on experimenting with both sight and sound in his second movie, *City Lights* (1931), and in *Dr Jekyll and Mr Hyde*, which, in spite of several later efforts, is still considered to be the best screen dramatization ever made of this famous story. When Mamoulian switched to musicals with the Chevalier-MacDonald *Love Me Tonight*, his witty touches and general expertise made it a landmark movie. Subsequently he directed Dietrich in *Song of Songs* and Garbo in *Queen Christina* (both in 1933). Following *Resurrection*, his *Becky Sharp* (1935), was notable for its new method of colour photography. Next he made *Gay Desperado* (1935), *High, Wide and*

Lee Marvin.

Handsome (1937), *Golden Boy* (1939) and remakes of *The Mark of Zorro* (1940) and *Blood and Sand*. After *Rings on Her Fingers* in 1942 he made only two more movies, *Summer Holiday* in 1948 and *Silk Stockings* in 1957. After that came two disastrous blows: after nearly a year's preparatory work on the film version of *Porgy and Bess*, Samuel Goldwyn gave the film to Otto Preminger to direct; and, in 1961, after filming footage in London for *Cleopatra*, he resigned from the film. During all this time he had a number of great stage successes, with such productions as Maxwell Anderson's *Lost in the Stars* (281 performances), *Oklahoma!* (which ran for five-and-a-half-years), *Carousel* (some 1500 performances) and many others. His retirement was spent with his wife of some 30 years, Azadia Newman, and their collection of cats, in considerable style in a Beverly Hills mansion. When in 1982 Mamoulian received the Directors' Guild of America's top honour, the D.W. Griffith

Award, *Variety* quoted Mamoulian as saying: 'The motion picture is a noble instrument which should serve noble causes . . . politics, religion, economics all seem to fail. So the last resort may be the fine arts.'

With his many film, television and stage successes, the strangest achievement for gravel-voiced tough guy **Lee Marvin** was topping the charts as a singer with his recording ('Wanderin' Star') from the 1969 musical *Paint Your Wagon*. Marvin, who died on 29 August 1987 as a result of a heart attack following a bad bout of 'flu, was 63; he appeared in just about the same number of films during his busy career. He became an actor almost by accident, his stage debut resulting from his being asked to fill the gap when an actor in the local summer repertory company was suddenly taken ill. The son of an advertising executive father and fashion editor mother, the young Marvin joined the US Marines in 1942, becoming a sniper and as such taking part in more

than a score of island battles against the Japanese. But a bullet in the spine ended his martial career and after a year in hospital he emerged to take a job as a plumber's assistant. But his unexpected stage debut had given him a taste for acting and he managed to land a series of small parts in out-of-town stage productions, before getting his first big breakthrough with a role in the Broadway production of *Billy Budd*. By the time he made his screen debut in *You're in the Navy Now* in 1951, in addition to his stage work he had some 200 TV performances to his credit. In his debut film year he appeared in no less than six movies, making the same number of appearances on the screen the following year. Initially typecast as a villain – usually in westerns like *Bad Day at Black Rock* and Ford's *The Man Who Shot Liberty Valance* – Marvin eventually managed to persuade the casting departments that he could play more sympathetic roles. In 1963 he won an Oscar for his dual role in *Cat Ballou*. Among his other good performances were those in *The Wild One*, *The Caine Mutiny* (both 1954), *Raintree County* (1957), *The Comancheros* (1961), *Donovan's Reef* (1963), *The Killers* (1964), *The Professionals* (1966), *The Dirty Dozen* (1967), *The Klansmen* (1974), *Shout at the Devil* (his only British film, made 1975), *Great Scout and Cathouse Thursday* (1976), *The Big Red One* (1979) and his final screen roles, *Gorky Park* (1983) and *The Delta Force* (1986). For the last three years Marvin had lived quietly on his Tucson ranch with his wife Pamela (whom he married in 1970), his son and three daughters. Marvin also had considerable success on TV, in both features and series; and in 1979 he hit the news headlines when he went to court in a landmark legal case after refusing to pay his live-in mistress of six years half his fortune; he won the sensational court wrangle that followed.

In her day **Colleen Moore** (whose real name was Kathleen Morrison), who died, aged 85, on 25 January 1988, was the highest-paid star in Hollywood. Born in Port Huron, Michigan, the favourite niece of the managing editor of the powerful *Chicago American* and a friend of D.W. Griffith, the convent-educated 14-year-old arrived in Hollywood in 1917, after studying the piano in Detroit. During her first year in the film colony she appeared in *The Bad Boys* and *Hands Up!*, the first of her 100-odd movies. Having starred in various B-movies and westerns (some of them opposite Tom Mix), at the age of 21 she suddenly changed her image completely to that of a lively, bob-haired, short-skirted flapper, starting a major fashion craze among the young-sters of her time. She switched image again in 1925 with her strong dramatic role in *So Big* (generally considered to be one of her best screen performances) but her public soon demanded her back in lighter roles. In 1929 she made her first talkie, *Smiling Irish Eyes*, which, according to a *Variety* report, she dis-missed as 'the most mediocre picture imaginable'. But she persevered with five more sound films before, having made *The Scarlet Letter* in 1934, she decided to call it a day. Her retirement was one of affluence, as she had shown a shrewd sense of investment (consider-ably helped, one imagines, by the fact that two of her four husbands were stockbrokers) and one of her four books was entitled *How Women Can Make Money in the Stock Market*. Her auto-biography was aptly called *Silent Star*; and another of her books, *Colleen Moore's Doll House*, was about her high-ly prized collection of miniature paint-ings. Her 'century' of movies included *Little Orphan Annie* (1919), *Flaming Youth* (1923), *The Perfect Flapper* (1924), *Naughty But Nice* (1927), *Synthetic Sin* (1929) and *The Power and the Glory* (1933).

Famous silent screen star **Pola Negri** (real name Barbara Apollonia Chalu-piec), who died in her sleep on 1 Au-gust 1987, aged about 87 (her published birthdate ranges between 1894 and 1904), had been diagnosed two years previously as having a brain tumour, for which she refused to have treat-ment. During her long career she made some 50 films, the majority either in her native Poland or in Germany. A product of the Warsaw slums, she in-itially studied ballet in Russia and made her dancing debut in *Swan Lake* in 1913, after which she decided to make drama her career and enrolled in the Imperial Academy of Dramatic Art in Warsaw. Her screen debut was in the 1914 Polish film *Love and Passion*. Af-ter two more Polish films she went to Germany, where she made seven films

for the up-and-coming Ernst Lubitsch. One of these, *Madame Dubarry*, proved such a success in America (where it was re-titled *Passion*) that Paramount offered her the then enormous sum of

Pola Negri.

£2,000 a week to make movies in Holly-wood. Having appeared in several in-different productions, she was again directed by Lubitsch, now also in Hol-lywood, and the result, *Forbidden Para-dise* (1924), became an enormous suc-cess. After finishing *The Woman He Scorned* in 1930 Miss Negri came to England to make *A Woman Commands*, then crossed the Channel to France to make *Fanatisme* in 1932, before return-ing to Berlin to make the big German success *Mazurka*. She made several more films in Germany but in 1938 went back to France for a period of idleness in her Paris and Riviera homes. *Variety* reported that by 1929 she had already earned some $5 million, but two years later, thanks largely to the US stock market crash, she had lost virtual-ly all of it. In 1941 she returned to Hollywood but now found work hard to get. She made only one further film there, 1943's *Hi Diddle Diddle*, then finally *The Moonspinners* for Walt Dis-ney, for which she came to Britain in 1964. Thereafter she lived in San Anto-nio. The daughter of a gipsy violinist who died in Siberian exile (according to some sources), Pola was one of the silent screen's greatest vamps and her private life matched her screen reputa-tion. Following her headline-hitting re-lationship with Chaplin she became en-gaged to Valentino ('the love of my life'), but within a year of his death she had married a penniless prince (her other husband was a count). Latterly

she had engaged in religious and cultu-ral duties as well as working for various charities.

Blonde, beautiful silent star **Eva Novak**, who died in late May 1988, was a real western gal, often appearing with Tom Mix and in other cowboy epics of the boots-and-saddle era. She also play-ed in some classic John Ford westerns including *Stagecoach*, *Fort Apache* and *She Wore a Yellow Ribbon*. With such credits it is strange how neglected she has been by the film reference books; even *Variety* seems to have failed to record her passing.

Hungarian **Emeric Pressburger**, who died in his adopted England on 5 February 1988 at the age of 85, was primarily a journalism-trained script-writer but in his later years tried, with reasonable success, directing and pro-ducing his own script (*Twice Upon a Time* in 1953). But it was for his col-laboration with director Michael Powell in their company 'The Archers', which produced fourteen films in sixteen years, that he is best known: starting with the classic *The Life and Death of Colonel Blimp*, they produced a string of successes including *A Canterbury Tale, I Know Where I'm Going, A Mat-ter of Life and Death, Black Narcissus, The Red Shoes, The Tales of Hoffman, The Small Back Room* and *The Battle of the River Plate*. In 1941 Pressburger won an Oscar for the writing of *49th Parallel*. After writing and producing *Miracle in Soho* in 1957 the Powell-Pressburger team got together again, for the last time, in 1972, to make a Children's Film Foundation feature called *The Boy Who Turned Yellow*. Pressburger wrote two novels, *A Mouse on Sunday* and *The Glass Pearls*.

A 'forties screen star, **Ella Raines** (real name Ella Wallace Raubes) died, aged 66, in Los Angeles on 30 May 1988. She was still a drama student in Washington when a new company formed by Charles Boyer and Howard Hawkes and called B-H Productions signed her up as its only contract star. Later B-H sold her contract to Univer-sal, for whom she made her best film, Robert Siodmak's *Phantom Lady*. She went on to the Sturges comedy *Hail the*

Conquering Hero (1944), *Tall in the Saddle* with John Wayne (1944), the Jules Dassin thriller *Brute Force* (1947) and *The Senator Was Indiscreet* with William Powell (1948). Thereafter her films became less distinguished and her last large-screen performance seems to have been in the British-made *Man in the Road* in 1956. After this she made rare appearances on TV and taught drama at the University of Washington.

Irene Rich.

Another of the silent screen stars who died this year was 96-year-old **Irene Rich** (real name Irene Luther), who made her first appearance on celluloid in Mary Pickford's *Stella Maris* in 1918. Miss Rich, who died on 22 April 1988, had some 70 films to her credit, both silent and sound (taking the latter in her stride), and co-starred with Will Rogers in several of his films before retiring temporarily in 1932 to concentrate on radio, which earned her universal popularity with her *Dear John* series. Six years later, after Broadway success, she returned to the film studios to play more mature roles in such movies as Deanna Durbin's *That Certain Age*, John Ford's *Fort Apache* and the screen version of *Joan of Arc* with Ingrid Bergman. In her career Irene Rich played opposite some of the screen's greatest names, among them Lon Chaney, Clive Brook, Ronald Colman and Lewis Stone. She will perhaps be best recalled for her brilliant performances in *Lady Windermere's Fan* (1923) and *Craig's Wife* (1938).

Albert S. Rogell, who died in Los Angeles on 7 April 1988 at the age of 86, directed about 100 movies and was famous for his string of competent B-pictures, including some early vintage westerns – for some reason never revived, even on TV – starring Jack Hoxie, Art Accord, Ken Maynard, Tom Mix etc. Latterly Rogell worked mostly for the small screen.

Renato Salvatori, the outstanding Italian actor whose best performance (of some 70 films) was almost certainly as the boxing brother in the classic *Rocco and His Brothers* in 1960, died in Rome, aged only 55, on 27 March 1988. Though his films were mostly Italian, Salvatori did appear in both French and American movies. He was in several films with his wife, Annie Girardot, notably in *The Gypsy – Le Gitan* in 1975. His final screen work was in *Asso – Ace* in 1981 and *Louisiana* in 1983, which, made for cable TV, is unlikely ever to get a cinema release.

Abraham Sofaer died aged 91 on 21 January 1988 after a stage, television and film career of more than half a century. Born in Rangoon, of Burmese-Jewish parents, he was a schoolteacher there and in England before making his stage debut in 1921. In addition to his popularity on radio, he had seasons at

Alice Terry.

the Old Vic and at Stratford, and in 1937 directed and starred (opposite Helen Hayes) in a West End production of *The Merchant of Venice*. He made a score of films starting with *Dreyfus* in 1931. He also had roles in *Rembrandt* (1936), *Pandora and the Flying Dutchman* (1951), *Quo Vadis* (the same year), *Elephant Walk* (1954), *Bhowani Junction* (1956), *The Greatest Story Ever Told* (1965) and, apparently his final screen credit, *Chisum* in 1970.

Possibly best recalled – at least by older moviegoers – as Rudolph Valentino's leading lady in *The Four Horsemen of the Apocalypse*, **Alice Terry** (real name Alice Frances Taaffe) died in Burbank on 22 December 1987 at the age of 87. Miss Terry played opposite Valentino again in *The Conquering Power* in 1921. Her first important part was in DeMille's *Old Wives For New* in 1918, but it was not until 1920 that her career really began to take off, with a small role in Rex Ingram's *Shores Acre*. Ingram gave her a more important part in his next film *Hearts Are Trumps* and when he directed the Valentino film he insisted that his protégée play opposite the star. His interest in Miss Terry had by now become more personal and he married her in 1921, from which time the two worked closely together as director and star in a number of films including *The Prisoner of Zenda* (1922), *Scaramouche* (1923), *The Arab* (1924) and *The Garden of Allah* (1927). With the advent of the sound film both their careers virtually ended, although they did make one more film together in 1933, *Love in Morocco*, which had the novelty of Ingram acting and Terry directing, and Ingram turned out a few more films in the tiny studio he had built in Nice. After some years the couple returned to Hollywood, where they lived in retirement on a small farm. Ingram died in 1950, after which his wife became something of a recluse, passing her time painting.

It was her stunning, dark-haired beauty that won **Raquel Torres** (real name Paula Marie Osterman) her first screen role at nineteen in Woody Van Dyke's 1928 movie *White Shadows in the South Seas*, a successful mixture of fiction and documentary and the first film to have fully synchronized dialogue, sound effects and music, which proved a big box-office hit. The Mexican-born, convent-educated star went on to make nine further films, including *The Bridge of San Luis Rey* (1929), *Under the Texas Moon* (1930), *Aloha* (1931) and, her final American movie, *Duck Soup* (1933). After her marriage at this point to a wealthy New York businessman (who became a film producer) she officially retired from the screen, although she did come to Britain in 1934 to appear in *The Red Wagon*. Five years after her husband died in 1954, she married actor Jon Hall, but later divorced him. She died, aged 78, from the aftermath of a stroke, on 10 August 1987.

Although he appeared in and otherwise contributed in various ways to a number of films, with considerable success, George **Emlyn Williams**, who died in London, following an operation for cancer, on 25 September 1987 at the age of 81, was essentially a man of the theatre, with more than a score of plays to his credit as a writer and some fine acting performances in his own and other writers' work. Born in Mostyn, North Wales, he was brought up in a mining community but escaped a working life down the pits thanks to his schoolteacher's ambition for him, which so helped his studies that he ended up with a scholarship to Oxford. Turning to acting, Emlyn made his stage debuts in London and New York the same year, 1927, at the age of 22. The following year he appeared on the

Emlyn Williams.

London stage in his own play *Glamour*; but it was in the 'thirties that his career really began to take off, with such big successes as *A Murder Has Been Arranged*, *Night Must Fall* and, of course, his autobiographical play *The Corn Is Green*. Williams made his film-acting debut in *Friday the 13th* (in 1932) and from that point appeared on the screen fairly regularly (often being involved in one way or another with the screenplays) in such films as *The Dictator* (1935), *Broken Blossoms* (1936), the unfinished *I, Claudius* (1937), *The Citadel* (1938), *The Stars Look Down* (1939), *Hatter's Castle* (1941), *Major Barbara* (the same year), *The Last Days of Dolwyn* (in 1949, the film in which he gave his fellow Welshman and friend Richard Burton his first film role), *The Magic Box* (1951), *Ivanhoe* (1952), *The Deep Blue Sea* (1955), *I Accuse* (playing Zola, 1958), *The Wreck of the Mary Deare* (1959), *The L-Shaped Room* (1962) and *David Copperfield* in 1970. As illustrated by the theme of many of his plays, Williams was fascinated by psychopathic murderers and his play *Beyond Belief* was based on the Moors Murders case. By general critical consent and audience acclaim, one of his

best screen performances was in *They Drive By Night* (1939). It was not widely known that Emlyn made a contribution to the script of Alfred Hitchcock's *The Man Who Knew Too Much*, or that Joseph Losey's film *Time Without Pity* was based on the Williams play *Someone Waiting*. In the 1950s Emlyn began his one-man stage shows of readings from Dickens and Dylan Thomas, which proved a great success on both sides of the Atlantic. Williams wrote two books of autobiography, *George* and *Emlyn*, and when he was 75 he wrote his only novel, published as *Headlong*. His marriage to Molly O'Shann in 1935 lasted until his death. Everything that Emlyn Williams did was intelligent and subtle and it is difficult to find anything of his that was not up to top standard. And who could forget his beguiling Welsh lilt?

Small, mobile-faced **Kenneth Williams**, the London-born comedian who was equally at home and equally popular on radio, television, stage and screen, died aged 62, seemingly from a

Kenneth Williams.

heart attack, on 15 April 1988. Williams started his career as a straight actor in the usual succession of repertory theatres, but by the time he achieved his London debut in the revue *Share My Lettuce* (in which, if memory serves me correctly, he, in a green suit, played the hilarious side-of-the-stage compere), his gift for comedy was firmly established. Other revues followed, as well as roles in such 'straight' productions as *Moby Dick* and *St Joan*. On TV and radio he was an instant success, so much so that when he appeared in some of Tony Hancock's *Half Hours* poor Tony, always so insecure, dispensed with his services. He was a stalwart of the *Carry On* films (none of which was more aptly titled than *Carry On Camping*), which accounted for more than twenty of his 30-odd films. Others included *The Beggar's Opera*, *The Hound of the Baskervilles* and *Raising the Wind*. Williams appeared in numerous TV and radio panel games and talk shows (he was always on top form in Radio 4's *Just a Minute*), generally stealing everyone else's thunder. But, like so many apparently extrovert comedians, once away from the cameras and the footlights he was a very serious character, extremely well read,

a loner who made few friends and adored his mother, who found him dead in his small, meticulously tidy London flat in which he lived alone and to which few were ever invited.

Though maybe not a familiar name to modern moviegoers, **Lois Wilson**, who died on 3 March 1988 at the age of about 93 (references to her birth date vary from 1896 to 1898) was a popular star of the silent screen. Initially a schoolteacher, Lois Wilson began her film career in the familiar way after winning a beauty contest; that was in 1915, just a year before her screen debut in *The Dumb Girl of Portici*. Her many other films included the original *Covered Wagon* in 1923, but there were other important successes in the total of 60 films in which she appeared. The list of titles makes amusing reading: among her movies were *What Every Woman Knows* (1921), *Is Matrimony a Failure?* (1922), *Let's Get Married* (1926), *Object – Alimony* (1928) and *Divorce in the Family* (1932). Miss Wilson, who never married, also starred in the original *Great Gatsby* (1926), *Ruggles of Red Gap* (1923) and *Monsieur Beaucaire* (1924). After retiring in 1941, Lois returned to the studios just once more, to play a character role in *The Girl from Jones Beach* in 1949.

Within three weeks of the death of Edgar Anstey, **Basil Wright**, another of Britain's famous documentary filmmakers and fellow graduate of John Grierson, died in London on 14 October at the age of 80. While still at Cambridge, Wright made a short film, *Standfast*, which so impressed Grierson that he suggested Wright join him at the Empire Film Marketing Board's Film Unit after graduating. That was in 1929, and after a couple of years in the editing rooms Wright was given his first directing assignment. When Grierson moved to take charge of the GPO film unit Wright went with him, leaving in 1937 to form his own film company, International Realist Films, with Cavalcanti, making documentaries for UNESCO and other organizations. Wright in his later years toured America and Africa lecturing on film and he wrote two books, *The Use of Film*, published in 1948, and *The Long View*, a critical history of the cinema, published in 1974. Two of Wright's films, now considered classic documentaries, were *Song of Ceylon* in 1934 and, in 1936 with Harry Watt, *Night Mail*. Other Basil Wright films, most of which he directed, wrote and often photographed, included *The Country Comes to Town* (1931), *Cargo from Jamaica* (1934), *The Face of Scotland* (1937), *Harvest Help* (1940), *This Was Japan* (1945), *World Without End* (which he made with Paul Rotha in 1950) and his final production, *A Place for Gold* in 1960.

Lois Wilson.

Film Books of the Year

IVAN BUTLER

Adventures with D.W. Griffith, Karl Brown, ed. Kevin Brownlow; Faber & Faber, £6.95

High among the most interesting of the year's reprints (first published in 1973, reviewed in *Film Review 1974–5* and now available in stout paperback), this is a fascinating account of D.W. Griffith at work. Karl Brown joined him in his teens as general dogsbody, became assistant cameraman to Billy Bitzer and parted company when Griffith left Hollywood to return east to Mamaronek – having worked on such masterpieces as *The Birth of a Nation*, *Intolerance*, and, more briefly, *Broken Blossoms*. He then went on to become a leading cameraman (on, for example, *The Covered Wagon*) and a director. His account of those pioneering days is vivid, amusing and moving by turns, and exciting throughout. Kevin Brownlow did a commendable job both in persuading the author to write the book and then in introducing and editing it.

As Time Goes By – The Life of Ingrid Bergman, Laurence Leamer; Sphere, £3.95

This is the paperback of the book first published in 1986, a good, sound biography, well indexed and fully documented.

Beasts and Behemoths, Roy Kinnard; Scarecrow Press, dist. Bailey Bros & Swinfen, £16.90

Subtitled 'Prehistoric Creatures in the Movies', this deals with some 30 films which have as their basis monsters of long, long ago. Titles range from *The Lost World* (1925) to *Baby* (1985), by way of *King Kong* and *Godzilla*. Interesting details as to their making, construction, etc., are given, together with cast-and-credits and critical commentaries. Two checklists are included, the second devoted to Japanese features. A useful little handbook for buffs of the genre.

Being and Becoming, Myrna Loy and James Kotsilibas-Davis; Bloomsbury, £14.95

This large-scale, generously illustrated co-biography is as delightful for its warmth and frankness as for the brilliant and often hilarious picture it paints of Hollywood from the 'twenties to the 'eighties, during which period Myrna Loy appeared in well over a hundred films. It is packed with good stories, shrewd judgements and generous appraisals.

Miss Loy has been fortunate in her co-writer, who has done an admirable and self-effacing job, skilfully retaining the colloquialisms which slipped in during what must have been a lengthy series of interviews, resulting in a pleasing informality. Only in the later pages, as we move in and out of the murky world of politics, where humour and generosity of spirit seem inevitably at a discount, does the flame flicker slightly; but even here 'cheerfulness keeps breaking in' – see the reference to Adolphe Menjou when he unexpectedly

played opposite her in *The Ambassador's Daughter*. Altogether, one of the more enjoyable memoirs of the year.

The Best of British, Maurice Sellar; Sphere, £8.95

A book based on a BBC series subtitled 'A Celebration of Rank Film Classics' may be expected to be somewhat bland – complimentary as well as complementary – in its approach. Fortunately, however, it does not hesitate to criticize when necessary. Apart from the films themselves, many of the best-known personalities are encountered and there are plenty of entertaining anecdotes.

Unfortunately, however, the whole book is spotted with an unacceptably high number of errors and examples of carelessness. Many names are misspelt: Sylvia 'Sydney', A.E. 'Mathews', 'Van' Guest, 'Marriot' Edgar, Valerie 'Dobson', 'Thex' Whistler, 'Anne' Todd, for example. The stills, very good in themselves, are often ruined by being insensitively split across two pages, and the captions contain errors: the actor on p.126 (twice) is Ernest Thesiger, not Felix Aylmer; the hussar on p.139 is Sandor Eles, not Nigel Green; the still on p.75 is from *The Wicked Lady*, not *The Man in Grey*. Many of the players appearing in the stills are not named, for example Griffith Jones on p.75; had he been named it might have saved the mistake in the title above. In this same still the girl in the centre is Patricia Roc, not Phyllis Calvert.

The book – unindexed – gives the impression of having been hastily cobbled together to meet a deadline.

The Big V, Anthony Slide; Scarecrow Press, dist. Bailey Bros & Swinfen, £29.50

Originally published in 1976, and now reissued in an updated and revised edition, this detailed and finely researched book traces the history of the pioneering Vitagraph Company which flourished under J. Stuart Blackton and Albert E. Smith from 1898 until its purchase by Warner Bros in 1925. About a third of the book is taken up with a concise history of the company, followed by a 'Who's Who' and a 'Necrology' (a slightly inaccurate term), and finally a complete 150-page list of film titles. A number of rare photographs rounds off this invaluable work of film reference.

Bing Crosby – A Discography, Radio Program List and Filmography, Timothy A. Morgereth; McFarland & Co., dist. Bailey Bros & Swinfen, £49.95

This enormous reference book offers 500 pages (plus another 50 of index) listing 2349 items of Crosby's output – recordings (with full lists of instrumentalists and even of rejected 'takes'), radio shows with many details (2271 in all), and feature films with brief cast and credit notes. In fact, though the author does not make the claim, this might justifiably be described as the complete Crosby record – a unique and essential illustrated compilation, set out with commendable clarity.

Blackface to Blacklist – Al Jolson, Larry Parks, and *The Jolson Story*, DougMcClelland; Scarecrow Press, dist. Bailey Bros & Swinfen, £22.15

An entire book devoted to *The Jolson Story* film might seem somewhat over-generous, but the author gives an interesting account of its genesis and life, including many side issues and personalities connected with its creation. Attention is focused mainly on Parks, while the notorious HUAC blacklist, though not dealt with in particular detail, hovers like a sinister shadow in the background. Plenty of good illustrations but no index.

Breaking Up, Nigel Williams; Faber & Faber, £4.95

The difference between a film made for the cinema and one made for television becomes ever more blurred, and it is good to find more TV screenplays appearing in printed form. The story of the break-up of a marriage between a haulage contractor and his wife, who have made the effort to send their son to a select private school, is movingly and often amusingly told, mainly from the viewpoint of the boy. It is simply and clearly set out to make for easy reading; a few stills, however, would have been welcome.

Britain Can Take It, Anthony Aldgate and Jeffrey Richards; Basil Blackwell, £15

Taking eleven key films as a basis, the authors have produced an absorbing examination of the British cinema during the Second World War. The film titles range from comedy (*Let George Do It*) through documentary (*Western Approaches*) to drama features such as *In Which We Serve*, *Thunder Rock* and *The Way to the Stars*. The underlying purposes of propaganda, the practical difficulties encountered in the actual making, the resultant values as entertainment and information, and various other aspects are all discussed in detail. Many other productions are also considered, and full accounts are given of the work of key figures such as Leslie Howard and Noël Coward, resulting in a valuable picture of British films during those vital years. The book forms a companion volume to Jeffrey Richards' account of the 1930s, *The Age of the Dream Palace*.

Charles Laughton – A Difficult Actor, Simon Callow; Methuen, £14.95

It is doubtful whether anyone will come closer to a true evaluation of the career and character of this complex and often tormented actor than the author of this absorbing, compassionate, appreciative but very frank biography. Every performance on stage and screen is covered in full, together with much about his associates, personal life and marriage to Elsa Lanchester. There is an engrossing account of his one great achievement as a director – the unforgettable and beautiful *Night of the Hunter*, and the author has a remarkable instinctive gift for recreating Laughton's early stage performances (notably *Payment Deferred* and *Portrait of a Man with Red Hair*) and bringing them to life again in the memories of those fortunate enough to have seen them at the time.

The book has some minor flaws: misspelt names ('Monte' Banks, 'Lilian' Gish, Derrick de 'Marne'); some apparent confusion over the American title of *Alibi*; an unfortunate misquotation from *King Lear*; and the author has a regrettable tendency to coin indigestible words, such as 'iconisation', 'transatlanticized' and 'phenomenality' (and how on earth does he pronounce 'colossality'?), presumably a lazy way to avoid rewriting the sentence more acceptably. Apart from such small blemishes, however, this is a valuable addition to the performing arts literature, which includes three excellent sections of illustrations.

The Cinema and Ireland, Anthony Slide; McFarland & Co., dist. Bailey Bros & Swinfen, £14.95

The influence of Ireland on the general world of cinema may be much greater than the Irish production itself, but in this brief but most interesting account adequate tribute is paid to both. Apart from the native output, Irish players, directors, producers and literary sources are discussed with this author's customary impeccable research and forthright opinions and comments. There are numerous good illustrations, a bibliography and full index.

Cinema and Literature in Society, Peter Miles and Malcolm Smith; Croom Helm, £25

Well documented and annotated, this survey of Britain in the 1920s and 1930s should be of considerable interest to the student of either sociology or the art of film, even though the writing is sometimes a bit heavy-handed, with a tendency to indulge in horrible non-words such as 'heroicization'. What a pity, though, that it should be presented in so unattractive a style – great blocks of unbroken paragraphs in far-from-pleasant type. At this price one might expect something less eye-straining.

City of Nets, Otto Friedrich; Headline, £14.95

A veritable feast of anecdotes, gossip, opinions (often caustic) and historical titbits covering, year by year, the Hollywood panorama of film-making, politics, business activities, private lives and public scandals, during the tumultuous decade of the 1940s. All the major events, such as the grubby days of the HUAC investigations, are covered in full, but among these serious matters are sprinkled countless minor (but equally entertaining) trivialities. Under the author's relentlessly sharp eye a number of reputations wither – Kazan, Brecht, Odets – while others (notably that of Ingrid Bergman, an obvious favourite) flourish almost unscathed. This is one of the most detailed (and invigorating) of all books on Hollywood, magnificently documented and with a full bibliography and an index.

Doing Their Bit, Michael S. Shull and David E. Wilt; McFarland & Co., dist. Bailey Bros & Swinfen, £29.95

Subtitled 'Wartime American Animated Short Films 1939–1945', this is a detailed examination of some 250 cartoons (out of 1000 produced during the period) which specifically or substantially refer to various aspects of the war. After an illustrated chronological survey, which includes a short section on the First World War, the bulk of the book is given up to a very full commentated filmography and concludes with several appendices. A useful reference book for the student of specialized film subjects and their social and political influences.

Double Take and Fade Away, Leslie Halliwell; Grafton, £14.95

This is indeed a vast treasure-house of marvellous extracts from the routines of the great comics of past and present – not a collection to be opened in a public place because of the impossibility of reading it without the embarrassment of bursting out into loud laughter. Halliwell deals with players in vaudeville, stage comedy and radio but, as might be expected, his book centres on the cinema and television. There is plenty of information in addition to the extracts, and plenty of comments also – sometimes quite acerbic. His dismissal of Woody Allen, for instance, though quite mild, will probably delight many who think him an overrated performer. The chapter headed 'America after 1945, television takes over' is a formidable – indeed appalling – list of title after title of mainly dreadful 'shows', demonstrating only too clearly how sadly comedy has deteriorated. Well illustrated, and with an excellent index.

Early Reagan, Anne Edwards; Hodder & Stoughton, £14.95

This substantial, well-balanced and painstakingly researched biography follows Reagan's life up to the end of his Hollywood days and his decision to run for the post of Governor of California. In immense detail and with apparent ease we are taken through his early years (when as lifeguard at Lowell Park he claimed to have saved 77 swimmers from drowning), his spells as radio sports commentator, his respectable but hardly outstanding film career (some 50 pictures, but only a handful of them memorable), and his growing interest in political and sociological matters. The Hollywood section is by far the longest in the book. In general, Anne Edwards presents the multifarious political and allied details with admirable clarity. Useful appendices and a first-class index.

Emotion Pictures, Hilton Tims; Columbus Books, £9.95

With countless books and articles emerging perennially from the presses on horror, science fiction, westerns, etc., it is a pleasure to find one devoted to an often overlooked genre, the 'women's picture', 1930–55. The author's range is generously wide, including not only such obvious female-star vehicles as the movies of Garbo, Davis, Garson, Hayward, Bergman and others but also more minor films of which it is equally pleasant to be reminded. Under such significant chapter headings as 'The Other Woman', 'The Food of Love', 'Silent Suffering' and 'Stiff Upper Lips', we are taken on an enjoyable journey through a nostalgic cinematic landscape; many of the films, of course, being still available on television or video. Illustrations are lavish and excellent.

Les Enfants du paradis, Marcel Carné and Jacques Prévert; Faber & Faber, £4.95

This film script first appeared in the Lorrimer series; it has long been out of print, and it is good to have it again available, integrated into Faber's own series of paperback cinema books. Before the days of video such well-produced scripts served as a useful guide to memory: now that many of the films can be obtained permanently the scripts are equally valuable for reference – and for checking that no inexcusable cuts have been made to the tape!

One complaint: many of the stills do not correspond to the reference numbers in the text – which can lead to considerable frustration.

Columbus Filmmakers Series:
Federico Fellini, Frank Burke; Columbus Books, £5.95
The Golden Age of French Cinema 1929–1939, John W. Martin; Columbus Books, £5.95
Lucino Visconti, Claretta Tonetti; Columbus Books, £5.95
Roman Polanski, Virginia Wright Wexman; Columbus Books, £5.95

Four further volumes in this handy series of *Filmmakers*, aimed particularly at the serious student, but useful to anyone with an interest in the subjects.

Fellini's career is covered up to and including *La Dolce Vita*, with a brief note on his contribution to the *Boccaccio '70* anthology and a reasonably lucid examination of a complex subject and personality. A further volume is promised, to cover the films from *8½* onwards.

The French films of the 1930s are discussed against the social and political backgrounds of their time – a time which saw some of the great cinematic masterpieces of any age or country: *L'Age d'or*, *Zéro de conduite*, *Le Jour se lève*, *Les Enfants du Paradis*, and the works of René Clair, to name but a few. It is strange that the editor considers *La Femme du boulanger*, *Un Carnet de bal*, *Poil de carotte* and the great Pagnol trilogy to be generally forgotten: certainly they are not by those fortunate enough to have seen them.

Visconti's work is discussed, after a brief chronological biography, with thoroughness and perception.

Bearing in mind that Roman Polanski's life and personal problems have caused many commentators to see his films only as forms of self-expression, Professor Wexford has focused on the films themselves. In her essays on each production up to and including *Tess* she puts forward a large number of fresh and fascinating analytic theories which should make all future viewings a stimulating experience. Her comparisons between Hardy's novel and Polanski's film of *Tess* are particularly valuable. The book was first published (in the USA) in 1985, and is thus too early for the inclusion of the controversial and elusive *Pirates*.

Full notes and filmographies are provided in each case. There are also a number of illustrations, but it is the texts that take first place.

Film Noir: Reflections in a Dark Mirror, Bruce Crowther; Columbus Books, £9.95

Film Noir is easier to recognize than to define. This is a thorough and detailed examination of the genre, with a mass of information clearly set out. All the best-known examples are discussed, but there are numerous others included that might be described as borderline cases or that contain *noir* elements, such as *Psycho*, *The Third Man*, *They Shoot Horses, Don't They?* and even *Citizen Kane*. The films are primarily grouped under stars ('Male Icons', 'Femmes Fatales'), minor players, directors, writers; and additional chapters deal with technique and origins, concluding with a surprisingly modest selection of 'classics'. This arrangement necessitates much use of the index, which fortunately is a sound one. There is a large number of good stills.

The Films of Gregory Peck, John Griggs; Columbus Books, £9.95

This follows the usual pattern: brief biography followed by cast-and-credits list and critical commentary (fuller than usual in this case) of every production featuring the star. The 49 films in which Peck appeared range from *Days of Glory* (1949) to *The Sea Wolves* (1980). American critic Judith Crist provides an introduction; stills and other photographs are copious and very well produced. A worthy record of a most likeable personality and memorable player.

The Films of Jack Nicholson, Douglas Brode; Columbus Books, £9.95

This large, stoutly made paperback follows the lines of the long-running Citadel series – biographical introduction, full coverage of every film with cast, credits and commentary, all lavishly illustrated with excellent stills and other photographs. It is a very good example of its kind, particularly as regards the commentaries. It is perhaps surprising to find that Nicholson has already appeared in well over 40 films, *Easy Rider* being a halfway mark.

Film Stars Don't Die in Liverpool, Peter Turner; Penguin, £2.95

The use throughout of invented (or at least recollected) dialogue gives this account of the tragic death through cancer of Gloria Grahame the appearance more of a novel than a factual record, but it is a moving story told by the friend and lover, twenty years her junior, who accompanied her during her last days in Liverpool in 1981. Best known for her Oscar-winning performance in *The Bad and the Beautiful* and her encounter with Lee Marvin in *The Big Heat*, Gloria Grahame in fact appeared in over 50 films.

The Films of Carol Reed, Robert F. Moss; Macmillan, £29.50

It is both surprising and discreditable that the work of Carol Reed should have had to wait so long for recognition in the form of a full-length study, and that it should then not have come from his own country. Fortunately Mr Moss's book is a worthy tribute – thorough, perceptive, enthusiastic but admirably balanced. Particularly valuable are his very detailed analyses of the 'big three': *Odd Man Out*, *The Fallen Idol* and *The Third Man*. There is a splendid bonus in the form of an excellent potted history of British cinema from 1895 to 1939, forming both a background and a breeding ground to Reed's work.

This said, it must be admitted that the book contains an unacceptable number of minor inaccuracies. Apart from numerous misprints we find misspelt names ('Demston' Tester – correct in index; Jean 'Cady') and wrong titles (*Our 'Father's' House*; *Love and Mr 'Windham'*): such an important and useful book deserves more careful preparatory scrutiny.

Five American Cinematographers, Scott Eyman; Scarecrow Press, dist. Bailey Bros & Swinfen, £25.00

The five cinematographers interviewed are Karl Struss, Joseph Ruttenberg, James Wong Howe, Linwood Dunn and William H. Clothier, all with famous films to their credit, and extending from 1917 to 1975. Under Scott Eyman's skilful handling they speak with fascinating frankness of their careers, their methods of working, their associates, their successes and failures. From this brief selection it would appear that cameramen are often at least as forthcoming, as trenchant and amusing as any of the stars and directors whose memoirs and opinions are much more frequently recorded. The result, illustrated with portraits and fine stills, is a highly entertaining and informative book.

5001 Nights at the Movies, Pauline Kael; Arena, £5.95

This large volume in the welcome series of paperback reprints of Pauline Kael's criticisms differs somewhat from the others, consisting of hundreds of reviews – long and short, early and recent – dating from the silent days to the late 'seventies, arranged alphabetically as a film and video guide. Nearly 700 pages; useful for either easy reference or a stimulating browse.

The French Through Their Films, Robin Buss; Batsford, £12.95

The author examines the French cinema against its sociological and historical background in a book which wears its scholarship lightly and is of equal interest as a study of society and of film. Avoiding the turgidity often found in such specialized analyses, Buss uses a wealth of examples in examining the mutual influences from early days (including the silents) until the present. Almost half the pages are taken up with a superb annotated filmography, with numbered references throughout the main text. There are over 50 good illustrations. Here is a book to be read for enjoyment as well as instruction and, despite a slightly patronizing attitude to the 'aesthetic' school of criticism, it must be ranked as among the best available in English on the cinema of France.

Fun in a Chinese Laundry, Josef von Sternberg; Columbus Books, £5.95

One of a handsome new paperback series of arts biographies, *The Lively Arts*, this reprint of the famous director's highly individual and often fiercely acerbic mixture of memoir and opinion is a most welcome reappearance of a book for too long unobtainable. His views on actors, in particular Emil Jannings and Charles Laughton, are, to put it mildly, stimulating; as also is his version of his relationship with Marlene Dietrich. How much cold reality is coloured by imagination may occasionally be open to question, but it makes for entertaining reading.

Gielgud, Robert Tanitch; Harrap, £14.95

A companion volume to the same author's *Olivier*, this is a complete survey of Gielgud's career, with a photograph accompanying almost every appearance in play, film and television production, together with brief comments and reviews (favourable and unfavourable) and a number of tributes from friends and colleagues. A chronology gives lists of performances, productions and awards, making this a comprehensive and handsomely produced record.

Great Movie Moments, John Russell Taylor; Conran Octopus, £14.95

After a very interesting and subtle essay on the magical linking of movie stills with memories of the films themselves, John Russell Taylor collects some 200 fine examples of the still photographer's art from the same number of equally notable films, accompanying each with a full caption. A suggestion: having read the introduction, turn straight to the index, select a film title at random, retain the instant memory that title conjures up, then look at the relevant still; the chances are that the two will closely coincide, even though the still itself may not exactly match the moment in the film which it represents. A treasure trove of items from the famous Kobal Collection.

The Great Spy Pictures, James Robert Parish and Michael R. Pitts; Scarecrow Press, dist. Bailey Bros & Swinfen, £27.50

First published in 1974 and now back in print, this is the first of the two-volume set, the second of which was reviewed in last year's *Film Review*. Despite being about 100 pages longer than its successor, its lower price has been retained. This book contains a 30-page history of the genre, reviews and commendably full cast-and-credit lists of over 460 films from the silent days to date, and a very wide coverage. Foreign films such as Fritz Lang's *Spione* are included, and even fringe comedies such as *Ma and Pa Kettle on Vacation*. As in the case of the second volume, there is also a lengthy bibliography. Together, the two well-illustrated books form a survey of this perennially popular film genre.

Halliwell's Film Guide (6th edition), Leslie Halliwell; Grafton, £19.95

This gargantuan guide proceeds on its impressive way with, we are assured, over 1,000 new entries (I have not ventured to count them), and no omission of previous ones. This has been accomplished with an addition of only 62 pages (now numbering 1,186) and no loss of clarity. Particular attention has been paid this time to the 1940s, and many serials between 1929 and 1955 are briefly included. The sections on 'Top Tens' and 'A Word on Shape' have been dropped, but the splendid essay on 'The Decline and Fall of the Movie' is retained. Fresh illustrations are included.

Henry Koster, interviewed by Irene Kahn Atkins; Scarecrow Press, dist. Bailey Bros & Swinfen, £20

This very enjoyable book is a fine example of what an 'oral history' (in question-and-answer form throughout) should be. The questions are unobtrusive and self-effacing, to the point and cleverly chosen to keep the reminiscences flowing smoothly. If Henry Koster is lucky in his questioner, then she is equally lucky in her subject. As she leads him through his early career in Germany and elsewhere, to his arrival in Hollywood as director in various studios, mainly Fox, a charming and forthcoming portrait emerges. The interviews are full of fascinating accounts of his early (often tough) struggles to assert himself in a foreign film world, of his association and work with stars such as Deanna Durbin (whose career he founded with *Three Smart Girls* and *100 Men and a Girl*), James Stewart, Marlene Dietrich, Loretta Young, Cary Grant and many others; and finally of his generous appraisals of his fellow filmmakers. Highly recommended.

Hitchcock and Selznick, Leonard J. Leff; Weidenfeld & Nicolson, £16.95

The uneasy, hot-and-cold, love-hate but productive partnership of these two leading figures of the great Hollywood years is compellingly told in this immensely readable book. The making of their four films (*Rebecca*, *Spellbound*, *Notorious* and *The Paradine Case*) together as director and producer is described in fascinating detail, with four long chapters covering every aspect of production from preliminaries to previews, and numerous glances on the way at some of the movies on which they worked separately. *Complete* filmographies of both men (occasionally a little short on cast lists) are included. A large number of rare photographs, full documentation and an excellent index are included.

Note: the original title of Patrick Hamilton's play, referred to here as *Rope's End*, which Hitchcock made as *Rope* was, in fact, also simply *Rope*.

Hollywood a Go-go, Andrew Yule; Sphere, £3.50

The first full account of Cannon, one of the most extraordinary phenomena of modern cinema history, the assets of which leapt from 20 cents in 1979 to about $371 in 1986, and included the acquisition of the once prestigious Classic Cinemas chain. During the period some of the feeblest films ever made emanated from the company, with titles rarely heard of and offering no inducement to further investigation, but it is undoubtedly correctly described on the book's cover as 'a massive international film empire'. An astonishing story, aptly titled and entertainingly told.

Hope and Glory, John Boorman; Faber & Faber, £4.95

The memoir and production details included with this delightful film script are as fascinating as the story itself – a personal reminiscence of Boorman's childhood in the London Blitz. The film won the Critics' Circle Best English Language Film Award and the *Evening Standard* Best Film Award. Embellished with many stills, production photographs and personal snapshots, the book is a pleasure to read from the first page to the last.

House of Games, David Mamet; Methuen, £4.95

Screenplay of the American writer's first film as director, which was seen at the London Film Festival in 1987. A few simple technical directions are incorporated, together with a section of stills, and an amusing introduction by Mamet recounts his experiences in making his first movie.

International Dictionary of Films and Filmmakers, Vol. 3, ed. James Vinson; Macmillan, £12.95

Dealing with actors and actresses, this is the third of a series originally entitled *The Macmillan Dictionary*. The first two (on films and directors) appeared in 1984 and were highly recommended in *Film Review 1985–6*. It follows the same lines as its predecessors – full acting credits (with directors), excellent biographical and critical paragraphs, lists of publications by both subject and author. Several hundred careers are covered in the 670 packed pages, mainly from Britain and America but with a sizeable proportion of foreign players. This particular volume is available in softback (Papermac) only, which unfortunately spoils the symmetry of the set, but it is splendid value at the lower price.

International Film Guide 1988, ed. Peter Cowie; Tantivy Press, £8.50

Resplendent in crimson and silver, the renowned annual reference cornucopia celebrates its quarter-century in grand style. Now with over 500 fully illustrated pages, it is as packed as ever with information, comments and criticisms on all relevant subjects worldwide. Advantage is taken of the 25th milestone to include many 'Ten Best' personal choices from 1962 to 1987 among the impeccably compiled features. Suitably, in view of the editor's pre-eminence in the subject, this year's Dossier (a splendid one) is on 'Scandinavian Cinema Now'. As Peter Cowie implies, the *IFG* can now press on to its Golden Jubilee.

Itinerant Cameraman, Walter Lassally; John Murray, £14.95

In contrast to stars and directors, books about cinematographers are rare indeed considering their vital role in film-making, and Mr Lassally's most enjoyable autobiography is therefore particularly welcome. His title is apt, for he has photographed features and documentaries in countries all over the world (*Zorba the Greek*, *Oedipus the King*, *Tom Jones*, *The Loneliness of the Long Distance Runner*, *Savages*, *Heat and Dust*, the underrated *The Adding Machine*, to name only a few), and describes his experiences with humour and an engaging modesty – together with occasional sharp comments on stars with inflated egos. Above all his book is of interest for its many technical details and tricks of the trade, all recounted so lucidly that they present few difficulties even to those whose knowledge of the secrets of his craft is minimal. Well illustrated and indexed.

The 'It's a Wonderful Life' Book, Jeanine Basinger; Pavilion Books, £9.95

This beautifully produced large-format softback contains the full shooting script of Frank Capra's favourite – and arguably best – film, interviews with star (James Stewart), photographer (Joseph Biroc) and Capra himself, the original story, notes on rejected screenplays and other relevant material. Embellished with a large number of superb stills and portraits, it is a wholly fascinating and complete record of the making of a famous and much-loved motion picture. Highly recommended for serious study and/or simple pleasure.

Jack Lemmon, His Films and Career, Joe Baltake; Columbus Books, £9.95

This large, stout paperback covers Lemmon's career up to 1986. After tributes and a lengthy biographical section (containing many personal quotations) each film is fully dealt with, given cast and technical credits, synopsis and a selection of critical comments. The latter are by no means unvaryingly complimentary, particularly when dealing with Lemmon's middle period, e.g. *The Out-of-Towners*. Finally, however, a fully rounded portrait of a gifted and very likeable star emerges. Stills and portraits are numerous and excellent, each film being given several illustrations, and a final section is devoted to his leading ladies.

A Life, Elia Kazan; André Deutsch, £17.95

This enormous autobiography (over 800 pages) grips the attention like a two-pronged fork. On the one hand one is the sheer scope and detail of his life and work in cinema and theatre; on the other is the outspoken, sometimes outrageously frank, often far from sweetness-and-light relationships with colleagues and associates. Though Kazan is frequently unsparing in his judgements, this is by no means a book without generosity. After all, the director of such plays as *A Streetcar Named Desire*, *The Skin of our Teeth*, *Death of a Salesman*, and films such as *East of Eden*, *On the Waterfront*, *Viva Zapata* and (again) *Streetcar*, may surely be permitted an occasional burst of egotism. He gives a spirited defence of his actions during the HUAC hearings; and parts of the book (including those which deal with the tragic deaths of his two wives) are deeply moving. Well illustrated and indexed, though a list of productions would have been welcome in this not inexpensive tome.

Louise Brooks – Portrait of an Anti-Star, ed. Roland Jaccard; Columbus Books, £9.95

This odd but attractive book, described as a tribute and a 'work of love', and based almost entirely on the actress's work with G.W. Pabst in *Pandora's Box* and *Diary of a Lost Girl*, is a collection of articles by and about the ever-fascinating Miss Brooks. The illustrations, many of them frame enlargements, are rare and excellent.

The Making of *The African Queen* – or how I went to Africa with Bogart, Bacall and Huston and almost lost my mind, Katharine Hepburn; Century Hutchinson, £10.95

Reading this highly enjoyable account of the making of this famous film, it is easy to imagine that the great Hepburn is simply sitting in the same room, comfortably chatting. It may be, as she says, her 'first book', but she certainly knows how to project her personality as sharply in print as on film. Even those whose admiration for her work may be firmly this side of idolatry must surely surrender to her spell here. Fully illustrated, attractively produced and even embellished with a helpful map, this hilarious memoir can be faulted in only one respect – it is too brief.

Marilyn Among Friends, Sam Shaw and Norman Rosten; Bloomsbury, £14.95

Of making many books about Marilyn Monroe (as the preacher might have said) there is no end – but apparently no slackening in demand either. Accompanying a lively and affectionate, if occasionally somewhat fulsome, text is a lavish collection of superb photographs, most of them entirely new. As the title indicates, they are in the main personal, rather than professional – intimate or social moments preserved in black-and-white or very attractive colour. The taking of the famous skirt-over-the-grating shot is illustrated in detail.

Marilyn Monroe, an Appreciation, Eve Arnold; Hamish Hamilton, £14.95

Yet another beautifully produced large-page photographic album on this apparently inexhaustible subject. The text is fuller than in many cases and contains interesting semi-technical details: 'As a subject she was unique, but there were days to make a photographer despair. She would look heavy, fat – as though if one put an apple in her mouth she could be served on a Christmas platter . . . Up close, around the periphery of her face there was a dusting of faint down. This light fuzz trapped light and caused an aureole to form, giving her a faint glow on film, a double plus.' Included among the many portraits, colour and black-and-white, are a number taken on location during the filming of *The Misfits*.

Mass-Observation at the Movies, ed. Jeffrey Richards and Dorothy Sheridan; Routledge & Kegan Paul, £35.95

This interesting and important addition to the 'Cinema and Society' series covers the years from the late 1930s to about 1943, and is a wide-reaching and extremely thorough contemporary survey of the cinema-going habits of the general (British) public, their reactions to a number of feature films, shorts (Ministry of Information and otherwise) and newsreels. The latter receive detailed treatment as to their influence both as propaganda and entertainment, their quality, reliability – and fakery. The longest single section of the book (over 100 out of 460 pages) is devoted to the comments, mainly brief, of several hundred filmgoers from a number of cinemas in the northern town of Bolton – nicknamed 'Worktown'. Among the films receiving special attention are *The Great Dictator*, *Ships with Wings*, George Formby's *Let George Do It* and the ludicrous propaganda effort *The Lion Has Wings*, in which an entire batch of enemy raiding planes turns tail at the sight of the balloon barrage. Other titles occurring frequently in the general comments include *Mrs Miniver*, Jessie Matthews's *Gangway*, *Victoria the Great*, *A Star is Born* and *In Which We Serve*. A wealth of statistical tables offers every kind of comparison.

Altogether this is a fascinating and engrossing chronicle – not least on account of the sharp and pithy judgements made by many of the observed 'mass'.

Meryl Streep, Eugene E. Pfaff Jr and Mark Emerson; McFarland & Co., dist. Bailey Bros & Swinfen, £14.20

Though it may seem somewhat early in the career of this competent actress for a full 'critical biography', this is a good, workmanlike account, well documented and with a detailed – if obviously brief – filmography. It should prove a useful preliminary summary of her early years, paving the way for a fuller study at a later date.

The Monogram Checklist, Ted Okuda; McFarland & Co., dist. Bailey Bros & Swinfen, £29.95

Monogram was one of the more important of the small B-feature-producing companies (merging briefly with Republic) and it is good to have this excellent comprehensive index, giving credits, casts, synopses etc. of 727 movies to its credit from 1931 to 1952. Comedies, drama, westerns, horror – all genres are represented, and quite a number of well-known names appear: Ava Gardner, Fay Wray, John Wayne, Kay Francis, Boris Karloff (in the *Mr Wong* series) and others, including Loretta Young's two sisters, Sally Blane and Polly Ann Young. Some British productions are featured among the releases. Interesting stills and advertisements, and a full index (based on the number of the film rather than the page) round off a useful reference book.

Movie Comedians – The Complete Guide, James L. Neibaur; McFarland & Co., dist. Bailey Bros & Swinfen, £25.95

The chief value of this survey is its comprehensiveness. Into a comparatively small space the author has packed an enormous number of facts, including long filmographies not only of leading figures such as Chaplin, Keaton and Lloyd, but also of Red Skelton, the Three Stooges, Jerry Lewis and others. It is pleasant to read his championship of Charley Chase, perhaps the most underrated of silent comedians, who has no fewer than ten pages of film titles allotted to him. Main entries are provided with a short but pithy commentary, 'significant minor comedians' are included for each decade, and a twenty-page appendix gives brief details of a large number of supporting players. More careful editing might have prevented name misspellings such as 'Jobyana' Ralston (Harold Lloyd's leading lady), Ann 'Rutheford' and other misprints, including on one occasion the omission of one or more whole lines.

The Movies, Mr Griffith and Me, Lillian Gish, with Anne Pinchot; Columbus Books, £5.95

One of the happiest events of the year is the return to availability, in the attractive *Lively Arts* series, of this engaging book which was first published in 1969. Almost as much a biography of D.W. Griffith as an autobiography of Lillian Gish, it is a vivid and wholly delightful evocation of the early Hollywood days. Though the period covered extends to the 1960s, the greatest part of the book is devoted to Lillian and Dorothy Gish's 'silent' days and the great (and lesser) names of the period. The portrait of Griffith himself, both as a person and as a sensitive (if sometimes ruthless) director, is disarmingly but never slavishly affectionate, with fascinating details about the making of such films as *The Birth of a Nation*, *Intolerance* and *Way Down East*. The index is excellent, and the photographic sections both generous and rare.

Olivier, Anthony Holden; Weidenfeld & Nicolson, £16

The author, known particularly for his notable biography of Prince Charles, states that this is neither an 'official' nor an 'authorized' work. It is, however, considerably the fullest account so far of Olivier's life and career, thoroughly researched, carefully documented, well illustrated and full of fascinating detail.

Past Forgetting, Peter Cushing; Weidenfeld & Nicolson, £9.95

After Peter Cushing's first autobiography appeared (see *Film Review 1986–7*) he apparently received numerous comments that not enough was included about his work in Hammer Films. Here he attempts to fill the gap, and even though far more is to be found than is indicated in the subtitle 'Memoirs of the Hammer Years' enough is described to satisfy most of the curious. What chiefly shines through this second volume, however, as notably as through the first, is the charm, humour and warmth of its author.

The Prophetic Soul, Leon Stover; McFarland & Co., dist. Bailey Bros & Swinfen, £29.95

This is a large-scale, exhaustive examination (described as a 'reading') of H.G. Wells's classic *Things to Come*. More than half the 300 pages is taken up by two vast appendices: the film treatment and the full release script, both published for the first time. The first part is a long, scholarly and absorbing essay on the film and on Wells's intentions, philosophy and beliefs. Written with both warm enthusiasm and cool judgement, it is an obvious 'must' for all devotees of Wells, and in addition should do much to counteract the somewhat belittling attitude sometimes adopted towards his famous film. The book is embellished with 50 excellent photographs.

Reel Politics, Terry Christensen; Basil Blackwell, £19.50

This ranks high among the best of the 'films against their sociological background' books – a detailed, in-depth study of American political movies from *The Birth of a Nation* to *Platoon*. The judgements, comments and analyses are balanced and perceptive, and written in an easy, unpretentious style that bears its scholarship lightly. A very large number of films are covered, on an equally wide range of subjects – the mere list of them fills ten pages.

Against these good points must be set some careless errors (including misspelt names) and a maddeningly inadequate index.

Screen World 1987, John Willis; Frederick Muller, £16.95

A little later than usual in arriving, but well worth waiting for, this invaluable reference and picture book continues the policy followed since 1949: no critical or other articles, but complete casts and credits, a thousand stills and portraits, biographical notes, obituary and other details, rounded off with a gargantuan index – a complete record of the cinema *in America* for the year 1986. Any fortunate owner of the complete set possesses a goldmine.

Screenwriting for Narrative Film and Television, William Miller; Columbus Books, £7.95

A scholarly work which examines in close detail every conceivable aspect of the subject: narrative techniques, structure, character portrayal, sequences, settings, dialogue, adaptations etc. A very large number of popular and readily available films are used as examples, and the whole is discussed lucidly and even entertainingly. Invaluable not only for the budding writer but for anyone interested in how a film is evolved and set down in written form.

Spencer Tracy – Tragic Idol, Bill Davidson; Sidgwick & Jackson, £12.95

Books on Spencer Tracy are fewer than on many less distinguished actors, and this competent biography is welcome. Much of the mystery of his life, in the author's words, remains unsolved, but at least this frank and sympathetic study provides a reasonably full and perceptive account of his life and career – though some may find the 'Open letter made public' by Katharine Hepburn a trifle embarrassing. With illustrations, a list of films and a notably full index.

Spiegel, Andrew Sinclair; Weidenfeld & Nicolson, £14.95

Apart from his four masterpieces, *Lawrence of Arabia*, *The African Queen*, *Bridge on the River Kwai* and *On the Waterfront*, producer Sam Spiegel was responsible for such notable movies as *Tales of Manhattan*, *The Chase* and *Night of the Generals*. Also to his credit is the little-known, and apparently fairly disastrous Buster Keaton film of 1935, *The Invader* (made in Britain), in which, it seems, Spiegel originally wished to cast Maurice Chevalier. In this comparatively brief biography his colourful personality and adventurous life are entertainingly depicted. The reference section contains a bibliography, lists of magazine and newspaper articles but, oddly, no filmography.

Sports Films: A Complete Reference, Harvey Marc Zucker and Lawrence J. Babich; McFarland & Co., dist. Bailey Bros & Swinfen, £30.95

The section headings of this massive 612-page book include such titles as 'Baseball', 'Boxing', 'Olympics', 'Skates' and 'Soccer' but the contents extend far beyond those films in which such activities are the main ingredient. To take a mere handful of entries: *The Rocking-horse Winner*, *Shadow of the Thin Man* and *Strangers on a Train* may be found here, together with comedy shorts from the earliest days, series such as *The Collegians* and *The Leather Pushers*, and even a tantalizing Mexican movie in 1961, *Invasion of the Zombies*, in which a masked wrestler takes on an entire army of zombies created by a mad scientist. British and foreign films are also included. Each of the 1827 films is given cast-and-credit lists, length, production company and plot summary. There is an 80-page supplement of athletes' biographies, together with a large bibliography, a number of illustrations and a comprehensive index. An excellent and easy-to-use addition to the reference shelf.

State of the Art, Pauline Kael; Arena, £5.95

A further volume in the useful stout paperback reprints of Pauline Kael's collected film reviews, covering the years 1983–5 under such intriguing subheadings as 'Silliness', 'Hysterics', 'Charismatic Half-and-halfs' and 'Plain and Simple'. Lively, often controversial, well indexed.

Striking Poses, Richard Schickel; Pavilion, £14.95

A gorgeous collection of the higher lunacies of film-star publicity photography, stunningly reproduced in brilliant colour, from the famous Kobal Collection. Grouped under such headings as 'Enigma Variations', 'Hats on their Belfries', 'Hey, Hey in the Hayloft' and 'All Alone by the Telephone', the Golden Age girls and boys are put through their smile-wreathed (and oddly asexual) paces. 'Don't laugh. These pictures are not meant to be funny,' says Mr Schickel in a no-nonsense – and indeed sobering – introduction, but he finally admits that we have to. What if fantasy and artifice triumph over reality? Such extravagances are, after all, as much part of the world of the cinema as the most solemn treatises on the *auteur* theory or the place of semiotics in the art of the film.

Talking Pictures, Barry Norman; Hodder & Stoughton, £14.95

Whereas a number of books have been published on the film against a background of sociological history, this might be described as a sociological history of Hollywood against a background of the films of the period – from the arrival of the talking picture up to the present day. The high spot is the account of the notorious HUAC and blacklist – the longest chapter in the book and a full and brilliant exposition of the complicated manoeuvering, subterfuges and generally reprehensible behaviour that went on during those less than admirable years, all set out with clarity and a commendable balance. Other chapters of particular interest are those on 'Hollywood and Crime' (including *film noir*) and on the B-movie. Barry Norman's style has all the wit and humour of his television series (on one of which it is based); indeed, one can almost hear his voice as one turns the pleasant and well-illustrated pages. Note: 'The business of America is business' was said by President Coolidge, not Hoover.

That Was Hollywood – The 1930s, Allen Eyles; Batsford, £14.95

General histories of the Hollywood 'thirties are available, but quick-reference books are not so plentiful, and this fact-packed summary is therefore all the more welcome. Covering some 500 films, it deals in month-by-month order with the most popular and/or critically esteemed. Information and commentaries are given for a film's first entry, and its title is repeated only if its popularity extends for a longer period. In addition there are lists of runners-up and Academy Awards, brief historical summaries, and details of such items as the Hays Code and American films in England. Illustrations include stills, advertisements, production and other photographs and a useful page of maps, all excellently reproduced.

The Third Man, Graham Greene; Faber & Faber, £3.95

Like *Les Enfants du Paradis*, this film script has long been out of print, having first appeared in the Lorrimer series. Its reappearance, integrated into Faber's own paperback cinema series, is very welcome.

This 'n' That, Bette Davis; Sidgwick & Jackson, £12.95

As the title implies, this is not a further chapter of autobiography but rather a fairly random collection of memories, opinions, advice and criticism, together with occasional and often amusing side-swipes at various colleagues and acquaintants. (After a dig or two at Ronald Reagan she has the frankness to admit to being a Democrat.) Among the more interesting chapters are those on the story of the Hollywood Canteen and on the making of *Whatever Happened to Baby Jane?* Among the less interesting (and indeed, at times, embarrassing) are the pages on her reactions to her daughter's marriage – including a rather awful twelve-verse 'lyric' – and her somewhat strained relations with her son-in-law. In part this section is intended, it appears, to 'put the record straight' after the publication of a *Mommie Dearest* type of book by her daughter – surely one of the least commendable forms of 'literature'. The appearance of the book was postponed owing to an operation and stroke from which Bette Davis most determinedly and courageously recovered.

Trevor Howard – A Gentleman and a Player, Vivienne Knight; Sphere, £3.50

Sadly, Trevor Howard died shortly before this paperback edition of an 'authorized biography' appeared. It is a warm, indeed affectionate, tribute, which nails some rumours (such as the reported 'hell-raising') and recounts many anecdotes – some interesting or amusing, some trivial. The writing is occasionally a bit flaccid and careless, but both career and personal life are well covered, and a full portrait emerges of a remarkably gifted, likeable and professional artiste. Note: Howard could not have seen *The Sin Flood* at the Dominion Theatre, London, in about 1924 – the building was not opened until 1929.

Vanity Will Get You Somewhere, Joseph Cotten; Columbus Books, £10.95

Joseph Cotten's autobiography is so full of wit and charm that the reader can only agree with the thankfulness he expresses in his foreword that 'clouded memory often diffuses cold fact into colorful form'. In any case, the many pages of obviously invented dialogue and neatly constructed 'events' are clearly based on sound and unclouded truth. The book is full of marvellous anecdotes, about great films such as *Citizen Kane* and *The Third Man* as well as those of perhaps slightly lower stature but equally fond remembrance. The details of his many travels, his relationship with family, friends and colleagues, his later confrontation with a terrifying affliction are by turn moving, amusing – and illuminated throughout with generosity and warmth.

Vivien, Alexander Walker; Methuen, £3.95

A paperback edition of the truly 'definitive' biography of Vivien Leigh, highly recommended in *Film Review 1987–8*, sensitively written, thoroughly documented and excellently indexed.

Wicked Women of the Screen, David Quinlan; Batsford, £12.95

In this lavishly illustrated paperback David Quinlan takes time off from compiling his comprehensive and invaluable 'Directories' (*Stars, Character Actors, Directors*) and indulges in an examination of all forms of feminine cinema sinners, from murderesses, psychos and crooks to schemers, horror baddies and mere bitches. Even cartoon villainesses are included. Hundreds of names are here, from the most famous, such as Bette Davis, to the equally accomplished but lesser known such as the fine British character actress Jean Cadell; from those who made a career of nastiness to those who slipped only occasionally. Apart from their actual ill-doings he supplies much about their general careers, with interesting snippets of minor information. A number of star filmographies are included, and one would gladly have seen more; but this is to quibble: it is a fascinating round-up, with over 200 (often rare) stills.

Wide Screen Movies, Robert E. Carr and R.M. Hayes; McFarland & Co., dist. Bailey Bros & Swinfen, £29.95

Another large volume on the lines of the same publisher's *Sports Movies* and *Western Movies*, this deals in immense and all-embracing detail with all aspects of the wide screen, and must surely become the definitive work on the subject. Both the history and the extraordinary ramifications of wide-screen filming contain surprises. The number of processes, for instance, running well into double figures, includes such awe-inspiring names (apart from VistaVision, CinemaScope and other familiar friends) as Plastorama, Showscan, Nikkatsuscope, Glamorama and Totalscope. Technical details are simply described and embellished with excellent charts, diagrams, stills and other illustrations. There are long lists of films in the various categories, a full index and a massive 200-page filmography: a valuable repository of curious information.

Wish You Were Here, David Leland; Faber & Faber, £4.95

The increasing number of films made available in printed form is to be welcomed, not only as memory-revivers but as a check on the infuriating cuts sometimes made on video (e.g. Polanski's *Cul-de-Sac*). This, one of a number from the same publisher, is a good example of how they should be presented for easy reading.

Awards and Festivals

While this feature cannot pretend to cover all the proliferating film festival and other awards, you will find all the major and many of the more interesting minor ones listed. A more or less complete advance list of the yearly film festivals is published periodically in *Variety*.

Nationality is stated only where films do not originate from the country in which the awards are given.

The American Academy of Motion Picture Arts and Sciences Awards and Nominations ('Oscars') for 1987, April 1988

Best Film: *The Last Emperor*. Nominations: *Broadcast News, Fatal Attraction, Hope and Glory, Moonstruck*.

Best Direction: Bernardo Bertolucci for *The Last Emperor*. Nominations: John Boor-

man, for *Hope and Glory*, Lasse Hallstrom, for *My Life As a Dog*, Norman Jewison, for *Moonstruck*, Adrian Lyne, for *Fatal Attraction*.

Best Actor: Michael Douglas in *Wall Street*. Nominations: William Hurt, in *Broadcast News*, Marcello Mastroianni, in *Dark*

Wu Tao in The Last Emperor, *which scooped nine of the 1987 Oscars.*

Eyes, Jack Nicholson, in *Ironweed*, Robin Williams, in *Good Morning, Vietnam*.

Best Actress: Cher, in *Moonstruck*. Nominations: Glenn Close, in *Fatal Attraction*, Holly Hunter, in *Broadcast News*, Sally Kirkland, in *Anna*, Meryl Streep, in *Ironweed*.

Best Supporting Actor: Sean Connery, in *The Untouchables*. Nominations: Albert Brooks, in *Broadcast News*, Morgan Freeman, in *Street Smart*, Vincent Gardenia, in *Moonstruck*, Denzel Washington, in *Cry Freedom*.

Best Supporting Actress: Olympia Dukakis, in *Moonstruck*. Nominations: Norma Aleandro, in *Gaby – A True Story*, Anne Archer, in *Fatal Attraction*, Anne Ramsey, in *Throw Momma from the Train*, Ann Sothern, in *The Whales of August*.

Best Original Screenplay: John Patrick Shanley, for *Moonstruck*. Nominations: Woody Allen, for *Radio Days*, John Boorman, for *Hope and Glory*, James L. Brooks, for *Broadcast News*, Louis Malle, for *Au Revoir, les enfants*.

Best Screenplay Adaptation of material from another medium: Mark Peploe, Bernardo Bertolucci, Enzo Ungari, for *The Last Emperor*. Nominations: James Dearden, for *Fatal Attraction*, Lasse Hallstrom, Reidar Jonsson, Brasse Brannstrom, Per Berglund, for *My Life As a Dog*, Tony Huston, for *The Dead*, Stanley Kubrick, Michael Herr, Gustav Hasford, for *Full Metal Jacket*.

Best Editing: Gabriella Cristiani, for *The Last Emperor*. Nominations: Michael Kahn, for *Empire of the Sun*, Michael Kahn, for *Fatal Attraction*, Richard Marks, for *Broadcast News*, Frank J. Urioste, for *RoboCop*.

Best Cinematography: Vittorio Storaro, for *The Last Emperor*. Nominations: Michael Ballhaus, for *Broadcast News*, Allen Daviau, for *Empire of the Sun*, Philippe Rousselot, for *Hope and Glory*, Haskell Wexler, for *Matewan*.

Best Foreign Language Film: *Babette's Feast* (Denmark). Nominations: *Au Revoir, les enfants* (France), *Course Completed* (Spain), *The Family* (Italy), *Pathfinder* (Lapland).

Best Art Direction/Set Direction: Ferdinando Scarfiotti, Bruno Cesari, for *The Last Emperor*. Nominations: Sando Loquasto, Carol Joffe, Les Bloom, George DeTitta Jr, for *Radio Days*, Anthony Pratt, Joan Woollard, for *Hope and Glory*, Norman Reynolds, Harry Cordwell, for *Empire of the Sun*, Patrizia Von Brandenstein, Hal Gausman, for *The Untouchables*.

Best Musical Score: David Byrne, Ryuichi Sakamoto, Cong Su, for *The Last Emperor*. Nominations: George Fenton, John Gwangwa, for *Cry Freedom*, Ennio Morricone, for *The Untouchables*, John Williams, for *Empire of the Sun*, John Williams, for *The Witches of Eastwick*.

Best Documentary Feature: *The Ten Year Lunch – The Wit and Legend of the Algonquin Round Table*. Nominations: *Eyes on the Prize (America's Civil Rights Years, Bridge To Freedom, 1965)*, *Hellfire – A Journey From Hiroshima*, *Radio Bikini*, *A Stitch in Time*.

Best Documentary Short: *Young at Heart*. Nominations: *Frances Steloff – Memoirs of a Bookseller*, *In the Wee Wee Hours*, *Language Says It All*, *Silver Into Gold*.

Short Subjects (Animated): *The Man Who Planted Trees*. Nominations: *George and Rosemary*, *Your Face*.

Short Subjects (Live-Action): *Ray's Male Heterosexual Dance Hall*. Nominations: *Making Waves*, *Shoeshine*.

Best Song: *Dirty Dancing*: '(I've Had) The Time of My Life'. Nominations: *Beverly Hills Cop II*: 'Shakedown', *Cry Freedom*: 'Cry Freedom', *Mannequin*: 'Nothing's Gonna Stop Us Now', *The Princess Bride*: 'Storybook Love'.

Best Costume Design: James Acheson, for *The Last Emperor*. Nominations: Jenny Beavan, John Bright, for *Maurice*, Dorothy Jeakins, for *The Dead*, Bob Ringwood, for *Empire of the Sun*, Marilyn Vance-Straker, for *The Untouchables*.

Best Makeup shared by: Rick Baker for *Harry and the Hendersons* and Bob Laden, for *Happy New Year*.

Best Sound: *The Last Emperor*. Nominations: *Empire of the Sun*, *Lethal Weapon*, *RoboCop*, *The Witches of Eastwick*.

Best Visual Effects: *Innerspace*. Nomination: *Predator*.

The Irving G. Thalberg Award went to Billy Wilder.

The 29th Australian Film Institute Awards, 1987

Best Film: *The Year My Voice Broke*; which also won the awards for Best Director and Best Original Screenplay (John Duigan), Best Supporting Actor: Ben Mendelsohn, and the AFI Members' Award.

Best Actor: Leo McKern, in *Travelling North*.

Best Actress: Judy Davis, in *High Tide*; which also won the award for Best Supporting Actress (Jan Adele).

Best Editing: David Pulbrook, for *Ground Zero*; which also won the awards for Best Cinematography (Steve Dobson) and Best Production Design (Brian Thomson).

The 38th Berlin International Festival Awards, February/March 1988

Golden Bear – Best Film: *Red Sorghum*, by Zhang Yimou (China).

Silver Bear – Special Jury Prize: *Commissar*, by Alexander Askoldov (USSR).

Silver Bear: *The Debt*, by Miguel Pereira (Argentina/UK).

Best Director: Norman Jewison, for *Moonstruck* (USA).

Best Actor shared by: Jorg Pose and Manfred Mock, in *Bear Ye One Another's Burdens* (East Germany).

Best Actress: Holly Hunter, in *Broadcast News* (USA).

Silver Bear for Outstanding Single Achievement: Janus Zaorski, writer-director of *Mother of Kings* (Poland).

Golden Bear for Best Short: Zdravko Barisic, for *The Power* (Yugoslavia).

The 1987 British Academy of Film and Television Arts Awards, March 1988

Best Film: *Jean de Florette*, by Claude Berri (France – the first time for fourteen years that a foreign film has won the Academy's top honour); which also won the awards for Best Supporting Actor (Daniel Auteuil) and Best Screenplay Adaptation (Gérard Brach and Claude Berri).

Best Direction: Oliver Stone, for *Platoon* (USA).

Best Actor: Sean Connery, in *The Name of the Rose* (West Germany/France/Italy).

Best Actress: Anne Bancroft, in *84 Charing Cross Road* (USA).

Best Supporting Actress: Susan Wooldridge, in *Hope and Glory*.

Best Original Screenplay: David Leland, for *Wish You Were Here*.

Best Film Music: Ennio Morricone, for *The Untouchables* (USA).

Best Foreign Language Film: *The Sacrifice*, by Andrei Tarkovsky (France/Sweden).

The Fellowship Award went to Ingmar Bergman, 'for more than 40 years of film achievement'.

The 9th Annual (British) Critics' Circle Film Section Awards, December 1987

Best English Language Film: *Hope and Glory*, by John Boorman.

Best Foreign Language Film: *Jean de Florette*, by Claude Berri (France).

Best Acting Performances: Sean Connery, in *The Name of the Rose* (West Germany/France/Italy) and *The Untouchables* (USA); and Gary Oldman, in *Prick Up Your Ears*.

Best Screenplay: Alan Bennett, for *Prick Up Your Ears*.

Best Director: Stanley Kubrick, for *Full Metal Jacket* (USA).

Film Music Award: Ennio Morricone, for *The Untouchables* (USA).

Special Awards: David Rose of Channel 4, Pinewood Studios and make-up artist Tommie Manderson.

The 1988 Academy of Canadian Cinema and Television ('Genie') Awards, March 1988

Best Film: *Night Zoo*; which also took the awards for Best Direction and Best Screenplay (Jean-Claude Lauzon), Best Actor (Roger le Bel), Best Supporting Actor (Germain Houde), Best Cinematography (Guy Dufaux), Best Art Direction (Jean-Baptiste Tard), Best Editing (Michael Arcand), and several others.

Best Actress: Sheila McCarthy, in *I've Heard the Mermaids Singing*; which also won the Best Supporting Actress Award (Paule Baillargeon).

Special Award to Norman Jewison for the founding of the Canadian Centre for Advanced Film Studies.

The Air Canada Award went to Rock Demers for his 'Outstanding Contribution to the Business of Filmmaking in Canada'.

The 41st Cannes Film Festival Awards, May 1988

Palme d'Or, Premier Award: *Pelle the Conqueror*, by Bille August (Denmark).

Special Jury Grand Prize: *A World Apart*, by Chris Menges (UK).

Best Direction: *The South*, by Fernando Solanas (Argentina).

Best Actor: Forest Whitaker, in *Bird* (USA).

Best Actress shared by: Barbara Hershey, Jodhi May and Linda Mvusi, in *A World Apart* (UK).

Best Artistic Contribution: *Drowning by Numbers*, by Peter Greenaway (UK).

Jury Prize: *Thou Shalt Not Kill*, by Krzysztof Kieslowski (Poland).

Camera d'Or: *Salaam Bombay* (India).

The Evening Standard Film Awards, January 1988

Best Film: *Hope and Glory*, by John Boorman.

Best Actor: Derek Jacobi, in *Little Dorrit*.

Best Actress: Emily Lloyd, in *Wish You Were Here*.

Best Screenplay: Alan Bennett, for *Prick Up Your Ears*.

Peter Sellars Award for Comedy: David Leland, for screenplays of *Personal Services* and *Wish You Were Here*.

Best Technical Achievement: Anthony Pratt, for the production design of *Hope and Glory*.

Most Promising Newcomer: Harry Hook, for *The Kitchen Toto*.

A Special Award to Zenith Films Co.

The 16th Fantasy Film Festival, Avoriaz, January 1988

Grand Prix: *The Hidden*, by Jack Sholder (USA).

Special Jury Prize: *A Chinese Ghost Story*, by Ching Siu-Tung (Hong Kong).

Critics' Prize: *Prince of Darkness*, by John Carpenter (USA).

Special (Excellence) Award: *RoboCop*, by Paul Verhoeven (USA).

Grand Prize – 'Fear' section: *Hellraiser*, by Clive Barker (UK).

The French Academy (César) Awards, March 1988

Best Film: *Au Revoir, les enfants*; which also won the awards for Best Direction and Best Screenplay (Louis Malle), Photography (Renato Berta), Editing (Emmanuelle Castro), Art (Willy Holt) and Sound (Jean-Claude Villand). The film had already been honoured with the Louis Deluc Prize and the French Film Critics' Award.

Best Actor: Richard Bohringer, in Jean-Lupe Hubert's *Le Grand Chemin*.

Best Actress: Anemone, in *Le Grand Chemin*.

Best Supporting Actor: Jean-Claude Brialy, in André Technine's *Les Innocents*.

Best Supporting Actress: Dominique Lavanant, in Jean-Pierre Mocky's *Agent Trouble*.

Best Foreign Film: *The Last Emperor*, by Bernardo Bertolucci (USA).

The Italian David Di Donatello Awards ('Davids'), Rome, June 1988

Best Film: *The Last Emperor* (USA); which also won the Best Direction and Best Screenplay awards (Bernardo Bertolucci), and took six other awards for photography, set design, production, costume, editing and best supporting actor (Peter O'Toole).

Best Foreign Film: *Au Revoir, les enfants* (France), which also won Louis Malle the awards for Best Direction and Best Screenplay in this category.

Best Italian Actor: Marcello Mastroianni, in *Dark Eyes*.

Best Italian Actress: Elena Sofonova, in *Dark Eyes*.

Best Foreign Actor: Michael Douglas, in *Wall Street* (USA).

Best Foreign Actress: Cher, in *Moonstruck* (USA).

The Locarno Film Festival Awards, August 1987

Golden Leopard for Best Film: *The Jester –*

O Bobo, by Josè Alvaro Morais (Portugal).

Silver Leopard: *The Terrorizers – Konbu Finze*, by Edward Yang (Taiwan).

Bronze Leopard: *Man's Solitary Voice – Odinokij Golos Celoveka*, by Aleksandr Sokurov (USSR).

Bronze Leopard for Best Acting Performance: Arpad Vermes, in *A Hungarian Fairy Tale – Hol Volt, Holm Nem Volt*, by Gyula Gazdak (Hungary).

Bronze Leopard for Best Technical Achievement: Gregg Araki, for writing, directing, photographing, editing and producing *Three Bewildered People in the Night* (USA).

Critics' Prize shared by: *Three Bewildered People in the Night* (USA) and *Long Goodbyes – Dolgie Provody*, by Kira Muratova (USSR).

The Madrid International Film Festival ('Imagfic') Awards, March 1988

Best Film: *Déja Vu – Veo Videno*, by Goran Markovic (Yugoslavia).

Best Direction: Wes Craven, for *The Serpent and the Rainbow* (USA); which also won the award for Best Screenplay (Richard Maxwell and A.R. Simoun).

Best Actor shared by: David Jacobson, in *The Beast* (USA) and Augustin Gonzalez, in *Blue Witness – Testigo Azul*.

Special Jury Prizes: *The Last of England*, by Derek Jarman (UK) and *About Princess Clara and the Flying Shoemaker – O Princazne Jasnence a Letajicim Sevci*, by Zdenek Troska (Czechoslovakia).

The Montreal Film Festival, August 1987

The Grand Prize of the Americas: *The Kid Brother*, by Claude Gagnon (Canada/USA/Japan).

Special Jury Award: *My General*, by Jaime de Arminan (Spain).

Jury Awards: *The Big Parade*, by Chen Kaige (China) and *George and Rosemary*, by Alison Snowden and David Fine.

Best Actor: Leo McKern, in *Travelling North* (Australia).

Best Actress: Irina Kupchenko, in *Lonely Woman Seeks Life Companion* (USSR).

Festival Award to Eric Rohmer, for his 'Comedies and Proverbs' series of films.

The Moscow Film Festival Awards, July 1987

Gold, Grand, Prize: *Intervista*, by Federico Fellini (Italy).

185

Silver Prizes: *Messenger Boy – Kurier*, by Karen Shaknazarov and *Hero of the Year – Bohater Roku*, by Feliks Falk (Poland).

Best Actor: Anthony Hopkins, in *84 Charing Cross Road* (USA).

Best Actress: Dorottya Udvaros, in *Love, Mother*.

Honorary Gold Prize for Documentary to the Soviet moviemakers who risked their lives filming the tragic events in Chernobyl.

Gold Prize for Best Children's Film: *The Journey of Natty Gann*, by Jeremy Paul Kagan (USA).

The 4th Rio Film Festival, November 1987

Best Film: *Out of Rosenheim*, by Percy Adlon (West Germany).

Best Direction: Pedro Almadovar, for *La Ley del Deseo* (Spain).

Best Actor: Denes Dobrei, in *Tolerance* (Hungary).

Best Actress: Wendy Hughes, in *Warm Nights on a Slow-Moving Train* (Australia).

Special Jury Prize: *Memoria Viva*, by Octavio Bezerra.

Critics' Prize: *Bouba*, by Zeev Revach (Israel).

The San Sebastian Festival Awards, September 1987

Golden Shell Award for Best Film: *Noce en Galilee*, by Michel Khleifi (France/Belgium/Palestine).

Silver Shell Awards: *Candy Mountain*, by Robert Frank and Rudy Wurlitzer (Switzerland/Canada) and *High Season*, by Clare Peploe (UK).

Best Actor: Imanol Arias, in *El Lute*.

Best Actress: Victoria Abril, in *El Lute*.

International Jury Critics' Prize: *The Raven's Strategy – Strateglia Surake*, by Zlatco Lavanic (Yugoslavia).

The Sitges Film Festival Awards, October 1987

Best Film: *A Hungarian Fairy Tale – Hol Volt, Hol Nem Volt*, by Gyula Gazdag (Hungary).

Best Director: Paul Verhoeven, for *RoboCop* (USA).

Best Actor: Michael Nouri, in *The Hidden* (USA).

Best Actress: Jill Schoelen, in *The Stepfather* (USA).

Best Screenplay: Martin Suter and Daniel Schmid, for *Jenatsch* (France/Switzerland).

Critics' Award for Best Film: *The Hidden*, by Jack Sholder (USA).

Best Photography: Moten Bruus and Jens Schlosser, for *The Dark Side of the Moon – Mandem Manen* (Denmark).

The 2nd Tokyo Film Festival Awards, September 1987

The Grand Prize and Governors' Award: *Old Well*, by Wu Tianming (China).

Special Jury Prize: *Housekeeping*, by Bill Forsyth (Canada); which also won the award for Best Screenplay.

Best Director: Lana Gogoberidze, for *Turnover* (USSR).

Best Actor: Zhang Yiou, in *Old Well*.

Best Actress: Rachel Ward, in *The Good Wife* (Australia).

Best Artistic Contribution to the Cinema: John Boorman, for *Hope and Glory* (UK).

Young Cinema Sakura Gold and Governor's Award: *The Kitchen Toto*, by Harry Hook (UK).

Young Cinema Silver: *Sweet Lorraine*, by Steve Gomer (USA).

International Critics' Award: *The Man With Three Coffins*, directed by Lee Chang-Ho (South Korea).

Special Festival Award to the late John Huston.

The Valencia Film Festival Prizes, October 1987

Gold Palm for Best Film: *Angel Dust – Poussière d'ange*, by Edouard Niermans (France).

Silver Palm: *Photography – I Photographia*, by Nikos Papatakis (Greece).

Bronze Palm shared by: *Hotel My Country – Anayurt Oteli*, by Omer Kavur (Turkey) and *An Italian Night – Una notte italiana*, by Carlos Mazzacurati (Italy).

Best Actress: Ksenija Pajic, in *An Officer With a Rose – Oficirs Ruzom* (Yugoslavia).

The 32nd Valladolid Film Festival Awards

Gold Sheaf for Best Film: *Tomorrow Was the War – Zavtra Bila Voina*, by Yuri Kara (USSR).

Silver Sheaf for Runner-up: *The Light – Yeelen*, by Souleymane Cissé (Mali).

Best Actor: Dennis Quaid, in *The Big Easy* (USA).

Best Actress: Leonor Manso, in *Made in Argentina* (Argentina).

Best Cinematography: Mikael Salomon, for *Early Spring – Barndommens Gade* (Denmark).

Special Jury Mention: Nikita Mikhalkov, for his *Dark Eyes – Oci Ciorne* (USSR).

François Truffaut Prize for Best First Film shared by: *Dragon Food – Drachenfutter*, by Jan Schutte (West Germany/Switzerland) and *Wish You Were Here*, by David Leland (UK).

The 44th Venice Film Festival Awards, September 1987

Golden Lion: *So Long, Children – Au Revoir, les enfants*, by Louis Malle (France).

Silver Lion shared by: *Maurice*, by James Ivory (UK) and *Long Live the Lady! – Lunga vita alla signora!*, by Ermanno Olmi.

Special Jury Award: *Hip, Hip, Hurrah*, by Kjell Grede (Scandinavia).

Best Actor shared by: James Wilby and Hugh Grant in *Maurice*.

Best Actress: Kang Soo-Yeon, in *Contract Mother* (Korea).

Special Mention: Miklos Jancso, for 'the coherence with which he carries on and renews his expressive research in a period of rapid evolution of film language'.

The Italian Senate Prize: *Plumbum, or A Dangerous Game*, by Vadim Abdrashitov (USSR).

Osella Prizes to: David Mamet, for Best Screenplay (*House of Games*); Richard Robbins, for Best Music (*Maurice*); Sten Holmberg, for Best Cinematography (*Hip, Hip, Hurrah*); Luciano Ricceri, for Best Art Direction (*The Gold-Rimmed Glasses*); and Nana Cecchi, for Best Costumes in the same film.

The Vevey Festival of Comedy Films, August 1987

Golden Cane, for Best Comedy Film: *Personal Services*, by Terry Jones (UK).

Golden Cane, for Best Comedy Performance: Sheila McCarthy, in *I've Heard The Mermaids Singing* (Canada).

Best First Feature: *Du Mich Auch*, by Helmut Berger, Daniel Levy and Anja Franks (Switzerland/West Germany).

Golden Cane – Audiences' Choice: *Satan's Empire*, by Salah Abou Seif (Egypt).

Index

Page numbers in *italic* refer to illustrations